Beginning Oracle PL/SQL

Second Edition

Donald J. Bales

〈IOUG〉
Independent oracle users group

Apress®

Beginning Oracle PL/SQL

ISBN-13 (pbk): 978-1-4842-0738-3

ISBN-13 (electronic): 978-1-4842-0737-6

Managing Director: Welmoed Spahr
Lead Editor: Jonathan Gennick
Development Editor: Douglas Pundick
Technical Reviewer: Michael Rosenblum
Editorial Board: Steve Anglin, Mark Beckner, Gary Cornell, Louise Corrigan, Jim DeWolf,
    Jonathan Gennick, Robert Hutchinson, Michelle Lowman, James Markham, Matthew Moodie,
    Jeffrey Pepper, Douglas Pundick, Ben Renow-Clarke, Gwenan Spearing, Matt Wade, Steve Weiss
Coordinating Editor: Jill Balzano
Copy Editor: Mary Behr
Compositor: SPi Global
Indexer: SPi Global
Artist: SPi Global
Cover Designer: Anna Ishchenko

Distributed to the book trade worldwide by Springer Science+Business Media New York,
233 Spring Street, 6th Floor, New York, NY 10013. Phone 1-800-SPRINGER, fax (201) 348-4505, e-mail orders-ny@springer-sbm.com, or visit www.springeronline.com. Apress Media, LLC is a California LLC and the sole member (owner) is Springer Science + Business Media Finance Inc (SSBM Finance Inc). SSBM Finance Inc is a Delaware corporation.

For information on translations, please e-mail rights@apress.com, or visit www.apress.com.

Apress and friends of ED books may be purchased in bulk for academic, corporate, or promotional use. eBook versions and licenses are also available for most titles. For more information, reference our Special Bulk Sales–eBook Licensing web page at www.apress.com/bulk-sales.

Any source code or other supplementary material referenced by the author in this text is available to readers at www.apress.com. For detailed information about how to locate your book's source code, go to www.apress.com/source-code/.

To my wife, Terry Moro,
you're the wind that feeds the flame

To my daughter, Kristyn,
"Every day, in every way, you get better and better!"

To Antoneo Bolagnao,
my Buddha

About IOUG Press

*IOUG Press is a joint effort by the **Independent Oracle Users Group (the IOUG)** and **Apress**
to deliver some of the highest-quality content possible on Oracle Database and related
topics. The IOUG is the world's leading, independent organization for professional users of
Oracle products. Apress is a leading, independent technical publisher known for developing
high-quality, no-fluff content for serious technology professionals. The IOUG and Apress
have joined forces in IOUG Press to provide the best content and publishing opportunities
to working professionals who use Oracle products.*

Our shared goals include:

- Developing content with excellence
- Helping working professionals to succeed
- Providing authoring and reviewing opportunities
- Networking and raising the profiles of authors and readers

To learn more about Apress, visit our website at **www.apress.com**. Follow the link for IOUG
Press to see the great content that is now available on a wide range of topics that matter to
those in Oracle's technology sphere.

Visit **www.ioug.org** to learn more about the Independent Oracle Users Group and its
mission. Consider joining if you haven't already. Review the many benefits at
www.ioug.org/join. Become a member. Get involved with peers. Boost your career.

www.ioug.org/join

Apress®

Contents at a Glance

Contents

About the Author

Donald Bales is an Information/Systems Architect, Business/Systems Analyst, Designer, and Programmer with over 30 years of professional experience in Business and Information Technology. He's an author of books and articles on Oracle, Java, and PL/SQL. His area of expertise is in the use of object-oriented analysis, design, and programming, along with service-oriented architecture, for scientific data analysis, business process modeling, enterprise application development and integration, most recently using Python Django, Ruby on Rails, Java JEE, XML, HTML, CSS, JavaScript, AJAX, Oracle, and Postgresql, to name a few. In addition, he possess more than 30 years of IT project management experience.

When he is not developing software applications, Don can often be found working with horses, or playing the piano or Native American flute. Don has had several careers, and has at various times been a mechanic, a general contractor, Mr. Mom, a developer, and a consultant. He is currently the Principal Technology Lead, Environmental Software and Data Management at Argonne National Laboratory. He has a bachelor of science degree in business from Elmhurst College in Illinois. Don resides in Downers Grove, Illinois, with his wife, Terry Moro. He can be contacted by e-mail at don@donaldbales.com.

About the Technical Reviewer

Michael Rosenblum is a Software Architect/Senior DBA at Dulcian, Inc. where he is responsible for system tuning and application architecture. Michael supports Dulcian developers by writing complex PL/SQL routines and researching new features. He is the co-author of *Oracle PL/SQL Performance Tuning Tips & Techniques* (McGraw-Hill, 2014) and *PL/SQL for Dummies* (Wiley Press, 2006), contributing author of *Expert PL/SQL Practices* (Apress, 2011), and author of a number of database-related articles (*IOUG Select Journal, ODTUG Tech Journal, OTech Magazine*) and conference papers. Michael is an Oracle ACE, a frequent presenter at various Oracle user group conferences (Oracle OpenWorld, ODTUG, IOUG Collaborate, RMOUG, NYOUG), and winner of the ODTUG Kaleidoscope 2009 Best Speaker Award. In his native Ukraine, he graduated summa cum laude from the Kiev National Economic University where he received a Master of Science degree in Information Systems.

Acknowledgments

Everything in the universe is constantly trying to change the behavior of everything else in the universe, all the time. Some behavioral modifications promote order; others promote chaos. So nothing we do–any of us–is actually a totally independent action. Whether we realize it or not, others as well as ourselves are taking part in both our successes and failures.

With that in mind, you should be able to understand why I say this book is the result of collaboration. Every person I've known, along with every situation I've experienced, has helped shape the text of this tutorial.

Since I have a seeming limited amount of memory, let me at least thank those who are directly responsible for bringing it to you:

Terry Moro, my wife, for reminding me how to maintain balance, even when I'm writing a book!

Jonathan Gennick, Lead Editor, for his friendship and leadership

Jill Balzano, Editor, for her encouragement

Michael Rosenblum, Technical Reviewer, for his excellent comments and suggestions

Mary Behr, Copy Editor, for making me look like a good writer

SPi Global, Compositor, Indexer, and Artist, for putting all the pieces together, for making it easy to dip into the book, and for making my artwork look good.

Foreword

I have some bad news and some good news. The bad news is: when you first meet Don Bales, he seems like an overly confident know-it-all. The good news is: he's not. Actually, he's a great teacher/author and perhaps does know it all when it comes to Oracle! I've not only read this book, but lived it. You see, I ended up working for him. Because of this, I think I am the perfect person to introduce you to *Beginning Oracle PL/SQL*.

A good programmer knows that the purpose of a good book, like this one, is to introduce the concepts of, the application of, and good examples of the subject: PL/SQL. *Beginning Oracle PL/SQL* goes above and beyond the call by explaining when you can use PL/SQL and when you should not. It starts with a low level understanding of basic SQL and builds your skills into understanding all types of complex PL/SQL.

My background may help you understand the profound effect that this book had on my career. I graduated with a computer science degree from a small private school. When I graduated, I had a basic understanding of databases and a good understanding of object-oriented programming languages.

My first job was at that same school, and it involved a lot of Java and a fair bit of PL/SQL. I was hired to be an object-oriented Java programmer and to hack through whatever else needed to be done. Although I never had formal training in it, or even understood the fundamentals of PL/SQL, I was able to hack together applications written in the language.

Before reading this book and working with Don, I had programmed in PL/SQL for five years. Working with Don reading this book changed the trajectory of my career. I looked both backward and forward to identify my mistakes and future direction. Since reading this book, I write much less PL/SQL to accomplish much more. It's amazing what a difference the strong fundamentals taught in *Beginning Oracle PL/SQL* provide to a person who has been effectively writing code for years, and that's not even who it was written for!

I believe Don asked me to write this forward because he saw my abilities before and after reading and learning from his book. I am the poster child for what his book can do for a programmer who has always been able to cobble things together. It turned me from someone who was able to accomplish a task into someone who can write PL/SQL in an efficient and consistent manner, and know when and why to use the various features of the language.

The nature of this book sets it apart from others in its category. PL/SQL is a procedural language. Therefore, it only makes sense that everything is taught in a procedural way, right? This is not the case, nor should it be. Don is able to apply object-oriented principles where they make sense to greatly enhance the use and effectiveness of PL/SQL.

Don is the perfect person to write this book. His background is unparalleled. He started off as a general contractor and was able to teach himself how to be a strong programmer. That's the least of it. Yes, his programming skills are superior, but he has two, much bigger, assets: building skills/getting the most out of others and delivering products that satisfy his customer's needs. He does both with this book. If you read and study it, your skills will be enhanced and you will become a confident PL/SQL programmer.

Don approached writing *Beginning Oracle PL/SQL* like everything else he does, by asking, "What is the goal?" The goal of this book is to teach you, the reader, everything you should know about PL/SQL. This is not an encyclopedia of every last Oracle function, procedure, etc. Instead, it's a great tool that will show you how to use PL/SQL, when to use PL/SQL, and what is possible with PL/SQL, when writing an application that utilizes Oracle.

—T.J. Eakle
Web Developer
Argonne National Laboratory

Introduction (The Big Picture)

This is a book about writing stored procedures for an Oracle database. A stored procedure in this context is a generic term for a program written in the Procedure Language extension for SQL (PL/SQL) that is stored inside the database when it is compiled. This means that you can then execute the program from inside the database. Why would you want to do this? Because your program will run faster inside the database.

Let's slow down for a minute, so I can explain what a stored procedure is and why you would want to use one.

What's a Stored Procedure?

In order for me to talk about stored procedures, I need to cover a little material on databases and networks first. By now, you've probably already seen three of the four diagrams I'm about to show you a few hundred times, but bear with me so I can make sure everyone is on the same page as we start out.

I'm going to assume, since you're ready to start writing programs against an Oracle database, that you already know what a relational database management system (RDBMS) is. For our purposes, an RDBMS, or database as I'll refer to it from here forward, is a hardware/software machine (server) that allows us to store, retrieve, and manipulate data in a predictable and organized manner using Structured Query Language (SQL).

SQL acts as the interface to the database. A client program, whether it exists on the same computer or on another, makes a connection to the database, sends a request in the form of SQL to the server, and in return gets back structured data, as in Figure I-1.

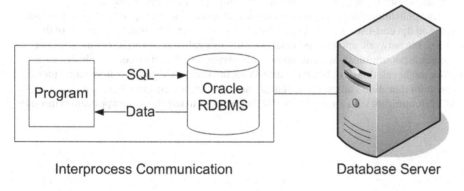

Figure I-1. *Client-server architecture on the same host*

A client program that utilizes Oracle on the same host computer, as in Figure I-1, is a client-server program because it accesses a server program to perform some of the client program's work. The communication between the two processes, client and server, takes place through an interprocess communication (IPC) system provided by the host operating system. This is typically done through memory. Suffice it to say that some communication overhead takes place when communicating between the client and the server in this fashion. This overhead takes time and operating system resources. Regardless, it's pretty fast.

But not everyone can run the program on the same computer, so some applications resort to the use of client-server architecture over a network. This is what is referred to when most people use the term client-server. Figure I-2 is a diagram that shows the communication between the client and server in a networked client-server architecture, specifically, a client-server diagram with one network connection in between the client (program) and server (database).

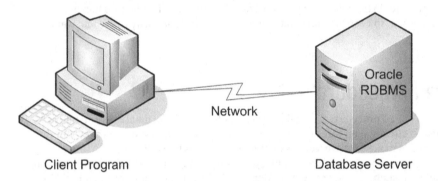

Figure I-2. *Client-server architecture over a network*

The communication between the two processes, client and server, in Figure I-2, is much slower than the architecture shown in Figure I-1, where IPC is used. Even with the best network hardware available, this connection is usually 20 times slower than IPC, or worse. Plus, a second software protocol stack, to allow the network communication, must be added to the use of resources. What's the net result? The connection between the two processes becomes the slowest, most time-consuming part of any application.

Nowadays, not every application can be run on a computer attached to a high-speed network. Nor can any one machine handle all the end-user requests, so architecture has effectively stretched the bus of the good old mainframe on to the network, and created what is commonly called n-tier architecture. In n-tier architecture, client programs communicate with an application server, which in turn communicates with one or more servers. You might call this Client-Server Gone Wild, but don't hold your breath waiting for the video. Figure I-3 is a diagram that shows an example of n-tier architecture where a notebook computer, a cell phone, and a tablet all communicate with an application server in order to use the same application through different devices.

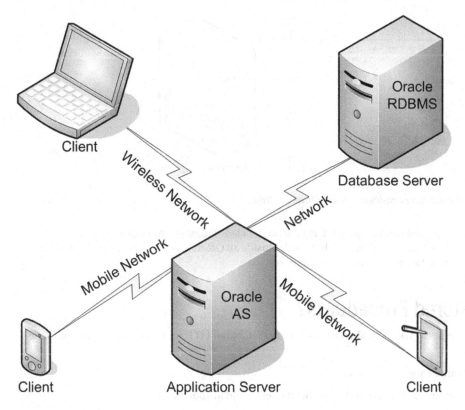

Figure I-3. *N-tier architecture over a network*

Now there are three different kinds of clients, with three different kinds of networks, using networked client-server architecture to communicate with an application server, which in turn uses networked client-server architecture to communicate with a database. Is this complex? Yes, but it's still just networked client-server architecture. Of course, this means that all the various networks involved conspire to slow down the response time of the application!

With the network being a bottleneck for any networked application, if we can perform some of our application's computer processing without using the network at all, that portion will simply run faster. With that in mind, examine Figure I-4. It's a diagram that shows how a stored procedure exists inside the database. Therefore, any computer processing that take place will occur inside the database before data is even sent to a client program, regardless of what type of client-server communication is used. In turn, that portion of the application will simply be more efficient and run faster.

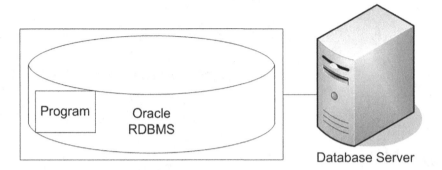

Figure I-4. *A stored procedure resides inside an Oracle database*

So what's a stored procedure? In Figure I-4, it's the box labeled "Program" that exists inside the database. So a stored procedure is a program that resides inside an Oracle database that manipulates data in the database before the data is used outside the database.

Why Use Stored Procedures?

Why use stored procedures? Well, I've already touched on that, haven't I? Here are my favorite reasons to use stored procedures:

> They eliminate the net in work.
>
> They allow you to more accurately model the real world in your database.
>
> They provide you with access to functionality that is not available through the standard database interface: SQL.

First, as I already stated in the previous section, using stored procedures allows you to eliminate the network from your data processing work. I can't emphasize this fact enough. If you write a Java Database Connectivity (JDBC) program that retrieves one million rows from the database, then queries the database for three related pieces of information, and then conditionally updates the retrieved rows, it can take days in Java; it will take only minutes inside Oracle using PL/SQL. That's a huge difference in performance. I often like to say, "The difference between any fast and slow application is that the fast application uses stored procedures."

Second, we basically use computers to automate what we do in the real world. Most people use databases to store only the characteristics of the real world, completely ignoring the behavior. Instead, behavior is temporarily kept in the code base for an application. If a change in the code is required, past behavior is lost forever. Yet no one would think of throwing away the data! What's going on here? Is the history of behavior unimportant or are we ignorant of the problem? I argue it's the latter. If you want to save both real-world characteristics and behavior, stored procedures allow you to do just that in either a pseudo-object-oriented or a truly object-oriented manner.

Finally, the standard database interface, SQL, is great, but its use is limited to four operations: insert, update, delete, and select. With stored procedures, you have unlimited possibilities. You are free to create as many new operations as are needed to satisfy requirements. The important point here is to perform work where it is done most efficiently. Presentation code should reside in the presentation layer, application code should reside in the application layer (the application server), and persistence code, like entity behavior, should reside in the persistence layer (the database).

Using PL/SQL, you can write stored procedures for the following:

Data processing

Data migration

Data warehousing

Entity behavior, including so-called business rules

Interfaces

Reports

Service-oriented-architecture routines

Now that you know the what and the why of stored procedures, are you still interested in learning PL/SQL? If so, then please read the next section, where I will tell you what this book is about, how I'm going to teach you PL/SQL, and why.

What's This Book About?

This book is not a reference. It's an immersion-based tutorial that teaches you how to program in PL/SQL by making you mimic successful PL/SQL programming.

Do you know that you have free access to outstanding reference materials directly from Oracle? If you download and install the database on your computer, these reference manuals will be accessible from the installation. Or you can download just the manuals to your computer. Oracle has always had superior technical documentation. I believe that has played a huge part in Oracle's success as a company and a product. Free access to Oracle's documentation and software for trial purposes has removed any barriers from anyone learning how to use Oracle.

How I'm Going to Teach You and Why

What do I mean by "an immersion-based tutorial?" I'm going to require you to read each and every program listing as part of the learning process. I'm going to start showing you program listings right away. Most listings will be complete contexts. By that, I mean there will be a lot of code in them that I have not yet discussed. I do this because I want you to get used to looking at the code and where things belong in the code from the get-go. Concentrate on the subject of the section and ignore the rest.

Whenever possible, I'm going to ask you to do an exercise that will make you think about and apply what I've just covered in the section. You should almost always be able to mimic (or copy and change) code that I've shown you before the exercise. I'm going to ask you to program all along. And the next section will often be dependent on you completing a prior exercise, so there's no skipping an exercise.

Why am I making you look at code, then read code, then try to understand my code, and then ask you to prove you understand my code by having you write code? For several reasons:

- You didn't learn how to speak by having those around you discuss the merits and drawbacks of various languages you might want to speak. You learned by mimicking those who spoke.

- You didn't learn how to read by talking about reading. You learned by reading.

- You don't learn a new language by reading about it. You need to speak it and then write it.

- You don't learn a new concept by reading about it. You must do your homework, where you actually use it.

So, how can you read a reference and be ready to solve business problems using a programming language? You can't. In the beginning, you must learn by mimicking someone else's work (hopefully, good examples)—something that someone has done before you. Then later, using your own creativity, you expand upon your basic knowledge with a reference.

But there's more to learning PL/SQL than just coding. I'm going to teach you good programming habits, such as these:

Document as you go.

Leave bread crumbs.

Keep it simple for the next person's sake.

Make it obvious by using prefixes or suffixes when it helps.

Make it obvious by using a coding style and sticking to it; consistency is important.

Make it obvious by adding comments to your code when it's not obvious.

Prepare for disaster ahead of time.

Prepare for testing ahead of time.

And finally, here are my assumptions:

You've programmed in another programming language, so you already know the difference between a function and a procedure.

You already know SQL.

I'm going to get you started down the right path, not tell you everything about PL/SQL. Your time is precious, so I'm not going to tell you anything that you don't need to know to get started (except for an occasional joke, or perhaps, my poor attempt at one). You may find my style terse. To me, that's a compliment.

This is not Oracle PL/SQL for Dummies. Remember that the examples are shown in a full-blown context. Pay attention to the subject; ignore the rest. You can do it!

What PL/SQL Am I Going to Teach You?

What am I going to teach you? Succinctly, how to get you, a programmer, from a novice to professional PL/SQL programmer in ten chapters." I've spent 25 years hiring programmers and then teaching them how to code properly, the past 15 years focusing on how to code in PL/SQL. In this book, I will apply the 80/20 rule in order to teach you the fundamentals of PL/SQL programming without bogging you down in the ever-so-increasing details.

As a scientist, I gather data about what I do all the time, so I have statistics about all the stored procedures that I and others have written since Oracle 7 became a production product. From these statistics, I've learned what's used often and not at all. In this book, I intend to touch on anything that is used 25% or more of the time when writing stored procedures.

Here, I'd like to share some interesting fun facts derived from over 30,000 stored procedures.

PL/SQL Pie, Anyone?

Figure I-5 shows that on average, only 31% of a stored procedure is actually logic. The rest is declaration, built-ins, and SQL. SQL makes up a whopping 26%. So if you don't know SQL, you're already behind the eight ball when you start to learn how to write stored procedures using PL/SQL.

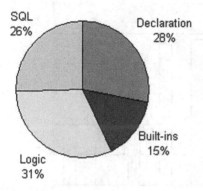

Figure I-5. *What is a PL/SQL stored procedure composed of?*

SQL, SQL, SQL!

The pretty little histogram in Figure I-6 shows the SQL keywords that are used in 25% or more of all stored procedures. So I need to start out with a SQL refresher for those of you who say you know SQL, but don't actually have much SQL experience. After all, I want you to buy this book and then go back and buy *Beginning Oracle SQL*, right?

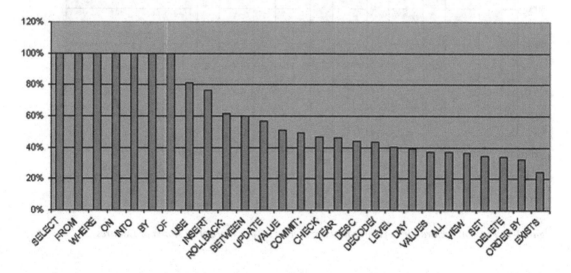

Figure I-6. *SQL keywords used in 25% or more of all stored procedures*

What About Those Declarations?

Figure I-7 shows the PL/SQL declaration keywords that are used in 25% or more of all stored procedures. Why teach any more than these to a beginner?

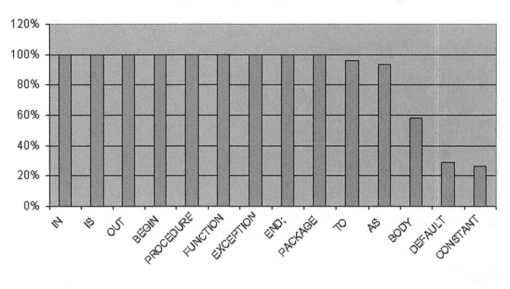

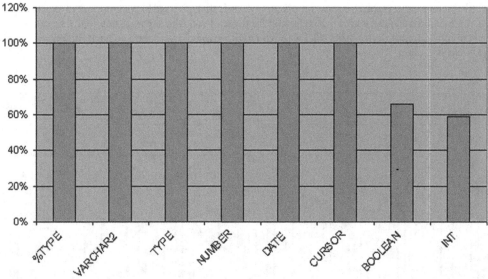

Figure I-7. *PL/SQL declaration keywords that are used in 25% or more of all stored procedures*

And How About Those Built-ins?

Figure I-8 shows the PL/SQL built-ins (functions and procedures that are part of the language) that are used in 25% or more of all stored procedures. Why teach any more than these to a beginner?

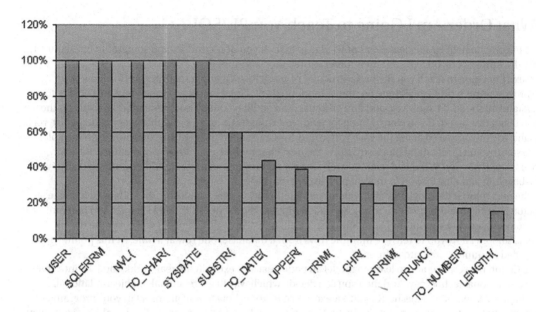

Figure I-8. *PL/SQL built-ins that are used in 25% or more of all stored procedures*

What Exactly Am I Supposed to Be Doing?

And last, but certainly not least, the histogram in Figure I-9 shows the PL/SQL keywords that are used in 25% or more of all stored procedures. The list isn't that large, so introducing these as we go will ease you right into coding logic.

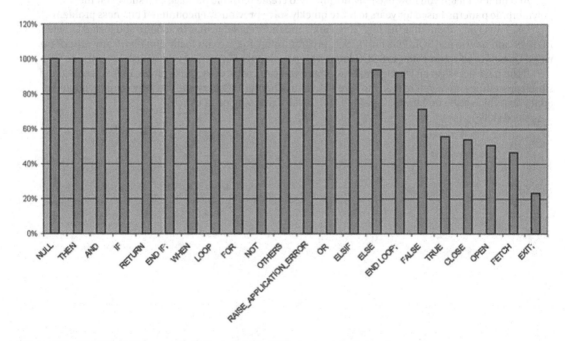

Figure I-9. *PL/SQL logic keywords that are used in 25% or more of all stored procedures*

In What Order Am I Going to Teach You PL/SQL?

First, I'm going to help you review your knowledge of SQL. If you don't understand something in Chapter 1, go buy the Apress book on SQL, as I mentioned earlier, then continue.

Next, I'm going to teach you the basic structure of every PL/SQL program unit type. I'll show you each program unit type. Concentrate on understanding PL/SQL block structure, and you'll be OK. Try to understand all the stuff I show you and don't discuss, and you'll be totally lost. Remember to focus on the subject being discussed. If you were mining for gold, you wouldn't stop and examine every grain of dirt, rock, and sand you encountered along the way; you would concentrate on the gold. So concentrate on the gold!

Assuming you understand block structure, the next chapter discusses the use of memory. Basically, it covers data types and variable declarations. You're a programmer, so there should be nothing really mind-boggling and new for you in this chapter, except maybe NULL.

The next topic is the singleton SQL statement. Whether it's a select, an insert, an update, or a delete, a singleton should always return one result. So what happens when it doesn't? Read Chapter 4 to find out!

From singletons to multitons? Something isn't right here. Anyway, Chapter 5 will cover the use of cursors. Cursors allow you to retrieve multiple rows from a database, one row at a time. At this point, you'll have coded a couple stored procedures.

In Chapter 6, you're going to learn to model an entity just as it exists in the real world. You'll be introduced to object-relational technology. And then you can decide which way to go: relational or object-relational.

Chapter 7 is about troubleshooting. It's always nice to know how to find an insect in your program. I'll also show you how to prevent insects in the first place. Oh yeah, did I tell you that I like to call defects defects, not bugs?

Professional programmers create programs with few defects. How do they do that? By testing. Chapter 8 is about automating the testing of your PL/SQL program units. Low error rates mean higher paychecks, too. So don't skip Chapter 8.

Concerning object-oriented development, it allows you to build reusable components, but reusable components are only valuable if you provide others with documentation, so they know the components exist and how they can use them! Professional programmers document as they go! That's what Chapter 9 is all about.

And finally, I'll tell you how use polymorphism to create reusable packages. I'll show you the polymorphic patterns I used for years to more quickly solve previously encountered business problems.

OK, I was lying about that "finally." The book's appendix explains how to acquire and install Oracle RDBMS, and how to use SQL*Plus for PL/SQL programming, in case you really don't have any experience with SQL before you start with PL/SQL (I knew it).

If you have access to an Oracle database where you can create objects like tables, indexes, types, and stored procedures, then you're ready to dive right in to Chapter 1. Otherwise, you may want to flip to the appendix, which tells you how to download and install a trial version of Oracle.

Good skill!

CHAPTER 1

■ ■ ■

Relational SQL

The question is, "Where do I start?" In the beginning, Codd created the paper "A Relational Model of Data for Large Shared Data Banks." Now the relational database was formless and empty, darkness was over the surface of the media, and the spirit of Codd was hovering over the requirements. Codd said, "Let there be Alpha," but as usual, the development team said, "Let there be something else," so SEQUEL (SQL) was created. Codd saw that SQL wasn't what he had in mind, but it was too late, for the Ellison separated the darkness from the SQL and called it Oracle. OK, that's enough of that silliness. But that's the short of it.

Did you know that about 25% of the average stored procedures written in the Procedural Language for SQL (PL/SQL) is, in fact, just SQL? Well, I'm a metrics junkie. I've kept statistics on every program I've ever written, and that's the statistic. After writing more than 30,000 stored procedures, 26% of my PL/SQL is nothing but SQL. So it's really important for you to know SQL!

OK, maybe you don't know SQL that well after all. If not, continue reading this light-speed refresher on relational SQL. Otherwise, move on to the exercises in the last section of the chapter ("Your Working Example").

This chapter covers Data Definition Language (DDL) and Data Manipulation Language (DML), from table creation to queries. Please keep in mind that this chapter is not a tutorial on SQL. It's simply a review. SQL is a large topic that can be covered fully only with several books. What I'm trying to accomplish here is to help you determine how familiar you are with SQL, so you'll be able to decide whether you need to spend some additional time learning SQL after or while you learn PL/SQL.

Tables

The core idea behind a relational database and SQL is so simple it's elusive. Take a look at Tables 1-1 and 1-2.

Table 1-1. *Relational Database Geniuses (Authors)*

ID	Name	Born	Gender
100	Edgar F Codd	1923	Male
200	Chris J Date	1941	Male
300	Hugh Darwen	1943	Male

Table 1-2. *Relational Genius's Publications (Author Publications)*

ID	Author ID	Title	Written
10	100	A Relational Model of Data for Large Shared Data Banks	1970
20	100	The Relational Model for Database Management	1990
30	200	An Introduction to Database Systems	2003
40	200	The Third Manifesto	2000
50	200	Temporal Data and the Relational Model	2002
60	200	Database in Depth: Relational Theory for Practitioners	2005
70	300	The Third Manifesto	2000
80	300	Temporal Data and the Relational Model	2002

You can find which publications were written by each genius simply by using the common datum in both of these tables: the ID. If you look at Codd's data in Table 1-1, you see he has ID 100. Next, if you look at ID 100's (Codd's) data in Table 1-2, you see he has written two titles:

- A Relational Model of Data for Large Shared Data Banks (1970)

- The Relational Model for Database Management (1990)

These two tables have a relationship, because they share an ID column with the same values. They don't have many entries, so figuring out what was written by each author is pretty easy. But what would you do if there were, say, one million authors with about three publications each? Yes! It's time for a computer and a database—*a relational database.*

A relational database allows you to store multiple tables, like Tables 1-1 and 1-2, in a database management system (DBMS). By doing so, you can manipulate the data in the tables using a query language on a computer, instead of a pencil on a sheet of paper. The current query language of choice is Structured Query Language (SQL). SQL is a set of nonprocedural commands, or language if you will, which you can use to manipulate the data in tables in a relational database management system (RDBMS).

A table in a relational database is a logical definition for how data is to be organized when it is stored. For example, in Table 1-3, I decided to order the columns of the database genius data just as it appeared horizontally in Table 1-1.

Table 1-3. *A Table Definition for Table 1-1*

Column Number	Column Name	Data Type
1	ID	Number
2	Name	Character
3	Birth Date	Date
4	Gender	Character

Perhaps I could give the relational table defined in Table 1-3 the name geniuses? In practice, a name like that tends to be too specific. It's better to find a more general name, like authors or persons. So how do you document your database design decisions?

An Entity-Relationship Diagram

Just as home builders have an architectural diagram or blueprint, which enables them to communicate clearly and objectively about what they are going to build, so do relational database builders. In our case, the architectural diagram is called an entity-relationship diagram (ERD).

Figure 1-1 is an ERD for the tables shown in Tables 1-1 and 1-2, now named authors and author_publications. It shows that one author may have zero or more publications. Additionally, it shows that an author's ID is his primary key (PK), or unique way to identify him, and an author's primary key is also used to identify his publications.

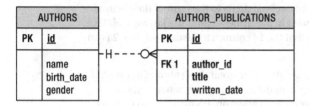

Figure 1-1. *An entity-relationship diagram for the authors and author publications tables*

ERDs, like blueprints, may have varying levels of detail, depending on your audience. For example, to simplify the ERD in Figure 1-1, I've left out the data types.

In an ERD, the tables are called *entities*. The lines that connect the tables—I mean entities—are called *relations*. So given an ERD, or even a narrative documentation as in Table 1-3, you can write a script to create a table.

Data Definition Language (DDL)

To create the authors table, as defined in Table 1-3, in Oracle, you'll need to create a SQL script (for SQL*Plus) that in SQL jargon is called Data Definition Language. That is, it's SQL for defining the relational database. Listing 1-1 shows the authors table's DDL.

Listing 1-1. DDL for Creating the Author Table, authors.tab

```
1  CREATE TABLE authors (
2  id                        number(38),
3  name                      varchar2(100),
4  birth_date                date,
5  gender                    varchar2(30) );
```

The syntax for the CREATE TABLE statement used in Listing 1-1 is as follows:

```
CREATE TABLE <table_name> (
<column_name_1>   <data_type_1>,
<column_name_2>   <data_type_2>,
<column_name_N>   <data_type_N> );
```

where <table_name> is the name of the table, <column_name> is the name of a column, and <data_type> is one of the Oracle data types.

The following are the Oracle data types you'll use most often:

- VARCHAR2: Allows you to store up to 32,767 bytes (4,000 in versions prior to 12c), data like *ABCD...*, in a column. You must define the maximum number of characters (or constrain the number of characters) by specifying the desired number in parentheses after the keyword VARCHAR2. For example, in Listing 1-1, line 3 specifies varchar2(100), which means a name can be up to 100 characters in length.

- NUMBER: Allows you to store a decimal number with 38 digits of precision. You do not need to constrain the size of a number, but you can. You can specify the maximum number of digits (1, 2, 3, 4 . . .) to the left of a decimal point, followed by a comma (,), and optionally the maximum number of decimal digits to the right of the decimal point, by specifying the desired constraint in parentheses after the keyword NUMBER. For example, if you want to make sure that the id column in Listing 1-1, line 2 is an integer, you could specify number(38).

- DATE: Allows you to store a date and time value. One great thing about Oracle DATE types is that they allow you to easily perform time calculations between dates; just subtract an earlier date from a later date. In addition, it's also easy to convert between VARCHAR2 and DATE values. For example, if you want to store the date and time of birth for someone born on January 1, 1980 at 8 a.m., you could use the Oracle to_date() function to convert a VARCHAR2 value in a proper format into a DATE data type as follows: to_date('19800101080000', 'YYYYMMDDHH24MISS').

Of course, there are other Oracle data types, but you'll end up using VARCHAR2, NUMBER, and DATE most of the time. The rest are specialized versions of these three, or they are designed for specialized uses.

It's Your Turn to Create a Table

OK, it's time to stop reading and start doing. This section gives you chance to put into practice some of what you've learned so far. I'll be asking you to perform exercises like this as we go along in order for you to verify that you understood what you just read well enough to put it into practice.

■ **Tip** First, if you don't have access to Oracle, see this book's appendix. Second, create a directory for the book's source code listings. Next, download the source code listings from the Source Code/Download section of the Apress web site (www.apress.com), and work within the book's source code listing directory structure for each chapter. Add your source code listings to the book's directory structure as you work. Last, create a shortcut, an icon, or whatever you want to call it, to start SQL*Plus from your working source code listing directory. Then you won't need to specify the entire path when trying to execute your scripts in SQL*Plus.

To create the author_publications table, follow these steps.

1. Start your Oracle database if it's not already running.

2. Start SQL*Plus, logging in as username RPS with password RPS.

3. Open your favorite text editor.

4. Write a DDL script to create a table for author_publications, as in Table 1-2.

5. Save the DDL script with the same filename as your table name, but with a `.tab` extension.

6. Execute your script in SQL*Plus by typing an at sign (@) followed by the filename at the SQL> prompt.

If you didn't have any errors in your script, the table will now exist in the database, just waiting for you to populate it with data. If it didn't work, try to make some sense out of the error message(s) you got, correct your script, and then try again.

Listing 1-2 is my try.

Listing 1-2. DDL for Creating the Publication Table, author_publications.tab

```
1  CREATE TABLE author_publications (
2  id                        number(38),
3  title                     varchar2(100),
4  written_date              date );
```

Now you know how to create a table, but what if you put a lot of data in those two tables? Then accessing them will be very slow, because none of the columns in the tables are indexed.

Indexes

Imagine, if you will, that a new phone book shows up on your doorstep. You put it in the drawer and throw out the old one. You pull the phone book out on Saturday evening so you can order some pizza, but when you open it, you get confused. Why? Well, when they printed the last set of phone books, including yours, they forgot to sort it by last name, first name, and street address. Instead, it's not sorted at all! The numbers show up the way they were put into the directory over the years—a complete mess.

You want that pizza! So you start at the beginning of the phone book, reading every last name, first name, and address until you finally find your local pizza place. Too bad it was closed by the time you found the phone number! If only that phone book had been sorted, or properly indexed.

Without an index to search on, you had to read through the entire phone book to make sure you got the right pizza place phone number. Well, the same holds true for the tables you create in a relational database.

You need to carefully analyze how data will be queried from each table, and then create an appropriate set of indexes. You don't want to index everything, because that would unnecessarily slow down the process of inserting, updating, and deleting data. That's why I said "carefully."

DDL Again

You should (*must*, in my opinion) create a unique index on each table's primary key column(s)—you know, the one that uniquely identifies entries in the table. In the authors table, that column is id. However, you will create a unique index on the id column when we talk about constraints in the next section. Instead, let's create a unique index on the name, birth_date, and gender columns of the authors table. Listing 1-3 shows the example.

Listing 1-3. DDL for Creating an Index on the Author Table, authors_uk1.ndx.

```
1  CREATE UNIQUE INDEX authors_uk1
2  on                  authors (
3  name,
4  birth_date,
5  gender );
```

The syntax for the CREATE INDEX statement is as follows:

```
CREATE [UNIQUE] INDEX <index_name>
on                    <table_name> (
<column_name_1>,
<column_name_2>,
<column_name_N> );
```

where <index_name> is the name of the index, <table_name> is the name of the table, and <column_name> is the name of a column. The keyword UNIQUE is optional, as denoted by the brackets ([ ]) around it. It just means that the database must check to make sure that the column's combination of the values is unique within the table. Unique indexes are old-fashioned; now it's more common to see a unique constraint, which I'll discuss shortly.

It's Your Turn to Create an Index

OK, it's time to stop listening to me talk about indexes, and time for you to start creating one. Here's the drill.

1. Write a DDL script to create a non-unique index on the author_publications table.

2. Save the DDL script with the same file name as your index name, but with an .ndx extension.

3. Execute your script in SQL*Plus by typing an at sign (@) followed by the file name at the SQL> prompt.

You should now have a non-unique index in the database, just waiting for you to query against it. If not, try to make some sense out of the error message(s) you got, correct your script, and then try again.

My shot at this is shown in Listing 1-4.

Listing 1-4. DDL for Creating an Index on the Title Column in the Publication Table, author_publications_k1.ndx

```
1  CREATE INDEX author_publications_k1
2  on            author_publications (
3  title );
```

Now you know how to create a table and an index or two, to make accessing it efficient, but what prevents someone from entering bad data? Well, that's what constrains are for.

Constraints

Constraints are rules for a table and its columns that constrain how and what data can be inserted, updated, or deleted. Constraints are available for both columns and tables.

Column Constraints

Columns may have rules that define what list of values or what kind of values may be entered into them. Although there are several types of column constraints, the one you will undoubtedly use most often is NOT NULL. The NOT NULL constraint simply means that a column must have a value. It can't be unknown, or blank, or in SQL jargon, NULL. Listing 1-5 shows the authors table script updated with NOT NULL constraints on the id and name columns.

Listing 1-5. DDL for Creating the Authors Table with NOT NULL Column Constraints, authors.tab

```
1   CREATE TABLE authors (
2   id                          number(38)                      not null,
3   name                        varchar2(100)                   not null,
4   birth_date                  date,
5   gender                      varchar2(30) );
```

Now if you try to insert data into the authors table, but don't supply values for the id or name column, the database will respond with an error message.

Table Constraints

Tables may have rules that enforce uniqueness of column values and the validity of relationships to other rows in other tables. Once again, although there are many forms of table constraints, I'll discuss only three here: unique key, primary key, and foreign key.

Unique Key Constraint

A unique key constraint (UKC) is a rule against one or more columns of a table that requires their combination of values to be unique for a row within the table. Columns in a unique index or unique constraint may be NULL, but that is not true for columns in a primary key constraint.

As an example, if I were going to create a unique key constraint against the authors table columns name, birth_date, and gender, the DDL to do that would look something like Listing 1-6.

Listing 1-6. DDL for Creating a Unique Constraint Against the Author Table, authors_uk1.ukc

```
1   ALTER TABLE authors ADD
2   CONSTRAINT  authors_uk1
3   UNIQUE (
4   name,
5   birth_date,
6   gender );
```

Primary Key Constraint

A primary key constraint (PKC) is a rule against one or more columns of a table that requires their combination of values to be unique for a row within the table. Although similar to a unique key, one big difference is that the unique key called the primary key is acknowledged to be the primary key, or primary index, of the table, and may not have NULL values. Semantics, right? No, not really, as you'll see when I talk about foreign keys in the next section.

You should have a primary key constraint defined for every table in your database. I say "should," because it isn't mandatory, but it's a really good idea. Listing 1-7 shows the DDL to create a primary key constraint against the authors table.

Listing 1-7. DDL to Create a Primary Key Constraint Against the Authors Table, authors_pk.pkc

```
1   ALTER TABLE authors ADD
2   CONSTRAINT  authors_pk
3   primary key (
4   id );
```

The syntax used in Listing 1-7 for creating a primary key constraint is as follows:

```
ALTER TABLE <table_name> ADD
CONSTRAINT  <constraint_name>
PRIMARY KEY (
<column_name_1>,
<column_name_2>,...
<column_name_N> );
```

where `<table_name>` is the name of the table, `<constraint_name>` is the name of the primary key constraint, and `<column_name>` is a column to use in the constraint.

Now that you have a primary key defined on the `authors` table, you can point to it from the `author_publications` table.

Foreign Key Constraint

A foreign key is one or more columns from another table that point to, or are connected to, the primary key of the first table. Since primary keys are defined using primary key constraints, it follows that foreign keys are defined with foreign key constraints (FKC). However, a foreign key constraint is defined against a dependent, or child, table.

So what's a dependent or child table? Well, in this example, you know that the `author_publications` table is dependent on, or points to, the `authors` table. So you need to define a foreign key constraint against the `author_publications` table, not the `authors` table. The foreign key constraint is represented by the relation (line with crow's feet) in the ERD in Figure 1-1.

Listing 1-8 shows the DDL to create a foreign key constraint against the `author_publications` table that defines its relationship with the `authors` table in the database.

Listing 1-8. DDL for Creating a Foreign Key Constraint Against the Author Publications Table, author_publications_fk1.fkc

```
1  ALTER TABLE author_publications ADD
2  CONSTRAINT  author_publications_fk1
3  FOREIGN KEY (author_id)
4  REFERENCES  authors (id);
```

The syntax used in Listing 1-8 for creating a foreign key constraint is as follows:

```
ALTER TABLE <table_name> ADD
CONSTRAINT  <constraint_name>
FOREIGN KEY (
<column_name_1>,
<column_name_2>,...
<column_name_N> )
REFERENCES <referenced_table_name> (
<column_name_1>,
<column_name_2>,...
<column_name_N> );
```

where `<table_name>` is the name of the table to be constrained, `<constraint_name>` is the name of the foreign key constraint, `<referenced_table_name>` is the name of the table to be referenced (or pointed to), and `<column_name>` is a column that is both part of the referenced table's key and corresponds to a column with the same value in the child or dependent table.

Now that you have a foreign key defined on the `author_publications` table, you can no longer delete a referenced row in the `authors` table. Or, put another way, you can't have any parentless children in the `author_publications` table. That's why the primary and foreign key constraints in SQL jargon are called *referential integrity constraints*. They ensure the integrity of the relational references between rows in related tables. In addition, it is a best practice to always create an index on a foreign key column or columns.

It's Your Turn to Create a Constraint

It's time to put you to work creating a primary key constraint against the `author_publications` table.

1. Write a DDL script to create a primary key constraint against the `author_publications` table.

2. Save the DDL script with the same file name as your constraint name, but with a `.pkc` extension.

3. Execute your script in SQL*Plus by typing an at sign (@) followed by the file name at the `SQL>` prompt.

The primary key constraint should now exist against the `author_publications` table in the database, just waiting for you to slip up and try putting in a duplicate row. Otherwise, try to make some sense out of the error message(s) you got, correct your script, and then try again.

My version of a DDL script to create a primary key constraint against the `author_publications` table is shown in Listing 1-9.

Listing 1-9. DDL for Creating a Primary Key Constraint Against the Author Publications Table, author_publications_pk.pkc

```
1  ALTER TABLE author_publications ADD
2  CONSTRAINT  author_publications_pk
3  PRIMARY KEY (
4  id);
```

Now you know how to create a table along with any required indexes and constraints, but what do you do if you need a really complex constraint? Or, what if you need other actions to be triggered when a row or column in a table is inserted, updated, or deleted? Well, that's the purpose of triggers.

Triggers

Triggers are PL/SQL programs that are set up to execute in response to a particular event on a table in the database. The events in question can take place FOR EACH ROW or for a SQL statement, so I call them row-level or statement-level triggers.

The actual events associated with triggers can take place BEFORE, AFTER, or INSTEAD OF an INSERT, an UPDATE, or a DELETE SQL statement. Accordingly, you can create triggers for any of the events in Table 1-4.

Table 1-4. Possible Trigger Events Against a Table

Event	SQL	Level
BEFORE	DELETE	FOR EACH ROW
BEFORE	DELETE	
BEFORE	INSERT	FOR EACH ROW
BEFORE	INSERT	
BEFORE	UPDATE	FOR EACH ROW
BEFORE	UPDATE	
AFTER	DELETE	FOR EACH ROW
AFTER	DELETE	
AFTER	INSERT	FOR EACH ROW
AFTER	INSERT	
AFTER	UPDATE	FOR EACH ROW
AFTER	UPDATE	
INSTEAD OF	DELETE	FOR EACH ROW
INSTEAD OF	DELETE	
INSTEAD OF	INSERT	FOR EACH ROW
INSTEAD OF	INSERT	
INSTEAD OF	UPDATE	FOR EACH ROW
INSTEAD OF	UPDATE	

So let's say we want to play a practical joke. Are you with me here? We don't want anyone to ever be able to add the name Jonathan Gennick (my editor, who is actually a genius in his own right, but it's fun to mess with him) to the list of database geniuses. Listing 1-10 shows a trigger created to prevent such an erroneous thing from happening.

Listing 1-10. A Trigger Against the Authors Table, authors_bir.trg

```
01  CREATE OR REPLACE TRIGGER authors_bir
02  BEFORE INSERT ON          authors
03  FOR EACH ROW
04
05  BEGIN
06    if upper(:new.name) = 'JONATHAN GENNICK' then
07      raise_application_error(20000, 'Sorry, that genius is not allowed.');
08    end if;
09  END;
10  /
```

The syntax used in Listing 1-10 is as follows:

```
CREATE [OR REPLACE] TRIGGER <trigger_name>
BEFORE INSERT ON             <table_name>
FOR EACH ROW
BEGIN
  <pl/sql>
END;
```

where `<trigger_name>` is the name of the trigger, `<table_name>` is the name of the table for which you're creating the trigger, and `<pl/sql>` is the PL/SQL program you've written to be executed BEFORE someone INSERTs EACH ROW. The brackets ([ ]) around the OR REPLACE keyword denote that it is optional. The OR REPLACE clause will allow you to re-create your trigger if it already exists.

Views

A view represents the definition of a SQL query (SELECT statement) as though it were just another table in the database. Hence, you can INSERT into and UPDATE, DELETE, and SELECT from a view just as you can any table. (There are some restrictions on updating a view, but they can be resolved by the use of INSTEAD OF triggers.)

Here are just a few of the uses of views:

- Transform the data from multiple tables into what appears to be one table.

- Nest multiple outer joins against different tables, which is not possible in a single SELECT statement.

- Implement a seamless layer of user-defined security against tables and columns.

Let's say you want to create a view that combines the authors and author_publications tables so it's easier for a novice SQL*Plus user to write a report about the publications written by each author. Listing 1-11 shows the DDL to create a view that contains the required SQL SELECT statement.

Listing 1-11. DDL to Create an Authors Publications View, authors_publications.vw

```
1  CREATE OR REPLACE VIEW authors_publications as
2  SELECT authors.id,
3         authors.name,
4         author_publications.title,
5         author_publications.written_date
6  FROM   authors,
7         author_publications
8  WHERE  authors.id = author_publications.author_id;
```

The syntax for the CREATE VIEW statement used in Listing 1-11 is as follows:

```
CREATE [OR REPLACE] VIEW <view_name> AS
<sql_select_statement>;
```

where `<view_name>` is the name of the view (the name that will be used in other SQL statements as though it's a table name), and `<sql_select_statement>` is a SQL SELECT statement against one or more tables in the database. Once again, the brackets around the OR REPLACE clause denote that it is optional. Using OR REPLACE also preserves any privileges (grants) that exist on a view.

That does it for your DDL review. Now let's move on to the SQL for manipulating data—SQL keywords like INSERT, UPDATE, DELETE, and SELECT.

Insert

At this point in your journey, you should have two tables—authors and author_publications—created in your Oracle database. Now it's time to put some data in them. You do that by using the SQL keyword INSERT.

INSERT is one of the SQL keywords that are part of SQL's Data Manipulation Language. As the term implies, DML allows you to manipulate data in your relational database. Let's start with the first form of an INSERT statement, INSERT...VALUES.

Insert . . .Values

First, let's add Codd's entry to the authors table. Listing 1-12 is a DML INSERT statement that uses a VALUES clause to do just that.

Listing 1-12. DML to Insert Codd's Entry into the Authors Table, authors_100.ins

```
01  INSERT INTO authors (
02          id,
03          name,
04          birth_date,
05          gender )
06  VALUES (
07          100,
08          'Edgar F Codd',
09          to_date('19230823', 'YYYYMMDD'),
10          'MALE' );
11  COMMIT;
```

The syntax for the INSERT VALUES statement used in Listing 1-12 is as follows:

```
INSERT INTO <table_name> (
      <column_name_1>,
      <column_name_2>, ...
      <column_name_N> )
VALUES (
      <column_value_1>,
      <column_value_2>,...
      <column_value_N> );
```

where <table_name> is the name of the table you wish to INSERT VALUES INTO, <column_name> is one of the columns from the table into which you wish to insert a value, and <column_value> is the value to place into the corresponding column. The COMMIT statement that follows the INSERT VALUES statement in Listing 1-12 simply commits your inserted values in the database.

So let's break down Listing 1-12 and look at what it does:

- Line 1 specifies the table to insert values into: authors.

- Lines 2 through 5 list the columns in which to insert data.

- Line 6 specifies the VALUES syntax.

- Lines 7 through 10 supply values to insert into corresponding columns in the list on lines 2 through 5.

- Line 11 commits the INSERT statement.

It's Your Turn to Insert with Values

Insert the entries for Codd's publications into the author_publications table. Here are the steps to follow.

1. If you haven't actually executed the scripts for the authors table yet, you need to do so now. The files are authors.tab, authors_uk1.ndx, authors_pk.pkc, and authors_100.ins. Execute them in that order.

2. Write a DML script to insert Codd's two publications from Table 1-2. (Hint: Use January 1 for the month and day of the written date, since you don't know those values.)

3. Save the DML script with the same file name as your table name, but with a _100 suffix and an .ins extension.

4. Execute your script in SQL*Plus by typing an at sign (@) followed by the file name at the SQL> prompt.

The author_publications table should now have two rows in it—congratulations! If it didn't work, try to make some sense out of the error message(s) you got, correct your script, and then try again.

Listing 1-13 shows how I would insert the publications into the table.

Listing 1-13. DML for Inserting Codd's Publications, author_publications_100.ins

```
01  INSERT INTO author_publications (
02        id,
03        author_id,
04        title,
05        written_date )
06  VALUES (
07        10,
08        100,
09        'A Relation Model of Data for Large Shared Data Banks',
10        to_date('19700101', 'YYYYMMDD') );
11
12  INSERT INTO author_publications (
13        id,
14        author_id,
15        title,
16        written_date )
```

```
17  VALUES (
18          20,
19          100,
20          'The Relational Model for Database Management',
21          to_date('19900101', 'YYYYMMDD') );
22
23  COMMIT;
24
25  execute SYS.DBMS_STATS.gather_table_stats(USER, 'AUTHOR_PUBLICATIONS');
```

There's a second form of the INSERT statement that can be quite useful. Let's look at it next.

Insert . . . Select

The second form of an INSERT statement uses a SELECT statement instead of a list of column values. Although we haven't covered the SELECT statement yet, I think you're intuitive enough to follow along. Listing 1-14 inserts Chris Date's entry using the INSERT ... SELECT syntax.

Listing 1-14. DML to Insert Date's Entry into the Author Table, authors_200.ins

```
01  INSERT INTO authors (
02          id,
03          name,
04          birth_date,
05          gender )
06  SELECT 200,
07          'Chris J Date',
08          to_date('19410101', 'YYYYMMDD')
09          'MALE'
10  FROM   dual;
11
12  COMMIT;
```

The syntax for the INSERT SELECT statement used in Listing 1-14 is as follows:

```
INSERT INTO <table_name> (
       <column_name_1>,
       <column_name_2>, ...
       <column_name_N> )
SELECT <column_value_1>,
       <column_value_2>,...
       <column_value_N>
FROM   <from_table_name> ...;
```

where <table_name> is the name of the table you wish to INSERT INTO, <column_name> is one of the columns from the table into which you wish to insert a value, <column_value> is the value to place into the corresponding column, and <from_table_name> is the table or tables from which to select the values. The COMMIT statement that follows the INSERT SELECT statement in Listing 1-14 simply commits your inserted values in the database.

Let's break down Listing 1-14:

- Line 1 specifies the table to insert values into: authors.

- Lines 2 through 5 list the columns in which to insert values.

- Line 6 specifies the SELECT syntax.

- Lines 6 through 9 supply values to insert into corresponding columns in the list on lines 2 through 5.

- Line 10 specifies the table or tables from which to select the values.

- Line 12 commits the INSERT statement.

So what's the big deal about this second INSERT syntax? First, it allows you to insert values into a table from other tables. Also, the SQL query to retrieve those values can be as complex as it needs to be. But its most handy use is to create conditional INSERT statements like the one in Listing 1-15.

Listing 1-15. Conditional INSERT ... SELECT Statement, authors_300.ins

```
01  INSERT INTO authors (
02          id,
03          name,
04          birth_date,
05          gender )
06  SELECT 300,
07          'Hugh Darwen',
08          to_date('19430101', 'YYYYMMDD')09          'MALE'
10  FROM    dual d
11  WHERE not exists (
12    SELECT 1
13    FROM    authors x
14    WHERE  x.id = 300 );
15
16  COMMIT;
```

The subquery in Listing 1-15's SQL SELECT statement, in lines 11 through 14, first checks to see if the desired entry already exists in the database. If it does, Oracle does not attempt the INSERT; otherwise, it adds the row. You'll see in time, as your experience grows, that being able to do a conditional insert is very useful!

THE DUAL TABLE

Have you noticed that I'm using a table by the name of dual in the conditional INSERT...SELECT statement? dual is a table owned by the Oracle database (owner SYS) that has one column and one row. It is very handy, because anytime you select against this table, you get one, and only one, row back.

So if you want to evaluate the addition of 1 + 1, you can simply execute the following SQL SELECT statement:

```
SELECT 1 + 1 FROM dual;
```

Oracle will tell you the answer is 2. Not so handy? Say you want to quickly figure out how Oracle will evaluate your use of the built-in function `length()`? Perhaps you might try this:

```
SELECT length(NULL) FROM dual;
```

Oh! It returns NULL. You need a number, so you try again. This time, you try wrapping `length()` in the SQL function `nvl()` so you can substitute a zero for a NULL value:

```
SELECT nvl(length(NULL), 0) FROM DUAL;
```

Now it returns zero, even if you pass a NULL string to it. That's how you want it to work!

See how using `dual` to test how a SQL function might work can be handy? It allows you to hack away without any huge commitment in code.

It's Your Turn to Insert with Select

It's time to practice inserting data once again. This time, insert the publications for Date and Darwen, but use the conditional `INSERT SELECT` syntax with detection for Darwen's publications.

1. Add Darwen's entry to the `authors` table by executing the script `authors_200.ins`.

2. Write the DML scripts to insert the publications by Date and Darwen from Table 1-2.

3. Save each DML script with the same file name as your table name, but with a _200 suffix for Date and a _300 suffix for Darwen, and add an `.ins` extension to both files.

4. Execute your scripts in SQL*Plus by typing an at sign (@) followed by the file name at the `SQL>` prompt.

The `author_publications` table should now have eight rows. And, if you run the Darwen script again, you won't get any duplicate-value errors, because the SQL detects whether Darwen's entries already exist in the database.

Listings 1-16 and 1-17 show my solutions.

Listing 1-16. DML for Inserting Date's Publications, author_publications_200.ins

```
01  INSERT INTO author_publications (
02          id,
03          author_id,
04          title,
05          written_date )
06  VALUES (
07          30,
08          200,
09          'An introduction to Database Systems',
10          to_date('20030101', 'YYYYMMDD') );
11
```

```
12  INSERT INTO author_publications (
13        id,
14        author_id,
15        title,
16        written_date )
17  VALUES (
18        40,
19        200,
20        'The Third Manifesto',
21        to_date('20000101', 'YYYYMMDD') );
22
23  INSERT INTO author_publications (
24        id,
25        author_id,
26        title,
27        written_date )
28  VALUES (
29        50,
30        200,
31        'Temporal Data and the Relational Model',
32        to_date('20020101', 'YYYYMMDD') );
33
34  INSERT INTO author_publications (
35        id,
36        author_id,
37        title,
38        written_date )
39  VALUES (
40        60,
41        200,
42        'Database in Depth: Relational Theory for Practitioners',
43        to_date('20050101', 'YYYYMMDD') );
44
45  COMMIT;
46
47  execute SYS.DBMS_STATS.gather_table_stats(USER, 'AUTHOR_PUBLICATIONS');
```

Listing 1-17. DML for Inserting Darwen's Publications, author_publications_300.ins

```
01  INSERT INTO author_publications (
02        id,
03        author_id,
04        title,
05        written_date )
06  SELECT 70,
07        300,
08        'The Third Manifesto',
09        to_date('20000101', 'YYYYMMDD')
```

```
10  FROM    dual
11  where not exists (
12    SELECT 1
13    FROM    author_publications x
14    WHERE   x.author_id = '300'
15    AND     x.title       = 'The Third Manifesto' );
16
17  INSERT INTO author_publications (
18          id,
19          author_id,
20          title,
21          written_date )
22  SELECT 80,
23         300,
24         'Temporal Data and the Relational Model',
25         to_date('20020101', 'YYYYMMDD')
26  FROM    dual
27  where not exists (
28    SELECT 1
29    FROM    author_publications x
30    WHERE   x.author_id = '300'
31    AND     x.title       = 'Temporal Data and the Relational Model' );
32
33  COMMIT;
34
35  execute SYS.DBMS_STATS.gather_table_stats(USER, 'AUTHOR_PUBLICATIONS');
```

It didn't work? Well, try, try again until it does—or look at the examples in the appropriate source code listing directory for the book.

Hey, you know what? I was supposed to put the data in the database in uppercase so we could perform efficient case-insensitive queries. Well, I should fix that. Let's use the UPDATE statement.

Update

An UPDATE statement allows you to selectively update one or more column values for one or more rows in a specified table. In order to selectively update, you need to specify a WHERE clause in your UPDATE statement. Let's first take a look at an UPDATE statement without a WHERE clause.

Fix a Mistake with Update

As I alluded to earlier, I forgot to make the text values in the database all in uppercase. Listing 1-18 is my solution to this problem for the authors table.

Listing 1-18. A DML Statement for Updating the Authors Table, authors.upd

```
1  UPDATE authors
2  SET    name = upper(name);
3
4  COMMIT;
```

The syntax used by Listing 1-18 is as follows:

```
UPDATE  <table_name>
SET     <column_name_1> = <column_value_1>,
        <column_name_2> = <column_value_2>,...
        <column_name_N> = <column_value_N>;
```

where <table_name> is the name of the table to update, <column_name> is the name of a column to update, and <column_value> is the value to which to update the column in question.

In this case, an UPDATE statement without a WHERE clause is just what I needed. However, in practice, that's rarely the case. And, if you find yourself coding such an SQL statement, think twice.

An unconstrained UPDATE statement can be one of the most destructive SQL statements you'll ever execute by mistake. You can turn a lot of good data into garbage in seconds. So it's always a good idea to specify which rows to update with an additional WHERE clause. For example, I could have added the following line:

```
WHERE   name <> upper(name)
```

That would have limited the UPDATE to only those rows that are not already in uppercase.

It's Your Turn to Update

I've fixed my uppercase mistake in the authors table. Now you can do the same for the author_publications table. So please update the publication titles to uppercase.

1. Write the DML script.

2. Save the DML script with the same file name as your table name, but add a .upd extension.

3. Execute your script in SQL*Plus.

The titles in the author_publications table should now be in uppercase—good job. Listing 1-19 shows how I fixed this mistake.

Listing 1-19. DML for Updating Titles in the Publications Table, author_publications.upd

```
1  UPDATE author_publications
2  SET    title = upper(title)
3  WHERE  title <> upper(title);
4
5  COMMIT;
```

UPDATE statements can be quite complex. They can pull data values from other tables, for each column, or for multiple columns using subqueries. Let's look at the use of subqueries.

Update and Subqueries

One of the biggest mistakes PL/SQL programmers make is to write a PL/SQL program to update selected values in one table with selected values from another table. Why is this a big mistake? Because you don't need PL/SQL to do it. And, in fact, if you use PL/SQL, it will be slower than just doing it in SQL!

You haven't yet had an opportunity to work with any complex data, nor have I talked much about the SQL SELECT statement, so I won't show you an example yet. But look at the possible syntax:

```
UPDATE <table_name> U
SET    U.<column_name_N> = (
  SELECT S.<subquery_column_name_N>
  FROM   <subquery_table_name> S
  WHERE  S.<column_name_N> = U.<column_name_N>
  AND    ...)
WHERE u.<column_name_N> = <some_value>...;
```

This syntax allows you to update the value of a column in table <table_name>, aliased with the name U, with values in table <subquery_table_name>, aliased with the name S, based on the current value in the current row in table U. If that isn't powerful enough, look at this:

```
UPDATE <table_name> U
SET    (U.<column_name_1>,
        U.<column_name_2>, ...
        U.<column_name_N> ) = (
  SELECT S.<subquery_column_name_1>,
         S.<subquery_column_name_2>, ...
         S.<subquery_column_name_N>
  FROM   <subquery_table_name> S
  WHERE  S.<column_name_N> = U.<column_name_N>
  AND    ...)
WHERE u.<column_name_N> = <some_value>...;
```

Yes! You can update multiple columns at the same time simply by grouping them with parentheses. The moral of the story is, don't use PL/SQL to do something you can already do with SQL. I'll be harping on this moral throughout the book, so if you didn't get my point, relax, you'll hear it again and again in the coming chapters.

Delete

In practice, data is rarely deleted from a relational database when compared to how much is input, updated, and queried. Regardless, you should know how to delete data. With DELETE, however, you need to do things backwards.

A Change in Order

So you don't think Hugh Darwen is a genius? Well I do, but for the sake of our tutorial, let's say you want to delete his entries from the database.

Since you created an integrity constraint on the author_publications table (a foreign key), you need to delete Darwen's publications before you delete him from the authors table. Listing 1-20 is the DML to delete Darwen's entries from the author_publications table.

Listing 1-20. DML to Delete Darwen's Publications, author_publications_300.del

```
1  DELETE FROM author_publications
2  WHERE  id = 300;
```

The syntax for the DELETE statement used in Listing 1-20 is as follows:

```
DELETE FROM <table_name>
WHERE   <column_name_N> = <column_value_N>...;
```

where <table_name> is the name of the table to DELETE FROM, and <column_name> is one or more columns for which you specify some criteria.

Did you happen to notice that I didn't include a COMMIT statement? I will wait until you're finished with your part first.

It's Your Turn to Delete

Now that I've deleted the publications, it's time for you to delete the author.

1. Write the DML script without a COMMIT statement.

2. Save the DML script with the same file name as your table name, suffix it with _300, and then add a .del extension.

3. Execute your script in SQL*Plus.

Darwen should no longer be in the database. Listing 1-21 shows how I got rid of him.

Listing 1-21. DML for Deleting Darwen from the Authors Table, authors_300.del

```
1  DELETE FROM authors
2  WHERE  id = 300;
```

Oops, no more Darwen. I changed my mind. Let's fix that quickly!

Type ROLLBACK; at your SQL*Plus prompt and then press the Enter key. The transaction—everything you did from the last time you executed a COMMIT or ROLLBACK statement—has been rolled back. So it's as though you never deleted Darwen's entries. You didn't *really* think I was going to let you delete Darwen, did you?

Now we are ready to review the most used SQL statement: SELECT.

Select

In the end, all the power of a relational database comes down to its ability to manipulate data. At the heart of that ability lies the SQL SELECT statement. I could write an entire book about it, but I've got only a couple of pages to spare, so pay attention.

Listing 1-22 is a query for selecting all the author names from the authors table. There's no WHERE clause to constrain which rows you will see.

Listing 1-22. DML to Query the Author Table, author_names.sql

```
1  SELECT name
2  FROM    authors
3  ORDER BY name;
```

```
NAME
------------------
CHRIS J DATE
EDGAR F CODD
HUGH DARWEN
```

Listing 1-22 actually shows the query (SELECT statement) executed in SQL*Plus, along with the database's response.

The syntax of the SELECT statement in Listing 1-22 is as follows:

```
SELECT  <column_name_1>,
        <column_name_2>,
        <column_name_N>
FROM    <table_name>
[ORDER BY <order_by_column_name_N>]
```

where <column_name> is one of the columns in the table listed, <table_name> is the table to query, and <order_by_column_name> is one or more columns by which to sort the results.

In Listing 1-23, I add a WHERE clause to constrain the output to only those authors born before the year 1940.

Listing 1-23. DML to Show Only Authors Born Before 1940, author_names_before_1940.sql

```
1  SELECT name
2  FROM   authors
3  WHERE  birth_date < to_date('19400101', 'YYYYMMDD')
4  ORDER BY name;
```

```
NAME
------------------
EDGAR F CODD
```

So while this is all very nice, we've only started to scratch the surface of the SELECT statement's capabilities. Next, let's look at querying more than one table at a time.

Joins

Do you remember that way back in the beginning of this chapter you went through the mental exercise of matching the value of the id column in the authors table against the author_id column in the author_publications table in order to find out which publications were written by each author? What you were doing back then was *joining* the two tables on the id column.

Also recall that to demonstrate views, I created an authors_publications view? In that view, I joined the two tables, authors and author_publications, by their related columns, authors.id and author_publications.author_id. That too was an example of joining two tables on the id column.

Joins in a Where Clause

Listing 1-24 shows the SQL SELECT statement from that view created in Listing 1-11 with an added ORDER BY clause. In this example, I am joining the two tables using the WHERE clause (sometimes called *traditional Oracle join syntax*).

Listing 1-24. DML to Join the Authors and Publications Tables, authors_publications_where_join.sql

```
SQL> SELECT a.id,
  2          a.name,
  3          p.title,
  4          p.written_date
  5  FROM    authors a,
  6          author_publications p
  7  WHERE   a.id = p.author_id
  8  ORDER BY a.name,
  9          p.written_date,
 10          p.title;
```

```
 ID NAME               TITLE
----- ------------------ --------------------------------------------------
 200 CHRIS J DATE       THE THIRD MANIFESTO
 200 CHRIS J DATE       TEMPORAL DATA AND THE RELATIONAL MODEL
 200 CHRIS J DATE       AN INTRODUCTION TO DATABASE SYSTEMS
 200 CHRIS J DATE       DATABASE IN DEPTH: RELATIONAL THEORY FOR PRACTITION
 100 EDGAR F CODD       A RELATION MODEL OF DATA FOR LARGE SHARED DATA BANK
 100 EDGAR F CODD       THE RELATIONAL MODEL FOR DATABASE MANAGEMENT
 300 HUGH DARWEN        THE THIRD MANIFESTO
 300 HUGH DARWEN        TEMPORAL DATA AND THE RELATIONAL MODEL

8 rows selected.
```

Line 7 in Listing 1-24 has this code:

```
WHERE   a.id = p.author_id.
```

Line 7 joins the authors table a with the author_publications table p, on the columns id and author_id respectively.

However, there's a second, newer form of join syntax that uses the FROM clause in a SQL SELECT statement instead of the WHERE clause.

Joins in a From Clause

Listing 1-25 shows the newer join syntax. The newer join syntax is part of the ANSI standard. If you use it, it may make it easier to move to another ANSI standard compliant SQL database in the future. The join takes place in lines 5 through 6 in the FROM...ON clause.

Listing 1-25. DML to Join the Authors and Publications Tables, authors_publications_from_join.sql

```
SQL> SELECT a.id,
  2          a.name,
  3          p.title,
  4          p.written_date
  5  FROM    authors a JOIN
  6          author_publications p
```

```
 7  ON      a.id = p.author_id
 8  ORDER BY a.name,
 9           p.written_date,
10           p.title;
```

Both forms of the join syntax give the same results. I suggest you use the syntax that is consistent with the previous use of join syntax in the application you're currently working on, or follow the conventions of your development team.

It's Your Turn to Select

It's time to for you to try to use the SELECT statement. Show me all the authors who have coauthored a book.

1. Write the DML script.

2. Save the DML script with the file name coauthors.sql.

3. Execute your script in SQL*Plus.

You should get results something like this:

```
NAME
------------------
CHRIS J DATE
HUGH DARWEN
```

Next, show me all the publications that have been coauthored along with the author's name. Save the script with the file name coauthor_publications.sql. You should get results like this:

```
TITLE                                               NAME
--------------------------------------------------  ------------------
TEMPORAL DATA AND THE RELATIONAL MODEL              CHRIS J DATE
TEMPORAL DATA AND THE RELATIONAL MODEL              HUGH DARWEN
THE THIRD MANIFESTO                                 CHRIS J DATE
THE THIRD MANIFESTO                                 HUGH DARWEN
```

You can find my solutions to these two exercises in the source code listings you downloaded for the book. If you had difficulty writing the queries for these two exercises, then you need more experience with SQL queries before you can be proficient with PL/SQL. You'll be able to learn and use PL/SQL, but you'll be handicapped by your SQL skills.

In fact, everything we just covered should have been a review for you. If any of it was new, I recommend that you follow up learning PL/SQL with some additional training in SQL. As I said when we started on this journey together, you need to know SQL really well, because it makes up about 25% of every PL/SQL stored procedure.

Now that we have reviewed the SQL basics, I need to introduce you to a fictional example that you will use in the rest of the book.

Your Working Example

I know it's a lot of work, but you really need to buy into the following fictional example in order to have something realistic to work with as you proceed through this book. I would love to take on one of your real business problems, but I don't work at the same company you do, so that would be very difficult. So let me start by telling you a short story.

Your Example Narrative

You're going to do some software development for a company called Very Dirty Manufacturing, Inc. (VDMI). VDMI prides itself with being able to take on the most environmentally damaging manufacturing jobs (dirty) in the most environmentally responsible way possible (clean).

Of course, VDMI gets paid big bucks for taking on such legally risky work, but the firm is also dedicated to preventing any of its employees from injury due to the work. The managers are so dedicated to the health and well-being of their workforce that they plan on having their industrial hygiene (IH), occupational health (OH), and safety records available on the Internet for public viewing (more on what IH and OH are about in just a moment).

Your job is the development of the worker demographics subsystem for maintaining the IH, OH, and safety records for VDMI. Internally, management will need to review worker data by the following:

- Organization in which a person works

- Location where the employee works

- Job and tasks the employee performs while working

For IH, environmental samples will be taken in the areas where people work to make sure they are not being exposed to hazardous chemicals or noise without the right protections in place. For OH, workers who do work in dirty areas will be under regular medical surveillance to make sure that they are not being harmed while doing their work. And last, any accidents involving workers will also be documented so that no similar accidents take place, and to ensure that the workers are properly compensated for their injuries.

Externally, the sensitivity of the information will prevent the company from identifying for whom the data presented exists, but the information will still be presented by the high-level organization, location, and job. Therefore, the same demographic data and its relationship to workers in the firm need to be in place.

Your Example ERD

Now that you have an overview of the situation, let's take a look at an architectural representation of the demographic subsystem. Figure 1-2 shows the ERD for the demographic subsystem.

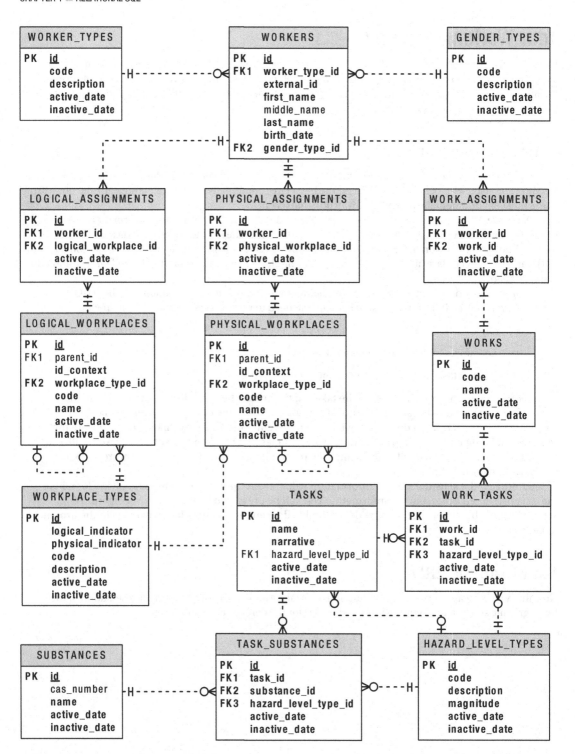

Figure 1-2. *VMDI's IH, OH, and safety demographic subsystem ERD*

In order for you to get a better understanding of the ERD, think of each table in the diagram as one of the following:

- Content
- Codes
- Intersections

What do these terms mean?

Content

Think of content as anything your users may actually need to type into the system, which varies greatly. For example, information like a worker's name and birth date changes a lot from one worker to the next. Since that data is kept in the WORKERS table, think of the WORKERS table as a content table.

Data in the WORKERS table is the kind of information that you're unlikely to translate into another language should you present the information in a report. I would also classify as content tables the LOGICAL_WORKPLACES, PHYSICAL_WORKPLACES, and WORKS tables, which describe the organization, location, and the job of a worker, respectively. However, you might also think of them as codes.

Codes

In order to make the categorization, classification, or typing of data specified in a content table consistent across all entries—for example, workers entered into the WORKERS table—I've added some code tables. There are only a limited number of types of workers, and definitely only a limited number of genders, so I've added a WORKER_TYPES code table and a GENDER_TYPES code table. Code tables act as the definitive source of categories, classes, types, and so on when specifying codified information in a content table like WORKERS.

Here are some of the reasons that it's important to use code tables:

- They constrain the values entered into a table to an authoritative list of entries. This improves quality.

- The primary key of a code table is typically an identifier (ID) that is a sequence-generated number with no inherent meaning other than it is the primary key's value. An ID value is a compact value that can then be stored in the content table to reference the much larger code and description values. This improves performance.

- Storing the sequence-generated ID of a code table in a content table will allow you to later change the code or description values for a particular code without needing to do so in the content table. This improves application maintenance.

- Storing the sequence-generated ID of a code table in a content table will also allow you to later change the code or description for a code on the fly for an internationalized application. This improves flexibility.

Think of the WORKER_TYPES, GENDER_TYPES, WORKPLACE_TYPES, and HAZARD_LEVEL_TYPES tables as code tables. They all have a similar set of behaviors that you will later make accessible with PL/SQL functions and procedures.

Intersections

Think of intersections as a means of documenting history. Understanding that there is a history of information is the single-most portion missing in the analyses of business problems. Most often, a many-to-many relationship table (an intersection) will be created that captures only the "current" relationship between content entities, but there's always a history, and the history is almost always what's actually needed to solve the business problem in question.

In the refresher earlier in this chapter, you worked with two tables (or entities) that did not require you to keep a history. However, in the example here, you definitely need to maintain a history of who workers reported to, where they actually did their work, and what they did. Intersections document timelines, as shown in Figure 1-3.

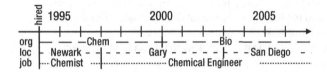

Figure 1-3. *An employment timeline*

Examining Figure 1-3, you can see that the employee in question has the following history:

- Worked in the Chemicals department from 1994 through 1999, and then in the Biologicals department since (logical assignment)

- Worked at the Newark, New Jersey location from 1994 through 1996, in Gary, Indiana through 2002, and then in sunny San Diego since (physical assignment)

- Worked as a chemist from 1994 through 1996, and then as a chemical engineer since (work assignment)

An intersection table has a beginning and end date for every assignment period. Think of the LOGICAL_ASSIGNMENTS, PHYSICAL_ASSIGNMENTS, and WORK_ASSIGNMENTS tables as history tables that hold an intersection in time between the WORKERS table and the LOGICAL_WORKPLACES, PHYSICAL_WORKPLACES, and WORKS tables, respectively.

Now that you're familiar with the ERD, you can start creating the tables.

Create a Code Table

Let's create some code tables. I'll write the script for the first code table, and then you do the other three. Listing 1-26 is a script to create the WORKER_TYPES code table.

Listing 1-26. DDL for Creating the WORKER_TYPES Code Table, worker_types.tab

```
01  rem worker_types.tab
02  rem by Donald J. Bales on 2014-10-20
03  rem
04
05  --drop   table WORKER_TYPES;
06  create table WORKER_TYPES (
07  id                              number(38)               not null,
08  code                            varchar2(30)             not null,
```

```
09  description                       varchar2(80)                        not null,
10  active_date                       date     default SYSDATE            not null,
11  inactive_date                     date     default '31-DEC-9999' not null);
12
13  --drop   sequence WORKER_TYPES_ID;
14  create sequence WORKER_TYPES_ID
15  start with 1;
16
17  alter  table WORKER_TYPES add
18  constraint   WORKER_TYPES_PK
19  primary key ( id )
20  using index;
21
22  alter  table WORKER_TYPES add
23  constraint   WORKER_TYPES_UK
24  unique ( code, active_date )
25  using index;
26
27  execute SYS.DBMS_STATS.gather_table_stats(USER, 'WORKER_TYPES');
```

This listing is more complex than the previous ones in this chapter. Here's the breakdown:

- Lines 1 through 3 document the name of the script, the author, and the date it was written. This is typical—everyone wants to know who to blame.

- Lines 5 and 13 have DROP statements that I've commented out. Those were really handy when I was in the iterative development cycle, where I had to edit my script to refine it and then recompile.

- Lines 6 through 11 contain the DDL to create the table WORKER_TYPES.

- Lines 14 and 15 contain the DDL to create WORKER_TYPES_ID, a sequence for the table's primary key column, id.

- Lines 17 through 20 contain the DDL to alter the table in order to add a primary key constraint.

- Lines 22 through 25 contain the DDL to alter the table in order to add a unique key constraint. This constraint will allow only unique code values in the code table.

Since it's a code table, I can seed it with some initial values. I've written a second script for that, shown in Listing 1-27.

Listing 1-27. DML Script to Populate the WORKER_TYPES Code Table, worker_types.ins

```
01  rem worker_types.ins
02  rem by Donald J. Bales on 2014-10-20
03  rem
04
05  insert into WORKER_TYPES (
06          id,
07          code,
08          description )
```

```
09  values (
10          WORKER_TYPES_ID.nextval,
11          'C',
12          'Contractor' );
13
14  insert into WORKER_TYPES (
15          id,
16          code,
17          description )
18  values (
19          WORKER_TYPES_ID.nextval,
20          'E',
21          'Employee' );
22
23  insert into WORKER_TYPES (
24          id,
25          code,
26          description )
27  values (
28          WORKER_TYPES_ID.nextval,
29          'U',
30          'Unknown' );
31
32  commit;
33
34  execute SYS.DBMS_STATS.gather_table_stats(USER, 'WORKER_TYPES');
```

Here's what's happening in Listing 1-27:

- In lines 1 through 3, I've added the author and written date.

- In lines 5 through 12, 14 through 21, and 23 through 30, I've added three DML INSERT VALUES statements in order to add three worker types to the WORKER_TYPES table.

- In lines 10, 19, and 28, I'm allocating a new sequence value from the primary key's sequence using the pseudo-column .nextval.

- In line 32, I commit the inserts so they are permanently accessible to everyone on the database.

After I execute these two scripts, I can query WORKER_TYPES and get results like this:

```
SQL> column code          format a4;
SQL> column description    format a13;
SQL> column active_date    format a13;
SQL> column inactive_date  format a13;
SQL>
SQL> select *
  2  from    WORKER_TYPES
  3  order by code;
```

```
   ID CODE DESCRIPTION    ACTIVE_DATE    INACTIVE_DATE
---------- ---- ------------- ------------- -------------
    1 C    Contractor     07-DEC-14      31-DEC-99
    2 E    Employee       07-DEC-14      31-DEC-99
    3 U    Unknown        07-DEC-14      31-DEC-99
```

CODING CONVENTIONS

Coding conventions (or standards) are something all professional programmers follow religiously.

SQL Coding Conventions

In the refresher part of this chapter, I capitalized the SQL keywords so it was easy for you to notice them in the syntax statement that followed their use. In practice, I don't do that. When I code SQL, I follow these simple rules:

- I type table names in all caps, literals in uppercase/lowercase/mixed case as required, and everything else in lowercase. Why? First, since SQL is table-centric, I want table names to stick out like a sore thumb. Second, lowercase is actually easier to read. And finally, lowercase is easier to type, and after 30 years of typing, you'll know why that's important.

- I format my code so column names, table names, and parameters in WHERE clauses all line up in nice left-justified columns. That way, the text is easy to scan.

- I name scripts with the same name as the object they are creating, dropping, inserting, updating, and so on, and an appropriate filename extension in order to make the names of the scripts as obvious as possible.

SQL Filename Extension Conventions

The following are the filename extensions I use:

- .tab: Create table
- .alt: Alter table (to add, modify, or drop a column)
- .ndx: Create index
- .pkc: Alter table/add constraint/primary key (usually included in the create table script)
- .fkc: Alter table/add constraint/foreign key (usually included in the create table script)
- .ukc: Alter table/add constraint/unique (usually included in the create table script)
- .drp: Drop table
- .ins: Insert into
- .upd: Update
- .del: Delete from
- .sql: Select from

It's Your Turn to Create Code Tables

Now that you've seen me do it, you should be able to code the scripts to do the same for the GENDER_TYPES, HAZARD_LEVEL_TYPES, and WORKPLACE_TYPES code tables. Code the scripts, saving them with the filenames gender_types.tab, hazard_level_types.tab, and workplace_types.tab, respectively. Then execute each script. You can see my solutions to these scripts in the book's source code directory for Chapter 1. Now let's move on to creating content tables.

Create a Content Table

This time, let's create some content tables. I'll write the first two scripts, and then you do the rest. Listing 1-28 is a script to create the WORKERS table.

Listing 1-28. DDL to Create the WORKERS Table, workers.tab

```
01  rem workers.tab
02  rem by Donald J. Bales on 2014-10-20
03  rem
04
05  --drop   table WORKERS;
06  create table WORKERS (
07  id                         number(38)                 not null,
08  worker_type_id             number(38)                 not null,
09  external_id                varchar2(30)               not null,
10  first_name                 varchar2(30)               not null,
11  middle_name                varchar2(30),
12  last_name                  varchar2(30)               not null,
13  name                       varchar2(100)              not null,
14  birth_date                 date                       not null,
15  gender_type_id             number                     not null );
16
17  --drop   sequence WORKERS_ID;
18  create sequence WORKERS_ID
19  start with 1;
20
21  --drop   sequence EXTERNAL_ID_SEQ;
22  create sequence EXTERNAL_ID_SEQ
23  start with 100000000 order;
24
25  alter  table WORKERS add
26  constraint   WORKERS_PK
27  primary key ( id )
28  using index;
29
30  alter  table WORKERS add
31  constraint   WORKERS_UK1
32  unique ( external_id )
33  using index;
34
```

```
35  alter  table WORKERS add
36  constraint    WORKERS_UK2
37  unique (
38  name,
39  birth_date,
40  gender_type_id )
41  using index;
42
43  alter  table WORKERS add
44  constraint    WORKERS_FK1
45  foreign key   ( worker_type_id )
46  references    WORKER_TYPES ( id );
47
48  alter  table WORKERS add
49  constraint    WORKERS_FK2
50  foreign key   ( gender_type_id )
51  references    GENDER_TYPES ( id );
52
53  execute SYS.DBMS_STATS.gather_table_stats(USER, 'WORKERS');
```

Looks familiar, doesn't it? It looks a lot like the code table scripts you created earlier. The exceptions are lines 43 through 46 and 48 through 51, where I've added DDL to create two foreign key constraints. The first foreign key creates an integrity constraint between the code table WORKER_TYPES, while the second does the same for code table GENDER_TYPES. These constraints will prevent anyone from deleting a code that is in use by the WORKERS table.

Listing 1-29 shows the code to create the LOGICAL_WORKPLACES table. I'm showing you this listing because this table has some interesting new columns: parent_id and id_context.

Listing 1-29. DDL to Create the LOGICAL_WORKPLACES Table, logical_workplaces.tab

```
01  rem logical_workplaces.tab
02  rem by Donald J. Bales on 2014-10-20
03  rem
04
05  --drop   table LOGICAL_WORKPLACES;
06  create table LOGICAL_WORKPLACES (
07  id                        number(38)                      not null,
08  parent_id                 number(38),
09  id_context                varchar2(100)                   not null,
10  workplace_type_id         number                          not null,
11  code                      varchar2(30)                    not null,
12  name                      varchar2(80)                    not null,
13  active_date               date      default SYSDATE       not null,
14  inactive_date             date      default '31-DEC-9999' not null );
15
16  --drop   sequence LOGICAL_WORKPLACES_ID;
17  create sequence LOGICAL_WORKPLACES_ID
18  start with 1;
19
```

```
20   alter   table LOGICAL_WORKPLACES add
21   constraint    LOGICAL_WORKPLACES_PK
22   primary key (
23   id )
24   using index;
25
26   alter   table LOGICAL_WORKPLACES add
27   constraint    LOGICAL_WORKPLACES_UK1
28   unique (
29   id_context )
30   using index;
31
32   alter   table LOGICAL_WORKPLACES add
33   constraint    LOGICAL_WORKPLACES_UK2
34   unique (
35   code,
36   name,
37   active_date )
38   using index;
39
40   alter   table LOGICAL_WORKPLACES add
41   constraint    LOGICAL_WORKPLACES_FK1
42   foreign key                ( parent_id )
43   references    LOGICAL_WORKPLACES ( id );
44
45   alter   table LOGICAL_WORKPLACES add
46   constraint    LOGICAL_WORKPLACES_FK2
47   foreign key    ( workplace_type_id )
48   references    WORKPLACE_TYPES ( id );
49
50   execute SYS.DBMS_STATS.gather_table_stats(USER, 'LOGICAL_WORKPLACES');
```

A logical workplace like a department may belong to a business unit, while its business unit may belong to a company. The parent_id column allows you to store the id of a department's parent business unit with the department, so you can document the organization hierarchy. With this information, you can present an organization chart, find everyone in a business unit, and so on.

The id_context column is a convenience or performance column for the mechanics of querying the database. You are going to write a PL/SQL function that will create an ID context string for this column. The ID context string will list all of the parent IDs, plus the logical workplace ID of the current row, separated by a known character, such as a period (.)—for example, 1.13.14. This will greatly improve the performance of any LIKE queries against the hierarchy of the organizations in the table.

It's Your Turn to Create Content Tables

Now that you've seen me do it, you should be able to code the scripts to do the same for the PHYSICAL_WORKPLACES , TASKS, and WORKS tables. So code the scripts, saving them with the filenames physical_workplaces.tab, tasks.tab, and works.tab, respectively. Then execute each script. You can view my solutions to these scripts in the book's source code directory for Chapter 1.

Now let's move on to creating intersection tables.

Create an Intersection Table

It's time to create some intersection tables. I'll write the first script, and then you write the rest. Listing 1-30 is a script to create the LOGICAL_ASSIGNMENTS table.

Listing 1-30. DDL to Create the LOGICAL_ASSIGNMENTS Table, logical_assignments.tab

```
01  rem logical_assignments.tab
02  rem by Donald J. Bales on 2014-10-20
03  rem
04
05  --drop   table LOGICAL_ASSIGNMENTS;
06  create table LOGICAL_ASSIGNMENTS (
07  id                          number(38)                    not null,
08  worker_id                   number(38)                    not null,
09  logical_workplace_id        number(38)                    not null,
10  active_date                 date      default SYSDATE      not null,
11  inactive_date               date      default '31-DEC-9999' not null );
12
13  --drop   sequence LOGICAL_ASSIGNMENTS_ID;
14  create sequence LOGICAL_ASSIGNMENTS_ID
15  start with 1;
16
17  alter  table LOGICAL_ASSIGNMENTS add
18  constraint   LOGICAL_ASSIGNMENTS_PK
19  primary key ( id )
20  using index;
21
22  alter  table LOGICAL_ASSIGNMENTS add
23  constraint   LOGICAL_ASSIGNMENTS_UK
24  unique (
25  worker_id,
26  active_date )
27  using index;
28
29  alter  table LOGICAL_ASSIGNMENTS add
30  constraint   LOGICAL_ASSIGNMENTS_FK1
31  foreign key   ( worker_id )
32  references   WORKERS ( id );
33
34  alter  table LOGICAL_ASSIGNMENTS add
35  constraint   LOGICAL_ASSIGNMENTS_FK2
36  foreign key   ( logical_workplace_id )
37  references   LOGICAL_WORKPLACES ( id );
38
39  execute SYS.DBMS_STATS.gather_table_stats(USER, 'LOGICAL_ASSIGNMENTS');
```

I know; you don't even need me to explain it anymore. I just wanted to make sure you have a nice pattern to mimic.

It's Your Turn to Create Intersection Tables

Just do it! Create tables PHYSICAL_ASSIGNMENTS, WORK_ASSIGNMENTS, and WORK_TASKS. Code your scripts with file names physical_assignments.tab, work_assignments.tab, and work_tasks.tab. Then execute your scripts.

Summary

By now you should have a fairly complete set of sample tables that you can work with when programming in PL/SQL. You've reviewed the basics of relational SQL, and then put that to work to create your working example. If you had any trouble with the SQL used so far, I sincerely encourage you to get some supplemental materials and/or training in order to improve your SQL skills. You've heard the old adage, "A chain is only as strong as its weakest link," haven't you?

So you think your SQL is up to the task of programming in PL/SQL? Well, let's get started!

CHAPTER 2

■ ■ ■

Blocks, Functions, and Procedures

In this chapter, as the title suggests, you'll learn about the foundational structures of PL/SQL: blocks, functions, and procedures. Blocks define the structures upon which functions and procedures are built. Functions and procedures are very similar, but distinct, in that a function returns a value to a calling function or procedure, while a procedure does not. So let's begin our discussion of PL/SQL by starting with its foundation: the block.

Blocks

The Procedure Language extension for SQL (PL/SQL) has a block structure. Every piece of code executes in a block, similar to Java, JavaScript, and PHP's try-catch clause; Python's try-except clause; or Ruby's begin-rescue-end clause. However, PL/SQL has four keywords:

- DECLARE: Every PL/SQL block has a declaration section. This is where you allocate memory for cursors, data type definitions, variables, embedded functions, and procedures (don't worry—you'll learn about all of these in this book, beginning with functions and procedures in this chapter). Sometimes when you code a PL/SQL program, you won't even use the declaration section, but it's still there.

- BEGIN: Every PL/SQL block has an executable section. It starts with the keyword BEGIN. BEGIN marks the beginning of where you put your program logic. And every PL/SQL program must have at least one line of executable code, even if it's the keyword NULL, which in this context means no operation.

- EXCEPTION: Every PL/SQL block has an exception-handling section. It starts with the keyword EXCEPTION. This is where you will catch any database or PL/SQL errors, or as they are affectionately known, *exceptions*. Like the declaration section, sometimes you won't even use an exception-handling section, but it's still there.

- END: Every PL/SQL block ends with the keyword END.

Anonymous Blocks

We'll start with an anonymous PL/SQL block. It's called *anonymous* because it's not going to be saved in the database, so it will never have a name. In practice, you won't find yourself using anonymous blocks in production, but you'll use them throughout the development process. They're perfect for creating test units that you'll eventually move into your stored PL/SQL blocks. You'll learn more about that in Chapter 8. For now, let's look at an example.

Anonymous Block Example

Listing 2-1 is an example of an anonymous PL/SQL block. Comments describe the different sections.

Listing 2-1. An Anonymous PL/SQL Block, anonymous.sql

```
01  -- This is an anonymous procedure, so it has no name
02  DECLARE
03    /*
04      You declare local cursors, variables, and methods here,
05      but you don't need to have a declaration section.
06    */
07  BEGIN
08    -- You write your executable code here
09
10    NULL;  -- Ahhh, you've got to have at least one command!
11  EXCEPTION
12    when NO_DATA_FOUND then
13      raise_application_error(-20000,
14        'Hey, This is in the exception-handling section!');
15  END;
16  /
17  -- the forward slash on a line by itself says execute this procedure
```

Let's go through Listing 2-1 line by line:

- Line 1 is a single-line comment. Single-line comments start with a double-dash (--), but line 1 is not part of the PL/SQL block or program because it exists outside the block structure.

- Line 2 starts the block with the keyword DECLARE. This anonymous PL/SQL block could have started with the keyword BEGIN because it doesn't have anything to declare.

- Lines 3 through 6 are a multiline comment in the declaration section. Multiline comments start with a slash and asterisk (/*) and end with an asterisk and slash (*/).

- Line 7 starts the PL/SQL executable section of the PL/SQL block with the keyword BEGIN.

- Line 8 is a single-line comment in the executable section.

- Line 10 is the PL/SQL keyword NULL followed by a single-line comment. NULL in this context means no operation. I put it there because every PL/SQL block must have at least one line of code, or it won't compile. The NULL command is terminated with a semicolon. In PL/SQL, a semicolon denotes the end of a command.

- Line 11 starts the exception-handling section with the keyword EXCEPTION. If you code an exception-handling section, you must catch at least one exception. In this case, I've coded a NO_DATA_FOUND exception, which will raise an application error with my message should a NO_DATA_FOUND exception occur.

- Line 15 ends the PL/SQL block or program with the keyword END.

- Line 16 has **a** *single forward slash (/), which is a signal to SQL*Plus* to execute the PL/SQL block. In this case—that is, with an anonymous PL/SQL block—the Oracle database will compile and then run the code in the PL/SQL block.

- Line 17 is another single-line comment that, too, exists outside the PL/SQL block.

It's Your Turn to Execute an Anonymous Block

Now it's time for you to execute an anonymous PL/SQL block/program.

1. Open SQL*Plus and connect to the database with username RPS.

2. At the SQL> prompt, type the following:

```
set serveroutput on size 1000000
begin
  SYS.DBMS_OUTPUT.put_line('Hi there genius!');
end;
/
```

After you type the forward slash on a line by itself, you will have executed your very first PL/SQL procedure, and a very complimentary one at that.

The first line tells SQL*Plus to echo the database's output for your session to the screen after the PL/SQL procedure is finished executing. Note that `set serveroutput on size 1000000` is a SQL*Plus command and is not part of the anonymous block.

The line that starts with `begin` starts your PL/SQL procedure's executable code section. The next line calls the `put_line` procedure in package (library of stored procedures) `DBMS_OUTPUT`, owned by user SYS:

```
sys.dbms_output.put_line('Hi there genius!');
```

Here, `put_line` stores your text in a buffer until the PL/SQL procedure ends. Then SQL*Plus displays the text from that buffer on the screen for you to see.

The fourth line, which starts with `end`, ends the anonymous PL/SQL procedure. Finally, as stated earlier, the forward slash (/) on a line by itself tells SQL*Plus to execute the procedure.

In this example, you didn't code declaration or exception-handling sections, but they're still there! If an error occurs between the `BEGIN` and `END` keywords, PL/SQL will use the default (invisible) exception handler to raise the error to the enclosing program unit, which, in this case, is SQL*Plus.

Exceptions

Exceptions allow you to catch errors as your PL/SQL program executes, so you have control over what happens in response to those errors. PL/SQL predefines more than 20 named exceptions, but you'll probably use only a few.

■ **Note**   After you've gained more PL/SQL experience, you may even want to define your own named exceptions. For more information about custom exceptions, see Oracle's *PL/SQL User's Guide and Reference*.

Common Exceptions

As you'll learn in future chapters, there are a handful of commonly seen exceptions. The rest occur only when there are catastrophic problems with the database, the network, or your PL/SQL code.

Two exceptions are very common:

- NO_DATA_FOUND: You'll get a NO_DATA_FOUND exception anytime you code a SQL SELECT statement that does not return any rows.

- TOO_MANY_ROWS: If you code a SELECT statement where you expect only one row but you get more than one, you'll get a TOO_MANY_ROWS exception.

Catching an Exception

You add the keyword EXCEPTION between the keywords BEGIN and END in order to add an exception-handling section to your PL/SQL block. Once you do that, any error that occurs between the keywords BEGIN and EXCEPTION will be handled by your exception-handling section.

Functions

A FUNCTION is a PL/SQL block or method that returns a value, so it can be used on the right-hand side of an assignment. Here is an example:

```
n_value := to_number('123.45');
```

In this line of PL/SQL code, n_value is a numeric variable (we'll cover variables in the next chapter). n_value is followed by an assignment operator, which is a colon followed by an equal sign (:=). Next is the PL/SQL built-in function to_number(text in varchar2), which parses a varchar2 data type, and then returns its numeric value—that is, if the varchar2 represents a number; otherwise, the function raises an INVALID_NUMBER exception.

Since a FUNCTION returns a value, you can also use it in a SQL statement, as in this example:

```
SQL> select to_number('A') from dual;
select to_number('A') from dual
          *
ERROR at line 1:
ORA-01722: invalid number
```

Look, there's that INVALID_NUMBER exception I was talking about!

Create a Function

Instead of dealing with errors when we try to convert a varchar2 (character string) to a number on the fly as in a SELECT statement, let's create an errorless to_number() function. Listing 2-2 is the DDL to do just that.

Listing 2-2. An Errorless to_number( ) Function, to_number_or_null.fun

```
01  CREATE OR REPLACE FUNCTION to_number_or_null (
02  aiv_number       IN      varchar2 )
03  return           number is
```

```
04  /*
05  to_number_or_null.fun
06  by Donald J. Bales on 2014-10-20
07  An errorless to_number( ) method
08  */
09  begin
10    return to_number(aiv_number);
11  exception
12    when OTHERS then
13      return NULL;
14  end to_number_or_null;
15  /
16  @fe.sql to_number_or_null;
```

The DDL syntax used in Listing 2-2 to create the function is as follows:

```
CREATE [OR REPLACE] FUNCTION <function_name> [(
<parameter_name_1>              [IN] [OUT] <parameter_data_type_1>,
<parameter_name_2>              [IN] [OUT] <parameter_data_type_2>,...
<parameter_name_N>              [IN] [OUT] <parameter_data_type_N> )]
RETURN                                     <return_data_type> IS
  --the declaration section
BEGIN
  -- the executable section
  return <return_data_type>;
EXCEPTION
  -- the exception-handling section
END;
/
```

where <function_name> is the name of the FUNCTION; <parameter_name> is the name of a parameter being passed IN, OUT, or IN and OUT; <parameter_data_type> is the PL/SQL data type of the corresponding parameter; and <return_data_type> is the PL/SQL data type of the value that will be returned by the FUNCTION when it completes its execution. The brackets ([ ]) around the keywords OR REPLACE denote that they are optional. The brackets around the parameters denote that they are optional, too.

The block structure of a FUNCTION is exactly the same as an anonymous procedure, except for the addition of the Data Definition Language (DDL) CREATE FUNCTION keywords, the optional parameters, and the RETURN clause.

Let's take a look at Listing 2-2 line by line:

- Line 1 has the DDL keywords to CREATE a stored FUNCTION. These take the place of the keyword DECLARE used earlier in the anonymous PL/SQL block.

- Line 2 declares one parameter, aiv_number, a varchar2 value passed INto the FUNCTION.

- Line 3 contains the RETURN clause. In this case, I'm returning a number.

- Lines 4 through 8 contain a multiline comment that lists the function's source code filename, the name of the author, the date the function was written, and a description of the function's purpose. So the only thing in the declaration section of this PL/SQL block is the multiline comment.

- On line 9, the keyword BEGIN starts the execution section of the PL/SQL block.

- On line 10, I return the built-in to_number( )'s return value for converting the varchar2 variable aiv_number to a number. Then the program ends. However, if the built-in to_number( ) raises an exception, the program's execution branches to the exception-handling section.

- On line 11, the keyword EXCEPTION starts the exception-handling section of this PL/SQL block.

- On line 12, the exception handler checks to see if the raised exception is the named exception OTHERS (a catch-all exception). If it is, it executes the code that follows it on line 13. It may have sufficed to use the execption INVALID_NUMBER; however, in practice, Oracle may define additional numeric conversion exceptions in the future, and consequently, my errorless routine might actually report an error!

- On line 13, I return NULL if there is an OTHERS, which includes INVALID_NUMBER, exception. That's what makes this an errorless to_number( ) function. If there are any *other* exceptions, the exception hander will not raise the error to the enclosing PL/SQL block or program, which in this case, will be SQL*Plus.

- On line 14, the keyword END denotes the end of the PL/SQL block, and hence the FUNCTION.

- On line 15, the single slash character (/) tells SQL*Plus to execute the DDL, which stores the PL/SQL in the database and then compiles it.

- Line 16 contains a helper SQL script that will list any compilation errors. Most of the time, this script will simply have one line of code that says show errors. However, if you're compiling into another schema (other than the username you're logged in with), you may need a more complex SQL script to display errors.

Now let's try using this errorless FUNCTION in a SELECT statement:

```
SQL> select to_number_or_null('A') from DUAL;
```

```
TO_NUMBER_OR_NULL('A')
----------------------
```

Ta da! It returned a NULL value since the letter *A* is not a number. Just in case you're a skeptic, here's a second test:

```
SQL> select to_number_or_null('234.56') from DUAL;
```

```
TO_NUMBER_OR_NULL('234.56')
---------------------------
                     234.56
```

Yes, indeed, it works correctly!

It's Your Turn to Create a Function

For this exercise, you'll create a function that returns a date value. You can use the function in Listing 2-2 as a model. This time, you'll pass this new function a varchar2 value that represents a date in the form *MM/DD/YYYY*. Your function will parse the varchar2 value and return a date data type if the varchar2 value is actually a date in the form *MM/DD/YYYY*; otherwise, it will return NULL.

You can use the PL/SQL built-in function to_date(text in varchar2, format in varchar2) in your function to do the actual parsing of the date. In the following form, to_date( ) will return a date value if it successfully parses the passed varchar2 value, or raise an exception if the passed varchar2 value is not a date in the format *MM/DD/YYYY*:

```
return to_date(aiv_date, 'MM/DD/YYYY');
```

Using this built-in function, create your function by following these steps.

1. Open your text editor, and code the DDL to create your function.

2. Save your new DDL script with the file name to_mmsddsyyyy_or_null.fun.

3. At your SQL*Plus prompt, type the at sign (@) followed by the name of your file in order to store and compile your new function.

4. Test your new function by using it in a SELECT statement against table DUAL.

Listing 2-3 shows my solution for this exercise.

Listing 2-3. An Errorless to_date( ) Function, to_mmsddsyyyy_or_null.fun

```
01  create or replace FUNCTION to_mmsddsyyyy_or_null (
02  aiv_date              in      varchar2 )
03  return                        date is
04  /*
05  to_mmsddsyyyy_or_null.fun
06  by Donald J. Bales on 2014-10-20
07  An errorless to_date( ) method
08  */
09  begin
10    return to_date(aiv_date, 'MM/DD/YYYY');
11  exception
12    /*
13    There are too many possible errors, for example:
14      ORA-01830: date format picture ends before
15                 converting entire input string
16      ORA-01843: not a valid month
17      ORA-01847: day of month must be between 1
18                 and last day of month
19      ORA-01858: a non-numeric character was found
20                 where a numeric was expected
21    so I used the exception OTHERS
22    */
23    when OTHERS then
24      return NULL;
25  end to_mmsddsyyyy_or_null;
26  /
27  @fe.sql to_mmsddsyyyy_or_null;
```

First, I'll test it using a SELECT statement against DUAL:

```
SQL> select to_mmsddsyyyy_or_null('A') from DUAL;
```

TO_MMSDDSYYYY_OR

Well, that worked. The to_mmsddsyyyy_or_null() function returned a NULL because the letter *A* is not a date in the form *MM/DD/YYYY*. So let's try a date string. This time, however, I'll execute the anonymous PL/SQL block in Listing 2-4 as a test unit in order to test the function.

Listing 2-4. A Test Unit for Function to_mmsddsyyyy_or_null( ), to_mmsddsyyyy_or_null.sql

```
01  rem to_mmsddsyyyy_or_null.sql
02  rem by Donald J. Bales on 2014-10-20
03  rem FUNCTION to_mmsddsyyyy_or_null() test unit
04
05  begin
06    sys.dbms_output.put_line(to_mmsddsyyyy_or_null('01/01/1980'));
07    sys.dbms_output.put_line(to_mmsddsyyyy_or_null('02/29/1980'));
08    sys.dbms_output.put_line(to_mmsddsyyyy_or_null('02/29/1981'));
09    sys.dbms_output.put_line(to_mmsddsyyyy_or_null('9/9/2006'));
10    sys.dbms_output.put_line(to_mmsddsyyyy_or_null('9/9/9999'));
11    sys.dbms_output.put_line(to_mmsddsyyyy_or_null('1/1/4712 BC'));
12  end;
13  /
```

The following output from executing function to_mmsddsyyyy_or_null()'s test unit shows that it's working great. The tests on lines 8 and 11 should have returned NULL because I passed invalid date strings, and they did!

```
SQL> @to_mmsddsyyyy_or_null.sql

01-JAN-80
29-FEB-80
09-SEP-06
09-SEP-99
PL/SQL procedure successfully completed.
```

Up to this point, you've seen an anonymous PL/SQL block and a function's PL/SQL block. The differences between the two are that an anonymous block is not permanently stored in the database with a name, nor can it return a value. Now let's take a look at PL/SQL blocks that do have names, but don't return values: procedures.

Procedures

PL/SQL procedures don't return a value. They just perform their instructions and return. Of course, this means that you can't use procedures on the right-hand side of an assignment statement like a function.

Create a Procedure

Listing 2-5 is a very simple example of a procedure. It's a wrapper around the Oracle SYS.DBMS_LOCK package's procedure sleep(seconds in number). This procedure will stop executing (or sleep) without using many CPU cycles for the number of seconds specified. I'll admit, it's kind of lame, but we're just starting out here, so I'm keeping things simple.

▪ **Note**   By default, the SYS.DBMS_LOCK package is not accessible by non-DBA users. The username creation script in this book's appendix will grant you access, but if you don't use that script, you may need to ask your DBA to explicitly grant you execute access to package SYS.DBMS_LOCK.

Listing 2-5. A Wrapper Procedure for SYS.DBMS_LOCK.sleep( ), wait.prc

```
01  CREATE OR REPLACE PROCEDURE wait(
02  ain_seconds        IN      number) is
03  /*
04  wait.prc
05  by Donald J. Bales on 2014-10-20
06  Wrapper for SYS.DBMS_LOCK.sleep()
07  */
08  begin
09    SYS.DBMS_LOCK.sleep(ain_seconds);
10  end wait;
11  /
12  @pe.sql wait
```

The DDL syntax used by Listing 2-5 is as follows:

```
CREATE [OR REPLACE] PROCEDURE <procedure_name> [(
<parameter_name_1>         [IN] [OUT] <parameter_data_type_1>,
<parameter_name_2>         [IN] [OUT] <parameter_data_type_2>,...
<parameter_name_N>         [IN] [OUT] <parameter_data_type_N> )] IS
  --the declaration section
BEGIN
  -- the executable section
EXCEPTION
  -- the exception-handling section
END;
/
```

where <procedure_name> is the name of the PROCEDURE; <parameter_name> is the name of a parameter being passed IN, OUT, or IN and OUT; and <parameter_data_type> is the PL/SQL data type of the corresponding parameter. The brackets around the keywords OR REPLACE denote that they are optional. In addition, just as with a function, the brackets around the parameters denote that they are optional.

The block structure of a PROCEDURE is exactly the same as an anonymous block, except for the addition of the DDL CREATE PROCEDURE keywords and the optional parameters. A procedure differs from a function in that it does not have a RETURN parameter.

Let's take a look at Listing 2-5, line by line:

- Line 1 contains the DDL keywords to CREATE a stored PROCEDURE.

- Line 2 passes in one parameter: the number of seconds to wait.

- Lines 3 through 7, in the declaration section, have a multiline comment that documents the procedure's source code filename, author, date the procedure was written, and finally a comment about what the procedure does.

- On line 8, the keyword BEGIN starts the executable section.

- On line 9, I call the procedure sleep() located in package DBMS_LOCK, owned by user SYS. sleep() calls the host operating system's sleep() or wait function and then returns sometime after the specified period in seconds.

- On line 10, the keyword END ends the executable section. Did you notice that there is no defined exception-handling section? Since I didn't code one, PL/SQL will use the default exception handler, which will simply raise the error to the enclosing program unit.

- On line 11, the slash (/) tells Oracle to store and then compile the procedure.

- Line 12 calls a helper script to show any compilation errors.

The PL/SQL block structure for the stored procedure in Listing 2-5 was really not that much different from the structure of the anonymous procedure and the stored function. The wait() procedure has a name and parameters, while an anonymous procedure does not. In addition, wait() does not return a value, while a stored function does.

It's Your Turn to Create a Procedure

Now you'll create a procedure that wraps the SYS.DBMS_OUTPUT.put_line() procedure, but uses a very short name. You'll end up using the SYS.DBMS_OUTPUT.put_line() procedure a lot. It gets tiresome to type a 24-character method name every time you want to display a line of text on the screen in SQL*Plus. So, to save keystrokes, you will give your SYS.DBMS_OUTPUT.put_line() wrapper procedure the name pl(), as in p for put and l for line.

You can use the procedure in Listing 2-5 as a model. Just replace the parameter on line 2 with aiv_text in varchar2, and write line 9 with a call to SYS.DBMS_OUTPUT.put_line(aiv_text).

1. Write the DDL to create your procedure.

2. Save your new DDL script with the file name pl.prc.

3. At your SQL*Plus prompt, type the at sign (@) followed by the name of your file to store and compile your new procedure.

4. Test your new procedure by using it in an anonymous procedure.

Listing 2-6 shows my solution for this exercise.

Listing 2-6. A Lazy Typist's SYS.DBMS_OUTPUT.put_line( ), pl.prc

```
01  create or replace PROCEDURE pl(
02  aiv_text              in      varchar2 ) is
03  /*
04  pl.prc
05  by Donald J. Bales on 2014-10-20
06  A wrapper procedure for SYS.DBMS_OUTPUT.put_line()
07  for the lazy typist.
08  */
09
10  begin
11    SYS.DBMS_OUTPUT.put_line(aiv_text);
12  end pl;
13  /
14  @pe.sql pl
```

Listing 2-7 is my test unit for procedure pl().I've named it with the same file name as my procedure, except for the extension: I used .prc for the stored procedure and .sql for the anonymous procedure, its test unit. Since this is a wrapper procedure, I'm simply testing the known limits of procedure SYS.DBMS_OUTPUT.put_line() to make sure pl() is working properly.

Listing 2-7. A Test Unit for Procedure pl( ), pl.sql

```
01  rem pl.sql
02  rem by Donald J. Bales on 2014-10-20
03  rem pl's test unit
04
05  declare
06
07    v_max_line varchar2(32767);
08
09  begin
10    -- The next three lines initialize the
11    -- variable v_max_line with 32,767 spaces.
12    for i in 1..32767 loop
13      v_max_line := v_max_line || ' ';
14    end loop;
15
16    pl('Test a line of text.');
17
18    pl('Test a number, such as 1?');
19    pl(1);
20
21    pl('Test a date, such as 01/01/1980?');
22    pl(to_date('19800101', 'YYYYMMDD'));
23
24    pl('Test a line <= 32767');
25    pl(v_max_line);
26
27    pl('Test a line  > 32767');
28    pl(v_max_line||' ');
29
```

```
30    pl('Test a multi-line');
31    pl('12345678901234567890123456789012345678901234567890'||
32        '12345678901234567890123456789012345678901234567890'||chr(10)||
33        '12345678901234567890123456789012345678901234567890'||
34        '12345678901234567890123456789012345678901234567890'||chr(10)||
35        '12345678901234567890123456789012345678901234567890'||
36        '12345678901234567890123456789012345678901234567890');
37  end;
38  /
```

Here's the output from my test unit:

```
SQL> @pl.sql
```

```
Test a line of text.
Test a number, such as 1?
1
Test a date, such as 01/01/1980?
01-JAN-80
Test a line <= 32767
Test a line  > 32767
declare
*
ERROR at line 1:
ORA-20000: ORU-10028: line length overflow, limit of 32767 bytes per line
ORA-06512: at "SYS.DBMS_OUTPUT", line 32
ORA-06512: at "SYS.DBMS_OUTPUT", line 91
ORA-06512: at "SYS.DBMS_OUTPUT", line 112
ORA-06512: at "RPS.PL", line 11
ORA-06512: at line 24
```

The line of text, number 1, date 01/01/1980, and line <= 32767 characters tests ran, but the last test, multiline, didn't because the > 32767 test threw an exception that was not handled. Let's see how the code can handle this problem.

Nested Blocks

You can, and should when necessary, nest PL/SQL blocks. To nest a PL/SQL block means to embed one or more PL/SQL blocks inside another PL/SQL block. Nesting PL/SQL blocks allows you greater control over your PL/SQL program's execution. You can wrap one or more PL/SQL or SQL statements in their own PL/SQL block, so you can catch an exception that is generated within that block. I call this "blocking" code. Let's look at an example.

An Example of Nesting Blocks

As you saw, the test unit for procedure pl() in Listing 2-7 stopped executing after line 28 because line 28 caused the following error:

```
ORA-20000: ORU-10028: line length overflow, limit of 32767 bytes per line
```

In Listing 2-8, I've recoded the pl( ) test unit. This time, I've blocked the lines that I expect to fail, so the program will catch any raised exceptions and continue processing the code all the way to the end of the source code listing.

Listing 2-8. The New, Improved pl( ) Test Unit, pl2.sql

```
01  rem pl2.sql
02  rem by Donald J. Bales on 2014-10-20
03  rem Test unit for procedure pl
04
05  declare
06    v_max_line varchar2(32767);
07
08  begin
09    -- The next three lines initialize a variable v_max_line with 32,767 spaces.
10    for i in 1..32767 loop
11      v_max_line := v_max_line || ' ';
12    end loop;
13
14    pl('Test a line of text.');
15
16    pl('Test a number, such as 1?');
17    pl(1);
18
19    pl('Test a date, such as 01/01/1980?');
20    pl(to_date('19800101', 'YYYYMMDD'));
21
22    pl('Test a line <= 32767');
23    pl(v_max_line);
24
25    pl('Test a line  > 32767');
26    begin
27      pl(v_max_line||' ');
28    exception
29      when OTHERS then
30        pl(SQLERRM);
31    end;
32
33    pl('Test a multi-line');
34    begin
35      pl('12345678901234567890123456789012345678901234567890'||
36         '12345678901234567890123456789012345678901234567890'||chr(10)||
37         '12345678901234567890123456789012345678901234567890'||
38         '12345678901234567890123456789012345678901234567890'||chr(10)||
39         '12345678901234567890123456789012345678901234567890'||
40         '12345678901234567890123456789012345678901234567890');
41    exception
42      when OTHERS then
43        pl(SQLERRM);
44    end;
45  end;
46  /
```

The changed lines (highlighted in the listing) are as follows:

- Line 26 starts a nested block with the keyword BEGIN around the PL/SQL statement that will actually test > 32767.

- Line 28 contains a corresponding keyword EXCEPTION in order to create an exception-handling section for the nested PL/SQL block.

- Line 29 has the phrase when OTHERS then in order to catch all exceptions that can be generated within the nested block.

- On line 30, I once again call procedure pl(), but this time I display the exception error message: SQLERRM.

- On line 31, the nested block ends with the keyword END.

- Once again, on lines 34 and 41 through 44, I create a nested block around the next PL/SQL statement that I expect may fail.

Let's see the results of these changes:

```
SQL> @pl2.sql
Test a line of text.
Test a number, such as 1?
1
Test a date, such as 01/01/1980?
01-JAN-80
Test a line <= 32767
Test a line  > 32767
ORA-20000: ORU-10028: line length overflow, limit of 32767 bytes per line
Test a multi-line
12345678901234567890123456789012345678901234567890123456789012345678901234567890...

PL/SQL procedure successfully completed.
```

Great! Now my test unit completed successfully, and it reported the errors I expected to see. As we move through the chapters ahead, you'll get plenty of experience nesting PL/SQL blocks.

Rules for Nesting

Here are the rules I employ when it comes to blocking PL/SQL code:

- Block every SQL statement except cursors (you'll learn about cursors in Chapter 5).

- Block any PL/SQL statement where you are converting from one data type to another, or moving a possibly larger character string into a smaller character string variable (you'll learn about variables in Chapter 3).

- Block any PL/SQL statement that you expect will raise an exception.

The important point about these nesting rules is that blocking will enable you to identify the reason for and the location of an exception when it is raised. In turn, that will make your software development easier and the resulting programs more robust.

Packages

In practice, you'll rarely create a stand-alone stored function or procedure. Instead, you'll use a package. What is a package? A package is a means to organize related functions and procedures together, like creating a library, but in PL/SQL jargon the library is called a *package*.

A PL/SQL package has two parts:

- A package specification

- A package body

A package specification (spec) is the public face to the package. It lists any globally accessible constants, cursors, functions, procedures, and variables. By "globally accessible," I mean those procedures, functions, and other items that other PL/SQL programs can access. If you consider a package as a sort of library, then the package spec describes what you can read from that library, while the package body contains the behind-the-scenes code that implements the package spec.

Create a Package Specification

Listing 2-9 is an example of a package spec. It shows the package spec for the package DATE_, which is a utility package for date-related constants and functions.

Listing 2-9. The DATE_ Package Spec, date_.pks

```
01   create or replace package DATE_ AS
02   /*
03   date_.pks
04   by Donald J. Bales on 2014-10-20
05   Additional DATE data type methods.
06   */
07
08   -- The maximum and minimum date values.
09
10   d_MAX                     constant date :=
11     to_date('99991231235959', 'YYYYMMDDHH24MISS');
12   d_MIN                     constant date :=
13     to_date('-47120101', 'SYYYYMMDD');
14
15
16   -- Returns the specified date with the time set to 23:59:59, therefore,
17   -- the end of the day.
18
19   FUNCTION end_of_day(
20   aid_date         in      date )
21   return           date;
22
23
24   -- Returns constant d_MAX. This is useful in SQL statements where the
25   -- constant DATE_.d_MAX is not accessible.
26
```

```
27  FUNCTION get_max
28  return          date;
29
30
31  -- Returns constant d_MIN. This is useful in SQL statements where the
32  -- constant DATE_.d_MIN is not accessible.
33
34  FUNCTION get_min
35  return          date;
36
37
38  -- Text-based help for this package. "set serveroutput on" in SQL*Plus.
39
40  PROCEDURE help;
41
42
43  -- Returns a randomly generated date that exists between the years specified.
44
45  FUNCTION random(
46  ain_starting_year  in      number,
47  ain_ending_year    in      number )
48  return                     date;
49
50
51  -- Returns the specified date with the time set to 00:00:00, therefore, the
52  -- start of the day.
53
54  FUNCTION start_of_day(
55  aid_date           in      date )
56  return                     date;
57
58
59  -- Test unit for this package.
60
61  PROCEDURE test;
62
63
64  end DATE_;
65  /
66  @se.sql DATE_
```

The DDL syntax used to create the package spec in Listing 2-9 is as follows:

```
CREATE [OR REPLACE] PACKAGE <package_name> AS
-- one or more: constant, cursor, function, procedure, or variable declarations
END <package_name>;
```

where <package_name> is the name of the package you're creating.

Not much to a package spec? Sure there is. Now, instead of using the DDL CREATE FUNCTION or CREATE PROCEDURE, you'll use the keywords FUNCTION and PROCEDURE for each PL/SQL method you want to declare globally.

Let's take a look at the package spec in Listing 2-9:

- Line 1 uses the DDL keywords to CREATE a stored PACKAGE specification.

- Lines 10 and 12 declare two global constants (ones available to any other PL/SQL stored procedure), d_MAX and d_MIN, which are the current maximum and minimum date values supported by Oracle.

- Lines 19, 27, 34, 45, and 54 declare five date functions. Please note that these are only declarations; they have no code. The code will be found in the package body.

- Lines 40 and 61 declare two "helper" procedures. I will discuss these helper procedures in great length in Chapters 7, 8, and 9.

- Line 64 ends the PACKAGE declaration with the keyword END.

- On line 65, I tell Oracle to store and compile the package spec.

- Line 66 calls a helper SQL script to show any errors.

You may also have noticed that I took the time to document the purpose of every declaration in the package spec. You should do the same. Documenting as you go is one of the major characteristics of a professional PL/SQL programmer.

It's Your Turn to Create a Package Specification

Do you remember the function to_number_or_null() in Listing 2-2? Now you will create a package called NUMBER_ that has it as one of its methods. Mimic what I just showed you as you follow these steps.

1. Write the DDL to create a package spec called NUMBER_.

2. Save your DDL script as number_.pks.

3. Execute your DDL script in SQL*Plus: SQL> @number_.pks.

4. Type desc number_ at the SQL*Plus prompt to verify that your package spec exists.

As usual, if you get any errors, figure out what's wrong so you can compile the script successfully. Remember to use the script in Listing 2-9 as a model. Listing 2-10 shows my solution.

Listing 2-10. The NUMBER_ Package Spec, number_.pks

```
01  create or replace package NUMBER_ as
02  /*
03  number_.pks
04  by Donald J. Bales on 2014-10-20
05  A utility package for the data type NUMBER
06  */
07
08  /*
09  Returns the passed varchar2 as a number if it represents a number,
10  otherwise, it returns NULL
11  */
```

```
12  FUNCTION to_number_or_null (
13  aiv_number           in      varchar2 )
14  return                       number;
15
16  end NUMBER_;
17  /
18  @se.sql
```

There's no way to test the package spec, because there's no code yet. The code goes in the package body.

Create a Package Body

A package body is the implementation for a package spec. It must contain the code for any functions or procedures declared in its corresponding package spec. In addition, the body can also contain any constant, cursor, function, procedure, or variable that should be accessible within the package body (that is, not publicly accessible). Let's take a look at the corresponding package body for package DATE_.

I'm about to show you a package body that has a lot of PL/SQL code that we haven't covered yet. Don't worry too much about the code itself. You won't understand it all now, but you'll be able to understand it after finishing this book. What you need to take away from this example is the package body structure, which is also a PL/SQL block structure. Let's look at Listing 2-11.

Listing 2-11. The DATE_ Package Body, date_.pkb

```
001  create or replace package body DATE_ AS
002  /*
003  date_.pkb
004  by Donald J. Bales on 2014-10-20
005  Additional DATE data type methods
006  */
007
008
009  FUNCTION end_of_day(
010  aid_date         in      date )
011  return                   date is
012
013  begin
014    return to_date(to_char(aid_date, 'SYYYYMMDD')||'235959',
015      'SYYYYMMDDHH24MISS');
016  end end_of_day;
017
018
019  FUNCTION get_max
020  return             date is
021
022  begin
023    return d_MAX;
024  end get_max;
025
026
```

```
027  FUNCTION get_min
028  return            date is
029
030  begin
031   return d_MIN;
032  end get_min;
033
034
035  FUNCTION random(
036  ain_starting_year in    number,
037  ain_ending_year   in    number )
038  return            date is
039
040  d_random               date;
041  n_day                  number;
042  n_month                number;
043  n_year                 number;
044
045  begin
046    n_year   := round(DBMS_RANDOM.value(
047      ain_starting_year, ain_ending_year), 0);
048    --pl('n_year='||n_year);
049    loop
050      n_month := round(DBMS_RANDOM.value(1, 12), 0);
051      --pl('n_month='||n_month);
052      n_day   := round(DBMS_RANDOM.value(1, 31), 0);
053      --pl('n_day='||n_day);
054      begin
055        d_random := to_date(lpad(to_char(n_year),  4, '0')||
056                            lpad(to_char(n_month), 2, '0')||
057                            lpad(to_char(n_day),   2, '0'),
058                            'YYYYMMDD');
059        exit;
060      exception
061        when OTHERS then
062          if SQLCODE <> -1839 then
063            pl(SQLERRM);
064          --else
065          --  pl('29-31');
066          end if;
067      end;
068    end loop;
069    return d_random;
070  end random;
071
072
073  FUNCTION start_of_day(
074  aid_date              in    date )
075  return                date is
076
```

```
077   begin
078     return trunc(aid_date);
079   end start_of_day;
080
081
082   -- Write up the help text here in this help method
083   PROCEDURE help is
084
085   begin
086   --    12345678901234567890123456789012345678901234567890123456789012345678901234567890
087     pl('============================= PACKAGE =============================');
088     pl(chr(9));
089     pl('DATE_');
090     pl(chr(9));
091     pl('--------------------------- CONSTANTS ---------------------------');
092     pl(chr(9));
093     pl('d_MAX');
094     pl(chr(9)||'Represents the maximum value for the DATE data type.');
095     pl('d_MIN');
096     pl(chr(9)||'Represents the minimum value for the DATE data type.');
097     pl(chr(9));
098     pl('--------------------------- FUNCTIONS ---------------------------');
099     pl(chr(9));
100     pl('DATE_.end_of_day(');
101     pl('aid_date          in     date)');
102     pl('return                    date;');
103     pl(chr(9)||'Returns the passed date with the time portion set to the end ');
104     pl(chr(9)||'of the day:');
105     pl(chr(9)||'23:59:59 (HH24:MI:SS).');
106     pl(chr(9));
107     pl('DATE_.get_max( )');
108     pl('return                    date;');
109     pl(chr(9)||'Returns the constant DATE_.d_MAX.');
110     pl(chr(9));
111     pl('DATE_.get_mim( )');
112     pl('return                    date;');
113     pl(chr(9)||'Returns the constant DATE_.d_MIN.');
114     pl(chr(9));
115     pl('DATE_.random(');
116     pl('ain_starting_year   in     number,');
117     pl('ain_ending_year     in     number)');
118     pl('return                         date;');
119     pl(chr(9)||'Returns a random date that exists between the specified years.');
120     pl(chr(9));
121     pl('DATE_.start_of_day(');
122     pl('aid_date          in     date)');
123     pl('return                    date;');
124     pl(chr(9)||'Returns the passed date with the time portion set to the start');
125     pl(chr(9)||'of the day:');
126     pl(chr(9)||'00:00:00 (HH24:MI:SS).');
127     pl(chr(9));
```

```
128    pl('----------------------------- PROCEDURES ----------------------------');
129    pl(chr(9));
130    pl('DATE_.help( );');
131    pl(chr(9)||'Displays this help text if set serveroutput is on.');
132    pl(chr(9));
133    pl('DATE_.test( );');
134    pl(chr(9)||'Built-in test unit. It will report success or error for each');
135    pl(chr(9)||'test if set');
136    pl(chr(9)||'serveroutput is on.');
137    pl(chr(9));
138  end help;
139
140
141  PROCEDURE test is
142
143  d_date              date;
144
145  begin
146    pl('============================== PACKAGE ==============================');
147    pl(chr(9));
148    pl('DATE_');
149    pl(chr(9));
150    pl('1. Testing constants d_MIN and d_MAX');
151    if d_MIN < d_MAX then
152     pl('SUCCESS');
153    else
154     pl('ERROR: d_MIN is not less than d_MAX');
155    end if;
156
157    pl('2. Testing end_of_day()');
158    if to_char(end_of_day(SYSDATE), 'HH24MISS') = '235959' then
159     pl('SUCCESS');
160    else
161     pl('ERROR: end_of_day is not 23:59:59');
162    end if;
163
164    pl('3. Testing get_max()');
165    if get_max() = d_MAX then
166     pl('SUCCESS');
167    else
168     pl('ERROR: get_max() is not equal to d_MAX');
169    end if;
170
171    pl('4. Testing get_min()');
172    if get_min() = d_MIN then
173     pl('SUCCESS');
174    else
175     pl('ERROR: get_min() is not equal to d_MIN');
176    end if;
177
```

```
178     pl('5. Testing random() 1000 times');
179     for i in 1..1000 loop
180       d_date := random(1, 9999);
181       --pl(to_char(d_date, 'YYYY-MM-DD HH24:MI:SS'));
182     end loop;
183     pl('SUCCESS');
184
185     pl('6. Testing start_of_day()');
186     if to_char(start_of_day(SYSDATE), 'HH24MISS') = '000000' then
187       pl('SUCCESS');
188     else
189       pl('ERROR: start_of_day is not 00:00:00');
190     end if;
191   end test;
192
193
194   end DATE_;
195   /
196   @be.sql DATE_
```

The DDL syntax used to create the package body in Listing 2-11 is as follows:

```
CREATE [OR REPLACE] PACKAGE BODY <package_name> AS
-- one or more constant, cursor, or variable declarations
-- one or more function, or procedure implementations
[BEGIN]
-- you can code a PL/SQL block called an initialization section that is
-- executed only once per session, when the package is first instantiated
-- into memory
[EXCEPTION]
-- you can code an exception-handling section for the initialization section
END <package_name>;
```

where <package_name> is the name of the package body you're creating.

Did you notice the two optional sections? If you have some initialization code that you want to run the first time a package is loaded into memory, you can use the keyword BEGIN to start an initialization section. And if you want an exception-handling section for your initialization section, you can add it by using the keyword EXCEPTION. This is classic PL/SQL block structure.

Your implementations of functions and procedures are actually embedded functions and procedures in the declaration section of a PL/SQL block! Any constant, cursor, or variable that you declare in the declaration section of the package body is accessible to all the declared functions and procedures in that section, but not globally to other stored procedures. Only the items you declared in the package spec are accessible to other stored procedures.

As I noted at the beginning of this section, Listing 2-11 contains a lot of code that we haven't yet discussed, so I'll leave its explanation for later chapters.

■ **Note** In Listing 2-11, if I had declared any package body (or instance) functions or procedures—ones not accessible outside the package body—I would take time to document the purpose of the instance declaration in the package body. You should do the same. Once again, I declare that professional PL/SQL programmers document as they go.

It's Your Turn to Create a Package Body

You should already have a package spec created for the NUMBER_ package, as in Listing 2-10. Now it's time create the corresponding package body. It's almost like the package spec, except for the keyword BODY in the DDL and the function to_number_or_null()'s implementation, as in Listing 2-2. Create your package body by following these steps.

1. Write the DDL to create a package body called NUMBER_.

2. Save your DDL script as number_.pkb.

3. Execute your DDL script in SQL*Plus: SQL> @number_.pkb.

4. Test your function using a SELECT statement, just as you did way back in the section on functions. This time, however, you'll prefix the function name with the name of your package.

Again, if you get any errors, work on your script until you figure out what's wrong so you can compile the script successfully. Listing 2-12 shows my solution.

Listing 2-12. The NUMBER_ Package Body, number_.pkb

```
01  create or replace package body NUMBER_ as
02  /*
03  number_.pkb
04  by Donald J. Bales on 2014-10-20
05  A utility package for the data type NUMBER
06  */
07
08  FUNCTION to_number_or_null (
09  aiv_number            in      varchar2 )
10  return                        number is
11  begin
12    return to_number(aiv_number);
13  exception
14    when OTHERS then
15      return NULL;
16  end to_number_or_null;
17
18  end NUMBER_;
19  /
20  @be.sql
```

Benefits of Using Packages

As I mentioned earlier, anything declared in a package spec can be seen by any username that has execute privileges on the package. Package specs also reduce dependency invalidation issues. What does that mean?

Say that procedure1 calls function1 and is called by procedure2. Then if you change function1, function1 becomes invalid, and so do procedure1 and procedure2. This means you need to recompile all three PL/SQL programs. This chain of dependency can be broken by using packages.

Now suppose that you use packages: package1.procedure1 calls package2.function1, and it is called by package3.procedure2. If you change the package implementation, or body, of package2.function1, it will not cause the invalidation of the function, nor any dependent PL/SQL blocks. You will cause dependent PL/SQL blocks to be invalidated only if you change the package spec.

Summary

Table 2-1 shows a side-by-side comparison of the syntax used for the various types of PL/SQL blocks covered in this chapter. The point here is that PL/SQL code always exists in a PL/SQL block, and that PL/SQL blocks are quite consistent in their structure. Even nested PL/SQL blocks are consistent with the ones shown in Table 2-1.

Table 2-1. *A Comparison of PL/SQL Block Syntax*

ANONYMOUS [DECLARE]	CREATE FUNCTION	CREATE PROCEDURE	CREATE PACKAGE	CREATE PACKAGE BODY
	[parameters]	[parameters]		
	RETURN			
[declaration section]	declaration section	declaration section	declaration section	declaration section
BEGIN	BEGIN	BEGIN		[BEGIN]
executable section	executable section	executable section		executable section]
[EXCEPTION]	[EXCEPTION]	[EXCEPTION]		[EXCEPTION]
[exception-handling section]	[exception-handling section]	[exception-handling section]		[exception-handling section]
END;	END;	END;	END;	END;
/	/	/	/	/

Now that you have a firm understanding of the block structure of PL/SQL, you're ready to move on to the next step: learning about PL/SQL data types and variables.

CHAPTER 3

■ ■ ■

Types, Variables, and Scope

This chapter is all about how to keep track of variables in a PL/SQL program. Before this chapter ends, you'll learn about PL/SQL data types, variables, scope, types, and parameters. Let's get started.

PL/SQL Data Types

Given that PL/SQL is the Procedural Language extension for SQL, you would think that it supports and uses the same data types as SQL does for the database, right? Right! It turns out that is almost the case, but not quite. PL/SQL can handle any database data type and also some data types of its own.

Do you remember the "Data Definition Language (DDL)" section in Chapter 1? In it, I talked about the three basic data types that you will use all the time: character (VARCHAR2), numeric (NUMBER), and time (DATE). Here's how those types work in PL/SQL:

- VARCHAR2: Just as in the database, most of the time you'll work with character strings in PL/SQL using the data type VARCHAR2. However, unlike the database VARCHAR2 type, a PL/SQL VARCHAR2 can hold as many as 32,767 characters, whereas the database type prior to Oracle12c only holds up to 4,000.

- NUMBER: Just as in the database, most of the time you'll work with numbers in PL/SQL using the data type NUMBER. And, just like the database, PL/SQL has additional numeric data types available. For example, you can use the type PLS_INTEGER, which has an integer range from –2147483648 to 2147483647. PLS_INTEGER also uses the computer's hardware to do its calculations instead of library routines, so it's faster. However, until you're comfortable writing stored procedures with PL/SQL, I don't think you need to bother with them. You can always take a look at them in Oracle's *PL/SQL User's Guide and Reference* when you're ready.

- DATE: Just as in the database, most of the time you'll work with dates and times in PL/SQL using data type DATE. Like NUMBER, PL/SQL has additional time-related data types. Check them out in Oracle's reference once you're up and coding confidently.

PL/SQL also has a BOOLEAN data type that allows you to store the logical values FALSE or TRUE in a variable. SQL has no equivalent. So you can pass BOOLEAN values between methods and use them as variables in your PL/SQL program units, but you can't store them in the database.

Of course, there are many more Oracle SQL and PL/SQL data types, but the ones I just covered are the ones you'll use most often.

Variables

Variables are named temporary storage locations that support a particular data type in your PL/SQL program. You must declare them in the declaration section of a PL/SQL block.

By "named," I mean that you give each of your variables a name. They are temporary because the values you assign to variables typically exist only in memory (or are accessible in memory) while the PL/SQL block in which they are declared is executing. They are storage locations in memory. And they are declared to store a particular data type so PL/SQL knows how to create, store, access, and destroy them.

Let's start by looking at how to name your variables.

Variable Naming

Like a SQL or database data type, PL/SQL variables must follow the identifier naming rules:

- A variable name must be less than 31 characters in length.

- A variable name must start with an uppercase or lowercase ASCII letter: A–Z or a–z. PL/SQL is not case-sensitive.

- A variable name may be composed of 1 letter, followed by up to 29 letters, numbers, or the underscore (_) character. You can also use the number (#) and dollar sign ($) characters.

As a matter of fact, all PL/SQL identifiers, like stored function and procedure names, must follow these naming rules!

I like to use the following conventions when naming variables:

- Use the two-character prefix for each data type, as defined in Table 3-1.

- Make its purpose obvious. If the variable will hold a value from the database, use the same name as in the database, but with the appropriate prefix.

***Table 3-1.** My PL/SQL Variable Naming Prefixes*

Prefix	Data Type
c_	CURSOR
d_	DATE
n_	NUMBER
r_	ROW
t_	TABLE
v_	VARCHAR2

For example, if I were to declare variables to hold data from the columns in the AUTHORS table, I would use the following identifier names:

- n_id

- v_name

- d_birth_date

- v_gender

The advantage of using these prefixes is that you'll always know the variable's data type and its scope. (I'll cover scope shortly.) In addition, since you made the name obvious, you'll also know where it comes from or where it's going.

By "obvious," I mean that you shouldn't use a synonym for an already existing identifier. For example, don't create variables named d_born, d_date_of_birth, and d_bday for a value from the birth_date column in the database. Why? All those name variations will just make what you're referring to unclear, and all professional PL/SQL programmers want to make it absolutely clear what is going on in their code!

Now that you know how to name your variables, let's look at how to declare them.

Variable Declarations

To declare a variable, type the variable name (identifier) followed by the data type definition, as you would use in SQL, terminated by a semicolon (;). The data type definition is the name of the data type, possibly followed by length constraints in a set of parentheses. For example, to declare variables to hold the data from columns in the AUTHORS table, I could code the following in a PL/SQL block's declaration section:

```
declare

    n_id                        number;
    v_name                      varchar2(100);
    d_birth_date                date;
    v_gender                    varchar2(30);

begin
    ...
end;
```

The DDL syntax used to declare the preceding variables is as follows:

```
<variable_name>  <data_type>;
```

where <variable_name> is the name of the variable (or identifier), and <data_type> is one of the PL/SQL data types.

You'll notice that if you get rid of the data type prefixes, variable declarations look just like the SQL in the table definition for AUTHORS in Chapter 1, and that's the whole point. They should! It wouldn't make much sense to declare varchar2 variables that are smaller than the ones in the database because that could cause an error. And it doesn't make much sense to name them differently than what they're named in the database because that would just make things confusing. That's why I use those prefixes shown in Table 3-1.

Most of the time, you'll end up declaring variables that temporarily hold values from or that are going into the database, and PL/SQL has a keyword for simplifying just that situation: %TYPE.

Variable Anchors

An *anchor* refers to the use of the keyword %TYPE to "anchor" a PL/SQL data type definition in a PL/SQL variable to the corresponding SQL data type definition of a column in a table. Steven Feuerstein coined the term *anchor*, and I've always liked it, so I use it whenever I talk about the keyword %TYPE.

Here's an example of the PL/SQL variables for the table AUTHORS declared using column anchors (the %TYPE keyword):

```
n_id                            AUTHORS.id%TYPE;
v_name                          AUTHORS.name%TYPE;
d_birth_date                    AUTHORS.birth_date%TYPE;
v_gender                        AUTHORS.gender%TYPE;
```

The syntax used to declare the preceding variables is as follows:

```
<variable_name>  <table_name>.<column_name>%TYPE;
```

where <variable_name> is the name of the variable (or identifier), <table_name> is the name of the table used to anchor the data type, and <column_name> is the name of the column used to anchor the data type.

Programming in PL/SQL just keeps getting better, doesn't it? By using anchors, you now know that the variables use the same data types and sizes as the table that will be the source of, or permanent storage for, each variable's value. Even when I use anchors, I still use data type prefixes in order to remind me of the variables' data types.

Now that you've seen how to declare variables, let's talk about how to assign values to them.

Variable Assignments

To assign a literal value to a variable in PL/SQL, you use the assignment operator, which is a colon (:) followed by an equal sign (=): :=. For example, I can make the following assignments:

```
declare
  ...
begin

  n_id         := 400;
  v_name       := 'STEVEN FEUERSTEIN';
  d_birth_date := to_date('19800101', 'YYYYMMDD');
  v_gender     := 'M';

end;
```

What do I mean by "a literal value"? OK, let's back up a second.

- A numeric literal is just a number without any formatting, such as 400.

- A character literal is just a string of characters enclosed in a pair of tick (') characters (or single quotes), such as 'STEVEN FEUERSTEIN'.

There is no such thing as a date literal. You can assign a character literal and hope the format you decided to use matches the current NLS_DATE_FORMAT (automatic type conversion—dangerous, very dangerous), or you can use the built-in function,

```
to_date(aiv_date in varchar2, aiv_date_format in varchar2)
```

A second way to assign a value to a variable is to use an INTO clause in a SQL SELECT statement. Here's an example:

```
select id,
       name,
       birth_date,
       gender
into   n_id
       v_name,
       d_birth_date,
       v_gender
from   AUTHORS
where  AUTHORS.id = (
  select AUTHOR_PUBLICATIONS.author_id
  from   AUTHRO_PUBLICATIONS
  where  title = 'ORACLE PL/SQL PROGRAMMING');
```

In this example, the PL/SQL keyword INTO moves the values from the SELECT statement's column list into the corresponding PL/SQL variables. I'll talk a lot more about this in Chapter 4.

By default, variables are uninitialized and hence are NULL. You can initialize them to a value when they are declared by simply assigning them a value in the declaration section. For example, you could initialize the AUTHORS variables as follows:

```
declare

  n_id         AUTHORS.id%TYPE         := 400;
  v_name       AUTHORS.name%TYPE       := 'STEVEN FEUERSTEIN';
  d_birth_date AUTHORS.birth_date%TYPE := to_date('19800101', 'YYYYMMDD');
  v_gender     AUTHORS.gender%TYPE     := NULL;

begin
  ...
end;
```

The syntax used to declare the preceding variables is as follows:

```
<variable_name>  <table_name>.<column_name>%TYPE := <value>;
```

where <variable_name> is the name of the variable (or identifier), <table_name> is the name of the table used to anchor the data type, <column_name> is the name of the column used to anchor the data type, and <value> is the initial value for the variable. But what exactly is NULL?

NULL Value

The term NULL *value* is a bit of a misnomer. The keyword NULL means *I don't know!* The keyword NULL means *you don't know!* The keyword NULL means *it is not possible to know what the value is,* so how can there be something such as a NULL value? Let's further define NULL:

- NULL is not equal to anything, not even NULL.

- NULL is not less than or greater than anything else, not even NULL.

- NULL means nothing knows, not even NULL.

You can test for NULL values in a SQL statement or PL/SQL code by using one of two phrases:

- is NULL

- is not NULL

Although the PL/SQL compiler may let you, you cannot use a logical operator with NULL, like

```
= NULL
```

or

```
<> NULL
```

and get the logical results you're seeking.

You must use is NULL and is not NULL. Remember this and you will save yourself many hours of troubleshooting erratic behavior.

It's Your Turn to Declare Variables

Now that you're familiar with the declaration of variables, let's put you to work. Create an anonymous PL/SQL procedure where you declare variables using anchors, and with default values, for the columns in the WORKERS table. Follow these steps.

1. Code your anonymous procedure.

2. Save it with the file name workers_variables.sql.

3. Execute your script in SQL*Plus: SQL> @workers_variables.sql.

Listing 3-1 is my solution for this problem.

Listing 3-1. An Anonymous PL/SQL Procedure with Variable Declarations, workers_variables.sql

```
01  declare
02    n_id                 WORKERS.id%TYPE               := 1;
03    n_worker_type_id     WORKERS.worker_type_id%TYPE   := 3;
04    v_external_id        WORKERS.external_id%TYPE       := '6305551212';
05    v_first_name         WORKERS.first_name%TYPE        := 'JANE';
06    v_middle_name        WORKERS.middle_name%TYPE       := 'E';
07    v_last_name          WORKERS.last_name%TYPE         := 'DOE';
08    v_name               WORKERS.name%TYPE              := 'JANEDOEE';
09    d_birth_date         WORKERS.birth_date%TYPE        :=
10      to_date('19800101', 'YYYYMMDD');
```

```
11   n_gender_type_id  WORKERS.gender_type_id%TYPE := 1;
12 begin
13   null;
14 end;
15 /
```

Let's break Listing 3-1 down line by line:

- Line 1 uses the keyword DECLARE to start an anonymous PL/SQL procedure.

- Lines 2 through 11 declare variables to hold the contents of the columns from the WORKERS table.

- Line 12 starts the executable section of the procedure with the keyword BEGIN.

- On line 13, I coded a no operation (NULL) so the block will compile.

- Line 14 ends the procedure with the keyword END.

- On line 15, I tell Oracle to compile and execute the procedure.

Now that you're an expert at declaring variables, let's take a look at when they are in scope.

Scope

In this context, *scope* refers to when a declared item can be seen by another PL/SQL block. And yes, I'm not just talking about variables here; I'm talking about any kind of declared item: a constant, cursor, function, procedure, or variable.

Scope Rules

The following is a list of rules for scope. As you go through the list, it may be helpful for you to examine Figure 3-1.

- Any item declared in the declaration section of a function or procedure is visible only within the same function or procedure.

- Any item declared in the declaration section of a package body is visible only within any other item in the same package body.

- Any item declared in a package specification is visible to any other stored function, stored procedure, and package for which the owner of the calling method has execute privileges.

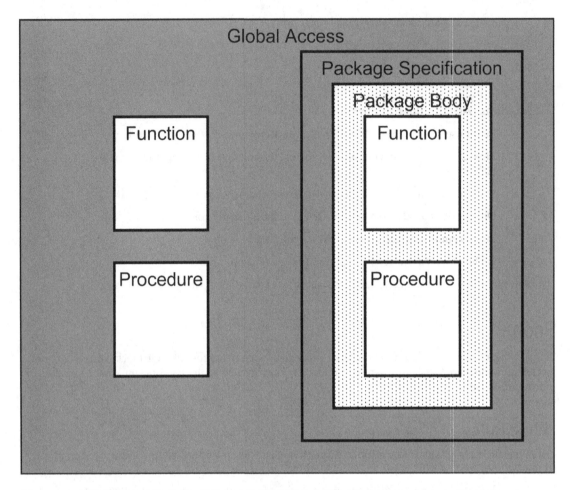

Figure 3-1. *Where an item is declared detemines its scope*

Listings 3-2 and 3-3 are a package spec and package body, respectively, to test scope. Listing 3-2 declares a global function, procedure, and variable in the package spec. Listing 3-3 declares an instance function, a procedure, and a variable. And, in the function and procedure implementations, I've declared local variables.

Listing 3-2. A Package Spec to Test Scope, scope.pks

```
01  create or replace package SCOPE as
02  /*
03  scope.pks
04  by Donald J. Bales on 2014-10-20
05  A package to test scope
06  */
07
```

```
08  -- Here's a global variable declaration
09  gv_scope                              varchar2(80) :=
10    'I''m a global (or package spec) variable';
11
12  -- Here's a global (or package spec) function declaration
13  FUNCTION my_scope_is_global
14  return                                varchar2;
15
16  -- Here's a global (or package spec) procedure declaration
17  PROCEDURE my_scope_is_global;
18
19
20  end SCOPE;
21  /
22  @se.sql SCOPE
```

Listing 3-3. *A Package Body to Test Scope, scope.pkb*

```
01  create or replace package body SCOPE as
02  /*
03  scope.pkb
04  by Donald J. Bales on 2014-10-20
05  A package to test scope
06  */
07
08  -- Here's an instance (or package body) variable declaration
09  iv_scope                              varchar2(80) :=
10    'I''m an instance (or package body) variable';
11
12
13  -- Here's an instance (or package body) function declaration
14  FUNCTION my_scope_is_instance
15  return                      varchar2 is
16  v_answer_1                  varchar2(3) := 'Yes';
17  begin
18    pl(chr(9)||'Can function my_scope_is_instance see variable gv_scope?');
19    pl(chr(9)||gv_scope);
20    return v_answer_1;
21  end my_scope_is_instance;
22
23
24  -- Here's a global (or package spec) function declaration
25  FUNCTION my_scope_is_global
26  return                      varchar2 is
27  v_answer_2                  varchar2(3) := 'Yes';
28  begin
29    pl(chr(9)||'Can function my_scope_is_global see variable iv_scope?');
30    pl(chr(9)||iv_scope);
31    return v_answer_2;
32  end my_scope_is_global;
```

```
33
34
35   -- Here's an instance (or package body) procedure declaration
36   PROCEDURE my_scope_is_instance is
37   v_answer_3                              varchar2(3) := 'Yes';
38   begin
39     pl(chr(9)||'Can procedure my_scope_is_instance see variable gv_scope?');
40     pl(chr(9)||gv_scope);
41     pl(v_answer_3);
42   end my_scope_is_instance;
43
44
45   -- Here's a global (or package spec) procedure declaration
46   PROCEDURE my_scope_is_global is
47   v_answer_4                              varchar2(3) := 'Yes';
48   begin
49     pl(chr(9)||'Can procedure my_scope_is_global see variable iv_scope?');
50     pl(chr(9)||iv_scope);
51     pl(v_answer_4);
52   end my_scope_is_global;
53
54
55   end SCOPE;
56   /
57   @se.sql SCOPE
```

Take some time to look over the two code listings. At this point, you should be able to understand the PL/SQL block structure of the package, and the methods declared and implemented in it, along with the variable declarations. The point now is to understand when a given function, procedure, or variable is in scope.

Listing 3-4 is an anonymous PL/SQL procedure that I wrote as a test unit for package SCOPE, specifically to help you understand when a declared item is in scope.

Listing 3-4. A Test Unit for Package SCOPE, scope.sql

```
01   rem scope.sql
02   rem by Donald J. Bales on 2014-10-20
03   rem Test unit for package scope
04
05   declare
06
07   -- ANONYMOUS PL/SQL BLOCK'S DECLARATION SECTION --
08
09   v_scope                              varchar2(40) :=
10     'I''m a local variable';
11
```

```
12  -- This is a local (or embedded) function
13  FUNCTION my_scope_is_local
14  return                                varchar2 is
15  v_answer_0                            varchar2(3) := 'Yes';
16  begin
17     return v_answer_0;
18  end my_scope_is_local;
19
20  -- This is a local (or embedded) procedure
21  PROCEDURE my_scope_is_local is
22  v_answer                             varchar2(3) := 'Yes';
23  begin
24    pl(v_answer);
25  end my_scope_is_local;
26
27  begin
28
29  -- ANONYMOUS PL/SQL BLOCK'S EXECUTABLE SECTION --
30
31    pl('Can I access my local variable?');
32    pl(v_scope);
33    pl('Can I access SCOPE'' global variable?');
34    pl(SCOPE.gv_scope);
35    pl('Can I access SCOPE'' instance variable?');
36    --pl(SCOPE.iv_scope);
37    pl('No!');
38
39    pl('Can I access my local function?');
40    pl(my_scope_is_local());
41    pl('Can I access SCOPE'' global function?');
42    pl(SCOPE.my_scope_is_global());
43    pl('Can I access SCOPE'' instance function?');
44    --pl(SCOPE.my_scope_is_instance());
45    pl('No!');
46
47    pl('Can I access my local procedure?');
48    my_scope_is_local();
49    pl('Can I access SCOPE'' global procedure?');
50    SCOPE.my_scope_is_global();
51    pl('Can I access SCOPE'' instance procedure?');
52    --SCOPE.my_scope_is_instance();
53    pl('No!');
54
55  end;
56  /
```

After I have compile scope.pks and scope.pkb, when I execute scopes.sql from Listing 3-4, I get the following output from SQL*Plus:

```
SQL> @scopes.sql
```

```
Can I access my local variable?
I'm a local variable
Can I access SCOPE' global variable?
I'm a global (or package spec) variable
Can I access SCOPE' instance variable?
No!
Can I access my local function?
Yes
Can I access SCOPE' global function?
        Can function my_scope_is_global see variable iv_scope?
        I'm an instance (or package body) variable
Yes
Can I access SCOPE' instance function?
No!
Can I access my local procedure?
Yes
Can I access SCOPE' global procedure?
        Can procedure my_scope_is_global see variable iv_scope?
        I'm an instance (or package body) variable
Yes
Can I access SCOPE' instance procedure?
No!

PL/SQL procedure successfully completed.
```

If you examine all three code listings and the SQL*Plus output carefully, you'll see that you can access any item

- Declared in a package specification, granted you have access to it.

- Declared in a package body, if the calling declared item also exists in the same package body.

- Declared in a function or procedure, if you're trying to access it from the same function or procedure.

Perhaps you would like to try testing the scope rules yourself?

It's Your Turn to Scope Things Out

There's nothing like hacking to see how things work. So put on your hacker's hat and take the anonymous procedure in scope.sql for a ride.

1. Compile scope.pks.

2. Compile scope.pkb.

3. Try alternatively removing the single-line comments characters on lines 36, 44, and 52 in scopes.sql, and then execute the script.

Each time you try to access a declared item that is out of scope, PL/SQL will let you know exactly where the coding problem exists in you source code.

Now that you have a firm understanding of scope, let's step it up a notch.

Types

No discussion of declaring variables would be complete, nor would any programming language itself be complete, without mentioning arrays. PL/SQL supports three kinds of arrays, or as they are known in PL/SQL jargon, *collections*. I will discuss only one kind here: *associative arrays*. Originally called PL/SQL tables, associative arrays provide you with the means to create a single-dimension array. Associative arrays can be based on almost any data type. However, you'll typically use one of the data types already covered.

Table Types

By table TYPEs, I'm not referring to SQL tables that are used to permanently store data, but PL/SQL tables (or associative arrays), which are used to temporarily store data in memory. Listing 3-5 is an anonymous PL/SQL procedure that demonstrates how to declare an associative array (or PL/SQL table). You'll see that declaring an associative array consists of two steps.

1. Declare the new TYPE.

2. Declare a new variable of that TYPE.

Listing 3-5. Declaring a PL/SQL Table with a Column Data Type, table.sql

```
01  rem table.sql
02  rem by Don Bales on 2014-10-20
03  rem An anonymous PL/SQL procedure to demonstrate
04  rem the elementary use of PL/SQL tables
05
06  declare
07
08  TYPE name_table IS TABLE OF WORKERS.name%TYPE
09  INDEX BY BINARY_INTEGER;
10
11  t_name                          name_table;
12
13  n_name                          binary_integer;
14
15  begin
16    t_name(1)  := 'DOE, JOHN';
17    t_name(10) := 'DOE, JANE';
18
19    pl(t_name(1));
20    pl(t_name(10));
21    pl('There are '||t_name.count()||' elements.');
22    n_name := t_name.first();
23    pl('The first element is '||n_name||'.');
24    n_name := t_name.next(n_name);
25    pl('The next element is '||n_name||'.');
26    n_name := t_name.last();
```

```
27    pl('The last element is '||n_name||'.');
28    n_name := t_name.prior(n_name);
29    pl('The prior element is '||n_name||'.');
30    if t_name.exists(1) then
31      pl('Element 1 exists.');
32    end if;
33    pl('I''m deleting element 10');
34    t_name.delete(10);
35    pl('There are '||t_name.count()||' elements.');
36    if not t_name.exists(10) then
37      pl('Element 10 no longer exists.');
38    end if;
39    pl('There are '||t_name.count()||' elements.');
40    pl('I''m deleting all elements');
41    t_name.delete();
42    pl('There are '||t_name.count()||' elements.');
43  end;
44  /
```

The syntax used in Listing 3-5 on lines 8 and 9 to declare the associative array is as follows:

```
TYPE <plsql_table_type_name> IS TABLE OF <data_type>
INDEX BY BINARY_INTEGER;
```

where <plsql_table_type_name> is the name you are giving to the new PL/SQL table TYPE, and <data_type> is the data type to use for the elements in the table (or associative array).

Then, on line 11, I declare an associative array based on the new type with the following syntax:

```
<variable_name>                    <plsql_table_type_name>;
```

where <variable_name> is an identifier for the PL/SQL table, and <plsql_table_type_name> is the name of the TYPE.

One of the unique characteristics of an associative array is that it can be sparsely populated. That means you don't need to add items consecutively to the array. Instead, you can add them to any index value between –2,147,483,647 and 2,147,483,647. Did you notice how I did just that in Listing 3-5, on lines 16 and 17? This can be very handy when copying values from a database table into a PL/SQL table because database tables are generally sparsely populated. You can then use the commands FIRST and NEXT to iterate through the list consecutively, or look up a value using the index randomly. (You can find more information about the FIRST and NEXT commands in the *PL/SQL User's Guide and Reference*.)

Table 3-2 lists the PL/SQL table built-in functions and procedures. With PL/SQL tables, it's also possible to use a varchar2 data type as the index value. So anywhere you see a reference to binary_integer, you can replace it with varchar2 (up to 32,767 characters long).

Table 3-2. *PL/SQL Table (Associative Array) Built-in Functions and Procedures*

Method	Description
count()	Returns the number of elements
delete(ain_index in binary_integer)	Deletes the specified element
delete()	Deletes all elements
exists(ain_index in binary_integer)	Returns TRUE if the element exists; otherwise, FALSE
first()	Returns the index of the first element
last()	Returns the index of the last element
prior(ain_index in binary_integer)	Returns the index of the first element before the specified element
next(ain_index in binary_integer)	Returns the index of the first element after the specified element

The following is the output from SQL*Plus when I execute table.sql from Listing 3-5:

```
SQL> @table.sql
```

```
DOE, JOHN
DOE, JANE
There are 2 elements.
The first element is 1.
The next element is 10.
The last element is 10.
The prior element is 1.
Element 1 exists.
I'm deleting element 10
There are 1 elements.
Element 10 no longer exists.
There are 1 elements.
I'm deleting all elements
There are 0 elements.

PL/SQL procedure successfully completed.
```

As you can see from the output, the procedure in the table.sql script exercises each of the associative array's methods.

Do you remember that I said it was possible to declare a PL/SQL table of almost any data type? Let's look at creating one with a composite data type next. Listing 3-6 is an example of a PL/SQL table (associative array) based on a row-level anchor.

Listing 3-6. Declaring a PL/SQL Table with a Row Type Anchor, row.sql

```
01  rem row.sql
02  rem by Don Bales on 2014-10-20
03  rem An anonymous PL/SQL procedure to demonstrate
04  rem the elementary use of PL/SQL tables
05
06  declare
07
08  TYPE name_table IS TABLE OF WORKERS%ROWTYPE
09  INDEX BY BINARY_INTEGER;
10
11  t_name                                name_table;
12
13  n_name                                binary_integer;
14
15  begin
16    t_name(1).name   := 'DOE, JOHN';
17    t_name(10).name  := 'DOE, JANE';
18    pl(t_name(1).name);
19    pl(t_name(10).name);
20    pl('There are '||t_name.count()||' elements.');
21    n_name := t_name.first();
22    pl('The first element is '||n_name||'.');
23    n_name := t_name.next(n_name);
24    pl('The next element is '||n_name||'.');
25    n_name := t_name.last();
26    pl('The last element is '||n_name||'.');
27    n_name := t_name.prior(n_name);
28    pl('The prior element is '||n_name||'.');
29    if t_name.exists(1) then
30      pl('Element 1 exists.');
31    end if;
32    pl('I''m deleting element 10');
33    t_name.delete(10);
34    pl('There are '||t_name.count()||' elements.');
35    if not t_name.exists(10) then
36      pl('Element 10 no longer exists.');
37    end if;
38    pl('There are '||t_name.count()||' elements.');
39    pl('I''m deleting all elements');
40    t_name.delete();
41    pl('There are '||t_name.count()||' elements.');
42  end;
43  /
```

A couple of new things are happening in Listing 3-6. First, line 8 uses the keyword %ROWTYPE to anchor to a composite record type based on the columns in the WORKERS table. Second, on lines 16 and 17 I appended the composite record's field name name with a dot operator (.) to the PL/SQL table's name and index, in order to store the name value in the associative array. Other than those items, the procedures in Listing 3-5 and Listing 3-6 are identical. I did this to point out how to address the fields in a PL/SQL record in a PL/SQL table, and also to show that the use of the PL/SQL table operators remains the same, regardless of which data type is used.

Perhaps you would like to declare your own composite record type. Let's see how you can do that next.

Record Types

Just as you can use the TYPE keyword to declare a new PL/SQL table, you can also use it to declare a PL/SQL record. Listing 3-7 is an example of doing just that.

Listing 3-7. Declaring a PL/SQL Record, record.sql

```
01   rem record.sql
02   rem by Don Bales on 2014-10-20
03   rem An anonymous PL/SQL procedure to demonstrate
04   rem the use of PL/SQL records
05
06   declare
07
08   TYPE name_record is record (
09   first_name                         WORKERS.first_name%TYPE,
10   middle_name                        WORKERS.middle_name%TYPE,
11   last_name                          WORKERS.last_name%TYPE );
12
13   TYPE name_table is table of name_record
14   index by binary_integer;
15
16   t_name                             name_table;
17
18   begin
19     t_name(1).first_name  := 'JOHN';
20     t_name(1).last_name   := 'DOE';
21     t_name(2).first_name  := 'JANE';
22     t_name(2).last_name   := 'DOE';
23
24     pl(t_name(1).last_name||', '||t_name(1).first_name);
25     pl(t_name(2).last_name||', '||t_name(2).first_name);
26   end;
27   /
```

The syntax used in Listing 3-7 to declare a PL/SQL record is as follows:

```
TYPE <plsql_record_type_name> IS RECORD (
<field_name_1>                    <data_type_1>,
<field_name_2>                    <data_type_2>,...
<field_name_N>                    <data_type_N>);
```

where <plsql_record_type_name> is the name for the new PL/SQL record type, <field_name> is the name of a field in the record, and <data_type> is the data type for the corresponding field.

As with the program in Listing 3-6, on lines 19 through 25 in Listing 3-7 I use the dot operator (.) followed by the name of the field in the record to address the composite data type values in the PL/SQL table.

WHAT'S WITH THIS NOMENCLATURE INCONSISTENCY ANYWAY?

I like things, especially programming code, to be consistent. Consistency makes things obvious. Obvious makes program code easy to maintain. Along those lines, I would feel much better if Oracle had called the syntax for creating a composite data type in a PL/SQL block a *row* instead of a *record*. Then we could refer to a *field* as *column*. The syntax would then be as follows:

```
TYPE <plsql_row_type_name> IS ROW (
<column_name_1>                    <data_type_1>,
<column_name_2>                    <data_type_2>,...
<column_name_N>                    <data_type_N>);
```

OK, now I feel better. I just needed to share how much that irritates me!

Multidimensional Arrays

Earlier, I said that associative arrays will support only a single dimension. In other words, you can't declare a multidimensional array and address it like this: t_name(1, 7).name. Well, there's a way around that limitation. Every good problem deserves a good hack. Listing 3-8 demonstrates how to use a PL/SQL table inside a PL/SQL record in order to work around the one-dimension limit.

Listing 3-8. A Hack to Work Around the PL/SQL Table One-Dimension Limit, multidimensional.sql

```
01   rem multidimensional.sql
02   rem Copyright by Don Bales on 2014-10-20
03   rem An anonymous PL/SQL procedure to demonstrate
04   rem the use of nested PL/SQL tables
05
06   declare
07
08   TYPE name_table is table of WORKERS.name%TYPE
09   index by binary_integer;
10
11   TYPE name_record is record (
12   dim2 name_table );
13
```

```
14  TYPE dim1 is table of name_record
15  index by binary_integer;
16
17  t_dim1                              dim1;
18
19  begin
20    t_dim1(1).dim2(1) := 'DOE, JOHN';
21    t_dim1(1).dim2(2) := 'DOE, JANE';
22
23    t_dim1(2).dim2(1) := 'DOUGH, JAYNE';
24    t_dim1(2).dim2(2) := 'DOUGH, JON';
25
26    pl(t_dim1(1).dim2(1));
27    pl(t_dim1(1).dim2(2));
28    pl(t_dim1(2).dim2(1));
29    pl(t_dim1(2).dim2(2));
30  end;
31  /
```

Here's how Listing 3-8 works:

- Lines 8 and 9 declare a table type, name_table, to hold a list of names.

- Lines 11 and 12 declare a record type, name_record, with one field named dim2, where the data type is name_table, a PL/SQL table.

- Lines 14 and 15 declare a second table type, dim1, which is based on record type dim2.

- On lines 20 through 29, with the pseudo-two-dimension table in place, I exercise accessing it using two indexes.

Since the use of arrays is a rather advanced topic, I'm going to skip the exercise here.

Next, let's look at the most temporary of variables, which aren't really variables at all: parameters.

Parameters

Parameters allow you to pass values into (IN), pass values out of (OUT), or pass values into and out of (IN OUT) a cursor, function, or procedure. (Cursors are covered in Chapter 5.) You've already seen parameters used in earlier code listings. I'm covering parameters here because they use declaration syntax similar to variables, and they themselves are variables.

Parameter Naming

Parameters follow the same PL/SQL identifier naming rules as variables. In practice, however, I like to use a couple of additional prefix characters on parameter names so I can also tell their scope, along with the data type. Table 3-3 is a list of those parameter prefix values.

Table 3-3. *My PL/SQL Parameter Naming Prefixes*

Prefix	Description
ai	Argument IN
ao	Argument OUT
aio	Argument IN OUT

For example, if I were to declare parameters to pass data from the columns in the AUTHORS table into and/or out of a method, I would use the identifier names in Table 3-4.

Table 3-4. *Parameter Name Examples Using My Prefixing Scheme*

Scope		
IN	OUT	IN OUT
ain_id	aon_id	aion_id
aiv_name	aov_name	aiov_name
aid_birth_date	aod_birth_date	aiod_birth_date
aiv_gender	aov_gender	aiov_gender

The advantage of using these prefixes is that you'll always know the scope and data type of the parameter with which you're working.

Parameter Declarations

Listing 3-9 and 3-10 create a package named PARAMETER, which I'll use to explain the parameter declaration syntax and parameter scope.

Listing 3-9. A Package Spec to Test Parameter Scope, parameter.pks

```
01  create or replace package PARAMETER as
02  /*
03  parameter.pks
04  by Donald J. Bales on 2014-10-20
05  A packge to test parameter scope
06  */
07
08  -- A function that execises the scope of parameters
09  FUNCTION in_out_inout(
10  aiv_in                    in     varchar2,
11  aov_out                        out varchar2,
12  aiov inout                in out varchar2)
13  return                           varchar2;
14
15
```

```
16   -- A procedure that execises the scope of parameters
17   PROCEDURE in_out_inout(
18   aiv_in                          in    varchar2,
19   aov_out                              out varchar2,
20   aiov_inout                      in out varchar2);
21
22
23   end PARAMETER;
24   /
25   @se.sql PARAMETER
```

The syntax used to declare the parameters in the function and procedure in Listing 3-9 is as follows:

```
(
<parameter_name_1>          [IN][OUT] <data_type_1>,
<parameter_name_2>          [IN][OUT] <data_type_2>,...
<parameter_name_N>          [IN][OUT] <data_type_N>)
```

where <parameter_name> is the name of the parameter; the scope is IN, OUT, or IN OUT; and <data_type> is the data type of the parameter. As you have already seen in previous listings, you can use column or row anchors to specify the data type (you know—%TYPE or %ROWTYPE). However, the value of the parameter will not be constrained by the specified size in the anchor. Only the data type is used from the anchor.

Parameter Scope

The parameter keywords IN and OUT determine the accessibility, or scope, of the parameters.

- IN makes your parameters' data available to the called cursor, function, or procedure.

- OUT allows the called function or procedure to set the parameter's value within the called PL/SQL block.

- The combination of IN and OUT allows both levels of accessibility.

Seeing is believing, so take some time to study Listings 3-10 and 3-11, and the output of Listing 3-11.

Listing 3-10. A Package Body to Test Parameter Scope, parameter.pkb

```
01   create or replace package body PARAMETER as
02   /*
03   parameter.pkb
04   by Donald J. Bales on 2014-10-20
05   A packge to test parameter scope
06   */
07
08   FUNCTION in_out_inout(
09   aiv_in                          in    varchar2,
10   aov_out                              out varchar2,
11   aiov_inout                      in out varchar2)
12   return                                 varchar2 is
```

```
13   begin
14     pl(chr(9)||'Before assignments...');
15     pl(chr(9)||'Inside function in_out_inout, aiv_in    = '||aiv_in);
16     pl(chr(9)||'Inside function in_out_inout, aov_out   = '||aov_out);
17     pl(chr(9)||'Inside function in_out_inout, aiov_inout = '||aiov_inout);
18     -- You can only assign a value (write) to an OUT
19     -- parameter, you can't read it!
20     aov_out   := 'OUT';
21
22     -- You can only read an IN parameter
23     aiov_inout := aiv_in;
24
25     -- You can read and write an IN OUT parameter
26     aiov_inout := aiov_inout||'OUT';
27
28     pl(chr(9)||'After assignments...');
29     pl(chr(9)||'Inside function in_out_inout, aiv_in    = '||aiv_in);
30     pl(chr(9)||'Inside function in_out_inout, aov_out   = '||aov_out);
31     pl(chr(9)||'Inside function in_out_inout, aiov_inout = '||aiov_inout);
32     return 'OK'; -- a function must return a value!
33   end in_out_inout;
34
35
36   PROCEDURE in_out_inout(
37   aiv_in                          in     varchar2,
38   aov_out                              out varchar2,
39   aiov_inout                   in out varchar2) is
40   begin
41     pl(chr(9)||'Before assignments...');
42     pl(chr(9)||'Inside procedure in_out_inout, aiv_in    = '||aiv_in);
43     pl(chr(9)||'Inside procedure in_out_inout, aov_out   = '||aov_out);
44     pl(chr(9)||'Inside procedure in_out_inout, aiov_inout = '||aiov_inout);
45     -- You can only assign a value (write) to an OUT
46     -- parameter, you can't read it!
47     aov_out   := 'OUT';
48
49     -- You can only read an IN parameter
50     aiov_inout := aiv_in;
51
52     -- You can read and write an IN OUT parameter
53     aiov_inout := aiov_inout||'OUT';
54     pl(chr(9)||'After assignments...');
55     pl(chr(9)||'Inside procedure in_out_inout, aiv_in    = '||aiv_in);
56     pl(chr(9)||'Inside procedure in_out_inout, aov_out   = '||aov_out);
57     pl(chr(9)||'Inside procedure in_out_inout, aiov_inout = '||aiov_inout);
58   end in_out_inout;
59
60
61   end PARAMETER;
62   /
63   @be.sql PARAMETER
```

Listing 3-11 is an anonymous PL/SQL procedure to test the scope defined by the use of IN, OUT, or IN OUT.

Listing 3-11. A Test Unit for Package PARAMETER, parameter.sql

```
01  rem parameter.sql
02  rem by Donald J. Bales on 2014-10-20
03  rem A test unit for package PARAMETER
04
05  declare
06
07  v_in                          varchar2(30) := 'IN';
08  v_out                         varchar2(30) :=
09    'Na na, you can''t see me!';
10  v_inout                       varchar2(30) :=
11    'But you can see me!';
12  v_return                      varchar2(30);
13
14  begin
15    pl('Before calling the function...');
16    pl('Inside test unit parameter v_in    = '||v_in);
17    pl('Inside test unit parameter v_out   = '||v_out);
18    pl('Inside test unit parameter v_inout = '||v_inout);
19    pl('Test function PARAMETER.in_out_inout(v_in, v_out, v_inout).');
20    v_return := PARAMETER.in_out_inout(v_in, v_out, v_inout);
21    pl(v_return);
22    pl('After calling the function...');
23    pl('Inside test unit parameter v_in    = '||v_in);
24    pl('Inside test unit parameter v_out   = '||v_out);
25    pl('Inside test unit parameter v_inout = '||v_inout);
26    pl('Resetting initial values...');
27    v_out   := 'Na na, you can''t see me!';
28    v_inout := 'But you can see me!';
29    pl('Before calling the procedure...');
30    pl('Inside test unit parameter v_in    = '||v_in);
31    pl('Inside test unit parameter v_out   = '||v_out);
32    pl('Inside test unit parameter v_inout = '||v_inout);
33    pl('Test procedure PARAMETER.in_out_inout(v_in, v_out, v_inout).');
34    PARAMETER.in_out_inout(v_in, v_out, v_inout);
35    pl('OK');
36    pl('After calling the procedure...');
37    pl('Inside test unit parameter v_in    = '||v_in);
38    pl('Inside test unit parameter v_out   = '||v_out);
39    pl('Inside test unit parameter v_inout = '||v_inout);
40  end;
41  /
```

Here's the SQL*Plus output from the `parameter.sql` script (Listing 3-11):

```
SQL> @parameter.sql
```

```
Before calling the function...
Inside test unit parameter v_in    = IN
Inside test unit parameter v_out   = Na na, you can't see me!
Inside test unit parameter v_inout = But you can see me!
Test function PARAMETER.in_out_inout(v_in, v_out, v_inout).
        Before assignments...
        Inside function in_out_inout, aiv_in    = IN
        Inside function in_out_inout, aov_out   =
        Inside function in_out_inout, aiov_inout = But you can see me!
        After assignments...
        Inside function in_out_inout, aiv_in    = IN
        Inside function in_out_inout, aov_out   = OUT
        Inside function in_out_inout, aiov_inout = INOUT
OK.
After calling the function...
Inside test unit parameter v_in    = IN
Inside test unit parameter v_out   = OUT
Inside test unit parameter v_inout = INOUT
Resetting initial values...
Before calling the procedure...
Inside test unit parameter v_in    = IN
Inside test unit parameter v_out   = Na na, you can't see me!
Inside test unit parameter v_inout = But you can see me!
Test procedure PARAMETER.in_out_inout(v_in, v_out, v_inout).
        Before assignments...
        Inside procedure in_out_inout, aiv_in    = IN
        Inside procedure in_out_inout, aov_out   =
        Inside procedure in_out_inout, aiov_inout = But you can see me!
        After assignments...
        Inside procedure in_out_inout, aiv_in    = IN
        Inside procedure in_out_inout, aov_out   = OUT
        Inside procedure in_out_inout, aiov_inout = INOUT
OK
After calling the procedure...
Inside test unit parameter v_in    = IN
Inside test unit parameter v_out   = OUT
Inside test unit parameter v_inout = INOUT

PL/SQL procedure successfully completed.
```

As you can verify from studying Listing 3-11 and the output from test unit `parameter.sql`,

- An `IN` parameter can be used to pass a value into a cursor, function, or procedure.
- An `OUT` parameter can be used to pass a value out of a function or procedure.
- An `IN OUT` parameter can be used to do both.

It's Your Turn to Declare Parameters

You'll have plenty of practice declaring parameters in the coming chapters. So I want you to do this instead:

1. Start on Chapter 4.

Summary

At this point, you should be a master of variable and parameter declarations. And you should understand the scope in which they are accessible. Next, let's start working with some SQL in your PL/SQL.

CHAPTER 4

■ ■ ■

Single Row Processing

Now you'll begin your journey of using SQL in PL/SQL. You'll start out slowly, inserting one row at a time, then updating one row at a time, then deleting one row at a time, and finally selecting one row at a time. I take this approach because you first have to insert data into a database before you can update, delete, or select it. I call these kinds of SQL statements *singletons* because they return one row of results. So let's get started by putting some data into the database.

Inserts

The context here is inserting data into a relational database. To insert data into a relational database from PL/SQL, you simply write a SQL INSERT statement, where the values are PL/SQL literals, PL/SQL variables, or SQL columns.

I begin with examples that represent what is most commonly done, and then continually improve the architecture and design as you progress through the chapter. To start out, you'll see what most PL/SQL programmers do, and then how to improve the code. Please keep in mind that there is a time and place for each of these solutions. In the end, you're the one who will need to make the decision about which is the best solution based on the business problem you're solving.

Rarely do you just perform a simple atomic INSERT statement in PL/SQL. You can do that using a SQL*Plus script, without using PL/SQL at all. More often, you'll want to insert or update depending on whether the data you intend to insert already exists in the database. If it does, you'll probably want to check if you need to update the values already in the database. So the process you decide to use to insert and/or update becomes a proverbial chicken vs. egg dilemma—which do you do first? Let's start by looking at what can happen if a duplicate row already exists.

You're going to see me use SELECT when I INSERT because, in a modern database design, you need to SELECT sequence and code ID values to use them in an INSERT statement. Let's check it out. Listing 4-1 is an anonymous PL/SQL procedure that inserts values into the WORKERS table.

Listing 4-1. An Insert Example Using PL/SQL Literals and Variables, insert.sql

```
001   rem insert.sql
002   rem by Donald J. Bales on 2014-10-20
003   rem An anonymous PL/SQL procedure to insert
004   rem values using PL/SQL literals and variables
005
006   set serveroutput on size 1000000;
007
008   declare
009
```

```
010   -- I declared these variables so I can get
011   -- the required ID values before I insert.
012   n_id                              WORKERS.id%TYPE;
013   n_worker_type_id                  WORKERS.worker_type_id%TYPE;
014   v_external_id                     WORKERS.external_id%TYPE;
015   n_gender_type_id                  WORKERS.gender_type_id%TYPE;
016
017   -- I'll use this variable to hold the result
018   -- of the SQL insert statement.
019   n_count                           number;
020
021   begin
022
023      -- First, let's get the WORKER_TYPES id for a contractor
024      begin
025        select id
026        into   n_worker_type_id
027        from   WORKER_TYPES
028        where  code = 'C';
029      exception
030        when OTHERS then
031          raise_application_error(-20002, SQLERRM||
032            ' on select WORKER_TYPES'||
033            ' in filename insert.sql');
034      end;
035
036      -- Next, let's get the  GENDER_TYPES id for a male
037      begin
038        select id
039        into   n_gender_type_id
040        from   GENDER_TYPES
041        where  code = 'M';
042      exception
043        when OTHERS then
044          raise_application_error(-20004, SQLERRM||
045            ' on select GENDER_TYPES'||
046            ' in filename insert.sql');
047      end;
048
049      -- Now, let's get the next WORKERS id sequence
050      begin
051        select WORKERS_ID.nextval
052        into   n_id
053        from   SYS.DUAL;
054      exception
055        when OTHERS then
056          raise_application_error(-20001, SQLERRM||
057            ' on select WORKERS_ID.nextval'||
058            ' in filename insert.sql');
059      end;
060
```

```
061    -- And then, let's get the next external_id sequence
062    begin
063      select lpad(to_char(EXTERNAL_ID_SEQ.nextval), 9, '0')
064      into   v_external_id
065      from   SYS.DUAL;
066    exception
067      when OTHERS then
068        raise_application_error(-20003, SQLERRM||
069          ' on select EXTERNAL_ID_SEQ.nextval'||
070          ' in filename insert.sql');
071    end;
072
073    -- Now that we have all the necessary ID values
074    -- we can finally insert a row!
075    begin
076      insert into WORKERS (
077            id,
078            worker_type_id,
079            external_id,
080            first_name,
081            middle_name,
082            last_name,
083            name,
084            birth_date,
085            gender_type_id )
086      values (
087            n_id,                            -- a variable
088            n_worker_type_id,                -- a variable
089            v_external_id,                   -- a variable
090            'JOHN',                          -- a literal
091            'J.',                            -- a literal
092            'DOE',                           -- a literal
093            'DOE, JOHN J.',                  -- a literal
094            to_date('19800101', 'YYYYMMDD'), -- a function
095            n_gender_type_id );              -- a variable
096
097      n_count := sql%rowcount;
098    exception
099      when OTHERS then
100        raise_application_error(-20005, SQLERRM||
101          ' on insert WORKERS'||
102          ' in filename insert.sql');
103    end;
104
105    pl(to_char(n_count)||' row(s) inserted.');
106  end;
107  /
108
109  commit;
```

The SQL INSERT syntax used in Listing 4-1 is as follows:

```
INSERT INTO <table_name> (
        <column_name_1>,
        <column_name_2>,...
        <column_name_N> )
VALUES (
        <column_value_1>,
        <column_value_2>,...
        <column_value_N> );
```

where <table_name> is the name of the table to INSERT VALUES INTO, <column_name> is the name of a column in the table, and <column_value> is the value for a corresponding <column_name>. The column values can be PL/SQL literals, variables, qualifying function results, or SQL column values.

You should always use a list of columns in your INSERT statements in order to maintain the validity of your code, in case someone later adds a column to a table definition (and, in practice, that happens).

Let's break down the code in Listing 4-1:

- Lines 12 through 15 declare four variables to hold the ID values from related sequence and code tables.

- Line 19 declares a number to hold the resulting row count from the INSERT statement.

- Lines 25 through 28 contain a SELECT statement to get the worker_type_id value for a contractor.

- On lines 24 through 34, I've blocked (put the code in a nested PL/SQL block) the SELECT statement so I can catch any catastrophic error, and report it to the presentation layer with an error number and message that are unique to the PL/SQL program. This practice greatly simplifies troubleshooting. You'll know exactly what went wrong and where it went wrong, and that's nice.

- On lines 37 through 47, I get the gender_type_id value for a male.

- On lines 50 through 59, I get the next id sequence value, storing that value in variable n_id.

- On lines 62 through 71, I get the next external_id value. I use the SQL function to_char() to do an explicit data type conversion from numeric to character. I wrap the character value with the SQL function lpad() in order to left-pad the number string with zeros so it's nine characters long.

- Lines 76 through 95 contain an INSERT statement to insert John Doe's data into the WORKERS table.

- Lines 77 through 85 list the names of the columns I'm going to insert values INTO. This is an important practice. If I didn't list the columns, the procedure would become invalid any time someone modified the WORKERS table.

- Lines 87 through 95 specify the column values using a combination of PL/SQL literals, PL/SQL variables, and even the return value of the SQL function to_date() for the value of column birth_date.

- On line 97, I store the result value of the INSERT statement, which is the number of rows inserted. To accomplish this, I use the pseudo-cursor name sql% and its variable rowcount.

- On lines 75 through 103 collectively, I've blocked the INSERT statement so I can detect and report the exact type and location of an error in the PL/SQL procedure.

The following is the output from the first time the insert.sql script is executed:

```
SQL> @insert.sql
```

```
1 row(s) inserted.
PL/SQL procedure successfully completed.
```

If you examine the code in Listing 4-1 and its output, you'll see that the procedure inserted one row into the database, as reported by the output from the INSERT statement through the sql%rowcount variable. But what happens if we run the script again? Here's the output from the script's second execution:

```
SQL> @insert.sql
```

```
declare
*
ERROR at line 1:
ORA-20005: ORA-00001: unique constraint (RPS.WORKERS_UK2) violated on insert WORKERS in
filename insert.sql
ORA-06512: at line 93
```

No PL/SQL procedure successfully completed message this time! An unhandled unique constraint exception was raised as an application error, number 20005, along with a meaningful message.

Now if you want to handle this particular kind of exception, you can use one of three tactics:

- Catch exception DUP_VAL_ON_INDEX (good).

- Use additional PL/SQL code to predetect the duplicate's presence (better).

- Use additional SQL code to predetect the duplicate's presence (best).

Let's take a look at these solutions, from good to best.

Catching a DUP_VAL_ON_INDEX Exception

When it comes to dealing with code that may raise a DUP_VAL_ON_INDEX exception (or any exception, for that matter), catching the exception is the laziest of solutions, yet perfectly legitimate. Actually, catching a DUP_VAL_ON_INDEX exception during an INSERT is the only way to determine that a duplicate row exists. So regardless of which process you use to insert a row, you always need to catch any possible exceptions during the execution of a SQL statement and handle them appropriately.

Figure 4-1 shows a simple process flow diagram for inserting a row and catching a DUP_VAL_ON_INDEX exception if a duplicate row already exists in the database. The process in Figure 4-1 starts out by executing a SQL INSERT statement. When you do this, Oracle will check for duplicate values in any existing unique index or unique key entries for the table in question. If a duplicate entry is found, PL/SQL will raise a DUP_VAL_ON_INDEX exception. So how do you handle that?

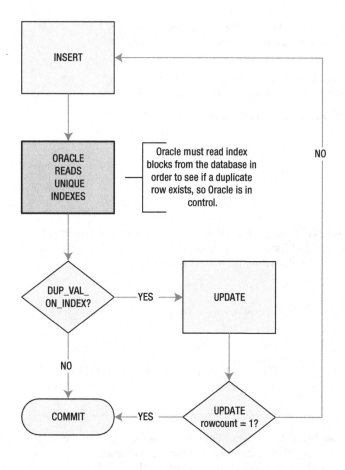

Figure 4-1. *Updating after an insert fails*

What you know at this point in your program is that a duplicate entry existed at the moment the SQL engine tried to insert your row. But that does not guarantee that the same duplicate row exists microseconds later in the exception handler. Someone or something else using the database could have deleted it in the meantime.

So perhaps you decide to try to UPDATE the supposedly existing entry. If you choose that tactic, you can be 100% sure that the entry was updated only if you examine sql%rowcount for the number of rows updated after your attempted update. If the row count isn't equal to one, then you need to try to insert the row again.

This "classic" solution is perfectly legitimate and arguably the only correct way to insert values. Or is it? I don't like this approach because it's a reactive solution where you are not in complete control of the process. Is it better to gain control after an error or to maintain control all along? Let's look at an example in order to get a better understanding of the problem, before you decide on a solution. Listing 4-2 shows a modified version of Listing 4-1, where the ORA-00001: unique constraint ... violated, or DUP_VAL_ON_INDEX exception, is handled.

Listing 4-2. An Insert Example, Modified to Catch DUP_VAL_ON_INDEX, insert_with_handled_exception.sql

```
073    -- Now that we have all the necessary ID values
074    -- we can finally insert a row!
075    begin
076      insert into WORKERS (
077            id,
078            worker_type_id,
079            external_id,
080            first_name,
081            middle_name,
082            last_name,
083            name,
084            birth_date,
085            gender_type_id )
086      values (
087            n_id,                              -- a variable
088            n_worker_type_id,                  -- a variable
089            v_external_id,                     -- a variable
090            'JOHN',                            -- a literal
091            'J.',                              -- a literal
092            'DOE',                             -- a literal
093            'DOE, JOHN J.',                    -- a literal
094            to_date('19800101', 'YYYYMMDD'),   -- a function
095            n_gender_type_id );                -- a variable
096
097      n_count := sql%rowcount;
098    exception
099      when DUP_VAL_ON_INDEX then
100        n_count := 0;
101        pl('Caught a DUP_VAL_ON_INDEX exception');
102      when OTHERS then
103        raise_application_error(-20005, SQLERRM||
104           ' on insert WORKERS'||
105           ' in filename insert_with_handled_exception.sql');
106    end;
```

■ **Note**   Listing 4-2 is a partial code listing. I'll use this technique whenever there's a lot of repeated code from one listing to the next. Because of this, you didn't have to pay as much for this book, nor did we have to kill as many trees; less paper, fewer dead trees, lower cost.

So what changed?

- Line 99 now has a WHEN DUP_VAL_ON_INDEX clause, which catches a DUP_VAL_ON_INDEX exception. The scope of the clause extends until the next use of the keyword WHEN or the keyword END for the enclosing PL/SQL block.

- On line 100, I set the row count variable, n_count, to 0 because lines 96 and 97 are not executed when an exception occurs. Instead, the program's execution jumps from line 95, where the error takes place, directly to line 98, in order to start handling exceptions.

- On line 101, I display a custom error message, but I don't raise the exception, so the program executes successfully.

Here's the output of the modified script, insert_with_handled_exception.sql:

```
SQL> @insert_with_handle_exception.sql
```

```
Caught a DUP_VAL_ON_INDEX exception
0 row(s) inserted.

PL/SQL procedure successfully completed.
```

But a nagging question remains. Is it better to gain control after an error or to maintain control all along? Let's take a look at tactic number two.

Using PL/SQL to Predetect a Duplicate

Using additional PL/SQL code to predetect the presence of duplicate values is, in my opinion, better than catching a DUP_VAL_ON_INDEX exception, for these reasons:

- You maintain control of your PL/SQL program's execution.

- You can conditionally decide how to handle duplicate values.

- You can use your detection scheme to acquire the primary key for the row that is a duplicate, and then update that row.

Figure 4-2 is a simple process flow diagram for predetecting a duplicate entry using PL/SQL, and then acting accordingly—that is, inserting or updating as needed. In this process, you start out by selecting the primary key value from the database for the table entry in question. If you find an existing entry, you can determine whether the entry needs to be updated, and then execute an UPDATE statement. Alternatively, you execute an INSERT statement if the SELECT statement raises a NO_DATA_FOUND exception.

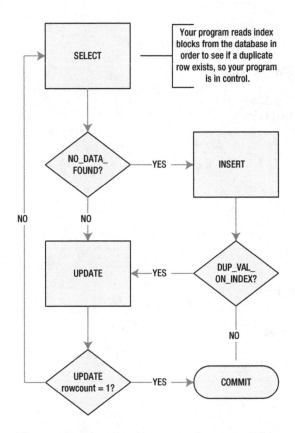

Figure 4-2. *Select, then insert or update as needed*

However, you cannot ignore the possibility that, even though a duplicate entry did not exist at the moment you executed a SELECT statement against the database, someone or something has since inserted a duplicate entry. This could happen in the microseconds between the raised exception and the execution of your INSERT statement, so you must still catch any possible exceptions on the execution of the INSERT statement and act accordingly.

This time, if the sql%rowcount variable is not equal to one, you need to try selecting the entry again.

So which solution is better? Once again, let's look at an example before you decide. Listing 4-3 is another modification of Listing 4-1. This time, I've added a nested block of PL/SQL code to detect possible duplicate values.

Listing 4-3. An Insert Example, Modified to Detect Duplicates with PL/SQL, insert_with_plsql_detection.sql

```
015  v_first_name                    WORKERS.first_name%TYPE;
016  v_middle_name                   WORKERS.middle_name%TYPE;
017  v_last_name                     WORKERS.last_name%TYPE;
018  v_name                          WORKERS.name%TYPE;
019  d_birth_date                    WORKERS.birth_date%TYPE;
...
027      v_first_name   := 'JOHN';
028      v_middle_name  := 'J.';
029      v_last_name    := 'DOE';
```

```
030    v_name          :=
031      rtrim(v_last_name||', '||v_first_name||' '||v_middle_name);
032    d_birth_date   :=
033      to_date('19800101', 'YYYYMMDD'); -- I'm guessing
...
061    -- Detect any existing entries with the unique
062    -- combination of columns as in this constraint:
063    -- constraint   WORKERS_UK2
064    -- unique (
065    -- name,
066    -- birth_date,
067    -- gender_type_id )
068    begin
069      select count(1)
070      into   n_count
071      from   WORKERS
072      where  name           = v_name
073      and    birth_date     = d_birth_date
074      and    gender_type_id = n_gender_type_id;
075    exception
076      when OTHERS then
077        raise_application_error(-20005, SQLERRM||
078          ' on select WORKERS'||
079          ' in filename insert_with_plsql_detection.sql');
080    end;
081
082    -- Conditionally insert the row
083    if n_count = 0 then
084      -- Now, let's get the next id sequence
085      begin
086        select WORKERS_ID.nextval
087        into   n_id
088        from   SYS.DUAL;
089      exception
090        when OTHERS then
091          raise_application_error(-20001, SQLERRM||
092            ' on select WORKERS_ID.nextval'||
093            ' in filename insert_with_plsql_detection.sql');
094      end;
095
096      -- And then, let's get the next external_id sequence
097      begin
098        select lpad(to_char(EXTERNAL_ID_SEQ.nextval), 9, '0')
099        into   v_external_id
100        from   SYS.DUAL;
101      exception
102        when OTHERS then
103          raise_application_error(-20003, SQLERRM||
104            ' on select EXTERNAL_ID_SEQ.nextval'||
105            ' in filename insert_with_plsql_detection.sql');
106      end;
107
```

```
108      -- Now that we have all the necessary ID values
109      -- we can finally insert a row!
110      begin
111        insert into WORKERS (
112                  id,
113                  worker_type_id,
114                  external_id,
115                  first_name,
116                  middle_name,
117                  last_name,
118                  name,
119                  birth_date,
120                  gender_type_id )
121          values (
122                  n_id,
123                  n_worker_type_id,
124                  v_external_id,
125                  v_first_name,
126                  v_middle_name,
127                  v_last_name,
128                  v_name,
129                  d_birth_date,
130                  n_gender_type_id );
131
132        n_count := sql%rowcount;
133      exception
134        when OTHERS then
135          raise_application_error(-20006, SQLERRM||
136              ' on insert WORKERS'||
137              ' in filename insert_with_plsql_detection.sql');
138      end;
139    else
140      n_count := 0;
141    end if;
```

Let's review the modifications:

- On lines 15 through 19, I've added variables to hold column values. I've done this because I need to specify the column values more than once. This way, I can set their values once, and then know that I will consistently use the same values twice.

- Lines 27 through 33 initialize the variables I added on lines 15 through 19. A particularly troublesome issue is the variable v_name for column WORKERS.name. It's a computed value that will be stored in the database in order to improve performance. This tactic will cause any relational database purist to have a hissy fit. But that's not what I find troublesome. Since it's a computed value, you must make sure it's always computed the same way. Hmm, that sounds like a job for a function dedicated to the WORKERS table. You'll create one to handle this issue in Chapter 5, so don't sweat it yet.

- Lines 68 through 80 contain a new nested PL/SQL block that queries the WORKERS table against the columns that make up the unique constraint in question, to see if an entry with duplicate values already exists in the table. The SQL statement simply counts the number of rows with duplicate values, storing the count in variable n_count.

- Line 83 has a new IF statement, which determines whether to insert a row. If the value of the variable n_count is 0, I go ahead and insert the row. Otherwise, on line 140, I set n_count to 0 in order to correctly report the number of rows inserted.

In Listing 4-3, I was able to maintain control of the execution of my PL/SQL program. But what if I wanted to update the row that already existed? Then I would have coded the detection block as shown in Listing 4-4.

Listing 4-4. An Insert Example, Modified to Detect Duplicates with PL/SQL for Update, insert_with_plsql_detection_for_update.sql

```
069    begin
070      select id
071      into   n_id
072      from   WORKERS
073      where  name            = v_name
074      and    birth_date      = d_birth_date
075      and    gender_type_id = n_gender_type_id;
076      exception
077        when NO_DATA_FOUND then
078          n_id := NULL; -- Is this really needed?
079        when OTHERS then
080          raise_application_error(-20003, SQLERRM||
081            ' on select WORKERS'||
082            ' in filename insert_with_plsql_detection_for_update.sql');
083      end;
084
085      -- Conditionally insert the row
086      if n_id is NULL then
087        -- Now, let's get the next id sequence
088        begin
089          select WORKERS_ID.nextval
090          into   n_id
091          from   SYS.DUAL;
092        exception
093          when OTHERS then
094            raise_application_error(-20004, SQLERRM||
095              ' on select WORKERS_ID.nextval'||
096              ' in filename insert_with_plsql_detection_for_update.sql');
097        end;
098
099        -- And then, let's get the next external_id sequence
100        begin
101          select lpad(to_char(EXTERNAL_ID_SEQ.nextval), 9, '0')
102          into   v_external_id
103          from   SYS.DUAL;
104        exception
105          when OTHERS then
```

```
106            raise_application_error(-20005, SQLERRM||
107              ' on select EXTERNAL_ID_SEQ.nextval'||
108                ' in filename insert_with_plsql_detection_for_update.sql');
109        end;
110
111      -- Now that we have all the necessary ID values
112      -- we can finally insert a row!
113      begin
114        insert into WORKERS (
115                id,
116                worker_type_id,
117                external_id,
118                first_name,
119                middle_name,
120                last_name,
121                name,
122                birth_date,
123                gender_type_id )
124          values (
125                n_id,
126                n_worker_type_id,
127                v_external_id,
128                v_first_name,
129                v_middle_name,
130                v_last_name,
131                v_name,
132                d_birth_date,
133                n_gender_type_id );
134
135        n_inserted := sql%rowcount;
136      exception
137        when OTHERS then
138          raise_application_error(-20006, SQLERRM||
139            ' on insert WORKERS'||
140            ' in filename insert_with_plsql_detection_for_update.sql');
141      end;
142    else
143      begin
144        update WORKERS
145        set    worker_type_id = n_worker_type_id
146        where  id             = n_id;
147
148        n_updated := sql%rowcount;
149      exception
150        when OTHERS then
151          raise_application_error(-20007, SQLERRM||
152            ' on update WORKERS'||
153            ' in filename insert_with_plsql_detection_for_update.sql');
154      end;
155    end if;
```

On lines 69 through 83, I've recoded the detection block to retrieve the primary key value for a row with duplicate values. If a duplicate row exists, variable n_id, initially NULL, will be set to the value of the primary key. Otherwise, if a duplicate row does not exist, a NO_DATA_FOUND exception will be raised. In turn, the exception will be handled by the WHEN NO_DATA_FOUND clause in the enclosing PL/SQL block's exception-handling section. There, in the EXCEPTION clause, I set the value of variable n_id to NULL to flag that I did not find a duplicate. I actually don't need to set it NULL because it remained NULL when the exception was raised. But the Oracle PL/SQL documentation does not explicitly guarantee this behavior, so I set it to NULL.

Also, on line 86, now I use the n_id variable to determine if I found a duplicate row. If n_id is NULL, I insert the row. Otherwise, on lines 143 through 154, I update the duplicate row with the worker_type_id value.

So if this was a better tactic, what's best? Before I answer that question, let's first digress a moment so I can finally explain the syntax of all those IF statements I've been using all along!

IF I Don't Tell You Now, When ELSE Can I?

This seems a good a time as any to finally get around to defining just what an IF statement is. Let's look at the IF statement syntax used in Listing 4-4:

```
IF <boolean_evaluation> THEN
  -- do this if it's TRUE
[ELSE
  -- do this if it's not TRUE]
END IF;
```

where <boolean_evaluation> is PL/SQL that evaluates to a Boolean value. If the <boolean_evaluation> is TRUE, then the lines of code between the THEN and ELSE keywords are executed. Otherwise, if the <boolean_evaluation> is not TRUE or NULL, then the lines of code between keywords ELSE and END IF are executed.

In Listing 4-4, on line 86, I evaluate id is NULL. If it's TRUE, PL/SQL executes lines 87 through 141; otherwise (ELSE), it executes lines 143 through 154. You can also use the following syntaxes:

```
IF <boolean_evaluation> THEN
  -- do this if it's TRUE
END IF;
```

or

```
IF     <boolean_evaluation> THEN

  -- do this if it's TRUE
[ELSIF <boolean_evaluation> THEN
  -- do this if it's TRUE
ELSIF ...

ELSE
  -- do this if it's not TRUE]
END IF;
```

Now, let's get back to the subject of inserting.

Using SQL to Predetect a Duplicate

It's almost always best to let SQL simply do its job! You can't imagine how much PL/SQL code I've seen that can be replaced by one SQL statement—for example, all the code you've seen so far in this chapter in Listings 4-1 through 4-4.

Figure 4-3 is a simple process flow diagram for predetecting a duplicate entry using SQL. In this process, SQL performs the work of predetection using an EXISTS clause. If a duplicate entry does not exist at the moment the EXISTS clause is executed, the SQL engine immediately follows with an INSERT. Regardless, this does not mean you can't get a DUP_VAL_ON_INDEX exception. In the microseconds between the evaluation of the EXISTS clause and the INSERT, it is possible that someone or something has inserted a duplicate value into the database. So you must still catch any exceptions from the SELECT...INTO statement and act accordingly.

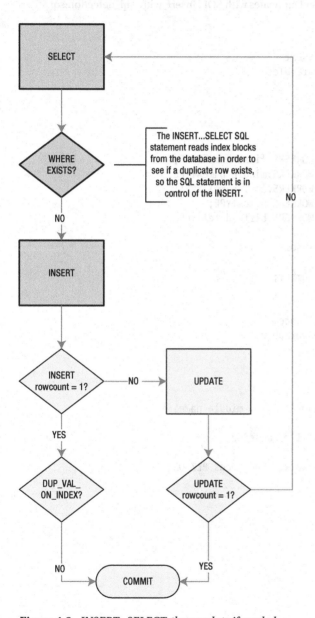

Figure 4-3. *INSERT...SELECT, then update if needed*

There appears to be no "perfect" solution, and indeed, that is the case. It's always possible that someone or something has deleted or inserted an entry in the database between your duplicate row detection and corresponding action. Now let's take a look at an example that uses SQL predetection.

Listing 4-5 is an example of letting SQL determine whether there's a duplicate row, and then conditionally inserting values into the WORKERS table.

Listing 4-5. An Insert Example, Modified to Detect Duplicates with SQL, insert_with_sql_detection.sql

```
01  rem insert_with_sql_detection.sql
02  rem by Donald J. Bales on 2014-10-20
03  rem An anonymous PL/SQL procedure to insert
04  rem values using PL/SQL literals and variables
05
06  set serveroutput on size 1000000;
07
08  declare
09
10  v_first_name                      WORKERS.first_name%TYPE;
11  v_middle_name                     WORKERS.middle_name%TYPE;
12  v_last_name                       WORKERS.last_name%TYPE;
13  v_name                            WORKERS.name%TYPE;
14  d_birth_date                      WORKERS.birth_date%TYPE;
15
16  -- I'll use this variable to hold the result
17  -- of the SQL insert statement.
18  n_count                           number;
19
20  begin
21    -- Since I use these values more than once,
22    -- I set them here, and then use the variables
23    v_first_name  := 'JOHN';
24    v_middle_name := 'J.';
25    v_last_name   := 'DOE';
26    v_name        :=
27      rtrim(v_last_name||', '||v_first_name||' '||v_middle_name);
28    d_birth_date  :=
29      to_date('19800101', 'YYYYMMDD'); -- I'm guessing
30
31    -- Now I can just let SQL do all the work.  Who needs PL/SQL!
32    begin
33      insert into WORKERS (
34            id,
35            worker_type_id,
36            external_id,
37            first_name,
38            middle_name,
39            last_name,
40            name,
41            birth_date,
42            gender_type_id )
43      select WORKERS_ID.nextval,
44            c1.id,
```

```
45                lpad(to_char(EXTERNAL_ID_SEQ.nextval), 9, '0'),
46                v_first_name,
47                v_middle_name,
48                v_last_name,
49                v_name,
50                d_birth_date,
51                c2.id
52        from   WORKER_TYPES c1,
53               GENDER_TYPES c2
54        where  c1.code = 'C'
55        and    c2.code = 'M'
56        and not exists (
57          select 1
58          from   WORKERS x
59          where  x.name            = v_name
60          and    x.birth_date      = d_birth_date
61          and    x.gender_type_id = c2.id );
62
63        n_count := sql%rowcount;
64      exception
65        when OTHERS then
66          raise_application_error(-20006, SQLERRM||
67            ' on insert WORKERS'||
68              ' in filename insert_with_sql_detection.sql');
69      end;
70
71      pl(to_char(n_count)||' row(s) inserted.');
72    end;
73    /
74
75    commit;
```

Listing 4-5 isn't a partial listing; it's the whole program! Where did all the PL/SQL go? Well, let's see. First, I'm using a different syntax for this program's INSERT statement, as follows:

```
INSERT INTO <insert_table_name> (
      <column_name_1>,
      <column_name_2>,...
      <column_name_N> )
SELECT <column_name_or_value_1>,
      <column_name_or_value_2>,...
      <column_name_or_value_N>
FROM   <select_table_name_1> <select_table_alias_1>,
       <select_table_name_2> <select_table_alias_2>,...
       <select_table_name_N> <select_table_alias_N>
WHERE  <where _clause>;
```

where <insert_table_name> is the name of the table to INSERT INTO, <column_name> is the name of a column in that table, <column_name_or_value> is the value for a corresponding <column_name> from one of the SELECT statement's tables, <select_table_name> is one of the tables being queried by the SELECT statement, <select_table_alias> is a corresponding table name alias, and <where_clause> is the SELECT statement's WHERE clause. The column values can be PL/SQL literals, variables, qualifying function results, or SQL column values.

I'll say it again: you should always use a list of columns in your INSERT statements in order to maintain the validity of your code in the event that someone later adds a column to the table.

Back to the SQL statement:

- On lines 54 and 55, since the WHERE clause selects one row from the WORKER_TYPES and GENDER_TYPES tables, the SELECT statement will return only one row of values.

- On lines 56 through 61, the NOT EXISTS subquery performs the detection of a duplicate entry and, accordingly, the conditional insert of a row.

All the work that was done by five other SQL SELECT statements is now accomplished in one INSERT SELECT statement. What's the moral of this story? Know thy SQL! Each solution presented here has its strengths and weaknesses. As I stated earlier, it's up to you to decide which is the best tactic to apply to each situation.

I favor predetection instead of postdetection (reacting to the DUP_VAL_ON_INDEX exception) because I can maintain control of my program. And I have never found a situation where my PL/SQL batch programs were working on inserting and/or updating the exact same set of data at the same time. So, in 20 plus years of writing stored procedures, and after more than 40,000 stored procedures, I've never seen a DUP_VAL_ON_INDEX exception when using predetection. This means you must also consider the nature of the business environment in which you are going to run your stored procedures when deciding whether to use postdetection or predetection.

■ **Tip** You should check out the functionality of the newer SQL DML statement MERGE. It can do a lot of what has already been covered in this chapter, using just SQL. However, it suffers from the same predetection issues I just covered.

It's Your Turn to Insert

Are you just going to watch me do all the work? No way! Here's what I need you to do, and you've got to do it, or the coming examples won't work.

1. Use whatever PL/SQL insert technique you want to code a script to insert rows into the WORKERS table for four workers: JANE J. DOE, her husband JOHN J. DOE, her daughter JANIE E. DOE, and her son JOHNNIE E. DOE.

2. Save your script as insert_the_doe_family.sql.

3. Execute your script.

4. Test your script by executing it again. Make sure you don't get any errors but still get the desired rows in the WORKERS table.

Listing 4-6 is my solution to this exercise.

Listing 4-6. An Anonymous Procedure to Insert the Doe Family into the Worker Table, insert_the_doe_family.sql

```
01  rem insert_the_doe_family.sql
02  rem by Donald J. Bales on 2014-10-20
03  rem An anonymous PL/SQL procedure to insert
04  rem values using PL/SQL literals and variables
05
```

```
06  set serveroutput on size 1000000;
07
08  declare
09
10  -- I'll use this variable to hold the result
11  -- of the SQL insert statement.
12  n_count                              number := 0;
13
14  -- I've declared this local (or embedded) function to
15  -- do the actual work of inserting values.  It uses
16  -- SQL detection to prevent DUP_VAL_ON_INDEX exceptions.
17  FUNCTION add_worker(
18  aiv_first_name                       WORKERS.first_name%TYPE,
19  aiv_middle_name                      WORKERS.middle_name%TYPE,
20  aiv_last_name                        WORKERS.last_name%TYPE,
21  aid_birth_date                       WORKERS.birth_date%TYPE,
22  aiv_gender_code                      GENDER_TYPES.code%TYPE,
23  aiv_worker_type_code                 WORKER_TYPES.code%TYPE)
24  return                               number is
25
26  v_name                               WORKERS.name%TYPE;
27
28  begin
29    v_name        :=
30      rtrim(aiv_last_name||', '||aiv_first_name||' '||aiv_middle_name);
31
32    -- Now I can just let SQL do all the work.  Who needs PL/SQL!
33    begin
34      insert into WORKERS (
35              id,
36              worker_type_id,
37              external_id,
38              first_name,
39              middle_name,
40              last_name,
41              name,
42              birth_date,
43              gender_type_id )
44      select WORKERS_ID.nextval,
45              c1.id,
46              lpad(to_char(EXTERNAL_ID_SEQ.nextval), 9, '0'),
47              aiv_first_name,
48              aiv_middle_name,
49              aiv_last_name,
50              v_name,
51              aid_birth_date,
52              c2.id
53      from    WORKER_TYPES c1,
54              GENDER_TYPES c2
55      where   c1.code = aiv_worker_type_code
56      and     c2.code = aiv_gender_code
```

```
57      and not exists (
58        select 1
59        from   WORKERS x
60        where  x.name          = v_name
61        and    x.birth_date    = aid_birth_date
62        and    x.gender_type_id = c2.id );
63
64      return sql%rowcount;
65    exception
66      when OTHERS then
67        raise_application_error(-20001, SQLERRM||
68          ' on insert WORKERS'||
69          ' in add_worker');
70    end;
71  end add_worker;
72
73  begin
74    -- All I have to do now, is call the add_worker function
75    -- four times with each Doe family member's values.
76    n_count := n_count + add_worker(
77      'JOHN',   'J.', 'DOE', to_date('19800101', 'YYYYMMDD'), 'M', 'C');
78    n_count := n_count + add_worker(
79      'JANE',   'J.', 'DOE', to_date('19800101', 'YYYYMMDD'), 'F', 'E');
80    n_count := n_count + add_worker(
81      'JOHNNY', 'E.', 'DOE', to_date('19980101', 'YYYYMMDD'), 'M', 'E');
82    n_count := n_count + add_worker(
83      'JANIE',  'E.', 'DOE', to_date('19980101', 'YYYYMMDD'), 'F', 'E');
84
85    pl(to_char(n_count)||' row(s) inserted.');
86  end;
87  /
88
89  commit;
```

In practice, you'll find that you primarily use an INSERT statement in PL/SQL when you do the following:

- Move data from one application to another for data migration

- Transform data for data processing

Beyond those two applications, a program written in some other programming language like Java or a data-loading utility like SQL*Loader will be used to insert values into the database.

Now that you have four entries in the WORKERS table, let's update a couple of them!

Updates

Here, I'm talking about updating a row or rows of data in a relational database from PL/SQL. Let's start with a simple update.

Updating a Row

Listing 4-7 is an example of using a SQL UPDATE statement in PL/SQL. It's just a good, old-fashioned UPDATE statement, where you can also use PL/SQL literals, PL/SQL variables, or SQL functions.

Listing 4-7. An Update Example Using Variables, insert_with_plsql_detection_for_update.sql

```
143      begin
144        update WORKERS
145        set    worker_type_id  = n_worker_type_id
146        where  id              = n_id;
147
148        n_updated := sql%rowcount;
149      exception
150        when OTHERS then
151          raise_application_error(-20007, SQLERRM||
152            ' on update WORKERS'||
153             ' in filename insert_with_plsql_detection_for_update.sql');
154      end;
```

The syntax used for the SQL UPDATE statement in Listing 4-7 is as follows:

```
UPDATE <table_name>
SET    <column_name_1> = <column_value_1>,
       <column_name_2> = <column_value_2>,...
       <column_name_N> = <column_value_N>
WHERE  <where_clause>;
```

where <table_name> is the name of the table to be updated, <column_name> is the name of a column to update, <column_value> is the corresponding value to use for the column, and <where_clause> is a WHERE clause that appropriately selects the rows to be updated.

I said it earlier, and I'll say it again: you should almost always have a WHERE clause with an UPDATE statement. I've seen some really catastrophic disasters in my day when someone has executed an UPDATE statement without a WHERE clause. I even go so far as to run a PL/SQL program against the database's source table, SYS.DBA_SOURCE, to look for UPDATE statements without WHERE clauses.

As for the code in this listing, well, there's nothing earth-shattering about it:

- Lines 144 through 146 contain a SQL UPDATE statement to update a worker's type if a duplicate row already exists in the database.

- Line 148 gets the result of the UPDATE statement: the number of rows updated.

- On lines 143 through 154 collectively, I've blocked the UPDATE statement in order to capture and report the exact type and location of any unexpected error.

The number one abuse of PL/SQL when used for data processing is using it to update values in a table in a row-by-row fashion. Why is that an abuse of PL/SQL? Because that's what SQL is for.

Using SQL to Perform Complex Updates

The SQL UPDATE statement is very powerful. It can update one or more columns for a predetermined set of rows in a single statement. Why am I spending so much time on this soapbox about knowing SQL? The whole purpose of PL/SQL is to control when to execute an appropriate SQL statement. It is *not* intended to replace SQL with a bunch of poorly performing PL/SQL statements.

You can update multiple columns at a time in a SQL UPDATE statement, as demonstrated in Listing 4-8.

Listing 4-8. Updating Multiple Columns with an UPDATE Statement, update_multiple.sql

```
1  update WORKERS u
2  set   ( u.worker_type_id,  u.gender_type_id ) = (
3  select c1.id,              c2.id
4  from   WORKER_TYPES c1,
5         GENDER_TYPES c2
6  where  c1.code = decode(instr(u.first_name, 'JOHN'), 0, 'E', 'C')
7  and    c2.code = decode(instr(u.first_name, 'JOHN'), 0, 'F', 'M') )
8  where  u.last_name = 'DOE';
```

The syntax used in the UPDATE statement in Listing 4-8 is as follows:

```
UPDATE <update_table_name>
SET ( <update_column_name_1>, <update_column_name_2>,... <update_column_name_N> ) =
(SELECT <select_column_name_1>, <select_column_name_2>,... <select_column_name_N>
FROM   <select_table_name_1>,
       <select_table_name_2>,...
       <select_table_name_N>
WHERE  <select_column_name_3> = <update_column_name_3>
AND    <select_column_name_4> = <update_column_name_4>
AND    <select_column_name_N> = <update_column_name_N> )
WHERE  <update_column_name_4> = ... ;
```

The UPDATE statement in Listing 4-8 will set the worker type and gender type to C (contractor) and M (male), respectively, for anyone with the first name John and the last name Doe. Yes, this is a silly example, but the point here is that the use of subqueries in the SET and WHERE clauses of a SQL UPDATE statement make it possible to update almost anything. All you should need PL/SQL for is deciding when to execute an appropriate SQL UPDATE statement.

Let's take a close look at Listing 4-8:

- Line 1 specifies the name of the table to be updated.

- Line 2 specifies a list of columns in that table to be updated. The list is enclosed in parentheses followed by an equal sign, and then an opening parenthesis, which is the start of a subquery.

- Lines 3 through 7 contain a subquery that will conditionally select which values to update the columns with based on information in the table to be updated.

- Line 3 has a list of the same number of values (columns) in the SELECT statement's column list as in the UPDATE statement's SET list.

- Lines 4 and 5 specify two code tables from which to draw update values.

- On line 6, I conditionally specify the code value for C (contractor) or E (employee), based on whether or not the worker's first_name contains the string 'JOHN'.

- On line 7, I conditionally specify the code value for F (female) or M (male), based on whether or not the worker's first name contains the string 'JOHN'.

- On line 8, I constrain the rows that will be updated to those with the last_name equal to 'DOE'.

The lesson here: know thy SQL!

As I stated earlier, in practice, you'll primarily use an UPDATE statement in PL/SQL in the following situations:

- The conditions for updating are too complex to be determined using a SQL WHERE clause; that is, you need a more procedural decision-making process.

- Deriving the values to use to update a table's column values is too complex to be done by SQL; that is, you need a more procedural decision-making process.

- You need to use a PL/SQL program unit's ability to formulate a larger and more complex multistatement transaction context.

Hence, the reason PL/SQL exists: to add procedure decision-making capabilities to the use of nonprocedural SQL statements!

Guess what? There's even less to say about deleting rows.

Deletes

In practice, the SQL DELETE command is rarely used when compared to its siblings INSERT, UPDATE, and SELECT. However, for completeness, let's look at how you use it in PL/SQL. Listing 4-9 is an example of using a DELETE statement in PL/SQL, where I use a PL/SQL literal, a SQL function, and a subquery that uses a PL/SQL variable.

Listing 4-9. A Delete Example Using a PL/SQL Literal and Variable, delete.sql

```
01  rem delete.sql
02  rem by Donald J. Bales on 2014-10-20
03  rem An anonymous PL/SQL procedure to delete
04  rem rows using PL/SQL literals and variables
05
06  set serveroutput on size 1000000;
07
08  declare
09
10  -- I'll use this variable to hold the result
11  -- of the SQL delete statement.
12  n_count                         number;
13
14  v_code                          GENDER_TYPES.code%TYPE := 'M';
15
16  begin
17
18    begin
19      delete from WORKERS d
20      where   d.name          = 'DOE, JOHN J.'            -- a literal
21      and     d.birth_date    = to_date('19800101', 'YYYYMMDD')  -- a function
22      and     d.gender_type_id = (                        -- a sub-query
23      select c.id
24      from    GENDER_TYPES c
25      where   c.code          = v_code );                 -- a variable
26
27      n_count := sql%rowcount;
28    exception
```

```
29      when OTHERS then
30        raise_application_error(-20001, SQLERRM||
31          ' on delete WORKERS'||
32          ' in filename delete.sql');
33    end;
34
35    pl(to_char(n_count)||' row(s) deleted.');
36  end;
37  /
38
39  commit;
```

The syntax for the SQL DELETE statement used in Listing 4-9 is as follows:

```
DELETE [FROM] <delete_table_name>
WHERE <where_clause> ;
```

where <delete_table_name> is the name of the table from which to delete rows, and <where_clause> is a SQL WHERE clause that appropriately specifies the rows within the table to delete.

On line 27, I capture the result of the SQL DELETE statement: the number of rows deleted. Just as with an UPDATE statement, every DELETE statement should have a WHERE clause.

Let's discuss how you might apply a DELETE statement in PL/SQL. In practice, you'll primarily use a DELETE statement in PL/SQL when the conditions for deleting are too complex to be determined by using a WHERE clause. So you'll find that you rarely use DELETE at all!

Finally, let's look at the SELECT statement.

Selects

The SQL SELECT statement is the most used SQL statement in PL/SQL, and for a good reason. PL/SQL is all about encompassing set-based operations with procedural logic. Yet a SQL SELECT statement is a nonprocedural construct, hence the need for the PL in PL/SQL. In this section, I'll discuss the singleton SELECT statement—the one that is supposed to return one row.

You've seen me use SELECT statements over and over again at this point. As I've said, I assume you already know SQL. Regardless, I've tried to take some time to review what you know about SQL, so you'll be ready for PL/SQL. Most PL/SQL stored procedures you write will have one or more SELECT statements in them. So what you can accomplish using PL/SQL—whether it's object-oriented architecture, service-oriented architecture, data processing, data migration, or reporting—will be constrained by your competency in writing a SQL SELECT statement.

Let's look back at the first source code listing in this chapter, Listing 4-3. For your convenience (and mine), I'm going to show part of it to you again in Listing 4-10.

Listing 4-10. An Example of Using Singleton SELECT Statements in PL/SQL, insert_with_plsql_detection.sql

```
048    -- Next, let's get the GENDER_TYPES id for a male
049    begin
050      select id
051      into   n_gender_type_id
052      from   GENDER_TYPES
053      where  code = 'M';
054    exception
055      when OTHERS then
```

```
056        raise_application_error(-20004, SQLERRM||
057          ' on select GENDER_TYPES'||
058          ' in filename insert_with_plsql_detection.sql');
059    end;
060
061    -- Detect any existing entries with the unique
062    -- combination of columns as in this constraint:
063    -- constraint   WORKERS_UK2
064    -- unique (
065    -- name,
066    -- birth_date,
067    -- gender_type_id )
068    begin
069      select count(1)
070      into   n_count
071      from   WORKERS
072      where  name          = v_name
073      and    birth_date    = d_birth_date
074      and    gender_type_id = n_gender_type_id;
075    exception
076      when OTHERS then
077        raise_application_error(-20005, SQLERRM||
078          ' on select WORKERS'||
079          ' in filename insert_with_plsql_detection.sql');
080    end;
081
082    -- Conditionally insert the row
083    if n_count = 0 then
084      -- Now, let's get the next id sequence
085      begin
086        select WORKERS_ID.nextval
087        into   n_id
088        from   SYS.DUAL;
089      exception
090        when OTHERS then
091          raise_application_error(-20001, SQLERRM||
092            ' on select WORKERS_ID.nextval'||
093            ' in filename insert_with_plsql_detection.sql');
094      end;
```

The syntax used for the SQL SELECT statements in Listing 4-10 is as follows:

```
SELECT <column_name_1>,
       <column_name_2>,...
       <column_name_N>
INTO   <plsql_variable_1>,
       <plsql_variable_2>,...
       <plsql_variable_N>
FROM   <table_name_1>,
       <table_name_2>,...
       <table_name_N>
WHERE  <where_clause>... ;
```

where <column_name> is the name of a column in one of the tables in the FROM list, <plsql_variable> is the corresponding variable to copy the column value to, <table_name> is a table to query, and <where_clause> is an appropriate WHERE clause.

Let's examine the three SQL SELECT INTO statements in Listing 4-10:

- Lines 50 through 53 get the corresponding gender_type_id value for the code 'M'.

- Line 50 selects the column name, GENDER_TYPES.id.

- Line 51 specifies the PL/SQL variable n_gender_type_id in the INTO clause.

- Line 52 specifies the code table's name, GENDER_TYPES.

- Line 53 specifies a WHERE clause, where the code is equal to 'M'.

- On lines 49 through 59 collectively, I block the SQL SELECT statement in order to catch and report any catastrophic errors (WHEN OTHERS). This is a SELECT statement where I don't expect any exceptions. I always expect the corresponding values to exist in the database.

- On lines 69 through 74, I use a SQL group operator, count(), to determine the number of rows in the table that match the criteria of the associated WHERE clause.

- On lines 68 through 80 collectively, I block the SQL SELECT statement for OTHERS. This is a safe SQL SELECT statement. It will always have a result, except in the case of some unforeseeable database error.

- Lines 86 through 88 get the next sequence value for the column id from sequence WORKERS_ID.

- On lines 85 through 94 collectively, I block the SQL SELECT statement for any unforeseeable errors, but I never expect this SQL SELECT statement to raise an exception.

But what do you do if you expect an error? For example, perhaps a row matching the WHERE clause criteria is not in the table! Or maybe too many rows match the WHERE clause criteria. What do you do then?

No Data Found

As I stated earlier when I first discussed exceptions in Chapter 2, there are two very commonly used exceptions. The most commonly used exception is NO_DATA_FOUND. When a singleton SELECT statement can't find a row to match its WHERE clause's criteria, it will raise a NO_DATA_FOUND exception. You saw an example of this earlier in Listing 4-4. Listing 4-11 highlights the SELECT statement in question.

Listing 4-11. An Example of a SELECT Statement That May Raise a NO_DATA_FOUND Exception, insert_with_plsql_detection_for_update.sql

```
069    begin
070      select id
071      into   n_id
072      from   WORKERS
073      where  name           = v_name
074      and    birth_date     = d_birth_date
075      and    gender_type_id = n_gender_type_id;
076    exception
077      when NO_DATA_FOUND then
```

```
078        n_id := NULL; -- Is this really needed?
079      when OTHERS then
080        raise_application_error(-20003, SQLERRM||
081          ' on select WORKERS'||
082          ' in filename insert_with_plsql_detection_for_update.sql');
083    end;
```

This SELECT statement may raise a NO_DATA_FOUND exception because the database might not contain a matching row. As a matter of fact, that's just what I'm trying to determine here. If the SELECT statement returns an id value, then the program knows that an entry already exists, so it will update the existing entry. Otherwise, the program will insert a new entry. It's the otherwise condition that will raise the exception.

When the NO_DATA_FOUND exception is raised, program execution jumps from the SELECT statement directly to the enclosing WHEN NO_DATA_FOUND clause. In this case, I set the n_id to NULL in that clause, and then later in the program, I use that fact to conditionally insert a new row.

Since the SELECT statement returns one set of columns—one row—from the database, there's no way for it to report the number of rows found, right? No, you can still get the number of rows returned from sql%rowcount. Take a look at Listing 4-12.

Listing 4-12. An Example of a SELECT Statement That Captures the Selected Row Count, select_no_data_found.sql

```
40    begin
41      select id
42      into   n_id
43      from   WORKERS
44      where  name            = v_name
45      and    birth_date      = d_birth_date
46      and    gender_type_id = n_gender_type_id;
47
48      n_selected := sql%rowcount;
49    exception
50      when NO_DATA_FOUND then
51        n_selected := sql%rowcount;
52        pl('Caught raised exception NO_DATA_FOUND');
53      when OTHERS then
54        raise_application_error(-20002, SQLERRM||
55          ' on select WORKERS'||
56          ' in filename select_no_data_found.sql');
57    end;
```

In Listing 4-12, I initially set the value of n_selected to –1 just so I can prove the value is changed later in the program. If the SELECT statement executes successfully, n_selected is equal to 1 because its value is set on line 48. However, if the SELECT statement raises the NO_DATA_FOUND exception, n_selected is equal to 0 because I set its value on line 51.

The number of rows returned from the SELECT statement is reported by the database, so why do I need a NO_DATA_FOUND exception? Why does it even exist? Quite frankly, I don't know. I think the exception exists as a matter of programming convenience. It's syntactic sugar. So even though it breaks my "You should always maintain control in your program" rule, it's commonly used to detect that no matching row was found for a WHERE clause's criteria. Even I use it.

I'll show you another tactic for detecting no data found for a singleton in the next chapter when I cover cursors. If you're going to rely on the NO_DATA_FOUND exception, you must keep in mind that any code that comes after your SELECT statement will not be executed if your SELECT statement raises NO_DATA_FOUND.

Next, let's look at the other singleton SELECT issue: too many rows are returned.

Too Many Rows

In the context of a singleton SELECT, PL/SQL is always going to expect your SELECT statement to return one and only one row. I just finished discussing what happens when a SELECT statement doesn't get at least one row. So what happens when a SELECT statement gets one (or more) too many? It raises the exception TOO_MANY_ROWS. Listing 4-13 is an example of a SELECT statement that will raise the exception TOO_MANY_ROWS.

Listing 4-13. An Example of a SELECT Statement That Raises a TOO_MANY_ROWS Exception, select_too_many_rows.sql

```
40    begin
41      select id
42      into   n_id
43      from   WORKERS;
44   -- Let's comment the WHERE clause so I get all the rows
45   --    where   name         = v_name
46   --    and     birth_date   = d_birth_date
47   --    and     gender_type_id = n_gender_type_id;
48        n_selected := sql%rowcount;
49      exception
50        when NO_DATA_FOUND then
51          n_selected := sql%rowcount;
52          pl('Caught raised exception NO_DATA_FOUND');
53        when TOO_MANY_ROWS then
54          n_selected := sql%rowcount;
55          pl('Caught raised exception TOO_MANY_ROWS');
56        when OTHERS then
57          raise_application_error(-20002, SQLERRM||
58            ' on select WORKERS'||
59            ' in filename select_too_many_rows.sql');
60      end;
```

In Listing 4-13, I've commented out the WHERE clause so the SELECT statement will see all four Doe family entries and will raise a TOO_MANY_ROWS exception. On lines 53 through 55, I've also added a WHEN TOO_MANY_ROWS clause to catch the raised exception and, in turn, capture the number of rows returned by the SELECT statement.

Guess what? On line 53, sql%rowcount reports that only one row was selected. So PL/SQL has no idea how many rows actually match the query. It only knows that more than one exists, and that's a problem—where will PL/SQL put the data from rows 2 and on? There's actually no place for the data, so PL/SQL appropriately throws an exception. After all, the query was supposed to be a singleton query!

You can add PL/SQL code to predetect too many rows, similar to the technique demonstrated in Listing 4-3, when I was trying to predetect a duplicate row.

If count() returns a value greater than one, the program will know that there's more than one row. But once again, PL/SQL provides some syntactic sugar that allows me to use an exception to detect a condition. Yes, again that syntactic sugar—catching a TOO_MANY_ROWS exception—breaks my rule of "You should always maintain control over your program!" I'll admit it, I use it. I catch the exception. I don't like it. But as I'll show you in the next chapter, you'll need to write a lot of extra code to maintain control, so PL/SQL programmers commonly use the exception TOO_MANY_ROWS.

Once again, if you're going to rely on the TOO_MANY_ROWS exception, you must keep in mind that any code that comes after your SELECT statement will not be executed if your SELECT statement raises TOO_MANY_ROWS!

That's enough of that. Now let's see you put what I just said to work.

It's Your Turn to Select

Your assignment is to write an anonymous procedure that displays the first name of each of the Doe family members from the WORKERS table—remember, the ones you added in the previous exercise? To that end, follow these steps.

1. Write you script using at least one singleton SELECT.

2. Save your script as select_the_doe_family.sql.

3. Execute your script.

4. Test your script by executing it again. Make sure you don't get any errors but still get the desired rows from the WORKERS table.

Listing 4-14 is my lousy solution. Why lousy? Because my solution involves repeatedly executing a singleton SELECT statement in order to read multiple rows from the WORKERS table. I really need a better way to handle this situation, and a better solution for this problem is just what I'll cover in the next chapter.

Listing 4-14. *A Really Bad Way to Select Multiple Rows from a Table, select_the_doe_family.sql*

```
01  rem select_the_doe_family.sql
02  rem by Donald J. Bales on 2014-10-20
03  rem An anonymous PL/SQL procedure to select
04  rem the first names for the Doe family from
05  rem the Worker table.
06
07  set serveroutput on size 1000000;
08
09  declare
10
11  v_first_name                        WORKERS.first_name%TYPE;
12  n_id                                WORKERS.id%TYPE;
13
14  -- A local function that will be called over-and-over again
15  -- to find the next first_name for the specified id
16  -- and last_name.
17  FUNCTION get_first_name(
18  aion_id                  in out WORKERS.id%TYPE,
19  aiv_last_name            in     WORKERS.last_name%TYPE)
20  return                          WORKERS.first_name%TYPE is
21
22  v_first_name                        WORKERS.first_name%TYPE;
23
24  begin
25    -- Use SQL pseudo-column rownum in order
26    -- to limit the SELECT to the first row
27    select id,
28           first_name
29    into   aion_id,
30           v_first_name
31    from   WORKERS
32    where  id              > aion_id
33    and    last_name like aiv_last_name||'%'
```

```
34    and     rownum      = 1;
35
36    return v_first_name;
37  exception
38    when NO_DATA_FOUND then
39      return v_first_name;
40    when OTHERS then
41      raise_application_error(-20001, SQLERRM||
42        ' on select WORKERS'||
43        ' in show_worker');
44  end get_first_name;
45
46  begin
47    -- Keep track of the primary key so you
48    -- only retrieve the SELECTed row once
49    n_id := 0;
50    -- Loop until there's NO_DATA_FOUND
51    loop
52      -- get the first name from the local function
53      v_first_name := get_first_name(n_id, 'DOE');
54      -- detect NO_DATA_FOUND
55      if v_first_name is NULL then
56        exit;  -- Exit the loop
57      end if;
58      -- show the first_name
59      pl(v_first_name);
60    end loop;
61  end;
62  /
```

In practice, you'll find that you primarily use a singleton SELECT statement in PL/SQL when you want to do the following:

- Select the IDs for some code values that you will reference repeatedly

- Allocate a sequence value for a new primary key value

- Predetect the presence of a matching row

Let's review what you've learned.

Summary

At this point, it should be evident that a singleton is a SQL statement that returns one row of results. Table 4-1 is a side-by-side comparison of the results returned by each of the singletons I've covered: INSERT, UPDATE, DELETE, and SELECT.

Table 4-1. *Singleton Results for INSERT, UPDATE, DELETE, and SELECT*

Statement	Returns	Common Exceptions
INSERT INTO	Row count	DUP_VAL_ON_INDEX
UPDATE	Row count	
DELETE FROM	Row count	
SELECT...INTO	Row count and column values	NO_DATA_FOUND, TOO_MANY_ROWS

When you're working with the INSERT INTO and SELECT...INTO statements, you may as well expect an exception and write your PL/SQL accordingly. Of the four singletons, you'll use the SELECT statement the most. After all, you are working with a database.

The last exercise left me looking for a better solution to selecting more than one row at a time. In the next chapter, I'll look at the PL/SQL solution to this problem: a CURSOR.

CHAPTER 5

■ ■ ■

Multirow Processing

In the last chapter, you left off trying to retrieve the first names of the Doe family members from table WORKERS using a singleton SELECT. As you may have already guessed, Oracle has a better way to handle this multi-row processing problem.

Cursors

A *cursor* in this context is a named SQL SELECT statement that you can use in your PL/SQL program to access multiple rows from a table, yet retrieve them one row at a time.

Cursor Declarations

You declare cursors in the declaration section of a PL/SQL block just as you declare functions, procedures, and variables. And you should declare them with parameters, if required, just as you do with functions and procedures.

Listing 5-1 is a better solution to the last exercise in Chapter 4, where you were assigned the task of listing the Doe family's first names.

Listing 5-1. An Example of Using a Cursor to Select Multiple Rows from a Table, cursor_the_doe_family.sql

```
01  rem cursor_the_doe_family.sql
02  rem by Donald J. Bales on 2014-10-20
03  rem An anonymous PL/SQL procedure to select
04  rem the first names for the Doe family from
05  rem the Worker table.
06
07  set serveroutput on size 1000000;
08
09  declare
10
11  cursor c_workers(
12  aiv_last_name              in      WORKERS.last_name%TYPE) is
13  select first_name
14  from   WORKERS
15  where  last_name like aiv_last_name||'%'
16  order by id;
17
```

```
18  v_first_name                              WORKERS.first_name%TYPE;
19
20  begin
21    open c_workers('DOE');
22    loop
23      fetch c_workers into v_first_name;
24
25      if c_workers%notfound then
26        close c_workers;
27        exit;
28      end if;
29
30      pl(v_first_name);
31    end loop;
32  end;
33  /
```

There's a lot of new PL/SQL in this example. Let's start with syntax. The syntax used in Listing 5-1 to declare CURSOR c_worker is as follows:

```
CURSOR <cursor_name> [(
<parameter_name_1>          [IN]       <parameter_data_type_1>,
<parameter_name_2>          [IN]       <parameter_data_type_2>,...
<parameter_name_N>          [IN]       <parameter_data_type_N> )] IS
<select_statement>;
```

where <cursor_name> is the name of the CURSOR, <parameter_name> is the name of a parameter being passed IN, <parameter_data_type> is the PL/SQL data type of the corresponding parameter, and <select_statement> is a SQL SELECT statement. The brackets ([ ]) around the parameters denote that they are optional.

Of course, there's more to using cursors than just declaring them. Read on, as the next few subsections tell you all about what you can accomplish using cursors.

Fetching Rows from a Cursor Manually

The procedural PL/SQL, or control structure, syntax used to retrieve rows using the declared CURSOR in Listing 5-1 is as follows:

```
OPEN <cursor_name> [(
  <parameter_value_1,
  <parameter_value_2>,...
  <parameter_value_N> )];

LOOP
  -- loop until you manually EXIT;
FETCH <cursor_name> INTO
  <variable_name_1>,
  <variable_name_2>,...
  <variable_name_N>;
```

```
END LOOP;

CLOSE <cursor_name>;

EXIT;
```

where <cursor_name> is the name of a declared CURSOR, <parameter_value> is a value to pass in to the CURSOR that will be utilized somewhere in its SQL SELECT statement, and <variable_name> is a PL/SQL variable to receive one of the SQL SELECT statement's column values from the CURSOR.

The keyword OPEN is used to pass parameters to, and then execute, the cursor's SQL SELECT statement. FETCH retrieves one row of column values from the cursor's SELECT statement into a comma-separated list of PL/SQL variables. CLOSE does just that—it closes a CURSOR, releasing the cursor's resources back to PL/SQL and the database.

The keyword LOOP is used to start an unconstrained loop. In this context, any PL/SQL code between the keywords LOOP and END LOOP will continue to be executed over and over again until you manually exit the loop with the keyword EXIT. It's what I call a manual loop.

Here's the output from the cursor_the_doe_family.sql script (Listing 5-1):

```
SQL> @cursor_the_doe_family
```

```
JOHN
JANE
JOHNNY
JANIE
```

```
PL/SQL procedure successfully completed.
```

Let's take a moment to look at Listing 5-1, line by line:

- Lines 11 through 16 declare CURSOR c_workers, which will select the first name column from the table WORKERS, where the last name is like the one passed in.

- Line 18 declares a variable to hold the column value from the cursor.

- On line 21, I open the cursor, passing it the last name 'DOE'. This should give me all the first names for anyone with a name like DOE.

- Line 22 starts a manual loop. Lines 23 through 30 will be repeated endlessly until I exit manually, as I do on line 27.

- On line 23, I fetch the value of the column first_name into variable v_first_name.

- On line 25, I test the cursor c_workers for %notfound. If the SELECT statement did not find a row in the database for the current loop, the cursor c_worker will report no data found through the cursor variable %notfound.

- On line 26, if there is no data found, I CLOSE the cursor, and then EXIT the loop on line 27.

- On line 30, if a row is found, I display the first name on the screen using pl().

- On line 31, the keywords END LOOP signify the end of the LOOP.

Using a cursor for this type of problem—that is, retrieving multiple rows one row at a time—is definitely a better solution, if for no other reason than it was easier to maintain control over the program. But PL/SQL's solutions to this problem are going to get even better.

Cursor Records

On line 18 in Listing 5-1, I declared the variable v_first_name to hold the value from the database during each iteration of the LOOP. You can also use the keyword %ROWTYPE to declare a record for a cursor. So with one declaration, you can declare a record that has as many columns as the cursor it is defined for, with the same field names as the column names in the SELECT statement of the cursor. For example, I could have declared a record for CURSOR c_workers on line 18 as follows:

```
r_worker                       c_workers%ROWTYPE;
```

Pretty neat, huh? You'll see an example of this later in the chapter in Listing 5-7. Now let's take a look at using a cursor as a singleton SELECT.

A Singleton Cursor

By using a cursor, you can eliminate having to give up control of your programs when a NO_DATA_FOUND exception is raised because one is never raised. Instead, you can check the cursor variable for the status %notfound. Listing 5-2 is an example of using a cursor for a singleton SELECT. As you will see as you review the listing, sometimes using a cursor to retrieve one row can cost more in code than it's worth.

Listing 5-2. An Example of Using a Cursor for a Singleton SELECT, insert_with_plsql_cursor_detection_for_update.sql

```
001   rem insert_with_plsql_cursor_detection_for_update.sql
002   rem by Donald J. Bales on 2014-10-20
003   rem An anonymous PL/SQL procedure to insert
004   rem values using PL/SQL literals and variables
005
006   set serveroutput on size 1000000;
007
008   declare
009
010   cursor c_worker_types(
011   aiv_code                  in     WORKER_TYPES.code%TYPE) is
012   select id
013   from    WORKER_TYPES
014   where   code = aiv_code;
015
016   cursor c_gender_types(
017   aiv_code                  in     GENDER_TYPES.code%TYPE) is
018   select id
019   from    GENDER_TYPES
020   where   code = aiv_code;
021
022   cursor c_workers(
023   aiv_name                  in     WORKERS.name%TYPE,
024   aid_birth_date            in     WORKERS.birth_date%TYPE,
025   ain_gender_type_id        in     WORKERS.gender_type_id%TYPE) is
026   select id
```

```
027  from     WORKERS
028  where    name           = aiv_name
029  and      birth_date     = aid_birth_date
030  and      gender_type_id = ain_gender_type_id;
031
032  cursor c_worker_ids is
033  select WORKERS_ID.nextval worker_id
034  from   SYS.DUAL;
035
036  cursor c_external_ids is
037  select lpad(to_char(EXTERNAL_ID_SEQ.nextval), 9, '0') external_id
038  from   SYS.DUAL;
039
040  -- I declared these variables so I can get
041  -- the required ID values before I insert.
042  n_id                              WORKERS.id%TYPE;
043  n_worker_type_id                  WORKERS.worker_type_id%TYPE;
044  v_external_id                     WORKERS.external_id%TYPE;
045  v_first_name                      WORKERS.first_name%TYPE;
046  v_middle_name                     WORKERS.middle_name%TYPE;
047  v_last_name                       WORKERS.last_name%TYPE;
048  v_name                            WORKERS.name%TYPE;
049  d_birth_date                      WORKERS.birth_date%TYPE;
050  n_gender_type_id                  WORKERS.gender_type_id%TYPE;
051
052  -- I'll use these variables to hold the result
053  -- of the SQL insert and update statements.
054  n_inserted                        number := 0;
055  n_updated                         number := 0;
056
057  begin
058    v_first_name  := 'JOHN';
059    v_middle_name := 'J.';
060    v_last_name   := 'DOE';
061    v_name        :=
062      rtrim(v_last_name||', '||v_first_name||' '||v_middle_name);
063    d_birth_date  :=
064      to_date('19800101', 'YYYYMMDD'); -- I'm guessing
065
066    -- First, let's get the worker_type_id for a contractor
067    begin
068      open  c_worker_types('C');
069      fetch c_worker_types
070      into  n_worker_type_id;
071      if    c_worker_types%notfound then
072       raise_application_error(-20001,
073         'Can''t find the worker types ID for Contractor.'||
074         ' on select WORKER_TYPES'||
075         ' in filename insert_with_plsql_cursor_detection_for_update.sql');
076      end if;
077      close c_worker_types;
```

```
078     exception
079       when OTHERS then
080         raise_application_error(-20002, SQLERRM||
081           ' on select WORKER_TYPES'||
082           ' in filename insert_with_plsql_cursor_detection_for_update.sql');
083     end;
084
085     -- Next, let's get the gender_id for a male
086     begin
087       open  c_gender_types('M');
088       fetch c_gender_types
089       into  n_gender_type_id;
090       if    c_gender_types%notfound then
091        raise_application_error(-20003,
092          'Can''t find the gender ID for Male.'||
093          ' on select GENDER_TYPES'||
094          ' in filename insert_with_plsql_cursor_detection_for_update.sql');
095       end if;
096       close c_gender_types;
097     exception
098       when OTHERS then
099         raise_application_error(-20004, SQLERRM||
100           ' on select GENDER_TYPES'||
101           ' in filename insert_with_plsql_cursor_detection_for_update.sql');
102     end;
103
104     -- Detect any existing entries with the unique
105     -- combination of columns as in this constraint:
106     -- constraint    WORKERS_UK2
107     -- unique (
108     -- name,
109     -- birth_date,
110     -- gender_id )
111     begin
112       open c_workers(v_name, d_birth_date, n_gender_type_id);
113       fetch c_workers
114       into  n_id;
115       if    c_workers%notfound then
116        n_id := NULL;
117       end if;
118       close c_workers;
119     exception
120       when OTHERS then
121         raise_application_error(-20005, SQLERRM||
122           ' on select WORKERS'||
123           ' in filename insert_with_plsql_cursor_detection_for_update.sql');
124     end;
125
```

```
126    -- Conditionally insert the row
127    if n_id is NULL then
128      -- Now, let's get the next worker_id sequence
129      begin
130      open  c_worker_ids;
131      fetch c_worker_ids
132      into  n_id;
133      close c_worker_ids;
134      exception
135        when OTHERS then
136          raise_application_error(-20006, SQLERRM||
137            ' on select WORKER_IDS.nextval'||
138            ' in filename insert_with_plsql_cursor_detection_for_update.sql');
139      end;
140
141      -- And then, let's get the next external_id sequence
142      begin
143      open  c_external_ids;
144      fetch c_external_ids
145      into  v_external_id;
146      if    c_external_ids%notfound then
147        v_external_id := NULL;
148      end if;
149      close c_external_ids;
150      exception
151        when OTHERS then
152          raise_application_error(-20006, SQLERRM||
153            ' on select EXTERNAL_ID_SEQ.nextval'||
154            ' in filename insert_with_plsql_cursor_detection_for_update.sql');
155      end;
156
157      -- Now that we have all the necessary ID values
158      -- we can finally insert a row!
159      begin
160        insert into WORKERS (
161                id,
162                worker_type_id,
163                external_id,
164                first_name,
165                middle_name,
166                last_name,
167                name,
168                birth_date,
169                gender_type_id )
170        values (
171                n_id,
172                n_worker_type_id,
173                v_external_id,
174                v_first_name,
175                v_middle_name,
176                v_last_name,
```

```
177                 v_name,
178                 d_birth_date,
179                 n_gender_type_id );
180
181       n_inserted := sql%rowcount;
182     exception
183       when OTHERS then
184         raise_application_error(-20007, SQLERRM||
185           ' on insert WORKERS'||
186           ' in filename insert_with_plsql_cursor_detection_for_update.sql');
187     end;
188   else
189     begin
190       update WORKERS
191       set    worker_type_id = n_worker_type_id
192       where  id             = n_id;
193
194       n_updated := sql%rowcount;
195     exception
196       when OTHERS then
197         raise_application_error(-20008, SQLERRM||
198           ' on update WORKERS'||
199           ' in filename insert_with_plsql_cursor_detection_for_update.sql');
200     end;
201   end if;
202
203   pl(to_char(n_inserted)||' row(s) inserted.');
204   pl(to_char(n_updated)||' row(s) updated.');
205 end;
206 /
207
208 commit;
```

Listing 5-2 doesn't have any new syntax, but it does show a different utilization of the keywords OPEN, FETCH, and CLOSE. You may recall seeing a form of this source code originally in Listing 4-4. Now it has been modified to use cursors for its singleton SELECT statements, so I can argue when it's a good idea to use cursors for singletons and when it's not.

Let's break down the listing:

- Lines 10 through 14 declare a cursor for table WORKER_TYPES.

- Lines 16 through 20 declare a cursor for table GENDER_TYPES.

- Lines 22 through 30 declare a cursor for table WORKERS. Later in the executable section, I'll pass parameters for the worker's name, birth date, and gender in order to try to find an existing row in the database.

- Lines 32 through 34 declare a cursor for allocating the next worker ID sequence value.

- Lines 36 through 38 declare a cursor for allocating the external ID sequence value.

- On line 68, I open the cursor for the worker type, passing the code value C as a parameter.

- On line 69 and 70, I try to fetch the corresponding worker_type_id value into variable n_worker_type_id.

- On line 71, I test the cursor variable c_worker_types%notfound to see if a corresponding ID value was found. If not, I raise an application error, which stops the execution of the program.

- Line 77 closes the cursor (that's a mandatory programming task).

- On lines 68 through 83 collectively, I've blocked OPEN, FETCH, and CLOSE in order to capture any unusual errors.

- On lines 86 through 102 collectively, I do the same for table GENDER_TYPES as I have done for table WORKER_TYPES. *My assessment: using a cursor for getting the code IDs gains me nothing.* I don't expect there to be an exception, so I really don't gain any more control over the program by using a cursor for singleton SELECT as in this situation.

- On lines 111 through 124 collectively, I use a cursor to select a matching id from WORKERS. *This time, there is an advantage in using a cursor for a singleton SELECT.* Since I expect that the SELECT may not find any data, I can query the cursor variable c_workers%notfound to determine this. If the SELECT statement did not find a matching entry in the table, I set variable n_id to NULL to flag that no matching entry exists. In this instance, I no longer needed to code a WHEN NO_DATA_FOUND exception.

- On lines 129 through 139, and 142 through 155 collectively, I've used cursors to select the next sequence values from the database. Once again, since I don't expect any possible errors, using cursors for singleton SELECT statements adds a lot of code but little value.

The moral of the story is that you may want to use a cursor for a singleton SELECT if you expect a NO_DATA_FOUND exception may be raised; otherwise, you may as well stick to a simple SELECT statement. In practice, I personally have no problem with utilizing the exception NO_DATA_FOUND, syntactic sugar that it is, but the choice is now yours.

It's Your Turn to Fetch Manually

In this section, your assignment is to write a program using cursors. But first, I'll present a point of view on why good use of cursors is so important.

Do you ever think about how many times you've written a given SQL statement? Do you ever find yourself writing the same statement more than once in your program? Just how many times should you write the same SQL statement? In my opinion, the answer is just once! There are a lot of reasons to avoid writing the same statement more than once. Let's start with these:

- One SQL statement to accomplish one goal means fewer cursors in use on your database, and that means better performance.

- One SQL statement to accomplish one task means consistent behavior across your application's presentation layers.

- One SQL statement to accomplish one requirement means it will be easier to maintain and modify your application's code.

- One SQL statement to attain the goals just mentioned means saving money, and saved money is profit.

To attain better performance, consistent behavior, more maintainable code, and profit, you're going to have to start thinking like an object-oriented programmer.

What's your assignment? Write three packages for three tables. I'll show you two out of the three so you have some models for your coding, but I expect you to stretch during the third exercise and it all on your own. Let's start by *modularizing* a code table.

A Code Table Package

In the listings in Chapter 4 and now Chapter 5, I've repeatedly coded the same SQL SELECT statement in order to get the corresponding ID value for a given code. So rather than keep writing the same code over and over, I've created a package called WORKER_TYPE for table WORKER_TYPES. This is what I call a pseudo-object-oriented approach to programming in PL/SQL. Listing 5-3 is the worker type codes package spec, and Listing 5-4 is its implementation, or package body.

Listing 5-3. The WORKER_TYPE Package Spec, worker_type.pks

```
01  create or replace PACKAGE WORKER_TYPE as
02  /*
03  worker_type.pks
04  by Don Bales on 2014-10-20
05  Code Table WORKER_TYPES' methods.
06  */
07
08
09  -- Returns the id for the specified code value.
10
11  FUNCTION get_id(
12  aiv_code                    in      WORKER_TYPES.code%TYPE )
13  return                              WORKER_TYPES.id%TYPE;
14
15
16  end WORKER_TYPE;
17  /
18  @se.sql WORKER_TYPE
```

In Listing 5-3, I've declared one function, get_id(aiv_code) return id. Now if programmers—whether they are coding in a PL/SQL program, a JDBC program, C, C++, Perl, PowerScript, and so on—want to get the id value for a corresponding code value, all they need to do is call the PL/SQL function WORKER_TYPE.get_id(), passing it an existing code value.

Listing 5-4. The WORKER_TYPE Package Body, worker_type.pkb

```
01  create or replace PACKAGE BODY WORKER_TYPE as
02  /*
03  worker_type.pkb
04  by Don Bales on 2014-10-20
05  Table WORKER_TYPES' methods
06  */
07
08
```

```
09  -- FUNCTIONS
10
11  FUNCTION get_id(
12  aiv_code                            in      WORKER_TYPES.code%TYPE )
13  return                                      WORKER_TYPES.id%TYPE is
14
15  n_id                                        WORKER_TYPES.id%TYPE;
16
17  begin
18    select id
19    into   n_id
20    from   WORKER_TYPES
21    where  code = aiv_code;
22
23    return n_id;
24  end get_id;
25
26
27  end WORKER_TYPE;
28  /
29  @be.sql WORKER_TYPE
```

Let's look at the implementation, Listing 5-4:

- Line 11 declares the implementation for function get_id().

- Line 12 specifies that a calling program must pass in a code value.

- Line 13 specifies that the function will return a worker type ID value.

- Line 15 declares a local variable called n_id to hold the ID value retrieved from the database.

- Lines 18 through 21 contain a SQL SELECT statement to retrieve a corresponding ID value for the given code value in parameter aiv_code.

- On line 23, I return the retrieved ID value to the calling program unit.

- Lines 11 through 24 collectively implement a SQL SELECT statement to retrieve an ID value for a corresponding code value. I have not blocked this SQL statement, so it will raise a NO_DATA_FOUND exception should one occur. This means the calling program may want to block the call to WORKER_TYPE.get_id() in order to be able to report the exact error and the location where it occurred in the program.

Now, anywhere I would have coded another SQL statement to select an ID from table WORKER_TYPES for a given code, I can simply code

```
n_worker_type_id := WORKER_TYPE.get_id('C');
```

or better yet

```
begin
  n_worker_type_id := WORKER_TYPE.get_id('C');
exception
  when OTHERS then
    raise_application_error(-20???, SQLERRM||
      ' on call WORKERT_TYPE.get_id()'||
      ' in <my_program_unit>');
end;
```

The latter example, although more code, will make it easier to troubleshoot your program when an error does occur.

So what's part one of your assignment? Create a code package for table GENDER_TYPES, and that includes compiling and testing it. When you're finished, continue reading for part two.

A Worker Table Package

In a similar fashion to the code tables, I've written SQL SELECT statements numerous times in order to allocate database-generated sequence values. So I've created package WORKER to hold functions and procedures for table WORKERS. The first function I've added is get_id(). However, this time, get_id() is called without parameters and returns the next available sequence number for the WORKERS id column.

Take a look at package WORKER. Listing 5-5 is its package spec, and Listing 5-6 is its implementation.

Listing 5-5. The WORKER Package Spec, worker.pks

```
01  create or replace PACKAGE WORKER as
02  /*
03  worker.pks
04  by Donald J. Bales on 2014-10-20
05  Table WORKERS' methods.
06  */
07
08
09  -- Return the next ID sequence value
10
11  FUNCTION get_id
12  return                              WORKERS.id%TYPE;
13
14
15  end WORKER;
16  /
17  @se.sql WORKER
```

In Listing 5-5, I've declared one function: get_id(). It will return the next WORKERS_ID sequence value.

Listing 5-6. The WORKER Package Body, worker.pkb

```
01  create or replace PACKAGE BODY WORKER as
02  /*
03  worker.pkb
04  by Donald J. Bales on 2014-10-20
05  Table WORKERS' methods
06  */
07
08
09  -- FUNCTIONS
10
11  FUNCTION get_id
12  return                              WORKERS.id%TYPE is
13
14  n_id                                WORKERS.id%TYPE;
15
16  begin
17    select WORKERS_ID.nextval
18    into   n_id
19    from   SYS.DUAL;
20
21    return n_id;
22  end get_id;
23
24
25  end WORKER;
26  /
27  @be.sql WORKER
```

In Listing 5-6, I've coded a function that queries and returns the sequence value from WORKERS_ID.nextval. Remember that the SYS.DUAL table has one row, so selecting any value against it will return one value.

Your assignment for part two is to add three functions to package WORKER:

- A get_external_id() function, which will return a value from sequence EXTERNAL_ID_SEQ as a properly zero-left-padded varchar2.

- A get_unformatted_name() function, which will return a concatenated value for three parameters: aiv_first_name, aiv_middle_name, and aiv_last_name. Use the concatenation operator—two vertical bars (||)—to concatenate the varchar2 values together. (Hint: I've already coded this concatenation time and time again in the previous listings.)

- An is_duplicate() function, which you will pass three parameters: aiv_name, aid_birth_date, and ain_gender_type_id. It should return a Boolean value of TRUE if a duplicate exists; otherwise, it should return FALSE.

Remember to test all three functions. Yes, write a test unit for each one!
Let's move on to part three of your assignment.

Write a Modularized Version of Insert with PL/SQL Detection

Do you remember Listing 4-3? Now that you have functions for five out of the five blocked singleton SELECT statements, rewrite Listing 4-3 (insert_with_plsql_detection.sql), but this time replace all the singletons and the creation of the value for v_name with function calls to the appropriate packages. Save your script as insert_with_modularity.sql. Then execute it until it works.

My Solution

Listing 5-7 is my solution to this third part of the exercise.

Listing 5-7. A Modular Approach to Inserting, insert_with_modularity.sql

```
01  rem insert_with_modularity.sql
02  rem by Donald J. Bales on 2014-10-20
03  rem An anonymous PL/SQL procedure to insert
04  rem values using PL/SQL functions
05
06  set serveroutput on size 1000000;
07
08  declare
09
10  -- I declared this record, so I can get
11  -- the required ID values before I insert.
12  r_worker                            WORKERS%ROWTYPE;
13
14  -- I'll use this variable to hold the result
15  -- of the SQL insert statement.
16  n_count                             number := 0;
17
18  begin
19    r_worker.first_name  := 'JOHN';
20    r_worker.middle_name := 'J.';
21    r_worker.last_name   := 'DOE';
22    -- Using the same function to get this derived value
23    -- from all programs will ensure its value is consistent
24    r_worker.name        := WORKER.get_formatted_name(
25      r_worker.first_name, r_worker.middle_name, r_worker.last_name);
26    r_worker.birth_date  :=
27      to_date('19800101', 'YYYYMMDD'); -- I'm guessing
28
29    -- First, let's get the worker_type_id for a contractor
30    begin
31      r_worker.worker_type_id := WORKER_TYPE.get_id('C');
32    exception
33      when OTHERS then
34        raise_application_error(-20001, SQLERRM||
35          ' on call WORKER_TYPE.get_id(''C'')'||
36          ' in filename insert_with_modularity.sql');
37    end;
38
```

```
39    -- Next, let's get the gender_id for a male
40    begin
41      r_worker.gender_type_id := GENDER_TYPE.get_id('M');
42    exception
43      when OTHERS then
44        raise_application_error(-20002, SQLERRM||
45          ' on call GENDER_TYPE.get_id(''M'')'||
46          ' in filename insert_with_modularity.sql');
47    end;
48
49    -- Detect any existing entries, and
50    -- then conditionally insert the row
51    if not WORKER.is_duplicate(
52      r_worker.name, r_worker.birth_date, r_worker.gender_type_id) then
53      -- I'm not going to block the next two calls,
54      -- because it's highly unlikely that I could
55      -- ever get an error allocating a sequnce.
56
57      -- Now, let's get the next id sequence.
58      -- no parameters, so no parentheses needed
59      r_worker.id          := WORKER.get_id;
60
61      -- And then, let's get the next external_id sequence
62      -- no parameters, so no parentheses needed
63      r_worker.external_id := WORKER.get_external_id;
64
65      -- Now that we have all the necessary ID values
66      -- we can finally insert a row!
67      begin
68        -- Since I declared r_worker based on WORKERS, I
69        -- can skip the column list and just use the record.
70        insert into WORKERS values r_worker;
71
72        n_count := sql%rowcount;
73      exception
74        when OTHERS then
75          raise_application_error(-20003, SQLERRM||
76            ' on insert WORKERS'||
77            ' in filename insert_with_modularity.sql');
78      end;
79    end if;
80
81    pl(to_char(n_count)||' row(s) inserted.');
82  end;
83  /
84
85  commit;
```

I'm not going to explain Listing 5-7 in detail, because it's well commented and you should be able to understand it by now. But I will say that, unless there's more you have to do between the selection of codes and sequences and before the insert, you're probably still better off using SQL to do all the work!

Now let me introduce you to the star of the PL/SQL show: CURSOR FOR LOOP.

Fetching Rows from a Cursor Automatically

CURSOR FOR LOOP is the heart and soul of PL/SQL's abilities. The CURSOR FOR LOOP allows you to work with a cursor that returns multiple rows, one row at a time, using a very nice and neat structure that does everything for you automatically.

Listing 5-8 is a revision of Listing 5-1. The difference is that Listing 5-8 utilizes the "automatic" CURSOR FOR LOOP, instead of the manually coded loop involving OPEN, FETCH, and CLOSE.

Listing 5-8. An Example of Using a CURSOR FOR LOOP, cursor_for_loop_the_doe_family.sql

```
01  rem cursor_for_loop_the_doe_family.sql
02  rem by Donald J. Bales on 2014-10-20
03  rem An anonymous PL/SQL procedure to select
04  rem the first names for the Doe family from
05  rem the Workers table.
06
07  set serveroutput on size 1000000;
08
09  declare
10
11  cursor c_workers(
12  aiv_last_name              in      WORKERS.last_name%TYPE) is
13  select first_name
14  from    WORKERS
15  where   last_name like aiv_last_name||'%'
16  order by id;
17
18  begin
19    for r_worker in c_workers('DOE') loop
20      pl(r_worker.first_name);
21    end loop;
22  end;
23  /
```

The CURSOR FOR LOOP syntax used in Listing 5-8 is as follows:

```
FOR <record_name> IN <cursor_name> [(<cursor_parameters>)] LOOP
  -- Put your PL/SQL to be executed for each row here
END LOOP;
```

where <record_name> is the name of the record that will contain fields that correspond to columns in the associated cursor's SELECT statement, <cursor_name> is the name of the associated CURSOR, and <cursor_parameters> is a list of zero or more parameters to be passed to the CURSOR. The brackets around the parameters denote that they are optional; they are needed only if the associated CURSOR was declared with parameters.

Listing 5-8 is short but powerful. In lines 11 through 16, I declare a CURSOR c_workers. Then, on line 19, I use the CURSOR FOR LOOP syntax to automatically OPEN the CURSOR and LOOP until there's no data found, placing any column values in an automatically declared record r_worker that is in scope only inside the FOR LOOP. If at least one row was retrieved from the database, the CURSOR FOR LOOP automatically CLOSEs the OPEN CURSOR when the LOOP ENDs. As I documented earlier in Table 3-1, I use the prefix c_ for cursors and the prefix r_ for records. This naming convention makes it easy to see exactly what is going on in PL/SQL.

I told you PL/SQL's solution to the last exercise in Chapter 4 was going to get even better. As you can see, the CURSOR FOR LOOP represents some powerfully compact syntax!

You can use a CURSOR FOR LOOP as long as you don't need the values of the fields in the automatically declared record outside the loop. And it will do you no good to declare the record outside the loop because the CURSOR FOR LOOP will still declare its own. If you do need the cursor values beyond the fetch, you'll need to assign the record values to variables declared outside the loop or use a manual loop, as I did earlier in Listing 5-1.

Enough talk—it's time you put CURSOR FOR LOOP to work for you.

It's Your Turn to Fetch Automatically

In the development process, you'll eventually need to test what you've built with some realistic data; otherwise, you won't know how your code will perform in production. So your assignment here is to create a PL/SQL procedure that will populate table WORKERS with test data.

If you combine 100 last names, 100 first names, and 26 different middle initials, you get 260,000 entries for table WORKERS. A quarter of a million entries in a table is a fair amount of data for testing.

To help you out with this assignment, I've created three scripts to create the TOP_100_FIRST_NAMES, TOP_100_LAST_NAMES, and A_THRU_Z tables for you. I've placed these table scripts in the downloaded source code directory for Chapter 5, as top_100_first_names.tab, top_100_last_names.tab, and a_thru_z.tab, respectively. You can create those tables by running these scripts.

In order to populate table WORKERS, I suggest you create a PL/SQL procedure that uses nested CURSOR FOR LOOPs to iterate through each table's entries, inserting an entry into the table for each loop, in the most nested FOR LOOP. Your executable code will look something like this:

```
begin
  for r_last in c_last loop
    for r_first in c_first loop
      for r_middle in c_middle loop
        -- initialize the variables to be used in the insert statement here.
        insert into WORKERS ...
      end loop;
    end loop;
  end loop;
end;
```

Of course, you'll need to supply values for other columns. For those, I suggest you do the following:

- For id, call function WORKER.get_id().

- For worker_type_id, use an IF statement to flip back and forth between the ID values for an employee vs. contractor on every other entry.

- For external_id, call function WORKER.get_external_id().

- For birth_date, call function DATES.random(1940, 1990); this will give you a randomly generated date between the years 1940 and 1990.

- For gender_type_id, use an IF statement to specify the correct ID value for the corresponding code found in the TOP_100_FIRST_NAME table.

Add a variable to keep track of how many inserts you've made, and then display that number on the screen when you're finished inserting. Save the script as worker cursor_for_loop.ins, and then execute it. I know this is a hard assignment, but you have everything you need to get it done.

Listing 5-9 is my solution to this exercise. When I ran this script on my computer, it inserted 260,000 rows in an average time of 72 seconds—that's about 3,611 rows per second.

Listing 5-9. Using CURSOR FOR LOOPs to Insert Test Data, workers _cursor_for_loop.ins

```
001  rem workers_cursor_for_loop.ins
002  rem by Donald J. Bales on 2014-10-20
003  rem Seed the Workers table with the top 100 names
004  rem 100 last x 100 first x 26 middle = 260,000 entries
005
006  set serveroutput on size 1000000;
007
008  declare
009
010  -- This is the cursor for the last names.
011  cursor c_last is
012  select last_name
013  from    TOP_100_LAST_NAMES;
014
015  -- This is the cursor for the first names.
016  cursor c_first is
017  select first_name,
018         gender_code
019  from    TOP_100_FIRST_NAMES;
020
021  -- This is the cursor for the middle initials.
022  cursor c_middle is
023  select letter
024  from    A_THRU_Z;
025
026  -- This is the number of seconds since midnight
027  -- I'll use it to profile my code's performance.
028  n_start                            number :=
029    to_number(to_char(SYSDATE, 'SSSSS'));
030
031  -- Here, I declare four psuedo-constants to hold the
032  -- ID values from the code tables, rather than look
033  -- them up repeatedly during the insert process.
034  n_G_FEMALE                         GENDER_TYPES.id%TYPE;
035  n_G_MALE                           GENDER_TYPES.id%TYPE;
036  n_WT_CONTRACTOR                    WORKER_TYPES.id%TYPE;
037  n_WT_EMPLOYEE                      WORKER_TYPES.id%TYPE;
038
039  -- I'll use this to keep track of the number of
040  -- rows inserted.
041  n_inserted                         number := 0;
042
043  -- Here, I declare a record anchored to the table so
044  -- I can set the column values and then insert using
045  -- the record.
046  r_worker                           WORKERS%ROWTYPE;
047
```

```
048   begin
049      -- Get the ID values for the codes
050      n_G_FEMALE      := GENDER_TYPE.get_id('F');
051      n_G_MALE        := GENDER_TYPE.get_id('M');
052      n_WT_CONTRACTOR := WORKER_TYPE.get_id('C');
053      n_WT_EMPLOYEE   := WORKER_TYPE.get_id('E');
054
055      -- Loop through the last names
056      for r_last in c_last loop
057
058         -- While looping through the last names,
059         -- loop through the first names
060         for r_first in c_first loop
061
062            -- While looping through the last and first names
063            -- loop through the 26 letters in the English
064            -- Alphabet in order to get middle initials
065            -- As an alternative, I could have used a FOR LOOP:
066   --          for i in ascii('A')..ascii('Z') loop
067            for r_middle in c_middle loop
068
069               -- Initialize the record
070
071               -- Get the PK using the table's package
072               r_worker.id               := WORKER.get_id();
073
074               -- Flip flop from contractor to employee and back again
075               if r_worker.worker_type_id = n_WT_CONTRACTOR then
076                  r_worker.worker_type_id := n_WT_EMPLOYEE;
077               else
078                  r_worker.worker_type_id := n_WT_CONTRACTOR;
079               end if;
080
081               -- Get the External ID using the table's package
082               r_worker.external_id      := WORKER.get_external_id();
083
084               -- The first, middle, and last names come from the cursors
085               r_worker.first_name       := r_first.first_name;
086   --          r_worker.middle_name      := chr(i)||'.';
087               r_worker.middle_name      := r_middle.letter||'.';
088               r_worker.last_name        := r_last.last_name;
089
090               -- get the name using the table's package
091               r_worker.name             := WORKER.get_formatted_name(
092                  r_worker.first_name, r_worker.middle_name, r_worker.last_name);
093
094               -- get a random date for a birth date
095               r_worker.birth_date       := DATES.random(
096                  to_number(to_char(SYSDATE, 'YYYY')) - 65,
097                  to_number(to_char(SYSDATE, 'YYYY')) - 18);
098
```

```
099              -- selecrt the corresponding ID value
100              if r_first.gender_code = 'F' then
101                 r_worker.gender_type_id := n_G_FEMALE;
102              else
103                 r_worker.gender_type_id := n_G_MALE;
104              end if;
105
106              -- Insert the row into the database
107              insert into WORKERS values r_worker;
108
109              -- keep track of the number of inserts
110              n_inserted := n_inserted + sql%rowcount;
111           end loop; -- c_middle
112    --         end loop; -- for i
113           commit;  -- commit every 26 rows
114
115       end loop; -- c_first
116
117    end loop; -- c_last
118    -- Display the results
119    pl(to_char(n_inserted)||' rows inserted in '||
120       (to_number(to_char(SYSDATE, 'SSSSS')) - n_start)||
121       ' seconds.');
122  end;
123  /
```

I won't elaborate on my solution here, because I've commented the code heavily. Notice that I've added a variable to hold the start time in seconds, so I can test the performance of this solution against others. You'll see me profile code this way as we move forward. It's part of the testing process. The question now is, "Can we make this PL/SQL procedure faster?"

In Oracle8, some additional functionality was added to PL/SQL to improve performance. Let's look at one of those additions next.

Bulk Collect

In this context, BULK COLLECT is about reducing the number of transitions between the PL/SQL engine and SQL engine in order to improve efficiency and speed of your PL/SQL program.

The idea is simple. Every time you execute SQL from your PL/SQL program, PL/SQL must hand off the SQL statement to the Oracle database's SQL engine. When the SQL engine is finished, it returns its result to the PL/SQL engine. Flip-flopping back and forth from PL/SQL to SQL and back again takes time.

Since version 8 of Oracle, you can reduce the number of transitions between PL/SQL and SQL by using the BULK COLLECT command. Rather than fetch one row at a time from the SQL engine, you can fetch perhaps 100 at a time into a PL/SQL collection, which can be a PL/SQL table (or array).

Although three types of PL/SQL collections exist, I'm going to cover only the use of associative arrays, or as they were once called, PL/SQL tables. Once you're comfortable programming in PL/SQL, I recommend you go back and learn about the other two in a good reference (such as *PL/SQL Programming* by Steven Feuerstein and Bill Pribyl).

Bulk Collect with a Cursor

Since we've been working with cursors, let's continue to talk about them. Listing 5-10 is yet another incarnation of Listing 5-1, the "select the Doe family" assignment. This time, however, it has been coded to use BULK COLLECT.

Listing 5-10. An Example of Using BULK COLLECT with a CURSOR, cursor_bulk_collect_the_doe_family.sql.

```
01  rem cursor_bulk_collect_the_doe_family.sql
02  rem by Donald J. Bales on 2014-10-20
03  rem An anonymous PL/SQL procedure to select
04  rem the first names for the Doe family from
05  rem the Workers table.
06
07  set serveroutput on size 1000000;
08
09  declare
10
11  cursor c_workers(
12  aiv_last_name                in      WORKERS.last_name%TYPE) is
13  select first_name
14  from    WORKERS
15  where   last_name like aiv_last_name||'%'
16  order by id;
17
18  TYPE c_worker_table is table of c_workers%ROWTYPE
19  index by binary_integer;
20
21  t_workers                            c_worker_table;
22
23  begin
24    open c_workers('DOE');
25    loop
26      fetch c_workers bulk collect into t_workers limit 2;
27
28      exit when t_workers.count = 0;
29
30      for i in t_workers.first..t_workers.last loop
31        pl(t_workers(i).first_name);
32      end loop;
33    end loop;
34  end;
35  /
```

The FETCH syntax used in the manual loop in Listing 5-10 is as follows:

```
FETCH <cursor_name> BULK COLLECT INTO <plsql_table_name> LIMIT <limit>;
```

where <cursor_name> is the name of an open cursor from which to fetch, and <plsql_table_name> is the name of the associative array in which to fetch the <limit> number of rows.

And the FOR LOOP syntax used in the listing is as follows:

```
FOR <index> IN <from_index>..<through_index> LOOP
  -- Put your PL/SQL code to execute during the loop here.
END LOOP
```

where <index> is an index value to use in the loop to address PL/SQL table elements, <from_index> is a valid index value to start with, and <through_index> is a valid index value to end with.

There's nothing like dissecting a program line by line to help explain it, so here it is:

- Lines 11 through 16 declare a cursor to select the first names of a specified family. There's nothing new here. You've seen this time and again.

- Lines 18 and 19 declare an associative array, or PL/SQL table, based on the row type of CURSOR c_workers.

- Line 21 declares a variable of TYPE c_worker_table that will be the target of the FETCH ... BULK COLLECT command.

- Line 24 opens the cursor c_workers.

- Line 25 starts a manual LOOP.

- On line 26, I fetch rows from the database, two rows at a time, into table t_workers. Because I've reduce the number of transitions, or context switches, by two, this PL/SQL program will run roughly twice as fast. I specified the number of rows to retrieve with the LIMIT clause at the end of the FETCH ... BULK COLLECT statement. I could have set the limit to 10, 100, 1000, 9999, or whatever. But keep in mind that the limit also determines how much memory will be consumed by holding the rows in memory between each call, so you need to use a reasonable value or bring your database to a screeching halt—it's your choice.

- On line 28, instead of checking the cursor variable c_workers%notfound, I need to check the PL/SQL table t_workers' %count variable to see how many rows were inserted into the table from the last FETCH. If t_workers%count is zero, there are no more rows to retrieve from the cursor, so I EXIT the LOOP.

- On line 30, now that the fetched data resides in PL/SQL table t_workers, I use a FOR LOOP to iterate through the entries, from the first, t_worker.first through (..) the last, t_worker.last. In this context, first and last are PL/SQL table variables that tell you the first and last rows in the table, respectively.

- Line 31, inside the FOR LOOP, displays the first names on the screen. However, this time, since the PL/SQL table was based on a cursor's row type, I need to use the form table name, index, dot, field name—t_workers(i).first_name—in order to address the field.

Using BULK COLLECT with a FETCH statement for a cursor can lead to a significant performance improvement if you set a moderately sized LIMIT. If you specify too large of a LIMIT, you'll use up memory needed for other database sessions.

Another thing to consider is that using BULK COLLECT requires additional programming. So is the extra memory consumption and additional programming worth the investment? Or will a simple CURSOR FOR LOOP do the job?

In practice, I always start out with a CURSOR FOR LOOP. If I find that a particular PL/SQL program is a performance bottleneck, or needs to run faster for business purposes, I take the extra time to transform the PL/SQL module to use BULK COLLECT. But then I test its performance gains against every other PL/SQL program's performance loss due to the additional consumption of memory. Yes, I test, test, and test again.

> ■ **Note** Oracle Database 10g introduced an "auto bulk collect" feature. I suggest you investigate this later by reading Oracle's PL/SQL *User's Guide and Reference* for a version of Oracle Database 10g or later.

Bulk Collect with a Select Statement

If you know that the result of your SQL SELECT statement will always be a small number of rows, you can simplify your PL/SQL programming by using BULK COLLECT with a SELECT statement. The result is a SELECT statement that looks a lot like a singleton SELECT, with the difference being that rather than returning only one row at a time, your use of BULK COLLECT allows the statement to return a number of rows at a time.

Listing 5-11 demonstrates the use of BULK COLLECT with a SELECT statement. The difference with this listing compared to Listing 5-10 is that I no longer use an explicit CURSOR.

Listing 5-11. An Example of Using BULK COLLECT with a SELECT statement, bulk_collect_the_doe_family.sql

```
01  rem bulk_collect_the_doe_family.sql
02  rem by Donald J. Bales on 2014-10-20
03  rem An anonymous PL/SQL procedure to select
04  rem the first names for the Doe family from
05  rem the Workers table.
06
07  set serveroutput on size 1000000;
08
09  declare
10
11  TYPE worker_table is table of WORKERS.first_name%TYPE
12  index by binary_integer;
13
14  t_workers                        worker_table;
15
16  begin
17    select first_name
18    BULK COLLECT
19    into    t_workers
20    from    WORKERS
21    where   last_name like 'DOE%'
22    order by id;
23
24    for i in t_workers.first..t_workers.last loop
25      pl(t_workers(i));
26    end loop;
27  end;
28  /
```

The BULK COLLECT syntax used in Listing 5-11 is as follows:

```
SELECT <column_list>
BULK COLLECT
INTO   <plsql_table_name>
FROM   <table_name>
WHERE  <where_clause>
ORDER BY <order_by_colunmn_list>;
```

where <column_list> is a single column name from the table or an asterisk (*) to denote all columns from the table (or row), <plsql_table_name> is the name of one or more associative array(s) declared to match the column list's data types, <table_name> is the name of the table to query, <where_clause> is an appropriate WHERE clause for the query, and <order_by_column_list> is a list of column(s) by which to order the SELECT statement's results.

Let's break down Listing 5-11:

- Lines 11 and 12 declare a TYPE based on the first_name column of the WORKERS table.

- Line 14 declares a table for the TYPE worker_table specified on lines 11 and 12.

- On lines 17 through 22, the magic occurs. This is where I've used the SELECT BULK COLLECT INTO syntax to load all the resulting rows from the query into the PL/SQL table t_workers in just one context switch!

- Lines 24 through 26 contain a FOR LOOP to iterate through the rows in PL/SQL table t_workers, displaying the results on the screen.

Sweet and simple, from disk to memory in one context switch, this is indeed a powerful syntax. However, it has all the same baggage as its CURSOR-based sibling in the previous section. So use it carefully, if at all.

In practice, I never use this syntax because I can't guarantee that the tables I'm coding against won't grow to require an unreasonable amount of memory for the BULK COLLECT. Instead, I play it safe and use the CURSOR BULK COLLECT syntax. But now it's your choice.

It's Your Turn to Bulk Collect

Now that you know how to make your code more efficient by using BULK COLLECT, put it to the test by taking your solution to the last exercise and modifying it to use BULK COLLECT. This means you'll get rid of the three cursors you declared in that solution and replace them with three TYPE and three PL/SQL table declarations. Next, you'll change your CURSOR FOR LOOPs to FOR LOOPs, as in the following example:

```
begin
  for l in t_last.first..t_last.last loop
    for f in t_first.first..t_first.last loop
      for m in t_middle.first..t_middle.last loop
        -- initialize the variables to be used in the insert statement here.
        insert into WORKERS ...
      end loop;
    end loop;
  end loop;
end;
```

Listing 5-12 is my solution to this exercise. When I ran this script on my computer, it inserted 260,000 rows in an average time of 65 seconds—that's about 4000 rows per second, for an 11% improvement. The small amount of improvement is understandable here, because while there were 223 context switches saved by using BULK COLLECT, there were still 260,000 context switches due to inserts.

Listing 5-12. Using BULK COLLECT to Improve the Insertion of Test Data, workers_bulk_collect.ins

```
001  rem workers_bulk_collect.ins
002  rem by Donald J. Bales on 2014-10-20
003  rem Seed the Workers table with the top 100 names
004  rem 100 last x 100 first x 26 middle = 260,000 entries
005
006  set serveroutput on size 1000000;
007
008  declare
009
010  -- Declare a type for a PL/SQL table of last names
011  TYPE last_name_table is table of TOP_100_LAST_NAMES%ROWTYPE
012  index by binary_integer;
013
014  -- Declare a type for a PL/SQL table of first names
015  TYPE first_name_table is table of TOP_100_FIRST_NAMES%ROWTYPE
016  index by binary_integer;
017
018  -- Declare a type for a PL/SQL table of middle initials
019  TYPE middle_name_table is table of A_THRU_Z%ROWTYPE
020  index by binary_integer;
021
022  -- This is the number of seconds since midnight
023  -- I'll use it to profile my code's performance.
024  n_start                            number :=
025    to_number(to_char(SYSDATE, 'SSSSS'));
026
027  -- Here, I declare four psuedo-constants to hold the
028  -- ID values from the code tables, rather than look
029  -- them up repeatedly during the insert process.
030  n_G_FEMALE                         GENDER_TYPES.id%TYPE;
031  n_G_MALE                           GENDER_TYPES.id%TYPE;
032  n_WT_CONTRACTOR                    WORKER_TYPES.id%TYPE;
033  n_WT_EMPLOYEE                      WORKER_TYPES.id%TYPE;
034
035  -- I'll use this to keep track of the number of
036  -- rows inserted.
037  n_inserted                         number := 0;
038
039  -- Here, I declare a record anchored to the table so
040  -- I can set the column values and then insert using
041  -- the record.
042  r_worker                           WORKERS%ROWTYPE;
043
044  -- Declare the three PL/SQL tables that replace cursors
045  t_first                            first_name_table;
```

```
046   t_middle                               middle_name_table;
047   t_last                                 last_name_table;
048
049   begin
050      -- Get the ID values for the codes
051      n_G_FEMALE      := GENDER_TYPE.get_id('F');
052      n_G_MALE        := GENDER_TYPE.get_id('M');
053      n_WT_CONTRACTOR := WORKER_TYPE.get_id('C');
054      n_WT_EMPLOYEE   := WORKER_TYPE.get_id('E');
055
056      -- Bulk collect the tables into the PL/SQL tables
057      select * bulk collect into t_last   from TOP_100_LAST_NAMES;
058      select * bulk collect into t_first  from TOP_100_FIRST_NAMES;
059      select * bulk collect into t_middle from A_THRU_Z;
060
061      -- Loop through the last names
062      for l in t_last.first..t_last.last loop
063
064         -- While looping through the last names,
065         -- loop through the first names
066         for f in t_first.first..t_first.last loop
067
068            -- While looping through the last and first names
069            -- loop through the 26 letters in the English
070            -- Alphabet in order to get middle initials
071            for m in t_middle.first..t_middle.last loop
072
073               -- Initialize the record
074
075               -- Get the PK using the table's package
076               r_worker.id               := WORKER.get_id();
077
078               -- Flip flop from contractor to employee and back again
079               if r_worker.worker_type_id = n_WT_CONTRACTOR then
080                  r_worker.worker_type_id := n_WT_EMPLOYEE;
081               else
082                  r_worker.worker_type_id := n_WT_CONTRACTOR;
083               end if;
084
085               -- Get the External ID using the table's package
086               r_worker.external_id      := WORKER.get_external_id();
087
088               -- The first, middle, and last names come from the cursors
089               r_worker.first_name       := t_first(f).first_name;
090               r_worker.middle_name      := t_middle(m).letter||'.';
091               r_worker.last_name        := t_last(l).last_name;
092
093               -- get the name using the table's package
094               r_worker.name             := WORKER.get_formatted_name(
095                  r_worker.first_name, r_worker.middle_name, r_worker.last_name);
096
```

```
097          -- get a random date for a birth date
098          r_worker.birth_date       := DATES.random(
099            to_number(to_char(SYSDATE, 'YYYY')) - 65,
100            to_number(to_char(SYSDATE, 'YYYY')) - 18);
101
102          -- selecrt the corresponding ID value
103          if t_first(f).gender_code = 'F' then
104            r_worker.gender_type_id := n_G_FEMALE;
105          else
106            r_worker.gender_type_id := n_G_MALE;
107          end if;
108
109          -- Insert the row into the database
110          insert into WORKERS values r_worker;
111
112          -- keep track of the number of inserts
113          n_inserted := n_inserted + sql%rowcount;
114        end loop; -- t_middle
115        commit;  -- commit every 26 rows
116
117      end loop; -- t_first
118
119    end loop; -- t_last
120    -- Display the results
121    pl(to_char(n_inserted)||' rows inserted in '||
122      (to_number(to_char(SYSDATE, 'SSSSS')) - n_start)||
123      ' seconds.');
124  end;
125  /
```

Once again, I won't elaborate on my solution here because I've commented the code heavily. The question remains, "Can we make this PL/SQL procedure faster?"

Well, we've already used BULK COLLECT. What else is in PL/SQL's bag of tricks?

FORALL

For the sake of completeness, I'm going to mention the FORALL statement here. It's kind of like the inverse of the BULK COLLECT statement. Given that you have a populated collection, like an associative array, you can bulk execute the same SQL statement for every entry or for selected entries in your collection(s).

For example, if you have 26 entries in your PL/SQL table, you can write a FORALL statement that will execute the same SQL statement 26 times, once for each row in your PL/SQL table. The assumption here is that you'll use the values from your PL/SQL table in each SQL statement.

The problem I have with FORALL is that the data for a collection usually comes from a table in the database in the first place. If that's the case, then a complex SQL statement can do everything a FORALL statement can do, with one context switch, just like FORALL, but using less memory. So why does FORALL exist? Frankly, I don't know. Perhaps it's syntactic sugar for PL/SQL programmers that have weak SQL skills. Or maybe I've just never run across a need for it. That's always possible. However, in practice, I never use it. I always seem to find a better solution using a complex SQL statement.

Let me show you what I mean. Listing 5-13 is a rewrite of the "populate the Worker table" assignment, where I use FORALL to bind 26 SQL statements per context switch. I could have rearranged my code some more so I could do 100 at a time, but the improvement from doing so is not significant.

Listing 5-13. Using FORALL to Improve the Insertion of Test Data, workers_forall.ins

```
001   rem workers_forall.ins
002   rem by Donald J. Bales on 2014-10-20
003   rem Seed the Workers table with the top 100 names
004   rem 100 last x 100 first x 26 middle = 260,000 entries
005
006   set serveroutput on size 1000000;
007
008   declare
009
010   -- Declare a type for a PL/SQL table of last names
011   TYPE last_name_table   is table of TOP_100_LAST_NAMES%ROWTYPE
012   index by binary_integer;
013
014   -- Declare a type for a PL/SQL table of first names
015   TYPE first_name_table  is table of TOP_100_FIRST_NAMES%ROWTYPE
016   index by binary_integer;
017
018   -- Declare a type for a PL/SQL table of middle initials
019   TYPE middle_name_table is table of A_THRU_Z%ROWTYPE
020   index by binary_integer;
021
022   -- Declare a type for a PL/SQL table of workers
023   TYPE worker_table      is table of WORKERS%ROWTYPE
024   index by binary_integer;
025
026   -- This is the number of seconds since midnight
027   -- I'll use it to profile my code's performance.
028   n_start                         number :=
029     to_number(to_char(SYSDATE, 'SSSSS'));
030
031   -- Here, I declare four psuedo-constants to hold the
032   -- ID values from the code tables, rather than look
033   -- them up repeatedly during the insert process.
034   n_G_FEMALE                      GENDER_TYPES.id%TYPE;
035   n_G_MALE                        GENDER_TYPES.id%TYPE;
036   n_WT_CONTRACTOR                 WORKER_TYPES.id%TYPE;
037   n_WT_EMPLOYEE                   WORKER_TYPES.id%TYPE;
038
039   -- I'll use this to keep track of the number of
040   -- rows inserted.
041   n_inserted                      number := 0;
042
043   -- Declare the four PL/SQL tables that replace cursors
044   -- and the worker record
045   t_first                         first_name_table;
046   t_middle                        middle_name_table;
047   t_last                          last_name_table;
048   t_workers                       worker_table;
049
050   begin
```

146

```
051    -- Get the ID values for the codes
052    n_G_FEMALE       := GENDER_TYPE.get_id('F');
053    n_G_MALE         := GENDER_TYPE.get_id('M');
054    n_WT_CONTRACTOR  := WORKER_TYPE.get_id('C');
055    n_WT_EMPLOYEE    := WORKER_TYPE.get_id('E');
056
057    -- Bulk collect the tables into the PL/SQL tables
058    select * bulk collect into t_last   from TOP_100_LAST_NAMES;
059    select * bulk collect into t_first  from TOP_100_FIRST_NAMES;
060    select * bulk collect into t_middle from A_THRU_Z;
061
062    -- Loop through the last names
063    for l in t_last.first..t_last.last loop
064
065      -- While looping through the last names,
066      -- loop through the first names
067      for f in t_first.first..t_first.last loop
068
069        -- While looping through the last and first names
070        -- loop through the 26 letters in the English
071        -- Alphabet in order to get middle initials
072        for m in t_middle.first..t_middle.last loop
073
074          -- Initialize the table's rows
075
076          -- Get the PK using the table's package
077          t_workers(m).id               := WORKER.get_id();
078
079          -- Flip flop from contractor to employee and back again
080          if t_workers(m).worker_type_id = n_WT_CONTRACTOR then
081            t_workers(m).worker_type_id := n_WT_EMPLOYEE;
082          else
083            t_workers(m).worker_type_id := n_WT_CONTRACTOR;
084          end if;
085
086          -- Get the External ID using the table's package
087          t_workers(m).external_id      := WORKER.get_external_id();
088
089          -- The first, middle, and last names come from the cursors
090          t_workers(m).first_name       := t_first(f).first_name;
091          t_workers(m).middle_name      := t_middle(m).letter||'.';
092          t_workers(m).last_name        := t_last(l).last_name;
093
094          -- get the name using the table's package
095          t_workers(m).name             := WORKER.get_formatted_name(
096            t_workers(m).first_name,
097            t_workers(m).middle_name,
098            t_workers(m).last_name);
099
```

```
100          -- get a random date for a birth date
101          t_workers(m).birth_date        := DATES.random(
102            to_number(to_char(SYSDATE, 'YYYY')) - 65,
103            to_number(to_char(SYSDATE, 'YYYY')) - 18);
104
105          -- select the corresponding ID value
106          if t_first(f).gender_code = 'F' then
107            t_workers(m).gender_type_id := n_G_FEMALE;
108          else
109            t_workers(m).gender_type_id := n_G_MALE;
110          end if;
111
112        end loop; -- t_middle
113
114        -- Now bulk bind the 26 insert statements
115        forall i in t_workers.first..t_workers.last
116          insert into WORKERS values t_workers(i);
117
118        n_inserted := n_inserted + sql%rowcount;
119
120      end loop; -- t_first
121
122    end loop; -- t_last
123    commit;
124    -- Display the results
125    pl(to_char(n_inserted)||' rows inserted in '||
126      (to_number(to_char(SYSDATE, 'SSSSS')) - n_start)||
127      ' seconds.');
128  end;
129  /
```

In Listing 5-13, the magic happens on lines 74 through 110, where I populate a PL/SQL table's records with values, and then, on lines 115 and 116, where I bulk bind the insert statements, so I have only one context switch for each set of 26 records. Using FORALL, my program now inserts 260,000 rows in an average time of 38 seconds. That's about 6,842 rows per second, for a 71% improvement. That's great, right? Well, what if I just use SQL?

Listing 5-14 is the "populate the Worker table" assignment, where I use a single SQL statement. How does it fare?

Listing 5-14. Using SQL to Improve the Insertion of Test Data, workers.ins

```
01  rem workers.ins
02  rem by Donald J. Bales on 2014-10-20
03  rem Seed the Worker table with the top 100 names
04  rem 100 last x 100 first x 26 middle = 260,000 entries
05
06  set serveroutput on size 1000000;
07
08  declare
09
10  -- This is the number of seconds since midnight
11  -- I'll use it to profile my code's performance.
```

```
12   n_start                                     number :=
13     to_number(to_char(SYSDATE, 'SSSSS'));
14
15   -- Here, I declare four psuedo-constants to hold the
16   -- ID values from the code tables, rather than look
17   -- them up repeatedly during the insert process.
18   n_G_FEMALE                                  GENDER_TYPES.id%TYPE;
19   n_G_MALE                                    GENDER_TYPES.id%TYPE;
20   n_WT_CONTRACTOR                             WORKER_TYPES.id%TYPE;
21   n_WT_EMPLOYEE                               WORKER_TYPES.id%TYPE;
22
23   -- I'll use this to keep track of the number of
24   -- rows inserted.
25   n_inserted                                  number := 0;
26
27   begin
28     -- Get the ID values for the codes
29     n_G_FEMALE      := GENDER_TYPE.get_id('F');
30     n_G_MALE        := GENDER_TYPE.get_id('M');
31     n_WT_CONTRACTOR := WORKER_TYPE.get_id('C');
32     n_WT_EMPLOYEE   := WORKER_TYPE.get_id('E');
33
34     -- Use an INSERT INTO SELECT SQL statement
35     insert into WORKERS (
36            id,
37            worker_type_id,
38            external_id,
39            first_name,
40            middle_name,
41            last_name,
42            name,
43            birth_date,
44            gender_type_id)
45     select WORKERS_ID.nextval,
46            decode(mod(WORKERS_ID.currval, 2),
47              0, n_WT_EMPLOYEE, n_WT_CONTRACTOR),
48            lpad(to_char(EXTERNAL_ID_SEQ.nextval), 9, '0'),
49            first_name,
50            letter||'.',
51            last_name,
52            WORKER.get_formatted_name(
53              first_name, letter||'.', last_name),
54            DATES.random(
55              to_number(to_char(SYSDATE, 'YYYY')) - 65,
56              to_number(to_char(SYSDATE, 'YYYY')) - 18),
57            decode(gender_code, 'F', n_G_FEMALE, n_G_MALE)
58     from   TOP_100_LAST_NAMES,
59            TOP_100_FIRST_NAMES,
60            A_THRU_Z;
61
62     n_inserted := n_inserted + sql%rowcount;
63
```

```
64    commit;
65
66    pl(to_char(n_inserted)||' rows inserted in '||
67       (to_number(to_char(SYSDATE, 'SSSSS')) - n_start)||
68       ' seconds.');
69  end;
70  /
```

In Listing 5-14, a single INSERT ... SELECT statement, albeit a complex one, does almost all the work done by lines and lines of PL/SQL. But how does it perform? It inserts 260,000 rows in an average time of 21 seconds. That's about 12,381 rows per second, for a 200% improvement. You can't get any faster than using plain-old SQL. So what's the moral of this story? Let me hear you say it. Know thy SQL!

When you're comfortable with PL/SQL and are up to challenging yourself, pull out a good PL/SQL reference and read up on FORALL. For now, I think you'll do better by improving your SQL skills instead.

Summary

In this chapter, you've gone from curs(or)ing, to fetching, to bulk collecting, to bulk binding, and then back to SQL again. CURSORs allow you to FETCH multiple rows from a SQL SELECT statement. You can FETCH rows manually or automatically, using a CURSOR FOR LOOP. You can use BULK COLLECT to improve the efficiency of loading an array with values from the database, and you can use FORALL to improve the efficiency of executing SQL statements with values from an array. But most important, you probably realize by now that when I stated in Chapter 1 that "knowing SQL is a prerequisite to learning PL/SQL," I wasn't joking.

All too often, I see poorly performing PL/SQL programs that are bloated with PL/SQL code that tries to do what SQL can simply do better. After all, it is the Procedural Language extension to SQL. PL/SQL's job is to handle the procedural tasks, while SQL's job is to handle manipulating data. Keep that in mind whenever you write a PL/SQL program.

Up to this point, although you've been keeping functions and procedures in a package for each table, you've still been acting as though these behaviors were something apart from the data they work with. In fact, in the real world, the opposite is true. Things in the real world don't keep their behavior or actions someplace away from themselves; they are part of a whole, and that's what you are going to look at next. You'll explore storing the behavior with the attributes, or as I like to think of it: object-relational technology.

CHAPTER 6

■ ■ ■

Object-Relational SQL

It was the philosopher George Santayana who stated, "Those who cannot remember the past are condemned to repeat it." Philosophy is an interesting pursuit from my point of view because it looks at very high-level abstract patterns of behavior. Patterns are repeated data or behavior of a simple or complex nature.

When we build an application, we attempt to model the workflow of the real world in order to automate or organize the workflow to improve how quickly or accurately we can perform its associated work. However, modeling is not only representing what data is used, but also recognizing the patterns of usage: behavior. Restated simply, we attempt to model the real world, and those who get modeling right profit from it the most.

Information Modeling

As business analysts and computer scientists, we have come a long way. Relational database technology has freed us from the tyranny of the high priests of database administration, so we are all capable of storing and retrieving data in sets of highly organized, two-dimensional tables. But, up to this point, we store only the data we use, for the most part ignoring the behavior.

As an analyst, I know that the accuracy of a real-world model depends on its use of the following:

- *Current data*: Data (words, numbers, and dates) about what happened last. I say "last" because usually, by the time you record the information, it's data about what just happened, not what's about to happen.

- *Hierarchical data*: Data about the relationships of like datum. For example, in a business organization, a department may belong to a subdivision, which may in turn belong to a division, which may in turn belong to a particular operating company; these are all levels of organization that have a hierarchical relationship to each other.

- *Historical data*: Multiple occurrences of "current" data; that is, data about what has happened over time, not just the last occurrence of behavior. Yes, data is about behavior.

- *Current behavior*: Methods (functions or procedures) used to accomplish the last act of work. Once again, I say "last" because by the time the act of work is recorded, these are the methods just used, not what will be used in the future.

- *Hierarchical behavior*: Methods used with hierarchical data.

- *Historical behavior*: Multiple occurrences of "current" methods; that is, methods used to accomplish acts of work at a particular point in time.

So I submit that in order for you to have an accurate model of the real world, you need to employ all six facets of information in your model. Is that what we do today? For the most part, no.

Today, simple applications store current data in a database and store current methods (behavior) in a presentation layer's codebase. When I say presentation layer, I mean the software you use to enter data into the application (data entry) or to view data from an application (reporting).

More sophisticated applications may store hierarchical data and try to separate the code (program logic) used to present information from the rules of work, or so-called business (busyness) rules. Then they have one database and two codebases: a database for the persistence of data, a codebase for the "current" business rules or behavior, and a second codebase for presenting or interfacing with a human role player. When business rules are changed in the mid-tier codebase, the old rules are lost forever.

Rarely do applications store the behavior that belongs to an entity with the entity. And even more rarely is the behavior that is stored with an entity temporal in nature; that is, sensitive to at what time the behavior takes place. Yet, that's how the real world is. No wonder business people have problems with our software solutions. We're not modeling the real world as it is!

To make matters worse, there's a disturbing trend toward the presentation layer defining the model. Mapping tools like Hibernate (java) or Django (Python) will create database entities for you. That's very convenient. However, what may be a convenient way to pass current data for data entry is not necessarily an accurate model of the real world.

Often, using the presentation layer to build the underlying real-world model leads to denormalized data, which leads to fat rows in a database, which because of physics, leads to poor performance. The mantra behind tools like Enterprise JavaBeans (EJB), Hibernate, Django and so on is database independence—as if to suggest that all databases are created equal, which they certainly are not.

Oracle is dominant among its peers because it is superior. It's that simple. If you're not going to use Oracle, I suggest checking out PostgreSQL, which is a high-quality, object-relational, open source alternative, but it's not Oracle by any stretch of imagination.

We've had the capability of modeling the real world accurately in object-relational databases for some time now, so why don't we? The following are my answers to that question:

- *"Lex I: Corpus omne perseverare in statu suo quiescendi vel movendi uniformiter in directum, nisi quatenus a viribus impressis cogitur statum illum mutare."*: Newton's first law translated for our purposes: everyone uses relational databases, so everyone will continue to use relational databases unless there is a compelling enough reason to move in a different direction.

- *Ignorance, not stupidity (business community)*: The level of awareness that the real world is a combination of fact and action, or data and methods, and the value of that information is not commonly understood by business people. Yet, they are the ones who drive the need for applications. If the business community doesn't understand its own work problems, then no information technology department within that community will ever understand the associated work problems either because the business community defines applications of business.

- *Ignorance, not stupidity (technical community)*: The level of awareness that technology developers have currently attained does not commonly include object-relational technology. Heck, most techies I talk to don't even know what *object-relational* means. You'll hear more evidence about this in this chapter.

In order for you to understand and communicate these newer ideas (my answers), you need to come up to speed on some technology jargon. Let's start with object orientation.

Object Orientation

What's the big deal about object orientation anyway? First and foremost, it's about modeling the real world. Here are some examples:

- Rather than being concerned about a particular process, the emphasis is on independent entities that can actually perform the process.

- Rather than write one large procedure that does everything, and would also need to be tossed if the process in question changed, it's about assigning the appropriate parts of a procedure to the various role players in the procedure.

- Instead of having one large program, it's about modularity—having multiple, independent, and reusable components that act appropriately together to complete an act of work.

So it's about teamwork.

Key Tenets

Object orientation has three key tenets:

- *Encapsulation*: This refers to packaging related data and methods together. Object orientation is the natural way to think about things; natural, as in nature. It's the way nature does it. Nature creates things that have both attributes and behavior. For example, I don't think about what I'd like to eat for dinner, and then you go eat it for me. It doesn't work that way. My thoughts about food affect me, not you. We are separate entities. All my attributes and behaviors are encapsulated in me. All your attributes and behaviors are encapsulated in you. If someone tells each of us to do something, odds are, we'll do it differently, or may not do it at all. How's that for modularity?

- *Inheritance*: This is the ability to reuse the data and methods of a more abstract type. If we continue on about the idea of asking each of us to perform a particular task, we'll most likely do it differently because we inherited different genetic attributes from our parents, and they taught us different behaviors, too. So we inherited different attributes and behaviors from our parents, upon which we will add new ones, or override what our parents taught us and do it our own way.

- *Polymorphism*: This refers to hiding different implementations behind a common interface. Polymorphism is the use of the same name for a particular behavior, yet knowing that each object, or person in our case, may perform the behavior differently. If I'm asked to clean the floor, I'll get out the vacuum cleaner, and then follow up by washing the floor with a bucket of clear water, while you may hire someone to do the job. All the same, the floor gets cleaned, and that's the behavior that was requested.

Using these three tenets, you can naturally model both the attributes and behavior, or data and methods, for any real-world entity. Let's talk more about reuse.

Reuse

What is reuse anyway? I consider it reuse any time you can abstract multiple lines of code into a larger block of code that will then be called by more than one actor. I also think there are multiple levels of reuse. Let's start with the smallest unit of reuse: method-level reuse.

Method-Level Reuse

I always tell programmers who I work with that if they must code the same lines of code more than once to accomplish the same task, then they need to create a method. That's what I call method-level reuse.

The trick is where to put the method. That's an easy question to answer for an object-oriented programmer: put the method with the entity that's executing the behavior! That's what object-orientation is all about.

Next up is what I call component-level reuse.

Component-Level Reuse

Component-level reuse is when you can reuse a particular class of an entity, or in SQL jargon, a TYPE. You can reuse a class in two ways: through direct application (composition) or inheritance. Direct application would be where you create a TYPE called PERSON, and then create a table based on that type, called PERSONS. In this case, you'll have used the TYPE PERSON directly.

On the other hand, you could create a sub-TYPE called WORKER based on TYPE PERSON. Now TYPE WORKER would inherit all the data attributes and methods from its parent PERSON, possibly adding some of its own attributes and methods. This would be a case where you reused component PERSON by using inheritance.

Finally, if you define these TYPEs, and then reuse them in more than one application, that's also an example of component reuse, and an example of reuse at the most intriguing level. For example, if a human resource information system (HRIS) uses the TYPE PERSON in its TYPE hierarchy for TYPE EMPLOYEE, and then a safety application on the same database uses PERSON in its TYPE hierarchy for TYPE WORKER, then both applications can TREAT their sub-TYPEs as a PERSON in order to share (or reuse) related information.

The last example sounds like it could also be called application-level reuse.

Application-Level Reuse

You can also design an entire set of applications such that they all use the same underlying abstract TYPEs. This allows each application to share a common set of applications that act as infrastructure for more complex applications. The use of common TYPEs in the inheritance hierarchy of sub-TYPEs would allow the common use of the same tables for all related applications. Now that's what I call reuse!

Service Orientation

Object-oriented programmers have been building service-oriented applications for ages. That's the entire nature of object-oriented programming. You build independent components that provide supporting services through their method calls. You test them, and then you don't have to recode the same service ever again.

Even if you continue to build relational instead of object-relational databases, you can still provide service-oriented routines by properly associating your methods with your data. That's what I've been having you do up to this point. I've asked you to create what I called a "table package" for each table. Each "table package" contains a set of methods that logically belong to the data that is stored in the associated table.

For example, I named the relational Worker table WORKERS. Then I asked you to create a package called WORKER that contained method for allocating a new primary key value. I've been using this pseudo-object orientation since PL/SQL became available, and it's a tactic that has worked well. Every programmer I've worked with has quickly come up to speed on the technique, and then reused the methods in the table package over and over again to accomplish the same logical task consistently every time.

In addition, although applications have been written in multiple programming languages and tools, all of them call the same "table package" methods to perform a particular service. Once again, even though different presentation layers are coded in different languages by different programmers, the same consistent behavior is seen across all presentations for all services—and that is reuse of the best kind.

Do these varying presentation layers recode the same behavior in varying languages? No. They all use the same code stored with the data. That's object orientation and service orientation in use. So how do you get there from here?

A Roadmap to Reality

So how do you get to using object-relational technology from relational technology? It's not as hard as you might think. Just like the function of life, $f(l)$, you'll get out whatever you put in to it. You can fully implement object-oriented technology in four progressive steps.

1. Create table packages.

2. Create user-defined types.

3. Create object views.

4. Create object tables.

Yes, you can implement four different levels of object orientation in your database, and based on what you implement, gain a level of consistency and reusability equal to your level of implementation.

Step 1: Table Packages

The first step is to start thinking in an object-oriented fashion, or as I call it, thinking naturally. This means organizing your data and methods in a related fashion, as I had you do earlier with table packages. I always name tables with a plural name, and then name their related packages with a singular name, so the package names are the singular of the table names. You can use whatever convention you want. By doing so, you should at least be able to employ encapsulation and polymorphism.

Table Method Encapsulation

You'll be employing encapsulation by gathering behavior and hiding it behind a public method call specification. Create a table package for every table in your database that has the same SQL statement executed on it more than once. Create a method for such a SQL statement, so the same behavior can be shared by multiple program units. Also, add any other related methods that perform calculations, concatenations, or locale-specific behavior.

Table Method Polymorphism

Next, look at the bigger picture. Notice the patterns of use of your table package methods, and use the same names for a particular pattern of use across all table packages.

For example, I use a FUNCTION named get_id() in every table package where I need a method that allocates a new primary key sequence value. Then, for a code table like WORKER_TYPES, if I need to get an ID value for a new entry, I call WORKER_TYPE.get_id(). Similarly, getting an ID value for a new WORKERS table entry will be a different package name, but the same method name: WORKER.get_id().

That's polymorphism in action.

Step 2: User-Defined Types

The second step is to create a new object type, a user-defined type, that encapsulates both data attributes and method call specifications in a permanent new "data" or object type in the database.

Gather the list of column names you use in the relational table, and then collect the methods you specify in each table's package specification. Use this information along with the keyword TYPE to create a new object type in the database.

Unlike the table's associated package specification, where all methods are essentially STATIC (always available), you'll need to decide whether methods will operate on an instance of an object, a MEMBER method, or will be available through the object's TYPE definition, a STATIC method. In addition, you may want to add your own CONSTRUCTOR method(s) in order to make it easier to create a new object instance. And you may also want to define a MAP MEMBER method to specify how objects are sorted.

When you create user-defined types, you have the opportunity to use all three facets of object orientation. As with table packages, you'll be employing encapsulation and polymorphism. But you may also be able to leverage inheritance, so keep on the lookout for higher-level patterns between user-defined types. If you see a high-level pattern, consider defining a super-TYPE, and then inheriting from that super-TYPE for similar sub-TYPEs.

If you stop at this level of implementation, you'll still be able to use data from relational tables as objects by TREATing the relational data as objects on the fly in your SQL statements. But, if you get this far, I would at least do step 3.

Step 3: Object Views

The third step involves creating object views for your relational tables. An object view presents the underlying relational table data as a table of the newly created user-defined object type.

If you use more than one table in an object view, you can write INSTEAD OF triggers that will then appropriately update the underlying relational tables if you execute a SQL INSERT, UPDATE, or DELETE statement against an object view.

One of the advantages to using object views is that you can still use object-relational-ignorant tools against the relational tables. But if I were you, and you went this far, I would go all the way and reap the full benefit of object-oriented technology in an Oracle database; I would do step 4.

Step 4: Object Tables

The last step is where you create an object-relational database or *objectbase*, one where real-world entities are accurately modeled for both attributes and behavior. I'm not advocating moving all of an application's code into the database—I mean objectbase; actually, just the opposite. The only items that should reside in the objectbase are the entities, along with their data attributes and methods that are in scope for the particular application.

This means that what is normally thought of as data in a relational database should be stored in the objectbase, along with its associated entity business rules. Whatever code is used to present the object-relational model—data-entry screens, reports, graphics, and so on—should continue to reside in an external codebase. Regardless of the presentation layer, any entity-related business rule should be executed in the objectbase, not in the presentation layer.

That may seem like a radical departure from what you're currently doing, or perhaps not. If you're using EJBs, you're already making a remote procedure call to employ business rules in a so-called middle tier. Why not do it correctly, and employ the authoritative rules that permanently reside side by side with the data attributes, instead of supposedly recoding the same rules again and again (with inconsistency) in another codebase?

A Change in Order

Building an object-relational database, or objectbase, calls for a change in order. When building a relational database, you follow this order:

1. Create tables with columns (attributes).

2. Create table packages with methods (behavior).

3. Code presentation by accessing the data in tables and the behaviors in their associated packages.

When you build an object-relational database, or objectbase, you follow this order:

1. Create user-defined types with attributes and behaviors.

2. Create tables based on your user-defined types.

3. Code presentation by accessing attributes and behaviors in user-defined type tables.

With that change of order in mind, I think it's time I actually show you example of what I'm talking about. Enough philosophy—it's time for action. We'll begin with how to create a new user-defined type, an object type.

Object Types

You remember the keyword TYPE from Chapter 3, right? You used it to declare the equivalent of an array in PL/SQL: a PL/SQL table. Well in this context, you're going to use it to permanently create a new user-defined data type in the database. Using the term *data type* is a bit of a misnomer. You're really going to be creating new types of classes of entities, or object types. Yes, here's a new word for your vocabulary: *object type*. An object type defines both data attributes and related methods. So the SQL keywords you'll use to create user-defined object types are CREATE TYPE.

By creating a user-defined type, you'll permanently marry data and its associated methods in the database so they can't be separated, not even accidentally. It's a marriage for life; no divorce allowed. Of course, you'll be able to change data and behavior over time, but you'll be coding behavior so it will be time-dependent, and therefore be coding behavior over time.

Some day, we will store universal behavioral executables the same way we store data. But today, the best we can do is to store our code with our data, not as separate entities, and to modify our code to be point-in-time-dependent, so we can reproduce behavior as it existed at any point in time.

Since you probably have little experience with this form of SQL, I'm going to show you two examples, with you doing some of the coding along the way. First, let's create a user-defined TYPE for one of your code tables: Gender Type.

■ **Note** In Chapters 1–5, you were using an Oracle username of RPS to log into the database. This meant you were using the RPS schema. In this chapter, you need to use Oracle username OPS to log into the database so you won't encounter naming conflicts. By the end of this chapter, you will have object-relational types and tables in schema OPS that have the same names as relational packages and tables in schema RPS.

Create a User-Defined Type Specification

Creating a user-defined type takes two steps. First, you create a specification, and then you create a type body, or implementation, similar to creating a package. Listing 6-1 is an example of a CREATE TYPE specification script for creating a user-defined type for code table Gender.

Listing 6-1. An Example of a CREATE TYPE Statement for a Code Table, gender_type.tps

```
01  create TYPE GENDER_TYPE as object (
02  /*
03  gender_type.tps
04  by Don Bales on 2014-10-20
05  Type GENDER's attributes and methods.
06  */
07  id                          number,
08  code                        varchar2(30),
09  description                 varchar2(80),
10  active_date                 date,
11  inactive_date               date,
12  /*
13  A constructor for creating a new instance of type GENDER_TYPE with NULL
14  values.
15  */
16  CONSTRUCTOR FUNCTION gender_type(
17  self                        in out gender_type)
18  return                      self as result,
19  /*
20  A constructor for creating a new instance of type GENDER_TYPE for insert.
21  */
22  CONSTRUCTOR FUNCTION gender_type(
23  self                        in out gender_type,
24  aiv_code                    varchar2,
25  aiv_description             varchar2)
26  return                      self as result,
27  /*
28  Gets the code and decription values for the specified id.
29  */
30  STATIC PROCEDURE get_code_descr(
31  ain_id                      in      number,
```

```
32  aov_code                        out varchar2,
33  aov_description                 out varchar2),
34  /*
35  Verifies that the passed code value is an exact or like match on the
36  date specified.
37  */
38  STATIC PROCEDURE get_code_id_descr(
39  aiov_code                 in out varchar2,
40  aon_id                        out number,
41  aov_description               out varchar2,
42  aid_on                 in     date),
43  /*
44  Verifies that the passed code value is currently an exact or like match.
45  */
46  STATIC PROCEDURE get_code_id_descr(
47  aiov_code                 in out varchar2,
48  aon_id                        out number,
49  aov_description               out varchar2),
50  /*
51  Returns a new primary key id value for a row.
52  */
53  MEMBER FUNCTION get_id
54  return                          number,
55  /*
56  Returns the id for the specified code value.
57  */
58  STATIC FUNCTION get_id(
59  aiv_code                  in     varchar2)
60  return                          number,
61  /*
62  Test-based help for this package.  "set serveroutput on" in SQL*Plus.
63  */
64  STATIC PROCEDURE help,
65  /*
66  Test units for this package.
67  */
68  STATIC PROCEDURE test,
69  /*
70  A MAP function for sorting at the object level.
71  */
72  MAP MEMBER FUNCTION to_varchar2
73  return                          varchar2
74  );
75  /
76  @se.sql GENDER_TYPE
```

The CREATE TYPE specification syntax used by Listing 6-1 is as follows:

```
CREATE [OR REPLACE] TYPE <type_name> AS OBJECT (
<attribute_name_1>               <attribute_type_1>,
<attribute_name_2>               <attribute_type_2>,...
<attribute_name_N>               <attribute_type_N>,
```

```
[MAP]MEMBER or STATIC FUNCTION or PROCEDURE <method_name> [(
SELF                          [IN OUT][NOCOPY]<type_name>,
<parameter_name_1>            [IN OUT] <parameter_type_1>,
<parameter_name_2>            [IN OUT] <parameter_type_2>,...
<parameter_name_N>            [IN OUT] <parameter_type_N>)]
[RETURN                                     <return_type>],
CONSTRUCTOR FUNCTION <type_name> (
SELF                          [IN OUT][NOCOPY]<type_name>,[
<parameter_name_1>            [IN OUT] <parameter_type_1>,
<parameter_name_2>            [IN OUT] <parameter_type_2>,...
<parameter_name_N>            [IN OUT] <parameter_type_N>)],
);
```

where

- `<type_name>` is the name of your user-defined TYPE.

- `<attribute_name>` is the name of a data item in your user-defined TYPE.

- `<attribute_type>` is a predefined scalar data type or a user-defined type.

- `<method_name>` is the name of a MEMBER or STATIC, FUNCTION or PROCEDURE.

- `<parameter_name>` is the name of a parameter being passed into or out of a method.

- `<parameter_type>` is a predefined scalar data type or a user-defined type.

- `<return_type>` is also a predefined scalar data type or a user-defined type to be returned by an associated FUNCTION.

Wow! As you can see by Listing 6-1, I've added a lot of methods to my Gender Type code user-defined TYPE. Let's take a look at the listing line by line:

- Line 1 uses the DDL keywords CREATE TYPE ... AS OBJECT to declare a new user-defined TYPE specification for my schema in the database. I call my new type GENDER_TYPE, as in it's the Gender Type code's user-defined object type.

- Lines 2 through 6 contain my usual source code preamble that documents the name of the source file, the author, date written, and purpose.

- On lines 7 through 11, I list the attributes for the TYPE. Theses are the names of the columns from the original relational table. Did you notice that I ended the last attribute with a comma (,), which means I intend to continue specifying attributes or methods for the TYPE?

- Lines 12 through 18 declare a user-defined CONSTRUCTOR method. You'll call a CONSTRUCTOR any time you want to create a new instance of a TYPE. For example, all user-defined TYPEs come with a default CONSTRUCTOR, where you pass in attribute values in the order they are specified in the TYPE specification. So to create a new instance of Gender Type using the default CONSTRUCTOR, you would code something like this:

  o_gender_type := GENDER_TYPE(3, 'U', 'Unknown', SYSDATE, NULL);

  The CONSTRUCTOR I've declared here will create an instance of the TYPE with all its attributes initialized to NULL values. This is handy when I want to access a member function without actually working with a permanent instance of a TYPE.

- Lines 12 through 15 hold a multiline comment that documents the purpose of the method. Remember to document as you go.

- Lines 19 through 26 declare a user-defined CONSTRUCTOR for coding convenience. Using it, you can create a new instance of Gender Type by simply passing the code and description like this:

  o_gender_type := GENDER_TYPE('U', 'Unknown');

- On lines 27 through 33, I specify my first STATIC method for the TYPE. If I specify a method as STATIC, it's available for execution through the TYPE's name, like a package, but not available through an instance of the type. For example, to execute PROCEDURE get_code_descr(), I would code GENDER_TYPE.get_code_desc(...), not using a variable of the TYPE in the method call like this: o_gender_type.get_code_desc(...).

- Skipping down, lines 50 through 54 declare a MEMBER method, get_id(), to allocate the next primary key value. This is the same method I asked you to create in a table package in Chapter 5. Now it has become a MEMBER method for the TYPE.

- Finally, lines 69 through 73 declare a MAP MEMBER FUNCTION. This method will be used by the Oracle database any time it needs to sort object-level instances of the TYPE.

Let's review. How did I get here, to a TYPE specification, from there, a relational table and associated table package? Here's what I did:

1. Took the columns from the relational table and made them the attributes of the TYPE.

2. Took the methods from the relational table's package specification and made them MEMBER or STATIC methods of the TYPE.

3. Added a MAP MEMBER FUNCTION for sorting.

4. Added user-defined CONSTRUCTOR FUNCTIONs for convenience.

Now that you've seen the specification, let's look at the implementation!

Create a User-Defined Type Implementation

Listing 6-2 is a CREATE TYPE BODY ... AS (implementation) script for the TYPE GENDER_TYPE specification shown in Listing 6-1. I'll cover all the methods implemented in this TYPE in subsequent chapters, when I take a polymorphic look at methods required by the TYPE and presentation layers: data entry, data migration, data processing, reporting, graphing, and so on. For now, it's important for you to focus on the method implementations that are unique to a TYPE, namely the MAP MEMBER and CONSTRUCTOR FUNCTIONs.

Listing 6-2. An Example of a CREATE TYPE BODY Statement for a Code Table, gender_type.tpb

```
001  create or replace TYPE BODY GENDER_TYPE as
002  /*
003  gender_type.tpb
004  by Don Bales on 2014-10-20
005  Type GENDER_TYPE's attributes and methods
006  */
007
```

```
008   CONSTRUCTOR FUNCTION gender_type(
009   self                          in out gender_type)
010   return                               self as result is
011
012   begin
013     id            := NULL;
014     code          := NULL;
015     description   := NULL;
016     active_date   := NULL;
017     inactive_date := NULL;
018     return;
019   end gender_type;
020
021
022   CONSTRUCTOR FUNCTION gender_type(
023   self                          in out gender_type,
024   aiv_code                            varchar2,
025   aiv_description                     varchar2)
026   return                               self as result is
027
028   begin
029     id            := get_id();
030     code          := aiv_code;
031     description   := aiv_description;
032     active_date   := SYSDATE;
033     inactive_date := DATE_.d_MAX;
034     return;
035   end gender_type;
036
037
038   STATIC PROCEDURE get_code_descr(
039   ain_id                        in      number,
040   aov_code                              out varchar2,
041   aov_description                       out varchar2 ) is
042
043   begin
044     select code,
045            description
046     into   aov_code,
047            aov_description
048     from   GENDER_TYPES
049     where  id = ain_id;
050   end get_code_descr;
051
052
053   STATIC PROCEDURE get_code_id_descr(
054   aiov_code                     in out varchar2,
055   aon_id                               out number,
056   aov_description                      out varchar2,
057   aid_on                        in      date ) is
058
059   v_code                               varchar2(30);
```

```
060
061  begin
062    select id,
063            description
064    into    aon_id,
065            aov_description
066    from    GENDER_TYPES
067    where   code = aiov_code
068    and     aid_on between active_date and nvl(inactive_date, DATE_.d_MAX);
069  exception
070    when NO_DATA_FOUND then
071      select id,
072              code,
073              description
074      into    aon_id,
075              v_code,
076              aov_description
077      from    GENDER_TYPES
078      where   code like aiov_code||'%'
079      and     aid_on between active_date and nvl(inactive_date, DATE_.d_MAX);
080      aiov_code := v_code;
081  end get_code_id_descr;
082
083
084  STATIC PROCEDURE get_code_id_descr(
085  aiov_code                    in out varchar2,
086  aon_id                       out number,
087  aov_description              out varchar2 ) is
088
089  begin
090   get_code_id_descr(
091    aiov_code,
092    aon_id,
093    aov_description,
094    SYSDATE );
095  end get_code_id_descr;
096
097
098  MEMBER FUNCTION get_id
099  return                       number is
100
101  n_id                         number;
102
103  begin
104    select GENDERS_ID.nextval
105    into ` n_id
106    from   SYS.DUAL;
107
108    return n_id;
109  end get_id;
110
111
```

163

```
112   STATIC FUNCTION get_id(
113   aiv_code                          in        varchar2 )
114   return                                      number is
115
116   n_id                                        number;
117
118   begin
119     select id
120     into   n_id
121     from   GENDER_TYPES
122     where  code = aiv_code;
123
124     return n_id;
125   end get_id;
126
127
128   STATIC PROCEDURE help is
129
130   begin
131    pl('No help at this time.');
132   end help;
133
134
135   STATIC PROCEDURE test is
136
137   begin
138     pl('No tests coded at this time');
139   end test;
140
141
142   MAP MEMBER FUNCTION to_varchar2
143   return                                      varchar2 is
144
145   begin
146     return description||to_char(active_date, 'YYYYMMDDHH24MISS');
147   end to_varchar2;
148
149
150   end;
151   /
152   @be.sql GENDER_TYPE
```

The CREATE TYPE BODY syntax used by Listing 6-2 is as follows:

```
CREATE [OR REPLACE] TYPE BODY <type_name> AS
[MAP]MEMBER or STATIC FUNCTION or PROCEDURE <method_name> [(
SELF                       [IN OUT][NOCOPY]<type_name>,
<parameter_name_1>         [IN OUT] <parameter_type_1>,
<parameter_name_2>         [IN OUT] <parameter_type_2>,...
<parameter_name_N>         [IN OUT] <parameter_type_N>),]
[RETURN                              <return_type>],
```

```
CONSTRUCTOR FUNCTION <type_name> (
SELF                            [IN OUT][NOCOPY]<type_name>,[
<parameter_name_1>              [IN OUT] <parameter_type_1>,
<parameter_name_2>              [IN OUT] <parameter_type_2>,...
<parameter_name_N>              [IN OUT] <parameter_type_N>),]
END;
```

where

- <type_name> is the name of your user-defined TYPE.

- <method_name> is the name of a MEMBER or STATIC, FUNCTION or PROCEDURE.

- <parameter_name> is the name of a parameter being passed INto or OUT of a method.

- <parameter_type> is a predefined scalar data type or a user-defined type.

- <return_type> is also a predefined scalar data type or a user-defined type to be returned by an associated FUNCTION.

As you can see by Listing 6-2, I've added quite a bit of behavior to my Gender Type code user-defined type. Let's break down the listing:

- Line 1 uses the DDL keywords CREATE TYPE BODY ... AS to create a TYPE BODY for TYPE specification GENDER_TYPE. The BODY consists of method implementations for the methods declare in the TYPE specification.

- Lines 9 through 19 implement a CONSTRUCTOR FUNCTION that will return an instance of a Gender Type object initialized to NULL values.

- Lines 22 through 35 implement a CONSTRUCTOR FUNCTION for coding convenience that requires you to pass in only a code and description in order to create a new Gender Type object instance. As you can see on line 29, the method initializes the id attribute using the MEMBER FUNCTION get_id().

- Lines 98 through 109 implement the MEMBER FUNCTION get_id() in order to allocate the next primary key value.

- Lines 198 through 203 implement the MAP MEMBER FUNCTION to_varchar2(), which returns the description for a given code along with its creation date, all as one long varchar2 value. Oracle will use this value to determine precedence when ordering object instances in a SQL SELECT statement. You don't need to declare and implement a MAP MEMBER FUNCTION, but I always do.

Which came first, the chicken or the egg? Now, if you're real sharp, you may have noticed that I have some dependency issues with the implementation. In order for the TYPE BODY to compile, an object table named GENDER_TYPES must already exist! Yes, the STATIC methods refer to an object table GENDER_TYPES, based on object TYPE GENDER_TYPE. This isn't a big problem. I can address it one of two ways:

- Compile the TYPE specification, create the object table based on the TYPE specification, and then compile the TYPE BODY.

- Use dynamic SQL in the STATIC methods so the dependent table name in the SQL statements doesn't get resolved until runtime.

I normally choose the first alternative, for performance reasons.

It's Your Turn to Create a User-Defined Type

Now that you've seen me transform the Gender Type table and table package into a user-defined TYPE, it's time for you to do the same for the Worker Type table.

1. Make sure to log into the database using username OPS, password OPS.

2. Get the list of columns from the relational SQL WORKER_TYPES table (from Chapter 5), and at least the one method you created in table package WORKER_TYPE, and use that information to code a WORKER_TYPE TYPE specification.

3. Save your specification script as worker_type.tps.

4. Compile your specification: @worker_type.tps.

5. Create a WORKER_TYPE TYPE BODY script, which will contain the implementation for your method get_id().

6. Save you body script as worker_type.tpb.

7. Compile your body: @worker_type.tpb.

8. Test your user-defined type to at least see that it compiled.

To test your user-defined type, you can use an anonymous PL/SQL procedure like the following.

```
declare
-- Declare a worker_type_o variable
o_worker_type                          WORKER_TYPE;

begin
  -- Now use the default constructor to create a new instance
  -- of the object
  o_worker_type := new WORKER_TYPE(
    NULL, 'H', 'A hard worker', SYSDATE, NULL);
  -- Now allocate a new ID using the member function get_id()
  o_worker_type.id := o_worker_type.get_id();
  -- Now show the values of the attributes in the instance
  pl('o_worker_type.id            = '||o_worker_type.id);
  pl('o_worker_type.code          = '||o_worker_type.code);
  pl('o_worker_type.description   = '||o_worker_type.description);
  pl('o_worker_type.active_date   = '||o_worker_type.active_date);
  pl('o_worker_type.inactive_date = '||o_worker_type.inactive_date);
end;
/
```

Your results should look something like this:

```
o_worker_type.id            = 111
o_worker_type.code          = H
o_worker_type.description   = A hard worker
o_worker_type.active_date   =  20070223 100918
o_worker_type.inactive_date =

PL/SQL procedure successfully completed.
```

Listings 6-3 and 6-4 demonstrate my solution for this exercise. Once again, I'm showing you a fully implemented TYPE.

Listing 6-3. A Worker Type Used-Defined TYPE Specification, worker_type.tps

```
01  create TYPE WORKER_TYPE as object (
02  /*
03  worker_type.tps
04  by Don Bales on 2014-10-20
05  Type WORKER_TYPE's attributes and methods.
06  */
07  id                              number,
08  code                            varchar2(30),
09  description                     varchar2(80),
10  active_date                     date,
11  inactive_date                   date,
12  -- Gets the code and decription values for the specified work_type_id.
13  STATIC PROCEDURE get_code_descr(
14  ain_id                    in      number,
15  aov_code                      out varchar2,
16  aov_description               out varchar2 ),
17  -- Verifies the passed aiov_code value is an exact or like match on the
18  -- date specified.
19  STATIC PROCEDURE get_code_id_descr(
20  aiov_code                 in out varchar2,
21  aon_id                        out number,
22  aov_description               out varchar2,
23  aid_on                    in      date ),
24  -- Verifies the passed aiov_code value is currently an exact or like match.
25  STATIC PROCEDURE get_code_id_descr(
26  aiov_code                 in out varchar2,
27  aon_id                        out number,
28  aov_description               out varchar2 ),
29  -- Returns a newly allocated id value.
30  MEMBER FUNCTION get_id
31  return                          number,
32  -- Returns the id for the specified code value.
33  STATIC FUNCTION get_id(
34  aiv_code                  in      varchar2 )
35  return                          number,
36  -- Test-based help for this package.  "set serveroutput on" in SQL*Plus.
37  STATIC PROCEDURE help,
38  -- Test units for this package.
39  STATIC PROCEDURE test,
40  -- A MAP function for sorting at the object level.
41  MAP MEMBER FUNCTION to_varchar2
42  return                          varchar2,
43  -- A constructor for creating a new instance of type WORKER_TYPE
44  -- with NULL values.
45  CONSTRUCTOR FUNCTION worker_type(
46  self                      in out worker_type)
47  return                          self as result,
```

```
48   -- A constructor for creating a new instance of type WORKER_TYPE
49   -- for insert.
50   CONSTRUCTOR FUNCTION worker_type(
51   self                           in out worker_type,
52   aiv_code                       in     varchar2,
53   aiv_description                in     varchar2)
54   return                                self as result
55   );
56   /
57   @se.sql WORKER_TYPE
```

Listing 6-4. A Worker Type User-Defined TYPE BODY, worker_type.tpb

```
001   create or replace TYPE BODY WORKER_TYPE as
002   /*
003   worker_type.tpb
004   by Don Bales on 2014-10-20
005   Type WORKER_TYPE's methods
006   */
007
008
009   MEMBER FUNCTION get_id
010   return                             number is
011
012   n_id                               number;
013
014   begin
015     select WORKER_TYPES_ID.nextval
016     into   n_id
017     from   SYS.DUAL;
018
019     return n_id;
020   end get_id;
021
022
023   STATIC FUNCTION get_id(
024   aiv_code                  in      varchar2 )
025   return                            number is
026
027   n_id                              number;
028
029   begin
030     select id
031     into   n_id
032     from   WORKER_TYPES
033     where  code = aiv_code;
034
035     return n_id;
036   end get_id;
037
038
```

```
039   STATIC PROCEDURE get_code_descr(
040   ain_id                          in      number,
041   aov_code                        out varchar2,
042   aov_description                 out varchar2 ) is
043
044   begin
045     select code,
046            description
047     into   aov_code,
048            aov_description
049     from   WORKER_TYPES
050     where  id = ain_id;
051   end get_code_descr;
052
053
054   STATIC PROCEDURE get_code_id_descr(
055   aiov_code                       in out varchar2,
056   aon_id                          out number,
057   aov_description                 out varchar2,
058   aid_on                          in      date ) is
059
060   v_code                          varchar2(30);
061
062   begin
063     select id,
064            description
065     into   aon_id,
066            aov_description
067     from   WORKER_TYPES
068     where  code = aiov_code
069     and    aid_on between active_date and nvl(inactive_date, DATE_.d_MAX);
070   exception
071     when NO_DATA_FOUND then
072       select id,
073              code,
074              description
075       into   aon_id,
076              v_code,
077              aov_description
078       from   WORKER_TYPES
079       where  code like aiov_code||'%'
080       and    aid_on between active_date and nvl(inactive_date, DATE_.d_MAX);
081
082       aiov_code := v_code;
083   end get_code_id_descr;
084
085
086   STATIC PROCEDURE get_code_id_descr(
087   aiov_code                       in out varchar2,
088   aon_id                          out number,
089   aov_description                 out varchar2 ) is
090
```

```
091   begin
092    get_code_id_descr(
093      aiov_code,
094      aon_id,
095      aov_description,
096      SYSDATE );
097   end get_code_id_descr;
098
099
100   STATIC PROCEDURE help is
101
102   begin
103    pl('No help coded at this time.');
104   end help;
105
106
107   STATIC PROCEDURE test is
108
109   begin
110     pl('No tests coded at this time.');
111   end test;
112
113
114   MAP MEMBER FUNCTION to_varchar2
115   return                            varchar2 is
116
117   begin
118     return description||to_char(active_date, 'YYYYMMDDHH24MISS');
119   end to_varchar2;
120
121
122   CONSTRUCTOR FUNCTION worker_type(
123   self                      in out worker_type)
124   return                           self as result is
125
126   begin
127     id           := NULL;
128     code         := NULL;
129     description  := NULL;
130     active_date  := NULL;
131     inactive_date := NULL;
132     return;
133   end worker_type;
134
135
136   CONSTRUCTOR FUNCTION worker_type(
137   self                      in out worker_type,
138   aiv_code                  in     varchar2,
139   aiv_description           in     varchar2)
140   return                           self as result is
141
```

```
142  begin
143    id           := get_id();
144    code         := aiv_code;
145    description  := aiv_description;
146    active_date  := SYSDATE;
147    inactive_date := DATE_.d_MAX;
148    return;
149  end worker_type;
150
151
152  end;
153  /
154  @be.sql WORKER_TYPE
```

Why don't we create an object view next!

Object Views

Think of this as a cloning project. You can seamlessly transition into the use of user-defined objects by intelligently overlaying your relational database structure with a set of object views. An object view takes the columns from one or more relational tables and morphs them into a pseudo-table of user-defined objects, complete with attributes and behavior.

Create an Object View

Listing 6-5 is a script to create an object view for the relational Gender Type code table GENDER_TYPES. This view automatically maps the column values in table GENDER_TYPES to the attributes of user-defined TYPE GENDER_TYPE, producing what appears to be a table of GENDER_TYPE objects called GENDER_TYPEZ.

Listing 6-5. An Example of an Object View Script for Table GENDER_TYPES, gender_typez.vw

```
01  rem gender_typez.vw
02  rem by Donald J. Bales on 2014-10-20
03  rem Create an object view for relational table GENDER_TYPES
04
05  create view GENDER_TYPEZ of GENDER_TYPE
06  with object identifier (id) as
07  select id,
08         code,
09         description,
10         active_date,
11         inactive_date
12  from   RPS.GENDER_TYPES;
```

The CREATE VIEW syntax used in Listing 6-5 is as follows:

```
CREATE [OR REPLACE] VIEW <view_name> OF <type_name>
WITH OBJECT IDENTIFIER (<primary_key_attributes>) AS
SELECT <column_name_1>,
       <column_name_2>,...
       <column_name_N>
FROM   <table_name>;
```

where

- `<view_name>` is the name of the view to create.

- `<type_name>` is the user-defined TYPE to map the columns to in the relational table.

- `<primary_key_attributes>` is one or more attributes in the user-defined TYPE that map to the primary key column(s) of the underlying table.

- `<column_name>` is the name of a column in the table to map to the attributes of the user-defined TYPE.

- `<table_name>` is the underlying table to map to the user-defined TYPE.

That wasn't much work, was it? OK, now let's test the view. Listing 6-6 is an anonymous PL/SQL procedure to test the object view. It's well commented, so you can see what is being tested. Note that you can execute INSERT, UPDATE, DELETE, and SELECT statements against an object view or its underlying table and get the same results. An object view therefore provides a means for your database to be both relational and object-oriented at the same time!

■ **Note** On line 12, I've added RPS. to GENDER_TYPES so the anchor points to the relational SQL schema's GENDER_TYPES table.

Listing 6-6. A Test Unit for View GENDER_TYPEZ, gender_typez.sql

```
01   rem gender_typez.sql
02   rem by Donald J. Bales on 2014-10-20
03   rem test unit for object view GENDER_TYPEZ
04
05   declare
06   -- Declare a variable of the user-define type
07   o_gender_type                        GENDER_TYPE;
08   -- Declare a variable for the underlying table
09   r_gender_type                        RPS.GENDER_TYPES%ROWTYPE;
10
11   begin
12     -- Insert a test object using the convenience constructor
13     insert into GENDER_TYPEZ
14     values ( GENDER_TYPE( 'T', 'Test') );
15
16     -- Now update the inactive date on the object
17     update GENDER_TYPEZ
18     set    inactive_date = SYSDATE
19     where  code          = 'T';
20
21     -- Retrieve the object in order to show its values
22     select value(g)
23     into   o_gender_type
24     from   GENDER_TYPEZ g
25     where  code          = 'T';
26
```

```
27     -- Show the object's values
28     pl('o_gender_type.id            = '||o_gender_type.id);
29     pl('o_gender_type.code          = '||o_gender_type.code);
30     pl('o_gender_type.description   = '||o_gender_type.description);
31     pl('o_gender_type.active_date   = '||o_gender_type.active_date);
32     pl('o_gender_type.inactive_date = '||o_gender_type.inactive_date);
33
34     -- Delete the test object
35     delete GENDER_TYPEZ
36     where  code          = 'T';
37
38     -- This time insert the test object using the instance variable
39     insert into GENDER_TYPEZ
40     values ( o_gender_type );
41
42     -- Now, select the values from the underlying relational table
43     select *
44     into   r_gender_type
45     from   RPS.GENDER_TYPES
46     where  code          = 'T';
47
48     -- Show the record's values
49     pl('r_gender_type.id            = '||r_gender_type.id);
50     pl('r_gender_type.code          = '||r_gender_type.code);
51     pl('r_gender_type.description   = '||r_gender_type.description);
52     pl('r_gender_type.active_date   = '||r_gender_type.active_date);
53     pl('r_gender_type.inactive_date = '||r_gender_type.inactive_date);
54
55     -- Last, delete the object from the relational table
56     delete RPS.GENDER_TYPES
57     where  code          = 'T';
58
59     -- Commit all these operations
60     commit;
61
62     -- Confirm that the test completed successfully
63     pl('Test completed successfully.');
64  end;
65  /
```

And, here are the results of the test unit in Listing 6-6:

```
SQL> @gender_ov.sql
```

```
o_gender.id            = 131
o_gender.code          = T
o_gender.description   = Test
o_gender.active_date   =  20070223 140020
o_gender.inactive_date =  20070223 140020
r_gender.id            = 131
r_gender.code          = T
r_gender.description   = Test
r_gender.active_date   =  20070223 140020
r_gender.inactive_date =  20070223 140020
Test completed successfully.

PL/SQL procedure successfully completed.
```

■ **Note**   On line 9, I've added RPS. to GENDER_TYPES%ROWTYPE so the anchor points to the relational SQL schema's GENDER_TYPES table.

It's Your Turn to Create an Object View

Yes, it's your turn. Can you guess what I'm going to ask you to do next? I thought so.

1. Make sure you are logged in to the database using Oracle username OPS.

2. Create a script to create an object view for table RPS.WORKER_TYPES that maps its values to user-defined type WORKER_TYPE. You know, the TYPE you just finished creating in the previous exercise.

3. Save your script as worker_typez.vw.

4. Execute your script to create the object view: @worker_typez.vw.

5. Create a test unit script and test your new object view.

Nope, I'm not going to show you my solution. This is so simple you don't need my help! Next, let's do step four of the four-step transformation to object-orientation.

Object Tables

Once you've created a TYPE, it's no harder to create an object (-relational) table than it is to build a relational table.

Create an Object Table

As a matter of fact, Listing 6-7 is nothing more than my table-creation script for the Gender Types table, gendertypes.tab, from Chapter 5, with a few minor changes.

Listing 6-7. An Example of an Object Table Script for GENDER_TYPES, gender_types.tab

```
01  rem gender_types.tab
02  rem by Donald J. Bales on 2014-10-20
03  rem Create an object table for the Gender Type codes
04
05  --drop   table GENDER_TYPES;
06  create table GENDER_TYPES of GENDER_TYPE;
07
08  --drop   sequence GENDERS_ID;
09  create sequence GENDERS_ID
10  start with 1;
11
12  alter  table GENDER_TYPES add
13  constraint   GENDER_TYPES_PK
14  primary key ( id )
15  using index;
16
17  alter  table GENDER_TYPES add
18  constraint   GENDER_TYPES_UK
19  unique ( code, active_date )
20  using index;
21
22  execute SYS.DBMS_STATS.gather_table_stats(USER, 'GENDER_TYPES');
```

The CREATE TABLE syntax used in Listing 6-7 is as follows:

```
CREATE TABLE <table_name> OF <type_name>;
```

where <table_name> is the name of the table to create, and <type_name> is the user-defined TYPE to use instead of column names for the table.

There isn't a lot of extra work to creating an object table vs. a relational table, now is there? Here's the rundown:

- On line 6, I use the new syntax to create a table of one user-defined TYPE instead of one or more predefined scalar data types.

- On lines 10 through 12, I create a sequence for the object (-relational) table.

- On lines 12 through 15, I create a primary key on the object table, just as I did on the relational table.

- On lines 17 through 20, I create a unique key on the object table, just as I did on the relational table.

It's Your Turn to Create an Object Table

Once again, it's your turn. For this exercise, create an object table named WORKER_TYPES for the Worker Type code table.

1. Write a script to create an object table based on user-defined TYPE WORKER_TYPE.

2. Save your script as worker_types.tab.

3. Execute your script to create the object view: @worker_types.tab.

4. Create a test unit script and test your new object table.

I'll indulge you. Listing 6-8 is my solution to this exercise.

Listing 6-8. An Example of an Object Table Script for WORKER_TYPES, worker_types.tab

```
01   rem worker_type.tab
02   rem copyright by Donald J. Bales on 2014-10-20
03   rem Create an object table for the Worker Type codes
04
05   --drop    table WORKER_TYPES;
06   create table WORKER_TYPES of WORKER_TYPE;
07
08   --drop    sequence WORKER_TYPES_ID;
09   create sequence WORKER_TYPES_ID
10   start with 1;
11
12   alter  table WORKER_TYPES add
13   constraint    WORKER_TYPES_PK
14   primary key ( id )
15   using index;
16
17   alter. table WORKER_TYPES add
18   constraint    WORKER_TYPES_UK
19   unique ( code )
20   using index;
21
22   execute SYS.DBMS_STATS.gather_table_stats(USER, 'WORKER_TYPES');
```

To test this object table, I just save my object view test unit as worker_types.sql, change the object view name to the object table name, and get rid of the relational table tests, and then ta da! Listing 6-9 shows my test unit for WORKER_TYPES.

Listing 6-9. A Test Unit for Table WORKER_TYPES, worker_types.sql

```
01   rem worker_types.sql
02   rem by Donald J. Bales on 2014-10-20
03   rem test unit for object table WORKER_TYPES
04
05   declare
06   -- Declare a variable of the user-define type
07   o_worker_type                        WORKER_TYPE;
08
```

```
09  begin
10      -- Insert a test object using the convenience constructor
11      insert into WORKER_TYPES
12      values ( WORKER_TYPE( 'T', 'Test') );
13
14      -- Now update the inactive date on the object
15      update WORKER_TYPES
16      set     inactive_date = SYSDATE
17      where   code          = 'T';
18
19      -- Retrieve the object in order to show its values
20      select value(g)
21      into    o_worker_type
22      from    WORKER_TYPES g
23      where   code          = 'T';
24
25      -- Show the object's values
26      pl('o_worker_type.id              = '||o_worker_type.id);
27      pl('o_worker_type.code            = '||o_worker_type.code);
28      pl('o_worker_type.description     = '||o_worker_type.description);
29      pl('o_worker_type.active_date     = '||o_worker_type.active_date);
30      pl('o_worker_type.inactive_date   = '||o_worker_type.inactive_date);
31
32      -- Delete the test object
33      delete WORKER_TYPES
34      where   code      = 'T';
35
36      -- This time insert the test object using the instance variable
37      insert into WORKER_TYPES
38      values ( o_worker_type );
39
40      -- Last, delete the object from the relational table
41      delete WORKER_TYPES
42      where   code      = 'T';
43
44      -- Commit all these operations
45      commit;
46
47      -- Confirm that the test completed successfully
48      pl('Test completed successfully.');
49  end;
50  /
```

The results of the test unit in Listing 6-9 should look something like this:

```
SQL> @worker_types.sql
```

```
o_worker_type.id            = 1
o_worker_type.code          = T
o_worker_type.description   = Test
o_worker_type.active_date   = 29-DEC-14
o_worker_type.inactive_date = 29-DEC-14
Test completed successfully.

PL/SQL procedure successfully completed.
```

Come on, you have to admit it. It's pretty easy to make a transition to object orientation, right? Perhaps, or perhaps not. Some argue that there is a problem between how object-oriented languages represent data and how data is stored in a relational database, calling it an *impedance mismatch*.

Impedance Mismatch?

I argue that if done properly, there is little so-called "mismatch" between the classes used in an object-oriented language like Java and object-relational user-defined types in Oracle—that is, if they both properly model the real world.

I have an entire section dedicated to the use of Java Database Connectivity (JDBC) and object-relational user-defined types in one of my previous books (*Java Programming with Oracle JDBC,* OReilly, 2001). My 30 plus years of experience in both programming with object-oriented languages and using relational and now object-relational databases has led me to the conclusion that the mismatch is one of improper analysis vs. the reality of the problem domain.

The only time I see a mismatch is when one of the following occurs:

- "Catchall" classes are used in the presentation layer, which make it easy to represent and move objects around in the presentation layer, but they don't actually model the real world at all.

- Denormalized attributes in classes, which once again make it easier to work with data in the presentation layer, but don't even remotely represent the cardinality of the real world.

- No time is taken to do a proper analysis. It's build a presentation and then create a database that fits it, or restated, shoot, ready, aim! Right.

- Target databases use a different programming language from the presentation layer's object-oriented programming environment, so the database programming language is misunderstood, misused, or ignored altogether.

Don't take these in any particular order, because there are more reasons than I am willing to list. I seem to remember the same phenomena—you know, all the reasons not to adopt better technology—years ago when relational technology first appeared, say 1984?

So what haven't I told you? There are, in fact, a few topics I have not covered yet. Let's delve into those next.

Nested Types and Collections

First, I haven't shown any examples with nested types. For example, I could create a TYPE ADDRESS for address information, and then use that TYPE as an attribute in another TYPE like CONTACT. You can do that; it's not a problem.

Nor have I shown you any examples of a TYPE that contain arrays of other TYPEs. That's certainly possible. You can create what is called a nested TYPE, and implement it as a nested table where you can have an unlimited number of entries, or as a varying array that has a fixed number of entries. I don't like the sound of the latter. It's not very relational in nature. And nesting is where all the so-called impedance mismatch occurs.

In the minds of some object-oriented programmers, it's necessary to create huge, complex, object types that contain everything remotely similar. You know this; if you're an object-oriented programmer, you've seen them, or worse, created them.

Consider Figure 6-1, a class diagram to replace the ERD for the problem domain from Chapter 1. Are all three historical entities—LocgicalAssignment, PhysicalAssignment, and WorkAssignment—part of Worker in an object-oriented setting? No, they may be related, but you won't find them on any particular worker, will you? They are actually stand-alone entities. However, in most cases, someone would create a class Worker that contained these three entities as arrays. There's the mismatch. It's a break between reality and programming convenience.

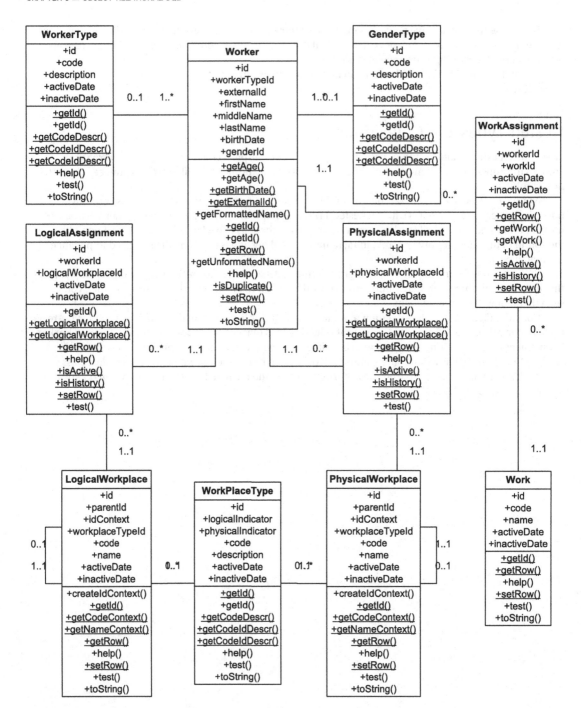

Figure 6-1. *A partial class diagram for the sample problem domain*

It's Your Turn to Prove There's No Impedance Mismatch

At this point, I've coded the scripts to create the Gender code object table, and you've done the same for the Worker Type object table. Now you can put these to work as you code the scripts for and create a Worker object table. Here's what to do.

1. Verify that you successfully executed the following scripts: gender_type.tps, gender_type.tpb, gender_types.tab, and gender_types.ins.

2. Verify that you successfully coded and executed the following scripts: worker_type.tps, worker_type.tpb, worker_types.tab, and worker_types.ins.

3. Write a script to create a TYPE specification for the Worker entity. You can get the attributes from the column names in file worker_types.tab from Chapter 5. You can get the method names from package file worker_type.pks from Chapter 5.

4. Save your script as worker.tps.

5. Compile your script: @worker.tps.

6. Write a script to create an object table named WORKERS using the user-defined type WORKER you just created.

7. Save your script as workers.tab.

8. Compile your script: @workers.tab.

9. Write a script to implement the TYPE BODY for the Worker entity. You can get the method implementations from package file worker_type.pkb from Chapter 5.

10. Save your script as worker.tpb.

11. Compile your script: @worker.tps.

12. At this point, you should have a valid WORKERS object table. So now modify the script you used to populate the WORKERS table in Chapter 5, workers.ins, to populate the WORKERS object table.

13. Save your script as workers.ins.

14. Execute your script in order to populate the object table: @workers.ins.

15. Create a test unit script and test your new object table.

Listings 6-10 through 6-13 show my solutions for this exercise. Listing 6-10 is my specification for the TYPE WORKER.

Listing 6-10. The Specification Script for User-Defined TYPE WORKER, worker.tps

```
001  create type WORKER as object (
002  /*
003  worker.tps
004  by Don Bales on 2014-10-20
005  Type WORKER's attributes and methods.
006  */
007  id                            number(38),
008  worker_type_id                number(38),
009  external_id                   varchar2(30),
```

```
010  first_name                          varchar2(30),
011  middle_name                         varchar2(30),
012  last_name                           varchar2(30),
013  name                                varchar2(100),
014  birth_date                          date,
015  gender_type_id                      number(38),
016  /*
017  Get the worker's current age.
018  */
019  MEMBER FUNCTION get_age
020  return                              number,
021  /*
022  Get the worker's age on the specified date.
023  */
024  MEMBER FUNCTION get_age(
025  aid_on                              date)
026  return                              number,
027  /*
028  Calculate a worker's age for the given birth date
029  and point in time.
030  */
031  STATIC FUNCTION get_age(
032  aid_birth_date            in     date,
033  aid_on                    in     date)
034  return                              number,
035  /*
036  Calculate a worker's current age for the given bith date.
037  */
038  STATIC FUNCTION get_age(
039  aid_birth_date            in     date)
040  return                              number,
041  /*
042  Get the specified worker's age at the given point in time.
043  */
044  STATIC FUNCTION get_age(
045  ain_id                    in     number,
046  aid_on                    in     date)
047  return                              number,
048  /*
049  Get the specified worker's current age.
050  */
051  STATIC FUNCTION get_age(
052  ain_id                    in     number)
053  return                              number,
054  /*
055  Get the specified worker's birth date.
056  */
057  STATIC FUNCTION get_birth_date(
058  ain_id                    in     number)
059  return                              date,
060  /*
```

```
061   Get the specified worker's external ID.
062   */
063   STATIC FUNCTION get_external_id
064   return                              varchar2,
065   /*
066   Calculate the locale specific formatted name.
067   */
068   STATIC FUNCTION get_formatted_name(
069   aiv_first_name               in     varchar2,
070   aiv_middle_name              in     varchar2,
071   aiv_last_name                in     varchar2)
072   return                              varchar2,
073   /*
074   Get the specified worker's formatted name.
075   */
076   STATIC FUNCTION get_formatted_name(
077   ain_id                       in     number)
078   return                              varchar2,
079   /*
080   Get the next primary key value for the table.
081   */
082   STATIC FUNCTION get_id
083   return                              number,
084   /*
085   Get the specified worker's internal ID.
086   */
087   STATIC FUNCTION get_id(
088   aiv_external_id              in     varchar2)
089   return                              number,
090   /*
091   Get the specified worker's row object.
092   */
093   STATIC FUNCTION get_row(
094   aio_worker                   in     WORKER)
095   return                              WORKER,
096   /*
097   Calculate the non-locale specific unformmated name.
098   */
099   STATIC FUNCTION get_unformatted_name(
100   aiv_first_name               in     varchar2,
101   aiv_middle_name              in     varchar2,
102   aiv_last_name                in     varchar2)
103   return                              varchar2,
104   /*
105   Display the help text for this TYPE.
106   */
107   MEMBER PROCEDURE help,
108   /*
109   Check to see if a worker with the same name, birth_date and
110   gender already exists in the database.
111   */
```

```
112  STATIC FUNCTION is_duplicate(
113  aiv_name                     in      varchar2,
114  aid_birth_date               in      varchar2,
115  ain_gender_type_id           in      varchar2)
116  return                               boolean,
117  /*
118  Set the specified worker's row object.
119  */
120  STATIC PROCEDURE set_row(
121  aioo_worker                  in out WORKER),
122  /*
123  Execute the test unit for this TYPE.
124  */
125  MEMBER PROCEDURE test,
126  /*
127  The MAP function for this TYPE.
128  */
129  MAP MEMBER FUNCTION to_varchar2
130  return                               varchar2,
131  /*
132  A convenience constructor for this TYPE.
133  */
134  CONSTRUCTOR FUNCTION worker(
135  self                         in out worker,
136  ain_worker_type_id           in      number,
137  aiv_first_name               in      varchar2,
138  aiv_middle_name              in      varchar2,
139  aiv_last_name                in      varchar2,
140  aid_birth_date               in      date,
141  ain_gender_type_id           in      number)
142  return                               self as result,
143  /*
144  A NULL values constructor for this TYPE.
145  */
146  CONSTRUCTOR FUNCTION worker(
147  self                         in out worker)
148  return                               self as result
149  );
150  /
151  @se.sql
```

Listing 6-11. The CREATE TABLE Script for Object Table WORKERS, workers.tab

```
01   rem worker_ot.tab
02   rem by Donald J. Bales on 2014-10-20
03   rem Create an object table for Workers
04
05   --drop   table WORKERS;
06   create table WORKERS of WORKER;
07
```

```
08   --drop    sequence WORKERS_ID;
09   create sequence WORKERS_ID
10   start with 1;
11
12   --drop    sequence EXTERNAL_ID_SEQ;
13   create sequence EXTERNAL_ID_SEQ
14   start with 100000000 order;
15
16   alter  table WORKERS add
17   constraint    WORKERS_PK
18   primary key ( id )
19   using index;
20
21   alter  table WORKERS add
22   constraint    WORKERS_UK1
23   unique ( external_id )
24   using index;
25
26   alter  table WORKERS add
27   constraint    WORKERS_UK2
28   unique (
29   name,
30   birth_date,
31   gender_type_id )
32   using index;
33
34   alter  table WORKERS add
35   constraint    WORKERS_FK1
36   foreign key   ( worker_type_id )
37   references    WORKER_TYPES ( id );
38
39   alter  table WORKERS add
40   constraint    WORKERS_FK2
41   foreign key   ( gender_type_id )
42   references    GENDER_TYPES ( id );
43
44   execute SYS.DBMS_STATS.gather_table_stats(USER, 'WORKERS');
```

Listing 6-12. The BODY Implementation Script for TYPE WORKER , worker.tpb

```
001   create or replace type body WORKER as
002   /*
003   worker.tpb
004   by Don Bales on 2014-10-20
005   TYPE WORKER's methods
006   */
007
008   MEMBER FUNCTION get_age(
009   aid_on                        in      date)
010   return                        number is
011
```

```
012  begin
013    return WORKER.get_age(birth_date, aid_on);
014  end get_age;
015
016
017  MEMBER FUNCTION get_age
018  return                              number is
019
020  begin
021    return WORKER.get_age(birth_date, SYSDATE);
022  end get_age;
023
024
025  STATIC FUNCTION get_age(
026  aid_birth_date               in      date,
027  aid_on                       in      date)
028  return                               number is
029
030  begin
031    if aid_birth_date is not NULL and
032       aid_on          is not NULL then
033      return trunc(months_between(aid_on, aid_birth_date) / 12);
034    else
035      return NULL;
036    end if;
037  exception
038    when OTHERS then
039      return NULL;
040  end get_age;
041
042
043  STATIC FUNCTION get_age(
044  aid_birth_date               in      date)
045  return                               number is
046
047  begin
048    return WORKER.get_age(aid_birth_date, SYSDATE);
049  end get_age;
050
051
052  STATIC FUNCTION get_age(
053  ain_id                       in      number,
054  aid_on                       in      date)
055  return                               number is
056
057  begin
058    return WORKER.get_age(WORKER.get_birth_date(ain_id), aid_on);
059  end get_age;
060
061
```

```
062   STATIC FUNCTION get_age(
063   ain_id                          in        number)
064   return                                    number is
065
066   begin
067     return WORKER.get_age(WORKER.get_birth_date(ain_id));
068   end get_age;
069
070
071   STATIC FUNCTION get_birth_date(
072   ain_id                          in        number)
073   return                                    date is
074
075   d_birth_date                    date;
076
077   begin
078     select birth_date
079     into    d_birth_date
080     from    WORKERS
081     where   id = ain_id;
082
083     return d_birth_date;
084   end get_birth_date;
085
086
087   STATIC FUNCTION get_external_id
088   return                                    varchar2 is
089
090   v_external_id                   varchar2(30);
091
092   begin
093     select lpad(to_char(EXTERNAL_ID_SEQ.nextval), 9, '0')
094     into    v_external_id
095     from    SYS.DUAL;
096
097     return v_external_id;
098   end get_external_id;
099
100
101   STATIC FUNCTION get_id
102   return                                    number is
103
104   n_id                            number;
105
106   begin
107     select WORKERS_ID.nextval
108     into    n_id
109     from    SYS.DUAL;
110
111     return n_id;
112   end get_id;
```

```
113
114
115   STATIC FUNCTION get_id(
116   aiv_external_id              in        varchar2)
117   return                                 number is
118
119   n_id                                   number;
120
121   begin
122      select id
123      into   n_id
124      from   WORKERS
125      where  external_id = aiv_external_id;
126
127      return n_id;
128   end get_id;
129
130
131   STATIC FUNCTION get_formatted_name(
132   aiv_first_name               in        varchar2,
133   aiv_middle_name              in        varchar2,
134   aiv_last_name                in        varchar2)
135   return                                 varchar2 is
136
137   begin
138    return aiv_last_name||', '||aiv_first_name||' '||aiv_middle_name;
139   end get_formatted_name;
140
141
142   STATIC FUNCTION get_formatted_name(
143   ain_id                       in        number)
144   return                                 varchar2 is
145
146   v_first_name                           varchar2(30);
147   v_middle_name                          varchar2(30);
148   v_last_name                            varchar2(30);
149
150   begin
151      select first_name,
152             middle_name,
153             last_name
154      into   v_first_name,
155             v_middle_name,
156             v_last_name
157      from   WORKERS
158      where  id = ain_id;
159
160      return get_formatted_name(
161             v_first_name,
162             v_middle_name,
163             v_last_name);
```

```
164   end get_formatted_name;
165
166
167   STATIC FUNCTION get_row(
168   aio_worker                     in      WORKER)
169   return                                 WORKER is
170
171   o_worker                               WORKER;
172
173   begin
174     if    aio_worker.id is not NULL then
175       -- retrieve the row by the primary key
176       select value(w)
177       into   o_worker
178       from   WORKERS w
179       where  id = aio_worker.id;
180     elsif aio_worker.external_id is not NULL then
181       -- retrieve the row by the external unique key
182       select value(w)
183       into   o_worker
184       from   WORKERS w
185       where  external_id = aio_worker.external_id;
186     else
187       -- retrieve the row by the name, birth_date, and gender
188       select value(w)
189       into   o_worker
190       from   WORKERS w
191       where  name         = worker.get_formatted_name(
192                               aio_worker.first_name,
193                               aio_worker.middle_name,
194                               aio_worker.last_name)
195       and    birth_date = aio_worker.birth_date
196       and    gender_type_id  = aio_worker.gender_type_id;
197     end if;
198     return o_worker;
199   exception
200     when NO_DATA_FOUND then
201       raise;
202     when OTHERS then
203       raise_application_error(-20001, SQLERRM||
204         ' on select WORKERS'||
205         ' in WORKER.get_row()');
206   end get_row;
207
208
209   STATIC FUNCTION get_unformatted_name(
210   aiv_first_name                 in      varchar2,
211   aiv_middle_name                in      varchar2,
212   aiv_last_name                  in      varchar2)
213   return                                 varchar2 is
214
```

189

```
215   begin
216     return upper(replace(replace(replace(replace(replace(
217       aiv_last_name||aiv_first_name||aiv_middle_name,
218         '''', NULL), ',', NULL), '-', NULL), '.', NULL), ' ', NULL));
219   end get_unformatted_name;
220
221
222   STATIC FUNCTION is_duplicate(
223   aiv_name                      in      varchar2,
224   aid_birth_date                in      varchar2,
225   ain_gender_type_id                in      varchar2)
226   return                              boolean is
227
228   n_selected                          number;
229
230   begin
231     execute immediate
232       'select count(1)
233       from    WORKERS
234       where   name       = aiv_name
235       and     birth_date = aid_birth_date
236       and     gender_type_id  = ain_gender_type_id'
237       into    n_selected
238       using   in aiv_name,
239               in aid_birth_date,
240               in ain_gender_type_id;
241
242     if nvl(n_selected, 0) > 0 then
243       return TRUE;
244     else
245       return FALSE;
246     end if;
247   end is_duplicate;
248
249
250   MEMBER PROCEDURE help is
251
252   begin
253   --    12345678901234567890123456789012345678901234567890123456789012345678901234567890
254     pl('================================= PACKAGE =====================================');
255     pl(chr(9));
256     pl('WORKER');
257     pl(chr(9));
258     pl('-------------------------------- FUNCTIONS ----------------------------------');
259     pl(chr(9));
260     pl('YOU GOTTA CODE THIS BUDDY WORKER.get_id');
261     pl('return                                number;');
262     pl(chr(9)||'Returns a newly allocated sequence value for id.');
263     pl(chr(9));
264     pl('WORKER.get_id(');
265     pl('aiv_external_id              in      varchar2 )');
```

```
266   pl('return                              number;');
267   pl(chr(9)||'Returns the corresponding id for the specified external_id.');
268   pl(chr(9));
269   pl('----------------------------- PROCEDURES -----------------------------');
270   pl(chr(9));
271   pl('WORKER.get_external_id_descr(');
272   pl('ain_id                       in    number,');
273   pl('aov_external_id                out varchar2,');
274   pl('aov_description                out WORKERS.description%TYPE );');
275   pl(chr(9)||'Gets the corresponding external_id and description for the specified');
276   pl(chr(9)||'id.');
277   pl(chr(9));
278   pl('WORKER.get_external_id_id_descr(');
279   pl('aiov_external_id                  in out varchar2,');
280   pl('aon_id                 out number,');
281   pl('aov_description                out WORKERS.description%TYPE,');
282   pl('aid_on                    in     WORKERS.active%TYPE );');
283   pl(chr(9)||'Gets the corresponding external_id, id, and description for');
284   pl(chr(9)||'the specified external_id.  First it trys to find an exact match.
      If one');
285   pl(chr(9)||'cannot be found, it trys to find a like match.  It may throw a');
286   pl(chr(9)||'NO_DATA_FOUND or a TOO_MANY_ROWS exception if a match cannot be');
287   pl(chr(9)||'found for the specified external_id and point in time.');
288   pl(chr(9));
289   pl('WORKER.get_external_id_id_descr(');
290   pl('aiov_external_id                in out varchar2,');
291   pl('aon_id                          out number,');
292   pl('aov_description                out WORKERS.description%TYPE );');
293   pl(chr(9)||'Gets the corresponding external_id, id, and description for');
294   pl(chr(9)||'the specified external_id.  First it trys to find an exact match.
      If one');
295   pl(chr(9)||'cannot be found, it trys to find a like match.  It may throw a');
296   pl(chr(9)||'NO_DATA_FOUND or a TOO_MANY_ROWS exception if a match cannot be');
297   pl(chr(9)||'found for the specified external_id at the current point in time.');
298   pl(chr(9));
299   pl('WORKER.help( );');
300   pl(chr(9)||'Displays this help text if set serveroutput is on.');
301   pl(chr(9));
302   pl('WORKER.test( );');
303   pl(chr(9)||'Built-in test unit.  It will report success or error for each test
      if set');
304   pl(chr(9)||'serveroutput is on.');
305   pl(chr(9));
306 end help;
307
308
309 STATIC PROCEDURE set_row(
310 aioo_worker                 in out WORKER) is
311
312 d_null                      constant date        := DATE_.d_MIN;
313 n_null                      constant number      := 0;
```

```
314   v_null                          constant varchar2(1) := ' ';
315   o_worker                                WORKER;
316
317   begin
318     -- set the formatted name
319     aioo_worker.name := worker.get_formatted_name(
320                           aioo_worker.first_name,
321                           aioo_worker.middle_name,
322                           aioo_worker.last_name);
323     -- get the existing row
324     begin
325       o_worker := get_row(aioo_worker);
326     exception
327       when NO_DATA_FOUND then
328         o_worker := NULL;
329     end;
330     -- if a row exists, update it if needed
331     if o_worker is not NULL then
332       aioo_worker.id := o_worker.id;
333       if nvl(o_worker.worker_type_id, n_null) <>
334            nvl(aioo_worker.worker_type_id, n_null) or
335          nvl(o_worker.external_id,    n_null) <>
336            nvl(aioo_worker.external_id,    n_null) or
337          nvl(o_worker.first_name,     v_null) <>
338            nvl(aioo_worker.first_name,     v_null) or
339          nvl(o_worker.middle_name,    v_null) <>
340            nvl(aioo_worker.middle_name,    v_null) or
341          nvl(o_worker.last_name,      v_null) <>
342            nvl(aioo_worker.last_name,      v_null) or
343          nvl(o_worker.birth_date,     d_null) <>
344            nvl(aioo_worker.birth_date,     d_null) or
345          nvl(o_worker.gender_type_id,     n_null) <>
346            nvl(aioo_worker.gender_type_id,     n_null) then
347         begin
348           update WORKERS
349           set    worker_type_id = aioo_worker.worker_type_id,
350                  external_id    = aioo_worker.external_id,
351                  first_name     = aioo_worker.first_name,
352                  middle_name    = aioo_worker.middle_name,
353                  last_name      = aioo_worker.last_name,
354                  name           = aioo_worker.name,
355                  birth_date     = aioo_worker.birth_date,
356                  gender_type_id = aioo_worker.gender_type_id
357           where  id             = aioo_worker.id;
358
359   --          n_updated := nvl(n_updated, 0) + nvl(sql%rowcount, 0);
360         exception
361           when OTHERS then
362             raise_application_error( -20002, SQLERRM||
363               ' on update WORKERS'||
364               ' in WORKER.set_row()' );
```

```
365          end;
366        end if;
367      else
368      -- add the row if it does not exist
369        begin
370          aioo_worker.id := get_id();
371          insert into WORKERS
372          values ( aioo_worker );
373
374  --         n_inserted := nvl(n_inserted, 0) + nvl(sql%rowcount, 0);
375        exception
376          when OTHERS then
377            raise_application_error( -20003, SQLERRM||
378              ' on insert WORKERS'||
379              ' in WORKER.set_row()' );
380        end;
381      end if;
382  end set_row;
383
384
385  MEMBER PROCEDURE test(
386  self                             in out nocopy worker) is
387
388  begin
389    pl('=============================== PACKAGE ====================================');
390    pl(chr(9));
391    pl('WORKER');
392    pl(chr(9));
393    pl(chr(9)||'No tests for WORKER at this time');
394  end test;
395
396
397  MAP MEMBER FUNCTION to_varchar2
398  return                           varchar2 is
399
400  begin
401    return rtrim(name||to_char(birth_date, 'YYYYMMDDHH24MISS'));
402  end to_varchar2;
403
404
405  CONSTRUCTOR FUNCTION worker(
406  self                     in out worker,
407  ain_worker_type_id       in     number,
408  aiv_first_name           in     varchar2,
409  aiv_middle_name          in     varchar2,
410  aiv_last_name            in     varchar2,
411  aid_birth_date           in     date,
412  ain_gender_type_id       in     number)
413  return                           self as result is
414
```

```
415   begin
416     id               := WORKER.get_id();
417     worker_type_id := ain_worker_type_id;
418     external_id     := WORKER.get_external_id();
419     first_name      := aiv_first_name;
420     middle_name     := aiv_middle_name;
421     last_name       := aiv_last_name;
422     name             := WORKER.get_formatted_name(
423       first_name, middle_name, last_name);
424     birth_date      := aid_birth_date;
425     gender_type_id := ain_gender_type_id;
426     return;
427   end worker;
428
429
430   CONSTRUCTOR FUNCTION worker(
431   self                              in out worker)
432   return                                self as result is
433
434   begin
435     id               := NULL;
436     worker_type_id := NULL;
437     external_id     := NULL;
438     first_name      := NULL;
439     middle_name     := NULL;
440     last_name       := NULL;
441     name             := NULL;
442     birth_date      := NULL;
443     gender_type_id := NULL;
444     return;
445   end worker;
446
447
448   end; --WORKER;
449   /
450   @be.sql WORKER
```

■ **Note**   Make sure you execute scripts gender_types.ins and worker_types.ins before executing workers.ins (Listing 6-13); otherwise, the script will be missing required code values.

Listing 6-13. The Populate Table Script for Object Table WORKERS, workers.ins

```
01   rem workers.ins
02   rem by Donald J. Bales on 2014-10-20
03   rem Seed the Worker table with the top 100 names
04   rem 100 last x 100 first x 26 middle = 260,000 entries
05
06   set serveroutput on size 1000000;
07
```

```
08  declare
09
10  -- This is the number of seconds since midnight
11  -- I'll use it to profile my code's performance.
12  n_start                              number :=
13    to_number(to_char(SYSDATE, 'SSSSS'));
14
15  -- Here, I declare four psuedo-constants to hold the
16  -- ID values from the code tables, rather `than look
17  -- them up repeatedly during the insert process.
18  n_G_FEMALE                           GENDER_TYPES.id%TYPE;
19  n_G_MALE                             GENDER_TYPES.id%TYPE;
20  n_WT_CONTRACTOR                      WORKER_TYPES.id%TYPE;
21  n_WT_EMPLOYEE                        WORKER_TYPES.id%TYPE;
22
23  -- I'll use this to keep track of the number of
24  -- rows inserted.
25  n_inserted                           number := 0;
26
27  begin
28    -- Get the ID values for the codes
29    n_G_FEMALE       := GENDER_TYPE.get_id('F');
30    n_G_MALE         := GENDER_TYPE.get_id('M');
31    n_WT_CONTRACTOR := WORKER_TYPE.get_id('C');
32    n_WT_EMPLOYEE    := WORKER_TYPE.get_id('E');
33
34    -- Use an INSERT INTO SELECT SQL statement
35    insert into WORKERS
36    select WORKER(
37          WORKERS_ID.nextval,
38          decode(mod(WORKERS_ID.currval, 2),
39            0, n_WT_EMPLOYEE, n_WT_CONTRACTOR),
40          lpad(to_char(EXTERNAL_ID_SEQ.nextval), 9, '0'),
41          first_name,
42          letter||'.',
43          last_name,
44          WORKER.get_formatted_name(
45            first_name, letter||'.', last_name),
46          DATE_.random(
47            to_number(to_char(SYSDATE, 'YYYY')) - 65,
48            to_number(to_char(SYSDATE, 'YYYY')) - 18),
49          decode(gender_code, 'F', n_G_FEMALE, n_G_MALE))
50    from  RPS.TOP_100_LAST_NAMES,
51          RPS.TOP_100_FIRST_NAMES,
52          RPS.A_THRU_Z;
53
54    n_inserted := n_inserted + sql%rowcount;
55
56    commit;
57
58    pl(to_char(n_inserted)||' rows inserted in '||
```

```
59      (to_number(to_char(SYSDATE, 'SSSSS')) - n_start)||
60      ' seconds.');
61 end;
62 /
63
64 execute SYS.DBMS_STATS.gather_table_stats(USER, 'WORKERS');
```

If you compare the three object tables—GENDER_TYPES, WORKER_TYPES, and WORKERS—against the class diagram in Figure 6-1, you'll see that you've fully implemented both the attributes and methods of the classes: GENDER_TYPE, WORKER_TYPE, and WORKER in the database using user-defined TYPEs. Congratulations.

Is there a performance penalty for using object-relational technology? Sure there is! You didn't think you could do extra work, that is, instatiating classes (TYPES) for free did you? How much of a performance penalty? Well, workers.ins inserted 260,000 objects in 126 seconds. That's 2063 objects per second, or about six times slower than its relational counterpart. Is it worth the extra functionality? I think so, but now it's up to you.

Summary

To sum it all up, the real world is made up of things, or objects. Objects have both attributes and behaviors. Using attributes alone, you can answer only the question "What was that?" But with behaviors, you can also answer the question "When did it behave that way?" So you decide which way to go. Try one, then the other!

Table 6-1 is a summary of the SQL and PL/SQL objects that are used in order to fully model a business, scientific, or any real-world problem accurately.

Table 6-1. *A Summary of SQL and PL/SQL Objects Used to Model the Real World*

Item	Data	Behavior
Relational table (SQL)	Columns	
Relational view (SQL)	Columns	
Table package (PL/SQL)		Methods
User-defined type (SQL and PL/SQL)	Attributes	Methods
Object view (SQL)	Columns mapped to attributes	Methods
Object table (SQL)	Attributes	Methods

The single most important point of this chapter is that you can't accurately model anything without attributes and behavior, or data and methods. And as the saying goes, "Those who cannot remember the past are condemned to repeat it." We, the business and technical community, can now accurately model the real world. So we can remember the past and no longer repeat our mistakes. We can profit from our knowledge, the information we have gathered, as we all move through time and space.

Now that you know how to write some PL/SQL, let's look at how you can see what's going on as your PL/SQL program executes.

CHAPTER 7

■ ■ ■

Troubleshooting

I believe programmers are no better than their knowledge of the debugging and troubleshooting tools available for the programming language they're using. Why? Well, first, all programmers make coding mistakes. I often remark that the day I code something that compiles and runs correctly the first time, I'm going to retire because that would be the peak of my programming career. Second, programmers make logic mistakes. When is the last time you had to write some parsing code? That's one of the toughest types of programming to get right the first, second, third, or nth time around.

To find and solve our mistakes, we need a means to be able to discover exactly what is going on in our programs at that point in time when an error occurs. Sadly enough, when PL/SQL first appeared and for quite some time after, there was virtually no way to debug a stored PL/SQL program unit. The best we could do was to use SYS.DBMS_OUTPUT.put_line() to display a bunch of messages on the screen after the stored procedure finished executing.

Then along came the package SYS.DBMS_PIPE, where the most adventurous of us could write our own utilities to monitor an executing stored PL/SQL program unit in "real time" from a second session. That was an improvement, but not one that most PL/SQL programmers could use. Next, the pragma autonomous transaction showed up, which allowed us to write logging utilities that used a second session in order to monitor a stored PL/SQL program unit, and could permanently save the monitoring messages to a table. That was better, but still not very good.

More recently, the package SYS.DBMS_DEBUG became available. It allows us to write our own programs to actually run a remote debugging utility against a stored PL/SQL program unit. And now Oracle has made a PL/SQL debugger freely available to its programming communities with a product (written in Java) called Oracle SQL Developer. Other vendors have followed suit, and now you can remotely debug from graphical user interface (GUI) integrated development environments (IDEs) like TOAD for Oracle and Visual Studio, to name just a few. With a real remote debugger in our hands, we can actually see just what's happening in our PL/SQL programs.

When it comes to SQL, we've had access to EXPLAIN PLAN and TKPROF for as long as I can remember. Both give us the means to see the plans that the Oracle SQL Optimizer is going to use to access the underlying objects that are part of our SQL statements. Once again, using these tools, we can actually see just what's happening in our SQL.

However, having access to these fine troubleshooting tools is not enough. You also need to prepare for trouble ahead of time. You need to build troubleshooting capabilities into your program units. To that end, I'm going to show you how to do the following:

- Prevent trouble in the first place

- Prepare for trouble so you're ready for troubleshooting when an error does occur

- Use SYS.DBMS_OUTPUT.put_line() to provide meaningful troubleshooting information after a program unit finishes executing

- Use a logging utility to provide meaningful troubleshooting information in real time

- Use a remote debugger to walk through a program unit as it executes

- Use EXPLAIN PLAN to troubleshoot the performance of your SQL statements

Let's start out with some prevention techniques.

Prevention

If you want to prevent problems, then assume nothing. A handful of capabilities built into PL/SQL are nothing but an invitation for trouble. They are all centered on data types and implicit conversion. What's implicit conversion? Let's say you have number held in a varchar2 data type variable, v_value. You try assigning n_value, a number data type variable, that value with the following line of code:

```
n_value := v_value;
```

That should work, right? Yes, it should, but when it doesn't, because you don't actually have a numeric literal stored in variable v_value, the implicit data type conversion will raise an "unexpected" exception in your program unit, which will be hard to identify. By "identify," I mean determine which line of code caused the error and why. Before we get to the solution for this problem, let's look at another example.

This time, let's say you want pass a date value to a function that will return the time in seconds since midnight, January 1, 1980. The function requires the date be passed as a varchar2 parameter in the form DD-MON-YY. Hey, no problem. Just pass the date variable like so:

```
...
d_value                          date := SYSDATE;
n_value                          number;

begin
  n_value := date_to_long(d_value);
...
```

Oracle's default date format is DD-MON-YY, so it will work fine, right? Not exactly. If the current NLS_DATE_FORMAT for the session is DD-MON-YY (the default), it will work, but not if it is YYYYMMDD HH24MISS, as I set mine every time I log in to SQL*Plus.

What's the solution? Use a combination of anchors, data type prefixes, and explicit conversions with blocking.

Anchors

I've already discussed anchors in Chapter 3. They are those wacky looking data type declarations that use the %TYPE or %ROWTYPE keyword. For example, here's a list of variables declared in a manner so they match the data types of their corresponding table columns:

```
...
d_birth_date                     WORKER.birth_date%TYPE;
n_gender_type_id                 WORKER.gender_type_id%TYPE;
v_name                           WORKER.name%TYPE;
...
```

How does using anchors help prevent errors? Since each variable is anchored to the data type of the column in a table for which it will be used to temporarily hold a value, SQL and PL/SQL will not need to perform an implicit data type conversion when values are moved between the SQL and PL/SQL. Explicitly anchoring the data types of variables to their database counterparts prevents implicit conversions. Preventing implicit conversions prevents errors.

But if you're going to anchor variables to their corresponding database columns or attributes, why use data type prefixes?

Data Type Prefixes

Data type prefixes help prevent errors in two ways. One is that when you declare a variable with a data type prefix, you're documenting that you understand that the data type is a date, number, or varchar2. You're saying, "Hey, I know what this is!" From that point in your coding forward, you can work with that assertion in place, to make sure that you're not doing any implicit conversions. Preventing implicit conversions prevents errors.

Data type prefixes also make it clear that a data type conversion is necessary. If you find yourself coding away in the far recesses of your stored procedure, and you come to a line where you're going to make an assignment and the data type prefixes are not the same, you know that you need to code an explicit data type conversion. In turn, coding an explicit data type conversion will prevent an implicit conversion. Again, preventing implicit conversions prevents errors.

So let's look at how you code an explicit data type conversion.

Explicit Conversions

When you perform an explicit conversion, you can wrap your PL/SQL statements in their own PL/SQL block, or as I like to say, "block your code." This allows you to catch any exceptions raised during the data type conversion, so you can do something intelligent with your newfound knowledge of the error.

You perform an explicit data type conversion by using one of the following functions:

- to_char(): Used to convert a date or number to a varchar2 data type

- to_date(): Used to convert a varchar2 to a date data type

- to_number(): Used to convert a varchar2 to a number data type

For example, to convert the value January 1, 1980 in variable d_date to a varchar2 data type for variable v_date in the form YYYYMMDD, you could use the following code:

```
v_date := to_char(d_date, 'YYYYMMDD');
```

It's unlikely that converting from a date (or number) to a varchar2 is ever going to cause an error as long as the receiving variable is declared large enough to hold the result, but, on the other hand, it's very likely an error will occur if you convert from a varchar2 to a date, as in the following:

```
...
  begin
    d_date := to_date(v_date, 'YYYYMMDD');
  exception
    when OTHERS then
      pl(SQLERRM);
      pl('Converting "'||v_date||'" to a date using format YYYYMMDD');
      raise_application_error(-20001, SQLERRM||
```

```
        ' converting v_date to d_date'||
        ' in my_program_unit.method');
  end;
...
```

■ **Note** Way back in Chapter 1 I created a script named `pl.prc` that created a procedure called `pl()` that calls `SYS.DBMS_OUTPUT.put_line()` because I'm a lazy programmer who does not like to type `SYS.DBMS_OUTPUT.put_line()` everywhere I want to post a message.

In this example, if the character representation of the date in variable `v_date` is not in the format YYYYMMDD, the `to_date()` function will raise an appropriate exception. The enclosing PL/SQL block will echo the details to the screen using `put_line()` via `pl()`, and then raise an application error that will report exactly where the error occurred in the program. This, in turn, will give you details as to why there was an error, so you are armed with good error information when you start troubleshooting, not some time after you are well into troubleshooting.

Just as `to_date()` and `to_char()` have formats they can use to specify the conversion parameters, so does `to_number()`. You can find the details on these formats in the freely available *PL/SQL User's Guide and Reference*. You can find this and the rest of the Oracle documentation set online at `http://otn.oracle.com`.

So the proper use of the combination of anchors, data type prefixes, and explicit conversion functions will prevent many unexpected errors. Next, let's see how you can better prepare for those that will still eventually arrive.

Preparation

Preparing for trouble ahead of time means preparing for troubleshooting ahead of time. How do you prepare for troubleshooting? You can do that by using blocks and bread crumbs.

You can block (wrap code in its own PL/SQL block) risky code ahead of time. When I say "risky code," I mean

- Explicit data type conversions

- Movement of larger character strings to shorter character variables

- Singleton SQL statements

And what about bread crumbs? You know the fairy tale about Hansel and Gretel, right? They dropped bread crumbs on the ground as they walked through the forest so they could find their way back. Well, I want you to drop code on your listings as you type through your program, so you, too, can find your way back— back to the source of a problem.

Let's start our discussion of blocking and bread crumbs with the former.

Blocking

I just showed you an example of blocking—wrapping a small piece of your PL/SQL in its own PL/SQL block in order to catch a raised exception and dealing with it—when I discussed explicit conversions. Now I'll show you another example, where I move a larger character string into a smaller character variable.

It's not uncommon when coding a data migration or data processing program to move a larger varchar2 variable into a smaller one. In such a situation, you can substring the larger variable in order to blindly truncate the larger string, or you can block the assignment so it raises an exception that you can deal with intelligently. Here's an example of the latter:

```
declare

v_large                         varchar2(80);
v_small                         varchar2(30);

begin
  -- I'm assigning the variable in the executable section because
  -- assignment errors in the declaration section are also very hard
  -- to troubleshoot!
  -- 12345678901234567890123456789012345678901234567890123456789012345678
  v_large :=
    'This is a large string of characters, at least longer than 30 bytes!';

  -- Now let's raise an exception
  begin
    -- This won't work!  68 bytes won't fit in 30 bytes!
    v_small := v_large;
  exception
    when OTHERS then
      pl(SQLERRM);
      pl('Moving v_large, length '||
        to_char(length(v_large))||' into v_small.');
      raise_application_error(-20001, SQLERRM||
        ' on v_small := v_large'||
        ' in my anonymous procedure');
  end;

  pl(v_small);
end;
/
```

Executing this example results in the following output from SQL*Plus:

```
ORA-06502: PL/SQL: numeric or value error: character string buffer too small
Moving v_large, length 68 into v_small.
declare
*
ERROR at line 1:
ORA-20001: ORA-06502: PL/SQL: numeric or value error: character string
buffer too small on v_small := v_large in my anonymous procedure
ORA-06512: at line 23
```

As you can see from the output, the first three lines come from the pl() messages, while the last four come from the raised application error. The important point here is that without the "extra" information displayed by pl() or the raised application error, you wouldn't know where in the program the assignment error occurred. So by "blocking" the code, you can use pl() or raise_application_error(), or both, in order to identify the location and reason for an error in your PL/SQL program.

This is invaluable information when troubleshooting. And, by now, you're probably tired of me stating that, but I can't impress on you enough how taking the time to add a few additional lines of PL/SQL code while you're programming can later drastically reduce the amount of time it takes to test and troubleshoot your code.

So how about those bread crumbs?

Bread Crumbs

What do I mean by "bread crumbs?" I mean adding columns to staging tables, adding logging from your PL/SQL programs, and so on, as you initially write your code, in preparation for trouble. I suppose you may think, "That's not a very optimistic way to think about my work." However, programming is highly detailed logical work. Therefore, human beings are bound to make mistakes, since we are, by nature, emotionally "big picture" thinkers.

With that in mind, here are some ideas for leaving behind bread crumbs:

- Never use WHEN OTHERS THEN NULL in an exception-handling section. OK, how about almost never use WHEN OTHERS THEN NULL. It's a rare occasion when you'll actually want to suppress all errors and do nothing. Think about it. The only example I've ever run into is my errorless to_number_or_null() and to_date_or_null() functions. If there are errors, you need to know, and you need to fix your program's logic so it deals with the errors intelligently, which means predictably.

- Never handle exceptions in a table package's methods or a type's methods. You want these to show up in the presentation layer so the end user (the programmer) can deal with them appropriately, which means predictably.

- Use SYS.DBMS_OUTPUT.put_line() to display success and error messages as the output of any data migration or data processing program unit.

- Use a procedure that utilizes pragma autonomous transaction to log your data migration or data processing program's progress to a table so you can see where in the process your program is currently executing or later review the program's execution.

- If you're involved in building interfaces that migrate data from another system into yours, add columns to the interface's staging tables, with the same names as the primary key columns in the destination tables. Then store the mappings used by your PL/SQL program (the primary key values) in the corresponding staging table columns when moving the data. This will allow you to see where your program moved the data.

You'll see some of these ideas in action in Chapter 10, when I talk about the polymorphic use of method names among the various table package methods and type methods.

I'll talk more about the use of put_line() and logging next. put_line() was the original means of debugging available to PL/SQL programmers, and even though it's not as powerful as a full-blown debugger, it remains useful. Let's see why.

After the Fact

Up to this point, you've seen the stored package procedure SYS.DBMS_OUTPUT.put_line() in action time and time again. Do you remember how, back in Chapter 2, I wrapped SYS.DBMS_OUTPUT.put_line() with a stored procedure named pl() so I wouldn't have to type that long name every time I wanted to display something on the screen?

Just because put_line() is the simplest of debugging tools in your arsenal does not by any means make it useless. If fact, because of its simplicity, it will probably be the first tool you use to debug any PL/SQL program unit. However, keep in mind that when you use put_line(), you're saying, "I can't wait to find out what's going on. OK, maybe I can." Why? Because you don't see any output from put_line() until your PL/SQL program unit has finished executing.

All the output from put_line() is stored in a temporary buffer until your PL/SQL program unit completes its execution, successfully or not. Then whatever tool you are using to execute your PL/SQL must query the DBMS_OUTPUT buffer and display your buffered messages on its screen. SQL*Plus does this for you automatically. However, if you were to write your own PL/SQL execution tool, you would need to program it to pull the messages from the DBMS_OUTPUT buffer after your PL/SQL program completed executing. The point is that put_line() messages appear after the fact.

In addition, you may be limited to the amount of message text you can output during any PL/SQL program unit's execution. You set this value in SQL*Plus using this command:

```
set serveroutput on size 1000000;
```

The size you specify is the maximum amount of memory to use for the DBMS_OUTPUT buffer. It used to be that you could specify 1,000,000 bytes at most, as in the preceding line. However, now you can use an unlimited amount, but is that a good idea?

And then there's the third limitation to put_line(). No single message can be more that 32,767 bytes in length. While that's not much of limitation, large messages can easily use up the buffer, so you must be careful about how you specify your messages.

In the end, the value of the information you get from put_line() is going to be equal to the quality of the messages you add to your PL/SQL code. So let's discuss that next.

Success Messages

It's just as important to display messages of successful operation as it is those related to failure. If you're writing a data processing or data migration program, it's likely that you'll leave your put_line() message in place. The thoughtful placement of success messages will narrow down the number of lines to investigate if an error does occur. For example, in Listing 7-1, I have five success messages. When an application error is raised on line 14, these messages will narrow the location of where the error actually took place.

Listing 7-1. An Example of Success Messages Narrowing the Scope of an Error, success.sql

```
01   rem success.sql
02   rem by Donald J. Bales on 2014-10-20
03   rem a script with success messages
04
05   declare
06
07   n_number                        number;
08
09   begin
10     pl('begin');
11
```

```
12    n_number := -1;
13
14    pl('No error here!');
15
16    n_number := 0;
17
18    pl('Still no error here!');
19
20    n_number := 'one';
21
22    pl('After the error.');
23
24    pl('end');
25  exception
26    when OTHERS then
27      raise_application_error(-20000, SQLERRM||
28        ' on assigning a value to n_number'||
29        ' in success.sql');
30  end;
31  /
```

When the script success.sql is executed, SQL*Plus outputs the following:

```
SQL> @success.sql
```

```
begin
No error here!
Still no error here!
declare
*
ERROR at line 1:
ORA-20000: ORA-06502: PL/SQL: numeric or value error: character to number
conversion error on assigning a value to n_number in success.sql
ORA-06512: at line 23
```

So, PL/SQL is reporting an ERROR at line 1:? That doesn't make much sense. Yet, further down it reports an error at line 23. Hey, that doesn't help much either. It's just a line number by the exception, but it can't be the error—it's a blank line! Where did the error occur? It took place somewhere in the block of PL/SQL code in scope for the exception-handling section.

Regardless, if we rely on our success messages, we can see that the error took place some time after the message Still no error here! and before After the error, and thus narrow down our search to lines 19 through 21. That helps.

In addition to using success messages to narrow the scope of an error, I like to keep track of the number of inserts, updates, deletes, and selects, and then display them at the end of the procedure to verify that something has actually happened.

If, on the other hand, you're writing table package or type service methods, you may use put_line() messages during the development process, and then manually comment them out before going into production. Why just comment them out and not delete them altogether? By leaving them commented out, you give support programmers a clue about a hard-to-understand or an error-prone section of code, and give them an opportunity to comment the put_line() back into play to help them debug your code in the future.

So how can you use failure messages?

Failure Messages

In practice, I rely on method raise_application_error() to send a meaningful error number and message to the presentation layer. I simply number application error messages from -20000 to -20199, from top down in my package body. The messages include the variable SQLERRM, a very brief note about what I was doing in the section of code, and the package and/or function or procedure name as a location of the error. The description in the message needs to be brief because raise_application_error() allows a maximum message size of only 2,048 bytes (255 bytes in earlier versions).

Since my message size is limited by raise_application_error(), I supplement the error message with extra lines of output using put_line() before the call to raise_application_error(). With the "extra" lines of output, I list the values of variables. By including the extra lines of error information, I can call the PL/SQL program unit that raised an error message with the same values as the presentation layer in order to re-create and then correct my code defect.

Now that you have some idea how to go about using put_line(), let's see you put it to use.

It's Your Turn to Use put_line()

It's your turn to put your knowledge of put_line() and raise_application_error() to work by following these steps.

1. Write an anonymous PL/SQL procedure that adds a number in a number variable to a "number" in a varchar2 variable together. Here's the hitch: you should spell out the second number in the varchar2 variable so it will raise an exception when added.

2. "Block" the line of code where you do your addition and then catch the error, list the contents of the variables with pl(), and then raise an application error.

3. Save your script as failure.sql.

4. Execute your script, @failure.sql.

Did your script and results turn out similar to mine? Listing 7-2 is my solution to this exercise.

■ **Note**   You won't get any output if you haven't executed the SQL*Plus command set serveroutput on size 1000000;, which I have already placed in the script login.sql that SQL*Plus executes every time it starts.

Listing 7-2. An Example of Using put_line() to List Variable Values, failure.sql

```
01  rem failure.sql
02  rem by Donald J. Bales on 2014-10-20
03  rem a script that fails on purpose
04
05  declare
06
07  n_number                            number;
08  v_number                            varchar2(30);
09
```

```
10   begin
11     pl('begin');
12
13     pl('before n_number assignment');
14
15     n_number := 1;
16
17     pl('after n_number assignment');
18
19     pl('before v_number assignment');
20
21     v_number := 'two';
22
23     pl('after v_number assignment');
24
25     pl('before addition');
26     begin
27       pl('n_number + v_number = '||to_char(n_number + to_number(v_number)));
28     exception
29       when OTHERS then
30         pl('n_number = '||to_char(n_number));
31         pl('v_number = '||v_number);
32         raise_application_error(-20000, SQLERRM||
33           ' on n_number + v_number'||
34           ' in failure.sql');
35     end;
36     pl('after addition');
37
38     pl('end');
39   end;
40   /
```

And here are the results from executing the `failure.sql` script:

```
SQL> @failure.sql
```

```
begin
before n_number assignment
after n_number assignment
before v_number assignment
after v_number assignment
before addition
n_number = 1
v_number = two
declare
*
ERROR at line 1:
ORA-20000: ORA-06502: PL/SQL: numeric or value error: character to
number conversion error on n_number + v_number in failure.sql
ORA-06512: at line 28
```

This time, since I blocked the one line where I'm performing the addition, the line number for the error reported by PL/SQL is fairly accurate. Still, the success messages do more to narrow the location of the error than does the error message from PL/SQL's `raise_application_error()`. In addition, since I use `pl()` to display the variable values, it's fairly easy to discern the reason for the program's error.

But what happens if you have a long-running procedure, and you want to get some ongoing feedback about its success? Then it's time to take advantage of logging from another session.

As It Happens

By utilizing the PL/SQL pragma `autonomous transaction`, you can build your own logging utility that can do the following:

- Insert and commit messages into a logging table from your PL/SQL program unit without committing your PL/SQL program's own transaction context

- Select the committed messages from a log table immediately after they are written from any other session

In essence, it's as if you're saying, "No, I've changed my mind. I can't wait after all." This technique of logging from another transaction context using an autonomous transaction allows you to see what's happening in your PL/SQL program unit almost in real time. You'll start by building your own logging utility, and then putting it to work in an example. First, you need a table to store messages.

A DEBUG Table

Should I build a relational example or an object-relational example? This time I'll build an object-relational example, and then you'll build its relational equivalent. So what do I need to store about a message? How about the list of attributes in Table 7-1?

Table 7-1. *Attributes for a Debugging Message Table*

Attribute	Description
id	A primary key column for the object table
text	The message to log from the calling PL/SQL program unit
unique_session_id	The unique session ID from the calling PL/SQL program unit
insert_user	The user from the calling PL/SQL program unit
insert_date	The date and time (SYSDATE) from the calling PL/SQL program unit

And don't forget about the behavior! What will my debug TYPE or package need to do for me? How about the list of behaviors in Table 7-2?

Table 7-2. *Behaviors for a Debugging Message Table*

Behavior	Description
get_id()	Allocate a primary key from the corresponding sequence
Null constructor	Return an object initialized to NULL values
Convenience constructor	Return an object initialized and ready for INSERT
Map method	Return a value to sort an object by
enable()	Enable set_text() for the specified program unit
disable()	Disable set_text() for the specified program unit
set_text()	Log the text to the debug table

Since I'm building the object-relational version, I need to create the TYPE first, the table second, and then the TYPE BODY last. Listing 7-3 is my source code for the object TYPE DEBUG_O.

Listing 7-3. Type DEBUG's Specification, ops.debug.tps

```
01  create type  DEBUG as object (
02  /*
03  debug.tps
04  by Donald Bales on 2014-10-20
05  Type DEBUG's specification:
06  A type for logging debug information
07  */
08  id                              number(38),
09  text                            varchar2(256),
10  unique_session_id               varchar2(24),
11  insert_user                     varchar2(30),
12  insert_date                     date,
13  -- Get the next primary key value
14  STATIC FUNCTION get_id
15  return                          number,
16  -- A NULL values constructor
17  CONSTRUCTOR FUNCTION debug(
18  self                    in out nocopy debug)
19  return                          self as result,
20  -- A convenience constructor
21  CONSTRUCTOR FUNCTION debug(
22  self                    in out nocopy debug,
23  ain_id                  in      number,
24  aiv_text                in      varchar2)
25  return                          self as result,
26  -- Override the default constructor
27  CONSTRUCTOR FUNCTION debug(
28  self                    in out nocopy debug,
29  id                      in      number,
30  text                    in      varchar2,
31  unique_session_id       in      varchar2,
```

```
32   insert_user                    in      varchar2,
33   insert_date                    in      date)
34   return                                 self as result,
35   -- Write to the debug object table
36   STATIC PROCEDURE set_text(
37   aiv_program_unit               in      varchar2,
38   aiv_text                       in      varchar2),
39   -- A map function
40   MAP MEMBER FUNCTION to_map
41   return                                 number
42   ) not final;
43   /
44   @se.sql
```

Let's take a close look at Listing 7-3.

- Lines 8 through 12 declare the five attributes for the TYPE.

- Lines 14 and 15 declare a static function get_id() to allocate the next primary key value. Since it's a static method, the function is executed using the TYPE rather than an instance of the TYPE.

- Lines 17 and 18 declare a constructor that returns an instance of the TYPE initialized to NULL values.

- Lines 21 through 25 declare a convenience constructor that will return a fully initialized instance of the TYPE, ready to be inserted into the DEBUGS table.

- Lines 27 through 34 declare a constructor that will override the default constructor definition provided by SQL.

- Lines 36 through 38 declare static procedure set_text(), which will insert an entry into the DEBUGS table using an autonomous transaction. This will allow me to commit the log entry without committing anything in the session where I'm using this method to log debug information.

- Lines 40 and 41 declare a MAP method used by SQL to compare and sort objects of this TYPE.

The next step in the development process is to create an object table based on the TYPE. You may have thought that I needed to code the TYPE's implementation first. In this case, I'm going to reference the object table in the TYPE BODY, so I must create the table first. Listing 7-4 is the DDL for creating an object table based on TYPE DEBUG.

Listing 7-4. DDL for Creating an Object Table Based on Type DEBUG, ops.debugs.tab

```
01   rem debugs.tab
02   rem by Donald Bales on 2014-10-20
03   rem Create debugging message table
04
05   -- drop table DEBUGS;
06   create table DEBUGS of DEBUG;
07
08   alter  table DEBUGS add
09   constraint   DEBUGS_PK
```

```
10  primary key (
11  id )
12  using index;
13
14  -- drop sequence DEBUGS_ID;
15  create sequence DEBUGS_ID
16  start with 1 order;
17
18  execute SYS.DBMS_STATS.gather_table_stats(USER, 'DEBUGS');
19
20  grant all on DEBUGS to PUBLIC;
```

Let's look at Listing 7-4 line by line:

- Line 6 creates object table DEBUGS based on TYPE DEBUG.

- Lines 8 through 12 create a primary key on the object table DEBUGS.

- Lines 15 through 16 declare a sequence to be used to allocate primary key values for table DEBUGS.

- On line 18, I analyze table DEBUGS to give the Optimizer some initial statistics to work with.

- On line 20, I grant all privileges to PUBLIC so anyone on the database can use the debug table facility I'm creating.

Now that the table exists, I can compile the TYPE BODY without dependency errors. Listing 7-5 is the TYPE BODY for TYPE DEBUG.

Listing 7-5. Type DEBUG's Implementation, debug.tpb

```
001  create or replace type body DEBUG as
002  /*
003  debug.tpb
004  by Donald Bales on 2014-10-20
005  Type DEBUG's implementation
006  A type for logging debug information
007  */
008
009  STATIC FUNCTION get_id
010  return                            number is
011
012  n_id                             number;
013
014  begin
015     select DEBUGS_ID.nextval
016     into   n_id
017     from   SYS.DUAL;
018
019     return n_id;
020  end get_id;
021
022
```

```
023  CONSTRUCTOR FUNCTION debug(
024  self                          in out nocopy debug)
025  return                                self as result is
026
027  begin
028    pl('debug(zero param)');
029    self.id                := NULL;
030    self.text              := NULL;
031    self.unique_session_id := NULL;
032    self.insert_user       := NULL;
033    self.insert_date       := NULL;
034
035    return;
036  end debug;
037
038
039  CONSTRUCTOR FUNCTION debug(
040  self                          in out nocopy debug,
041  ain_id                        in      number,
042  aiv_text                      in      varchar2)
043  return                                self as result is
044
045  begin
046    pl('debug(two params)');
047    self.id                := ain_id;
048    self.text              := aiv_text;
049    self.unique_session_id := SYS.DBMS_SESSION.unique_session_id;
050    self.insert_user       := USER;
051    self.insert_date       := SYSDATE;
052
053    return;
054  end debug;
055
056
057  -- Override the default constructor.  To do so, you must
058  -- use the same attributes names for the parameter names
059  -- and use them in the order specified in the type spec.
060  CONSTRUCTOR FUNCTION debug(
061  self                          in out nocopy debug,
062  id                            in      number,
063  text                          in      varchar2,
064  unique_session_id             in      varchar2,
065  insert_user                   in      varchar2,
066  insert_date                   in      date)
067  return                                self as result is
068
069  begin
070    pl('debug(five params)');
071    self.id                := id;
072    self.text              := text;
073    self.unique_session_id := unique_session_id;
```

```
074    self.insert_user        := insert_user;
075    self.insert_date        := insert_date;
076
077    return;
078  end debug;
079
080
081  STATIC PROCEDURE set_text(
082  aiv_program_unit              in      varchar2,
083  aiv_text                      in      varchar2) is
084
085  pragma autonomous_transaction;
086
087  v_text                              varchar2(256);
088
089  begin
090    v_text := substrb(aiv_program_unit||': '||aiv_text, 1, 256);
091
092    insert into DEBUGS
093    values (DEBUG(DEBUGS_ID.nextval, aiv_text));
094  -- A defect in SQL prevented me from using the
095  -- function get_id() as follows:
096  --   values (DEBUG(DEBUG.get_id(), aiv_text));
097    commit;
098  end set_text;
099
100
101  MAP MEMBER FUNCTION to_map
102  return                              number is
103
104  begin
105    return id;
106  end to_map;
107
108
109  end;
110  /
111  @be.sql DEBUG
```

Listing 7-5 doesn't have any new code, so I'll just point out two details. The first centers around the second constructor found on lines 39 through 51. In this constructor, I should be able to code line 47 to read as follows:

```
self.id                 := DEBUG.get_id();
```

However, in SQL the constructor is called repeatedly, seemingly the number of times that there are attributes in the TYPE. Accordingly, SQL calls the constructor for this TYPE five times. I consider this a defect. It causes extra CPU and memory consumption, along with the wasted allocation of sequence values that will not be used if implemented in a reasonably object-oriented fashion. I've left in some troubleshooting pl() statements to prove that the constructors are called multiple times. To work around this defect, I've added parameter ain_id on line 41, and used the sequence directly in the SQL—for example, on line 93.

How long it will take Oracle to get around to fixing this problem is anyone's guess. I first pointed out this error in 2006, and it's still not fixed, so for the time being, I'm coding the convenience constructor for two parameters instead of one. So, I've just shown you an example of using pl() to help troubleshoot a problem.

The second item to notice is the use of the following on line 85:

```
pragma autonomous_transaction;
```

This effectively executes method set_text() in its own session, so committing the inserted debugging information will not affect the transaction state in the calling program unit.

My next step is to test what I've coded. To do that, I actually have three listings. Listing 7-6 is a test unit for TYPE DEBUG.

Listing 7-6. Type DEBUG's Test Unit, ops.debug.sql

```
01  rem debug.sql
02  rem by Donald J. Bales on 2014-10-20
03  rem A test unit for type DEBUG
04
05  declare
06
07  begin
08    DEBUG.set_text('DEBUG.SQL', 'before the loop');
09    for i in 1..10 loop
10      DEBUG.set_text('DEBUG.SQL', 'loop '||to_char(i)||' before sleep');
11      SYS.DBMS_LOCK.sleep(3);
12      DEBUG.set_text('DEBUG.SQL', 'loop '||to_char(i)||' after sleep');
13    end loop;
14    DEBUG.set_text('DEBUG.SQL:', 'after the loop');
15  end;
16  /
```

When executed, Listing 7-6 will log debug messages to object table DEBUGS. But before you execute it, you may want to determine your session's unique ID so you can specify that value from a second session in order to filter the debug messages that appear as your program executes.

Listing 7-7 is a very short anonymous PL/SQL program to get your session's unique ID. Then when you want to see what's going on with the program from which you're debug logging, you can specify your first session's unique session ID on the SQL*Plus command line when you execute the SQL query from Listing 7-8.

Listing 7-7. An Example of How to Get Your Unique Session ID, usi.sql

```
1  rem usi.sql
2  rem by Donald J. Bales on 2014-10-20
3  rem Show me my unique session ID
4
5  execute pl('unique_session_id='||SYS.DBMS_SESSION.unique_session_id);
```

For example, if I execute usi.sql in SQL*Plus from my first session, session 1, it reports the following:

```
SQL> @usi.sql
```

```
unique_session_id= 000487240001
```

```
PL/SQL procedure successfully completed.
```

Next, I open a second session, session 2. I execute the following at the SQL> prompt:

```
@debug_a_session.sql 000487240001
```

Of course, I get no rows selected because I haven't started my test unit in session 1. So I go back to session 1 and execute the following at the SQL> prompt:

```
@debug.sql
```

Then I switch back to session 2 and simply type a forward slash at the SQL> prompt to see the PL/SQL program in session 1's progress:

```
SQL> @debug_a_session.sql 000487240001
```

```
old   4: where  unique_session_id = upper('&unique_session_id')
new   4: where  unique_session_id = upper('000487240001')
```

```
no rows selected
```

```
SQL> /
```

```
old   4: where  unique_session_id = upper('&unique_session_id')
new   4: where  unique_session_id = upper('000487240001')
```

```
        ID TEXT
---------- -------------------------------------------------
       203 before the loop
       204 loop 1 before sleep
       205 loop 1 after sleep
       206 loop 2 before sleep
```

```
SQL> /
```

```
old   4: where  unique_session_id = upper('&unique_session_id')
new   4: where  unique_session_id = upper('000487240001')
```

```
        ID TEXT
---------- ------------------------------------------------------------
       203 before the loop
       204 loop 1 before sleep
       205 loop 1 after sleep
       206 loop 2 before sleep
       207 loop 2 after sleep
       208 loop 3 before sleep
       209 loop 3 after sleep
       210 loop 4 before sleep
       211 loop 4 after sleep
       212 loop 5 before sleep
       213 loop 5 after sleep
       214 loop 6 before sleep

12 rows selected.
```

```
SQL> /
```

```
old    4: where  unique_session_id = upper('&unique_session_id')
new    4: where  unique_session_id = upper('000487240001')

        ID TEXT
---------- ------------------------------------------------------------
       203 before the loop
       204 loop 1 before sleep
       205 loop 1 after sleep
       206 loop 2 before sleep
       207 loop 2 after sleep
       208 loop 3 before sleep
       209 loop 3 after sleep
       210 loop 4 before sleep
       211 loop 4 after sleep
       212 loop 5 before sleep
       213 loop 5 after sleep
       214 loop 6 before sleep
       215 loop 6 after sleep
       216 loop 7 before sleep
       217 loop 7 after sleep
       218 loop 8 before sleep
       219 loop 8 after sleep
       220 loop 9 before sleep
       221 loop 9 after sleep
       222 loop 10 before sleep
       223 loop 10 after sleep
       224 after the loop

22 rows selected.
```

As you can see from the preceding output, I reexecuted the SQL SELECT statement three times (using the forward slash, /) during the 33 seconds it took to run the test unit, and I got more debug information as the program unit executed.

If you examine Listing 7-8, which I used to query the table DEBUGS, you can see that I am limiting the information to a specified unique session ID and for the last ten minutes (the expression (10/(24*60)) means ten minutes).

Listing 7-8. An Example of How to Check on Progress in Real Time, ops.debug_a_session.sql

```
01  rem debug_a_sesion.sql
02  rem by Donald J. Bales on 2014-10-20
03  rem Query DEBUGS uing the specified unique session ID
04
05  define unique_session_id=&1;
06
07  select id,
08         text
09  from   DEBUGS
10  where  unique_session_id = upper('&unique_session_id')
11  and    insert_date       > SYSDATE - (10/(24*60))
12  order by id;
```

A debug table can be very handy. It gives you the kind of information you get from put_line(), but as it happens. Now you can just add the following command to your code as needed:

```
DEBUG.set_text(<aiv_program_unit>, <aiv_text>);
```

However, you'll need to wrap set_text() in an IF statement if you want to turn it on or off as needed. I have a better solution. How about a debug package?

A DEBUGGER Package

I'm going to create a DEBUGGER package in order to extend the table DEBUGS and its underlying TYPE DEBUG's functionality. I have two methods that I wasn't able to add to TYPE DEBUG because there's no way to maintain temporary state in a TYPE's BODY. That's not the case for a package, so I'm going to create a "role" package DEBUGGER for table DEBUGS, which will implement methods disable(), enable(), and a conditional set_text().

Method enable() will add a specified program unit to a list of program units for which to log debug information to table DEBUGS. If a program calls DEBUGGER.enable(), passing its name, then any calls to DEBUGGER.set_text() will be logged to table DEBUGS. If a program doesn't enable debug logging, nothing will happen when it calls DEBUGGER.set_text(). Conversely, method DEBUGGER.disable() will remove a specified program unit from the "debug logging enabled" list. Listing 7-9 is the package specification, and Listing 7-10 is its corresponding package body.

Listing 7-9. A Role Package Specification for Object Table DEBUGS, ops.debugger.pks

```
01  create or replace package DEBUGGER as
02  /*
03  debugger.pks
04  by Donald J. Bales on 2014-10-20
05  Object Table DEBUGS's package
06  */
07
```

```
08   -- Disable debug logging for the specified program unit
09   PROCEDURE disable(
10   aiv_program_unit                 in      varchar2);
11
12   -- Enable debug logging for the specified program unit
13   PROCEDURE enable(
14   aiv_program_unit                 in      varchar2);
15
16   -- Conditionally log the debug information for the specified
17   -- program unit, if it is enabled
18   PROCEDURE set_text(
19   aiv_program_unit                 in      varchar2,
20   aiv_text                         in      DEBUGS.text%TYPE);
21
22
23   end DEBUGGER;
24   /
25   @se.sql DEBUGGER;
```

Listing 7-10. A Role Package Body for Object Table DEBUGS, ops.debugger.pkb

```
01   create or replace package body DEBUGGER as
02   /*
03   debugger.pkb
04   by Donald J. Bales on 2014-10-20
05   Object Table DEBUGS' package
06   */
07
08   -- Declare a table type and then table to hold the
09   -- enabled program units
10   TYPE program_unit_table is table of varchar2(1)
11   index by varchar2(30);
12
13   t_program_unit                       program_unit_table;
14
15
16   PROCEDURE disable(
17   aiv_program_unit            in      varchar2) is
18
19   v_program_unit                       varchar2(30);
20
21   begin
22     v_program_unit := upper(aiv_program_unit);
23
24     if t_program_unit.exists(v_program_unit) then
25       t_program_unit.delete(v_program_unit);
26     end if;
27   end disable;
28
29
30   PROCEDURE enable(
31   aiv_program_unit            in      varchar2) is
32
```

217

```
33  v_program_unit                              varchar2(30);
34
35  begin
36    v_program_unit := upper(aiv_program_unit);
37
38    if not t_program_unit.exists(v_program_unit) then
39      t_program_unit(v_program_unit) := NULL;
40    end if;
41  end enable;
42
43
44  PROCEDURE set_text(
45  aiv_program_unit              in      varchar2,
46  aiv_text                      in      DEBUGS.text%TYPE) is
47
48  v_program_unit                        varchar2(30);
49
50  begin
51    v_program_unit := upper(aiv_program_unit);
52
53    if t_program_unit.exists(v_program_unit) then
54      DEBUG.set_text(v_program_unit, aiv_text);
55    end if;
56  end set_text;
57
58
59  end DEBUGGER;
60  /
61  @be.sql DEBUGGER;
```

Let's take a detailed look at Listing 7-10:

- Lines 10 and 11 declare a PL/SQL table TYPE indexed by a varchar2. You can't do this with older versions of Oracle, but you can now. I'm taking advantage of that fact, so PL/SQL can do the work instead of me writing a lot more code.

- Line 13 declares an "enabled program unit list" table, which will temporarily hold a list of program units for which to log debug information to table DEBUGS.

- Lines 16 through 27 implement method disable(). This method looks to see if an entry exists in the "enabled program unit" PL/SQL table for the specified program unit. If it does exist, it deletes the PL/SQL table entry, effectively disabling debug logging for the specified program unit.

- Lines 30 through 41 implement the enable() method. This method looks to see if an entry exists in the "enabled program unit" PL/SQL table for the specified program unit. If it does not exist, the method adds an entry to the PL/SQL table, effectively enabling debug logging for the specified program unit.

- Lines 44 through 56 implement the set_text() method. This method simply calls the autonomous procedure set_text() in the underlying TYPE DEBUG if the program unit in question is enabled.

"Big deal—so what?" you say. The implications are staggering. You can add DEBUGGER.set_text() calls to your long-running or complicated PL/SQL programs and leave them there to be enabled as needed when trouble rears its ugly head!

Listing 7-11 is a test unit for package DEBUG_OTS that turns debug logging on then off, repeating the same test twice.

Listing 7-11. A Test Unit for Package DEBUGGER, ops.debugger.sql

```
01  rem debugger.sql
02  rem by Donald J. Bales on 2014-10-20
03  rem A test unit for package DEBUGGER
04
05  declare
06
07  begin
08    -- Enable debug output
09    DEBUGGER.enable('DEBUGGER.SQL');
10    -- Test
11    DEBUGGER.set_text('DEBUGGER.SQL', 'before the loop ');
12    for i in 1..10 loop
13      DEBUGGER.set_text('DEBUGGER.SQL', 'loop '||to_char(i)||' before sleep');
14      SYS.DBMS_LOCK.sleep(3);
15      DEBUGGER.set_text('DEBUGGER.SQL', 'loop '||to_char(i)||' after sleep');
16    end loop;
17    DEBUGGER.set_text('DEBUGGER.SQL', 'after the loop ');
18
19    -- Disable debug output
20    DEBUGGER.disable('DEBUGGER.SQL');
21    -- Test
22    DEBUGGER.set_text('DEBUGGER.SQL', 'before the loop ');
23    for i in 1..10 loop
24      DEBUGGER.set_text('DEBUGGER.SQL', 'loop '||to_char(i)||' before sleep');
25      -- SYS.DBMS_LOCK.sleep(3);
26      DEBUGGER.set_text('DEBUGGER.SQL', 'loop '||to_char(i)||' after sleep');
27    end loop;
28    DEBUGGER.set_text('DEBUGGER.SQL', 'after the loop ');
29  end;
30  /
```

Given that you have your unique session ID and start debugger.sql in session 1, and then switch to session 2 and query table DEBUGS with debug_a_session.sql, you'll see output like this:

```
SQL> @debug_a_session.sql 000487240001

old   4: where  unique_session_id = upper('&unique_session_id')
new   4: where  unique_session_id = upper('000487240001')

        ID TEXT
---------- -------------------------------------------------------
       225 before the loop
       226 loop 1 before sleep
       227 loop 1 after sleep
       228 loop 2 before sleep

4 rows selected.
```

```
SQL> /
```

```
old   4: where  unique_session_id = upper('&unique_session_id')
new   4: where  unique_session_id = upper('000487240001')

        ID TEXT
---------- --------------------------------------------------
       225 before the loop
       226 loop 1 before sleep
       227 loop 1 after sleep
       228 loop 2 before sleep
       229 loop 2 after sleep
       230 loop 3 before sleep
       231 loop 3 after sleep
       232 loop 4 before sleep
       233 loop 4 after sleep
       234 loop 5 before sleep
       235 loop 5 after sleep
       236 loop 6 before sleep
       237 loop 6 after sleep
       238 loop 7 before sleep
       239 loop 7 after sleep
       240 loop 8 before sleep
       241 loop 8 after sleep
       242 loop 9 before sleep
       243 loop 9 after sleep
       244 loop 10 before sleep
       245 loop 10 after sleep
       246 after the loop

22 rows selected.
```

In the preceding output, you see the first half of the test unit where the program unit was enabled, but not the second half of the program unit where it was disabled. This means you can turn debug logging on and off programmatically as needed. That's a powerful troubleshooting tool!

Now that you've seen me do the object-relational version, it's your turn to do the relational version.

It's Your Turn to Use Debug Logging

Your assignment is to create a relational debug table and table package that incorporate the same functionality as the object-relational example I just showed you. Yes, you should also include the test unit. Follow these steps.

1. Write a DDL script to create a relational table called DEBUGS with the same columns as the attributes found in TYPE DEBUG.

2. Save your script as rps.debugs.tab.

3. Create your table DEBUGS by executing script @rps.debugs.tab.

4. Write a DDL script to create a table package specification for DEBUG. You should have three methods: disable(), enable(), and set_text().

5.   Save your script as rps.debug.pks.

6.   Create your package specification by executing script @rps.debug.pks.

7.   Write a DDL script to create a table package body for DEBUG. Remember to use the pragma autonomous_transaction; in set_text()!

8.   Save your script as rps.debug.pkb.

9.   Create your package body by executing script @rps.debug.pkb.

10. Write a test unit for package DEBUG, saving your script as rps.debug.sql.

11. Open two SQL*Plus sessions. Get the unique session ID from the first session by executing script usi.sql. Then start your test unit in the first session by executing script @rps.debug.sql.

12. Quickly switch to session 2, and then execute a SELECT statement against table DEBUGS so you can see the output of your test unit as it executes.

Listings 7-12 through 7-15 are my solution to this exercise. Listing 7-12 is a script to create a relational table for debug logging output.

Listing 7-12. A DDL Script to Create Table DEBUGS, rps.debugs.tab

```
01  rem debugs.tab
02  rem by Donald Bales on 2014-10-20
03  rem Create debugging message table
04
05  --drop    table DEBUGS;
06  create table DEBUGS (
07  id                              number                          not null,
08  text                            varchar2(256),
09  unique_session_id               varchar2(24)                    not null,
10  insert_user                     varchar2(30)  default USER      not null,
11  insert_date                     date          default SYSDATE   not null );
12
13  alter   table DEBUGS add
14  constraint   DEBUGS_PK
15  primary key (
16  id )
17  using index;
18
19  --drop    sequence DEBUGS_ID;
20  create sequence DEBUGS_ID
21  start with 1 order;
22
23  execute SYS.DBMS_STATS.gather_table_stats(USER, 'DEBUGS');
24
25  grant all on DEBUGS to PUBLIC;
```

Listing 7-13 is the specification for the table package for table DEBUG. I've declared three methods: disable(), enable(), and conditional set_text().

Listing 7-13. A DDL Script to Create Table Package Spec DEBUG, rps.debug.pks

```
01  create or replace package DEBUG as
02  /*
03  debug.pks
04  by Donald J. Bales on 2014-10-20
05  Table DEBUGS's package
06  */
07
08  n_id                                  number := 0;
09
10  -- Get the next primary key value for the table
11  FUNCTION get_id
12  return                                DEBUGS.id%TYPE;
13
14  -- Enable debug output for the specified program unit
15  PROCEDURE enable(
16  aiv_program_unit            in      varchar2);
17
18  -- Disable debug output for the specified program unit
19  PROCEDURE disable(
20  aiv_program_unit            in      varchar2);
21
22  -- Log debug output if enabled for the specified program unit
23  PROCEDURE set_text(
24  aiv_program_unit            in      varchar2,
25  aiv_text                    in      DEBUGS.text%TYPE);
26
27
28  end DEBUG;
29  /
30  @se.sql DEBUG
```

Listing 7-14 is the body for table package DEBUG. In it, I've declared a PL/SQL table TYPE and PL/SQL table to hold the "enabled program units," and then implemented methods disable(), enable(), and set_text().

Listing 7-14. A DDL Script to Create Table Package Body DEBUG, rps.debug.pkb

```
01  create or replace package body DEBUG as
02  /*
03  debug.pkb
04  by Donald J. Bales on 2014-10-20
05  Table DEBUGS's package
06  */
07
08  -- A table to hold the list of program units for which
09  -- to store debug information
10  TYPE program_unit_table is table of varchar2(1)
11  index by varchar2(30);
12
```

```
13   t_program_unit                          program_unit_table;
14
15
16   FUNCTION get_id
17   return                                  DEBUGS.id%TYPE is
18
19   n_id                                    DEBUGS.id%TYPE;
20
21   begin
22     select DEBUGS_ID.nextval
23     into    n_id
24     from    SYS.DUAL;
25
26     return n_id;
27   end get_id;
28
29
30   PROCEDURE disable(
31   aiv_program_unit             in      varchar2) is
32
33   v_program_unit                     varchar2(30);
34
35   begin
36     v_program_unit := upper(aiv_program_unit);
37
38     if t_program_unit.exists(v_program_unit) then
39       t_program_unit.delete(v_program_unit);
40     end if;
41   end disable;
42
43
44   PROCEDURE enable(
45   aiv_program_unit             in      varchar2) is
46
47   v_program_unit                     varchar2(30);
48
49   begin
50     v_program_unit := upper(aiv_program_unit);
51
52     if not t_program_unit.exists(v_program_unit) then
53       t_program_unit(v_program_unit) := NULL;
54     end if;
55   end enable;
56
57
58   PROCEDURE set_text(
59   aiv_program_unit             in      varchar2,
60   aiv_text                     in      DEBUGS.text%TYPE) is
61
62   pragma autonomous_transaction;
63
```

```
64  v_program_unit                              varchar2(30);
65
66  begin
67    v_program_unit := upper(aiv_program_unit);
68
69    if t_program_unit.exists(v_program_unit) then
70      insert into DEBUGS (
71              id,
72              text,
73              unique_session_id )
74      values (
75              DEBUG.get_id(),
76              substrb(v_program_unit||': '||aiv_text, 1, 256),
77              SYS.DBMS_SESSION.unique_session_id);
78    end if;
79    commit;
80  end set_text;
81
82
83  end DEBUG;
84  /
85  @be.sql DEBUG
```

In Listing 7-14, method set_text() logs information to table DEBUGS only if the specified program unit is "enabled." Listing 7-15 is a test unit for table package DEBUG.

Listing 7-15. An Anonymous PL/SQL Script to Test Table Package DEBUG, rps.debug.sql

```
01  rem debug.sql
02  rem by Donald J. Bales on 2014-10-20
03  rem Test unit for package DEBUG
04
05  declare
06
07  v_program_unit                              varchar2(30) :=
08    'debug.sql';
09
10  begin
11    DEBUG.enable(v_program_unit);
12    DEBUG.set_text(v_program_unit, 'before the loop ');
13    for i in 1..1000 loop
14      DEBUG.set_text(v_program_unit, 'loop '||to_char(i)||' before sleep');
15      SYS.DBMS_LOCK.sleep(3);
16      DEBUG.set_text(v_program_unit, 'loop '||to_char(i)||' after sleep');
17    end loop;
18    DEBUG.set_text(v_program_unit, 'after the loop ');
19    DEBUG.disable(v_program_unit);
20    DEBUG.set_text(v_program_unit, 'before the loop ');
21    for i in 1..1000 loop
```

```
22      DEBUG.set_text(v_program_unit, 'loop '||to_char(i)||' before sleep');
23      -- SYS.DBMS_LOCK.sleep(3);
24      DEBUG.set_text(v_program_unit, 'loop '||to_char(i)||' after sleep');
25    end loop;
26    DEBUG.set_text(v_program_unit, 'after the loop ');
27  end;
28  /
```

The following is the output from a query against the debug table DEBUGS:

```
SQL> select * from debugs;

        ID TEXT
---------- ------------------------------------------------
       313 debug.sql: before the loop
       314 debug.sql: loop 1 before sleep
       315 debug.sql: loop 1 after sleep
       316 debug.sql: loop 2 before sleep


SQL> /

        ID TEXT
---------- ------------------------------------------------
       313 debug.sql: before the loop
       314 debug.sql: loop 1 before sleep
       315 debug.sql: loop 1 after sleep
       316 debug.sql: loop 2 before sleep


SQL> /

        ID TEXT
---------- ------------------------------------------------
       313 debug.sql: before the loop
       314 debug.sql: loop 1 before sleep
       315 debug.sql: loop 1 after sleep
       316 debug.sql: loop 2 before sleep
       317 debug.sql: loop 2 after sleep
       318 debug.sql: loop 3 before sleep
       319 debug.sql: loop 3 after sleep
       320 debug.sql: loop 4 before sleep
       321 debug.sql: loop 4 after sleep
       322 debug.sql: loop 5 before sleep
       323 debug.sql: loop 5 after sleep
       324 debug.sql: loop 6 before sleep

12 rows selected.
```

```
SQL> /

        ID TEXT
---------- -------------------------------------------------
       313 debug.sql: before the loop
       314 debug.sql: loop 1 before sleep
       315 debug.sql: loop 1 after sleep
       316 debug.sql: loop 2 before sleep
       317 debug.sql: loop 2 after sleep
       318 debug.sql: loop 3 before sleep
       319 debug.sql: loop 3 after sleep
       320 debug.sql: loop 4 before sleep
       321 debug.sql: loop 4 after sleep
       322 debug.sql: loop 5 before sleep
       323 debug.sql: loop 5 after sleep
       324 debug.sql: loop 6 before sleep
       325 debug.sql: loop 6 after sleep
       326 debug.sql: loop 7 before sleep
       327 debug.sql: loop 7 after sleep
       328 debug.sql: loop 8 before sleep
       329 debug.sql: loop 8 after sleep
       330 debug.sql: loop 9 before sleep
       331 debug.sql: loop 9 after sleep
       332 debug.sql: loop 10 before sleep
       333 debug.sql: loop 10 after sleep
       334 debug.sql: after the loop

22 rows selected.
```

As you can see from this output, you are able to view the progress of the test unit as it executes. Armed with this troubleshooting tool, you can monitor your long-running or short-running data processing or data migration programs.

In practice, I've even found this technique useful in some table package or TYPE methods that are called by the presentation layer. One example is when I worked with a table package that built SQL statements dynamically using information from the database, and then passed them back to the presentation layer. If a user got an error, I could see what SQL was passed back to his web page by looking in the debug table in the database. It didn't take long for me to figure out that I had some data-entry errors in the tables used to build the dynamic queries, but it would have been next to impossible to identify the problem in the presentation layer.

As an alternative to debug logging, you may decide to use package SYS.DBMS_TRACE to trace the execution of a session to a file that you can later examine, line by line, or using a utility like TKPROF. However, I've found that DBMS_TRACE creates too much information to be useful. With it, you have limited control of the volume of information collected. In contrast, with a debug logging utility, you determine what information is logged and when.

Another alternative package you may want to investigate is SYS.DBMS_ERRLOG. With this package, you can write debug information to a table anytime an exception occurs in your PL/SQL program unit. I still find the use of my "homegrown" debug logging to be more useful.

Debug logging is a good tool, but in some situations, a real debugging tool is more appropriate. Let's look at Oracle's debugger next.

One Step at a Time

After what seemed an eternity, PL/SQL programmers now have a real, honest-to-goodness debugger. What's a debugger? It allows you to step through your PL/SQL code as it executes, one step at a time, line by line, inspecting the value of variables, and seeing how your program executes your logic. It's a remote debugger—remote in the fact that your PL/SQL program unit must be stored in the database, and it must be executable. By "executable," I mean it must be a stored function, procedure, or packaged function or procedure.

So how did this revolution come about? It started with a PL/SQL package called SYS.DBMS_DEBUG. Oracle database PL/SQL package DBMS_DEBUG provides communication hooks into the PL/SQL debugger layer in the database. Using this package, you can build your own remote debugger, but it's much easier to use Oracle SQL Developer.

Debugging with Oracle SQL Developer

Oracle SQL Developer is an SQL and PL/SQL development tool for the Oracle database. You can download a free copy from the Oracle Technology Network site, http://otn.oracle.com.

I'm not going to give you a lesson on how to use Oracle SQL Developer here, because that would be a book in itself, but I will show you some highlights to debugging with it.

Your first step in using a remote debugger with Oracle is to grant debugging rights to the username for which you intend to debug a stored program unit. That's done by the system administrator or DBA using the following syntax:

```
grant debug connect session to <username>;
grant debug any procedure to <username>;
```

where <username> is the name of the user for which to grant the debug privileges.

Your next step is to recompile the stored program units in question with the DEBUG option, using the appropriate syntax for the object type from the following list:

```
alter function  <name> compile debug;
alter package   <name> compile debug package;
alter package   <name> compile debug specification;
alter package   <name> compile debug body;
alter procedure <name> compile debug;
alter trigger   <name> compile debug;
alter type      <name> compile debug specification;
alter type      <name> compile debug body;
```

Alternatively, you can recompile the code from Oracle SQL Developer! Let me show you an example of debugging (of all things) the DEBUG TYPE and the DEBUGGER package. In this example, I've already started Oracle SQL Developer and logged in to database ORCL, where, incidentally, I have already granted debug connect session and debug any procedure rights to the username.

In Figure 7-1, I used the tree view on the left side of the screen to drill down and select the BODY for TYPE DEBUG. From there, I right-clicked and chose Edit. That action displayed the tab DEBUG Body, where I subsequently added a breakpoint to the constructor.

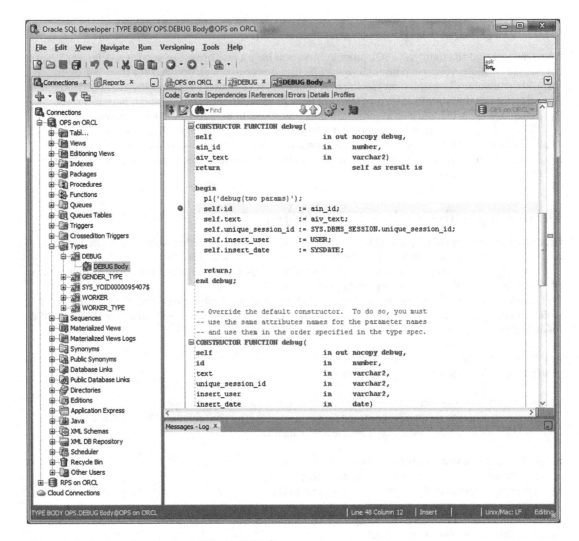

Figure 7-1. *Setting a breakpoint in TYPE DEBUG's constructor*

In Figure 7-2, I used the tree view to find the package body for DEBUGGER. Next, I right-clicked and selected Edit. That action displayed the tab DEBUGGER Body, where I added a breakpoint for procedure set_text(). Then I clicked the icon to recompile the item with debug.

Figure 7-2. Setting a breakpoint in package body method DEBUGGER.set_text( )

At this point, I've set two breakpoints: one in TYPE DEBUG's constructor and a second in package body DEBUGGER's set_text() method. Now when I execute a program unit that calls either DEBUG's constructor or DEBUGGER.set_text(), the debugger will stop execution so I can inspect variable values or single-step through each line of code.

My next task is to select an executable target and then debug it. That's what I did in Figure 7-3. Once again, I used the tree view to select the package specification for DEBUGGER. Then I right-clicked and selected Edit. That action displayed the tab DEBUGGER. From there, I clicked the debug icon. Since I'm in a package specification, the target is runnable, so Oracle SQL Developer prompts me for an anonymous procedure that I can use to execute the target.

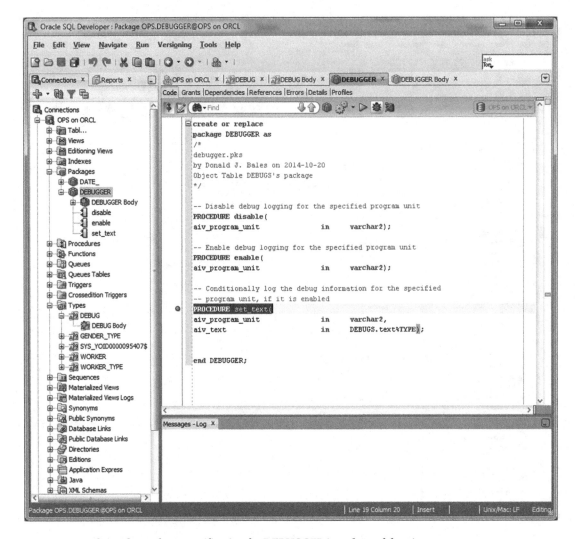

Figure 7-3. *Editing the package specification for DEBUGGER in order to debug it*

When I clicked the debug icon in Figure 7-3, the Debug PL/SQL dialog box appeared, as shown in Figure 7-4. Here, I selected the target method to debug—in this case, set_text. Next, I needed to modify the anonymous PL/SQL procedure stub presented by Oracle SQL Developer or select one from the file system by clicking the From File button. Since I already had a test unit script written, ops.debug.sql, I selected it from the file system, deleted the remark lines and the trailing compile slash, and then clicked the OK button to start the procedure, thus starting the debugging session.

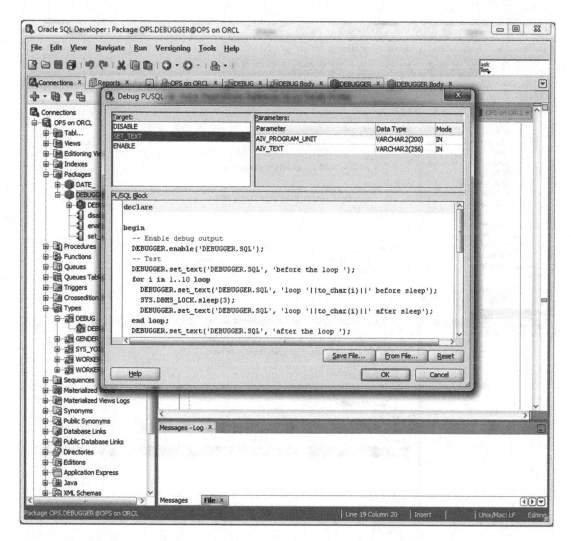

Figure 7-4. *Specifying the anonymous PL/SQL script to execute the runnable target*

In Figure 7-5, the debugger stopped the execution of the program when it encountered the breakpoint set on method set_text(). From there, I clicked the Step Into icon in order to execute the code line by line. In the lower-right corner of the screen, you can see the value of variable v_program_unit because I set up a watch on that variable.

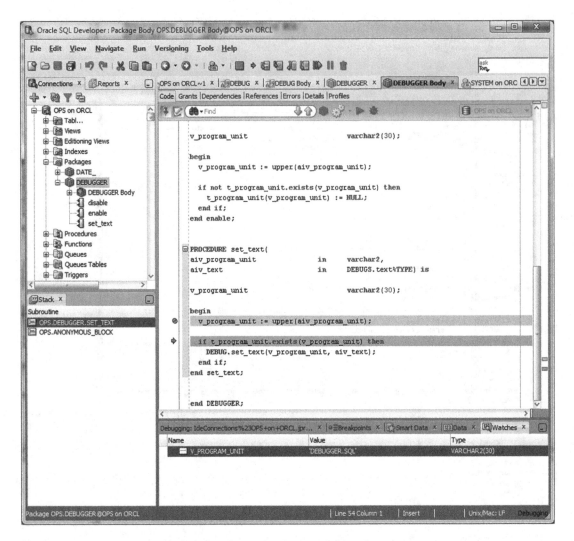

Figure 7-5. *Stepping into code after a breakpoint has been encountered*

As you can see from this short example, you have total access to both the values of variables and how program logic is being executed when you're in a debugger. This is the ultimate troubleshooting tool. Or is it?

For a simple troubleshooting task, you are probably better off using put_line(). For a long-running program unit, you're probably better off using debug logging. Then once you've narrowed down the problem, if you haven't already solved it, you may want to use a debugger. Why?

Using a debugger requires a great deal of setup, arranging access to the username of the stored program unit, grants for debugging, and the creation of an access control list. And it can take a lot of time to use for the simple fact that stepping through a program line by line can be extremely time-consuming. It's up to you to use the appropriate tool at the appropriate time.

Debugging Anonymous PL/SQL

So far, I've been talking only about debugging stored program units. What about anonymous PL/SQL procedures? Sorry, you cannot debug anonymous PL/SQL program units. And that should not be a big deal. If you have an anonymous PL/SQL program that's so big that it needs debugging, it probably needs to be permanently stored in the database. Once you store it in the database, you can use Oracle SQL Developer to debug it.

Debugging with TOAD for Oracle

TOAD for Oracle is a very popular SQL and PL/SQL development tool by Quest Software. There's a freeware version available for download from Dell (formerly Quest Software) at http://software.dell.com/products/toad-for-oracle/. However, the free version does not include debugging capability. To get a copy of TOAD with a debugger, you must download the trial version. The TOAD debugger has almost the same set of debugging features as Oracle SQL Developer, but I prefer Oracle SQL Developer.

Debugging with Visual Studio

Oracle has a plug-in module that allows you to use the remote debugger from Microsoft's Visual Studio. Once again, you can download this plug-in from Oracle's Technology Network web site at http://otn.oracle.com.

It's Your Turn to Use a Debugger

I know I haven't taken the time to show you how to use the PL/SQL debugger; I've only walked through an example. As a professional, it will be invaluable for you to know how to use the PL/SQL debugger. So, follow these somewhat loosely defined steps to install the PL/SQL debugger and get some experience using it.

1. Go to http://otn.oracle.com and search for "Oracle SQL Developer download." This should bring you to the Oracle SQL Developer page, where you can download a copy of the software, get its installation instructions, and access tutorials for using the product.

2. Download Oracle SQL Developer.

3. Print a copy of the tutorials "Creating a database connection" and "Loading, executing and debugging PL/SQL."

4. Install Oracle SQL Developer.

5. Run Oracle SQL Developer and create a connection to the database you're using for username RPS for working on your exercises.

6. Using the "Loading, executing and debugging PL/SQL" tutorial as your guide, find table package DEBUG in the tree view.

7. Edit the package body by right-clicking its name in the tree view, and then recompile it with debug.

8. Create breakpoints in DEBUG's three methods: disable(), enable(), and set_text().

9. Edit the package specification, and click the ladybug icon to run the debugger.

10. When the Debug PL/SQL dialog box appears, click the From File button, and then load your test unit script, `rps.debug.sql`.

11. Remove the comment lines at the top of test unit script and the trailing compile slash at the end of the script, and then click OK to start your debug session.

12. After the first breakpoint is triggered, click the Step Into icon to walk through the code line by line.

13. Add some watches so you can see the variable's values change as the program executes.

14. Sit back and think how helpful this tool can be in your future.

At this point, you should now have three tools in your troubleshooting arsenal: `put_line()`, table package `DEBUG`, and a real live debugger! With these tools, you should be able to troubleshoot any logic problem, but what about performance?

If you have a long-running or large stored procedure, how do you know where in its code it's slow? You can get this information with runtime profiling, our next topic.

Profiling PL/SQL

Profiling in this context is about collecting runtime statistics from your PL/SQL program units in order to determine which lines of code are consuming the most resources, usually in a unit of time. Armed with these statistics, you can quickly see what part of your PL/SQL program is taking the most time to execute, so you can concentrate your efforts on improving performance on those lines of code that are poor performers.

In days of yore, you had to write your own profiling package in order to collect runtime statistics. Then you had to sprinkle your code with calls to your profiling package in order to collect the statistics. In fact, I did just that, creating a profiling package with architecture similar to the debug logging package.

Nowadays, you have access to a built-in profiling package, `SYS.DBMS_PROFILER`, which can hook itself into you session and profile your PL/SQL code line by line, without you needing to add many lines of code to your listings. Here, you'll look at the three tables where `DBMS_PROFILER` stores its collected statistics, the package's methods, and an example of its use. Then you'll finish up this section by profiling your own code.

Profiler's Tables

The profiling package `DBMS_PROFILER` stores the statistics it collects during its use in memory, until you call its `flush_data()` method, at which point it moves the statistics to three tables:

- `PLSQL_PROFILER_RUNS`: Holds information about a particular run

- `PLSQL_PROFILER_UNITS`: Holds the names of program units for a particular run

- `PLSQL_PROFILE_DATA`: Holds the profiling statistics for every line of each program unit accessed in a particular run

Your Oracle system administrator or DBA must create these tables globally using the profload.sql script, or in the schema you're logged in to using the proftab.sql script, before you try to use the profiler. In addition, you must have the same rights granted to your username as you need for debugging.

You can find detailed information about the `DBMS_PROFILER` package and these three tables in Oracle's *PL/SQL Packages and Types Reference*. Let's look at the package's methods next.

Profiler's Methods

The DBMS_PROFILER package has seven methods, of which you must use at least three to profile an application. Here are the three I am referring to:

- start_profiler(): Initializes and starts a profiling "run" in order to collect statistics. You can specify a description for the run so you can identify the run number after the run, or you can use an overloaded version of the method that returns the run number when you start the run.

- stop_profile(): Stops a previously started run.

- flush_data(): Stores the statistics for the current run into three tables: PLSQL_PROFILER_RUNS, PLSQL_PROFILER_UNITS, and PLSQL_PROFILER_DATA.

To start a profiling session, you need to execute procedure start_profiler() in your PL/SQL program unit where you want to start collecting performance statistics. To stop collecting statistics, you need to execute stop_profile(), usually followed by flush_data(), in order to permanently store the statistics in the profiler's tables.

Listing 7-16 is a SQL*Plus script that can run any anonymous PL/SQL script with profiling turned on.

Listing 7-16. A Script to Execute Another Script with Profiling, run_profile.sql

```
01   rem run_profile.sql
02   rem by Donald J. Bales on 2014-10-20
03   rem Capture DBMS_PROFILER information for the specified script
04
05   define script="&1";
06
07   set verify off;
08
09   declare
10
11   n_run_number                          number;
12
13   begin
14     DBMS_PROFILER.start_profiler(
15       '&script'||' on '||to_char(SYSDATE, 'YYYYMMDD HH24MISS'),
16       ' ',
17       n_run_number);
18
19     pl('DBMS_PROFILER run_number = '||to_char(n_run_number));
20   end;
21   /
22
23   @&script
24
25   execute DBMS_PROFILER.stop_profiler;
26   execute DBMS_PROFILER.flush_data;
27
28   set verify on;
```

To execute the script, type the name of the script in Listing 7-16 followed by the name of the script you wish to execute after the SQL*Plus prompt, as follows:

```
SQL> @run_profile.sql <script_name>
```

For example, to profile TYPE DEBUG and role package DEBUGGER, I first log in with username OPS, create the profiler tables by executing script C:\oracle12c\product\12.1.0\dbhome_1\RDBMS\ADMIN\proftab.sql, and then execute the script run_profile.sql, passing in the name of my test unit script, ops.debugger.sql:

```
SQL> @run_profile.sql ops.debugger.sql
```

Here's the output from executing the script in SQL*Plus:

```
SQL> @run_profile ops.debugger.sql


DBMS_PROFILER run_number = 4

PL/SQL procedure successfully completed.

PL/SQL procedure successfully completed.

PL/SQL procedure successfully completed.

PL/SQL procedure successfully completed.
```

run_profile.sql displays the run number for a profile run on the screen, so you can then run a report to view the profiling data.

Profiling Reports

I find two profiling reports helpful: one to display the average percent of processing time in descending order, and another to order average time consumption by program unit and line number. The SQL*Plus script avg_profile.sql, shown in Listing 7-17, displays what percent of processing time was consumed by each program unit and line of code, in the descending order of time consumption.

Listing 7-17. A Script to Create an Average Percent Profiling Report, avg_profile.sql

```
01   rem avg_profile.sql
02   rem by Donald J. Bales on 2014-10-20
03   rem Create a DBMS_PROFILER report by avg desc
04
05   define runid="&1";
06
07   column avg_pct    format 990.99;
08   column line#      format 9999;
09   column occur      format 9999
10   column text       format a42 trunc;
11   column unit_name  format a11;
12
13   set linesize  1000;
```

```
14   set newpage   1;
15   set pagesize  32767;
16   set trimspool on;
17   set verify    off;
18
19   spool avg_profile_&runid..txt;
20
21   select v.unit_name,
22          round(v.avg_time/t.avg_time*100, 2) avg_pct,
23          v.occur,
24          v.line#,
25          ltrim(s.text) text
26   from   SYS.ALL_SOURCE s,
27        ( select u.runid,
28                 u.unit_owner,
29                 u.unit_type,
30                 u.unit_name,
31                 d.min_time,
32                 to_number(decode(d.total_occur,
33                   NULL, NULL,
34                   0,    0,
35                   round(d.total_time/d.total_occur))) avg_time,
36                 d.max_time,
37                 d.total_time,
38                 d.total_occur occur,
39                 d.line#
40          from   PLSQL_PROFILER_UNITS u,
41                 PLSQL_PROFILER_DATA d
42          where  u.runid       = d.runid
43          and    u.unit_number = d.unit_number
44          and    d.runid       = &runid ) v,
45        ( select sum(to_number(decode(d.total_occur,
46                   NULL, NULL,
47                   0,    0,
48                   round(d.total_time/d.total_occur)))) avg_time
49          from   PLSQL_PROFILER_UNITS u,
50                 PLSQL_PROFILER_DATA d
51          where  u.runid       = d.runid
52          and    u.unit_number = d.unit_number
53          and    d.runid       = &runid ) t
54   where  v.unit_owner  = s.owner(+)
55   and    v.unit_type   = s.type(+)
56   and    v.unit_name   = s.name(+)
57   and    v.line#       = s.line(+)
58   and    v.avg_time    > 0
59   order by v.avg_time desc,
60          v.unit_name,
61          v.line#;
62
63   spool off;
64
65   set verify on;
```

The avg_profile.sql script produces a report that shows the following information:

- The program unit's name

- Its average consumption of time

- How many times the line was executed during the run

- The line number and text from the PL/SQL program unit in question

Listing 7-18 is an example of a report created by avg_profile.sql from Listing 7-17.

Listing 7-18. An Average Percent Time Consumption Report for Test Unit ops.debugger.sql

```
UNIT_NAME    AVG_PCT OCCUR LINE# TEXT
-----------  ------- ----- ----- ------------------------------------------
DEBUG         39.72    22    92 insert into DEBUGS
DEBUG         15.28    22    97 commit;
<anonymous>    9.53     2     1
<anonymous>    6.57     1     5
<anonymous>    6.11    18     1
<anonymous>    5.06     1    11
<anonymous>    1.56     2     1
<anonymous>    1.28    10    11
DEBUGGER       0.97     1    36 v_program_unit := upper(aiv_program_unit);
DEBUG          0.86   132    46 pl('debug(two params)');
<anonymous>    0.83    10     9
DEBUG          0.82   132    49 self.unique_session_id := SYS.DBMS_SESSION
DEBUG          0.80   132    50 self.insert_user       := USER;
<anonymous>    0.75    10    10
PL             0.75   133    11 SYS.DBMS_OUTPUT.put_line(aiv_text);
DEBUG          0.65   132    53 return;
DEBUG          0.62    22    89 begin
DEBUG          0.59    22    90 v_text := substrb(aiv_program_unit||': '||
DEBUGGER       0.54     1    25 t_program_unit.delete(v_program_unit);
DEBUG          0.46    22    98 end set_text;
DEBUGGER       0.43     1    30 PROCEDURE enable(
DEBUGGER       0.43     1    39 t_program_unit(v_program_unit) := NULL;
DEBUGGER       0.40    22    54 DEBUG.set_text(v_program_unit, aiv_text);
DEBUG          0.34   132    39 CONSTRUCTOR FUNCTION debug(
DEBUGGER       0.32     1    22 v_program_unit := upper(aiv_program_unit);
DEBUGGER       0.32     1    38 if not t_program_unit.exists(v_program_uni
DEBUGGER       0.32    44    51 v_program_unit := upper(aiv_program_unit);
DEBUG          0.28    22    81 STATIC PROCEDURE set_text(
DEBUGGER       0.28    44    44 PROCEDURE set_text(
DEBUGGER       0.25    44    53 if t_program_unit.exists(v_program_unit) t
DEBUG          0.24   132    51 self.insert_date       := SYSDATE;
<anonymous>    0.23    10    20
<anonymous>    0.22     1    16
<anonymous>    0.22     1    18
<anonymous>    0.22     1    25
DEBUGGER       0.22     1    16 PROCEDURE disable(
DEBUGGER       0.22     1    24 if t_program_unit.exists(v_program_unit) t
DEBUG          0.20   132    54 end debug;
```

```
DEBUG           0.16   132   47 self.id                  := ain_id;
<anonymous>     0.13    10   22
<anonymous>     0.11     1    7
<anonymous>     0.11     1   12
<anonymous>     0.11     1   13
DEBUGGER        0.11     1   27 end disable;
DEBUGGER        0.11     1   41 end enable;
<anonymous>     0.09    11    8
PL              0.08   133   12 end pl;
DEBUGGER        0.05    44   56 end set_text;
DEBUG           0.05   132   48 self.text                := aiv_text;
<anonymous>     0.04    11   19
```

```
50 rows selected.
```

Looking at Listing 7-18, it's easy to see that the bulk of time consumption is taken by the INSERT statement. This is typical. The slowest portion of any PL/SQL procedure is usually one or more SQL statements. That's why it's important to always maximize the efficiency of your SQL statements. You'll learn about one of the tools you can use to do that shortly, in the section about EXPLAIN PLAN. For now, it's important for you to understand just how valuable this report is when considering how to approach performance enhancements to your PL/SQL program units. With data like this, you can significantly narrow down the lines of code for which you need to improve performance, and not waste a lot of time guessing which ones are the poor performers.

A second report I like to use orders the average time consumption by program unit and line number. The script I execute for this report is named ord_profile.sql (you can find the listing for this report in the downloadable source code for the book). Just as with avg_profile.sql, you execute the script at the SQL*Plus prompt, passing in the run number as a parameter. Here's an example:

```
SQL> @ord_profile.sql 4
```

This command produced the report example shown in Listing 7-19. This report is helpful because it shows which lines in your program were actually executed. And even more interesting, you can add up the statistics for a function or procedure call by totaling the statistics from the line where the method is defined down to the line where it ends. For example, doing this for the constructor debug in Listing 7-19, you can calculate that it consumed 38,265 nanoseconds of processing time.

Listing 7-19. An Average Time Consumption Report by Program Unit and Line Number for Test Unit ops.debugger.sql

```
UNIT_NAME      AVG_TIME OCCUR LINE# TEXT
------------- --------- ----- ----- ----------------------------------------
<anonymous>      14497     2     1
<anonymous>      56766    18     1
<anonymous>          0     0     1
<anonymous>      88482     2     1
<anonymous>          0     0     1
<anonymous>      60987     1     5
<anonymous>          0     0     6
<anonymous>        999     1     7
<anonymous>        818    11     8
<anonymous>       7698    10     9
<anonymous>       6999    10    10
```

<anonymous>	11898	10	11
<anonymous>	46990	1	11
<anonymous>	999	1	12
<anonymous>	999	1	13
<anonymous>	1999	1	16
<anonymous>	1999	1	18
<anonymous>	364	11	19
<anonymous>	2100	10	20
<anonymous>	1200	10	22
<anonymous>	0	1	24
<anonymous>	1999	1	25
DEBUG	0	0	9 STATIC FUNCTION get_id
DEBUG	0	0	14 begin
DEBUG	0	0	15 select DEBUGS_ID.nextval
DEBUG	0	0	19 return n_id;
DEBUG	0	0	20 end get_id;
DEBUG	0	0	23 CONSTRUCTOR FUNCTION debug(
DEBUG	0	0	27 begin
DEBUG	0	0	28 pl('debug(zero param)');
DEBUG	0	0	29 self.id := NULL;
DEBUG	0	0	30 self.text := NULL;
DEBUG	0	0	31 self.unique_session_id := NULL;
DEBUG	0	0	32 self.insert_user := NULL;
DEBUG	0	0	33 self.insert_date := NULL;
DEBUG	0	0	35 return;
DEBUG	0	0	36 end debug;
DEBUG	3174	132	39 CONSTRUCTOR FUNCTION debug(
DEBUG	0	132	45 begin
DEBUG	8029	132	46 pl('debug(two params)');
DEBUG	1469	132	47 self.id := ain_id;
DEBUG	477	132	48 self.text := aiv_text;
DEBUG	7604	132	49 self.unique_session_id := SYS.DBMS_SESSI
DEBUG	7445	132	50 self.insert_user := USER;
DEBUG	2197	132	51 self.insert_date := SYSDATE;
DEBUG	6037	132	53 return;
DEBUG	1833	132	54 end debug;
DEBUG	0	0	60 CONSTRUCTOR FUNCTION debug(
DEBUG	0	0	69 begin
DEBUG	0	0	70 pl('debug(five params)');
DEBUG	0	0	71 self.id := id;
DEBUG	0	0	72 self.text := text;
DEBUG	0	0	73 self.unique_session_id := unique_session
DEBUG	0	0	74 self.insert_user := insert_user;
DEBUG	0	0	75 self.insert_date := insert_date;
DEBUG	0	0	77 return;
DEBUG	0	0	78 end debug;
DEBUG	2636	22	81 STATIC PROCEDURE set_text(
DEBUG	5726	22	89 begin
DEBUG	5453	22	90 v_text := substrb(aiv_program_unit||': '
DEBUG	368832	22	92 insert into DEBUGS
DEBUG	141880	22	97 commit;

```
DEBUG         4226    22    98 end set_text;
DEBUG            0     0   101 MAP MEMBER FUNCTION to_map
DEBUG            0     0   104 begin
DEBUG            0     0   105 return id;
DEBUG            0     0   106 end to_map;
DEBUGGER         0     0     1 package body DEBUGGER as
DEBUGGER      1999     1    16 PROCEDURE disable(
DEBUGGER         0     1    21 begin
DEBUGGER      2999     1    22 v_program_unit := upper(aiv_program_unit
DEBUGGER      1999     1    24 if t_program_unit.exists(v_program_unit)
DEBUGGER      4998     1    25 t_program_unit.delete(v_program_unit);
DEBUGGER         0     1    26 end if;
DEBUGGER       999     1    27 end disable;
DEBUGGER      3999     1    30 PROCEDURE enable(
DEBUGGER         0     1    35 begin
DEBUGGER      8998     1    36 v_program_unit := upper(aiv_program_unit
DEBUGGER      2999     1    38 if not t_program_unit.exists(v_program_u
DEBUGGER      3999     1    39 t_program_unit(v_program_unit) := NULL;
DEBUGGER         0     1    40 end if;
DEBUGGER       999     1    41 end enable;
DEBUGGER      2636    44    44 PROCEDURE set_text(
DEBUGGER         0    44    50 begin
DEBUGGER      2931    44    51 v_program_unit := upper(aiv_program_unit
DEBUGGER      2363    44    53 if t_program_unit.exists(v_program_unit)
DEBUGGER      3726    22    54 DEBUG.set_text(v_program_unit, aiv_text)
DEBUGGER         0    44    55 end if;
DEBUGGER       500    44    56 end set_text;
DEBUGGER         0     0    59 end DEBUGGER;
PL               0     0     1 PROCEDURE pl(
PL            6953   133    11 SYS.DBMS_OUTPUT.put_line(aiv_text);
PL             729   133    12 end pl;
```

93 rows selected.

Utilizing the statistics provided by DBMS_PROFILER, you can easily determine any bottlenecks in your PL/SQL programs and approach performance tuning in an efficient manner. DBMS_PROFILER data can also be used to detect defects in your code, in a fashion similar to debug logging.

Did you notice that, in both reports, the constructor for DEBUG was called 132 times, yet the INSERT statement was executed only 22 times? That means that SQL executed the constructor six times during each insert, clearly a defect in the SQL layer of the database, and subsequently a performance problem.

Now that I've profiled the object-relational version of the debug logger, it's your turn to profile the relational version.

It's Your Turn to Profile

The value of profiling code grows with the number of lines of code you're profiling. Still, you'll start out small by using DBMS_PROFILER on a smaller set of program units: your own code.

Before you begin, it's a good idea to see if DBMS_PROFILER is installed and if there are tables that it can store its data into when method flush_data() is called. To that end, execute a script like is_profiler.sql, as shown in Listing 7-20.

Listing 7-20. A Script to Detemine If SYS.DBMS_PROFILER Is Installed Properly, is_profiler.sql

```
01  rem is_profiler.sql
02  rem by Donaled J. Bales on 2014-10-20
03  rem Check to see if the profiler is installed and accessible
04
05  declare
06
07  n_major                             number;
08  n_minor                             number;
09  n_package                           number;
10  n_local                             number;
11  n_global                            number;
12
13  begin
14    select count(1)
15    into   n_package
16    from   SYS.ALL_OBJECTS
17    where  object_type = 'PACKAGE'
18    and    object_name = 'DBMS_PROFILER'
19    and    owner       = 'SYS';
20
21    if n_package > 0 then
22      SYS.DBMS_PROFILER.get_version(n_major, n_minor);
23
24      pl('DBMS_PROFILER Version '||
25        to_char(n_major)||'.'||
26        to_char(n_minor));
27
28      pl('DBMS_PROFILER.internal_version_check = '||
29        to_char(SYS.DBMS_PROFILER.internal_version_check));
30    else
31      pl('Sorry, either the profile does not exist, or you'||
32          'don''t have access to it.  Contact your DBA!');
33    end if;
34
35    select count(1)
36    into   n_local
37    from   SYS.ALL_OBJECTS
38    where  object_type = 'TABLE'
39    and    object_name in (
40      'PLSQL_PROFILER_RUNS',
41      'PLSQL_PROFILER_UNITS',
42      'PLSQL_PROFILER_DATA')
43    and    owner = USER;
44
45    if n_local = 3 then
46      pl('You have access to locally defined profiler tables '||
47        'for your current username: '||USER);
48    end if;
49
50    select count(1)
```

```
51    into    n_global
52    from    SYS.ALL_OBJECTS
53    where   object_type = 'TABLE'
54    and     object_name in (
55      'PLSQL_PROFILER_RUNS',
56      'PLSQL_PROFILER_UNITS',
57      'PLSQL_PROFILER_DATA')
58    and     owner = 'SYS';
59
60    if n_global = 3 then
61      pl('You have access to gloablly defined profiler tables '||
62        'under username SYS');
63    end if;
64
65    if n_local  <> 3 and
66       n_global <> 3 then
67      pl('Sorry, either the profile tables do not exist, or you'||
68        'don''t have access to them.  Contact your DBA!');
69    end if;
70
71  end;
72  /
```

You should see SQL*Plus output like this:

```
SQL> @is_profiler.sql
```

```
DBMS_PROFILER Version 2.0
DBMS_PROFILER.internal_version_check = 0
You have access to locally defined profiler tables for your current username: RPS

PL/SQL procedure successfully completed.
```

Given that you have access to the profiler, profile your relational version of the debug logger by following these steps.

1.   Profile your debug logger by executing the following at the SQL*Plus prompt:

     ```
     SQL> @run_profile.sql rps.debug.sql
     ```

     This profiles your debug logging table package by executing your test unit for said package. The run_profiler.sql script should have displayed the run number on the screen. Jot down this number because you'll need it to run the two profiling reports next.

2.   Create an "average percent consumption" report by executing the following at the SQL*Plus prompt:

     ```
     SQL> @avg_profile.sql <run_number>
     ```

     where <run_number> is the run number you got from executing script run_profile.sql.

3. Examine the file avg_profile_<run_number>.txt. Ask yourself, "What's the biggest consumer of resources?"

4. Create an "order by program unit and line number" report by executing the following at the SQL*Plus prompt:

   ```
   SQL> @ord_profile.sql <run_number>
   ```

5. Examine the file ord_profile_<run_number>.txt. Scan down the report. Find where your methods start and stop. Add up the average time consumption in nanoseconds. Ask yourself, "What's the biggest consumer of resources?"

Interestingly enough, in both cases, when you ask yourself to identify the biggest consumer of resources, you'll see that the answer is your SQL statements. Yes, we're back to dealing with SQL again. It's important to verify that your PL/SQL program logic is sound and it performs well, but it's even more important to make sure that your SQL is efficient. So let's see how you can determine just what's going on in a SQL statement next.

Profiling SQL

It's undeniable. You must make sure your SQL statements are as efficient as possible and that they are doing as much of the data manipulation work as is possible because SQL is more efficient at manipulating data than PL/SQL. So how do you see what's going on when it comes to a SQL statement?

Oracle provides two tools that you can use to examine the underlying access plan generated by the Oracle SQL Optimizer:

- EXPLAIN PLAN: Shows the execution plan generated by the Optimizer for a SQL statement you execute under the Oracle keywords EXPLAIN PLAN

- TKPROF: A utility program that can produce execution plans for all SQL statements executed again a database

Let's start out by looking at EXPLAIN PLAN.

Explain Plan

"Why does this take so long to run?" EXPLAIN PLAN will tell you, in just a bit more time than it takes you wrap your SQL statement in the keywords EXPLAIN PLAN FOR, exactly how the database intends to execute your SQL statement. Armed with this information, you can quickly determine if you need to do any of the following:

- Add an index to a table (or remove it)

- Rewrite your SQL statement

- Break your data processing into smaller chunks of work

- Just live with what you have

Given what you just learned in the section on profiling about performance in a PL/SQL program, your first step should always be to use EXPLAIN PLAN on every SQL statement in your PL/SQL program unit. So how do you do that?

1. Execute your SQL statement prefixed with the keywords EXPLAIN PLAN FOR.

2. Query the table PLAN_TABLE to extract the statistics.

In the olden days, you had to write your own SQL statements to query the PLAN_TABLE, but now you have access to package SYS.DBMS_XPLAN, which will do all the work of formatting the statistics for you.

Listing 7-21 is a SQL*Plus script named xp.sql that will explain the Optimizer's plan for a SQL statement stored in a file, with the filename passed to the script as the first parameter.

Listing 7-21. A Script to Explain the Optimizer Plan for SQL Statements, xp.sql

```
01  rem xp.sql
02  rem by Donald J. Bales on 2014-10-20
03  rem Display the execution plan for the last executed cursor
04
05  define script="&1";
06
07  set linesize  1000;
08  set newpage   1;
09  set pagesize  0;
10  set trimspool on;
11  set verify    off;
12
13  EXPLAIN PLAN FOR
14  select 1 from DUAL;
15
16  spool &script..pln;
17
18  EXPLAIN PLAN FOR
19  @&script
20
21  set echo off;
22
23  select * from table(SYS.DBMS_XPLAN.DISPLAY);
24
25  spool off;
26
27  set pagesize  32767;
28  set verify    on;
```

For example, first I save the following simple query in file select_workers_equlato.sql:

```
select *
from    WORKERS
where   name = 'DOE, JOHN J.'
order by 1;
```

Next, I execute xp.sql in SQL*Plus, passing it the filename as follows:

```
SQL> @xp.sql select_workers_equalto.sql
```

This produces the following plan:

```
Explained.

Plan hash value: 2276017427

----------------------------------------------------------------------------
| Id  | Operation                            | Name         | Rows  | Bytes |
----------------------------------------------------------------------------
|   0 | SELECT STATEMENT                     |              |     1 |    66 |
|   1 |  SORT ORDER BY                       |              |     1 |    66 |
|   2 |   TABLE ACCESS BY INDEX ROWID BATCHED| WORKERS      |     1 |    66 |
|*  3 |    INDEX RANGE SCAN                  | WORKERS_UK2  |     1 |       |
----------------------------------------------------------------------------
```

```
-------------------------
| Cost (%CPU)| Time      |
-------------------------
|     6  (17)| 00:00:01 |
|     6  (17)| 00:00:01 |
|     5   (0)| 00:00:01 |
|     3   (0)| 00:00:01 |
-------------------------
```

```
Predicate Information (identified by operation id):
---------------------------------------------------

   3 - access("NAME"='DOE, JOHN J.')

15 rows selected.
```

If you examine the plan, you'll see that the query is retrieving the values from the database by first scanning index WORKERS_UK2. Since I know how the indexes were built, I can be assured by looking at the plan that the Optimizer has chosen the best plan for accessing the WORKERS table. Now let's see what the Optimizer decides to do when I change the query from an "equal to" to a "like literal ending with a wildcard" query.

First, I save the following query in file select_workers_likepct.sql:

```
select *
from    WORKERS
where   name like 'DOE%'
order by 1;
```

Next, I execute xp.sql against that filename as follows:

```
SQL> @xp.sql select_workers_likepct.sql
```

This produces the following plan:

```
Explained.

Plan hash value: 2276017427
```

```
-----------------------------------------------------------------------
| Id  | Operation                            | Name        | Rows | Bytes |
-----------------------------------------------------------------------
|   0 | SELECT STATEMENT                     |             |    1 |   66 |
|   1 |  SORT ORDER BY                       |             |    1 |   66 |
|   2 |   TABLE ACCESS BY INDEX ROWID BATCHED| WORKERS     |    1 |   66 |
|*  3 |    INDEX RANGE SCAN                  | WORKERS_UK2 |    1 |      |
-----------------------------------------------------------------------
```

```
------------------------
| Cost (%CPU)| Time     |
------------------------
|    6  (17)| 00:00:01 |
|    6  (17)| 00:00:01 |
|    5   (0)| 00:00:01 |
|    3   (0)| 00:00:01 |
------------------------
```

```
Predicate Information (identified by operation id):
---------------------------------------------------

   3 - access("NAME" LIKE 'DOE%')
       filter("NAME" LIKE 'DOE%')

16 rows selected.
```

The Optimizer chose the same plan for this query as it did that last one.

Now let's try a worst-case scenario for any LIKE statement. I'll use the (%) wildcard on both sides of the literal. I would assume that this SQL statement will lead to a *full index scan*, instead of an *index range scan*. Does it?

First, I save the following query in file select_workers_pctlikepct.sql:

```
select *
from    WORKERS
where   name like '%DOE%'
order by 1;
```

Next, I pass the filename to xp.sql as follows:

```
SQL> @xp.sql select_workers_pctlikepct.sql
```

This produces the following plan:

```
Explained.

Plan hash value: 412163233

--------------------------------------------------------------
| Id  | Operation            | Name    | Rows  | Bytes |TempSpc|
--------------------------------------------------------------
|   0 | SELECT STATEMENT     |         | 13000 |  837K |       |
|   1 |  SORT ORDER BY       |         | 13000 |  837K | 1144K |
|*  2 |   TABLE ACCESS FULL  | WORKERS | 13000 |  837K |       |
--------------------------------------------------------------


-------------------------
| Cost (%CPU)| Time      |
-------------------------
|  1065   (1)| 00:00:01 |
|  1065   (1)| 00:00:01 |
|   856   (1)| 00:00:01 |
-------------------------

Predicate Information (identified by operation id):
---------------------------------------------------

   2 - filter("NAME" LIKE '%DOE%' AND "NAME" IS NOT NULL)

14 rows selected.
```

No, it doesn't use an index at all. Instead, it resorted to the worst of all options: a *full table scan*. Ouch! The cost went from 6 to 1065. That means it will take about 177 times longer for this query to respond than the first two. It looks like if I want to maintain performance in my application, I'm going to have to devise another solution for allowing my end users to find someone with a name like %<name>%. Is there something I can do in Oracle to improve this situation? Yes, sometimes there is.

Physics vs. Explain Plan

If you have a table that has much larger row sizes than an applicable index, you can use simple physics to improve your query response time. For example, the average row size for the table WORKERS is 87 bytes. The average row size for index WORKERS_UK2 is 17 bytes. If I add a hint to the query forcing it to full scan the index WORKERS_UK2, the database will be able to retrieve five times as many index blocks per retrieval that it can table blocks. What does the Optimizer have to say about this plan? Let's find out.

First, I save the following query as select_workers_pctlikepct2.sql:

```
select /*+ INDEX(WORKERS WORKERS_UK2) */
       *
from    WORKERS
where   name like '%DOE%'
order by 1;
```

In this query, I've added the hint /*+ INDEX(WORKERS WORKERS_UK2) */, which tells the Optimizer to use index WORKERS_UK2. Next, I use xp.sql to do explain the Optimizer's plan as follows:

```
SQL> xp.sql select_workerS_pctlikepct2.sql
```

This produces the following plan:

```
Explained.

Plan hash value: 2470337875
```

```
--------------------------------------------------------------------------
| Id  | Operation                          | Name        | Rows  | Bytes |
--------------------------------------------------------------------------
|   0 | SELECT STATEMENT                   |             | 13000 |  837K|
|   1 |  SORT ORDER BY                     |             | 13000 |  837K|
|   2 |   TABLE ACCESS BY INDEX ROWID BATCHED| WORKERS   | 13000 |  837K|
|*  3 |    INDEX FULL SCAN                 | WORKERS_UK2 | 13000 |       |
--------------------------------------------------------------------------
```

```
------------------------------------
|TempSpc| Cost (%CPU)| Time         |
------------------------------------
|       | 14787   (1)| 00:00:01 |
| 1144K | 14787   (1)| 00:00:01 |
|       | 14579   (1)| 00:00:01 |
|       |  1576   (1)| 00:00:01 |
------------------------------------
```

```
Predicate Information (identified by operation id):
---------------------------------------------------

   3 - filter("NAME" LIKE '%DOE%' AND "NAME" IS NOT NULL)

15 rows selected.
```

Indeed, the Optimizer understands my hint and is prepared to scan the index, but the cost is astronomical! Well guess what—*the Optimizer is wrong*. It doesn't understand the underlying physics involved.

Since there are 260,000 rows of data, with an average length of 87 bytes, if the Oracle database retrieves the data in 4KB blocks, it will require the retrieval of at least 5,500 blocks from the disk drive. On the other hand, it will require the retrieval of only about 1,080 blocks to identify which data rows to retrieve. Since, in this context, searching for part of a name will return a small set of rows, the application's performance can permanently benefit from the use of the hint, regardless of how the Optimizer feels about it. But the proof is in testing. And that is testing a snapshot of a fully loaded production database, not your development database. It's not until there are millions of rows in tables that you will probably need to "out think" Oracle's optimizer.

If I execute the first query select_worker_ot_pctlikepct.sql, which does not have the hint, against 260,000 rows, it takes on average three seconds to retrieve the matching rows. If I execute the second query, select_worker_ot_pctlikepct2.sql, which does have the hint to scan the index, it takes on average one second to retrieve the matching rows.

What's the moral of this story? The Optimizer doesn't always know the best way to retrieve data. It works with what it knows—basically statistics gathered when you analyze a table. On the other hand, you're an intelligent programmer who is much more knowledgeable and can therefore consider things like physics.

It's Your Turn to Use Explain Plan

Do you remember the section on FORALL in Chapter 5? That's where I nailed down the value of using the power of SQL instead of writing a whole lot of PL/SQL code to do the same work. The following SQL statement comes from Listing 5-14:

```
insert into WORKERS (
       worker_id,
       worker_type_id,
       external_id,
       first_name,
       middle_name,
       last_name,
       name,
       birth_date,
       gender_id)
select WORKERS_ID.nextval,
       decode(mod(WORKER_ID_SEQ.currval, 2),
         0, n_WT_EMPLOYEE, n_WT_CONTRACTOR),
       lpad(to_char(EXTERNAL_ID_SEQ.nextval), 9, '0'),
       first_name,
       letter||'.',
       last_name,
       WORKER.get_formatted_name(
         first_name, letter||'.', last_name),
       DATE_.random(
         to_number(to_char(SYSDATE, 'YYYY')) - 65,
         to_number(to_char(SYSDATE, 'YYYY')) - 18),
       decode(gender_code, 'F', n_G_FEMALE, n_G_MALE)
from   TOP_100_LAST_NAMES,
       TOP_100_FIRST_NAMES,
       A_THRU_Z;
```

In this code, I use pseudo-constants n_WT_EMPLOYEE, n_WT_CONTRACTOR, n_G_FEMALE, and n_G_MALE, which were preselected from the database, instead of selecting those values from the database in the SQL INSERT statement. Why?

It's another one of those tricks I've learned along the way. After years of using EXPLAIN PLAN on every SQL statement I've written, I noticed that I can improve the performance of a SQL statement if I reduce the number of tables accessed in the statement. If a SQL statement has three or less tables being selected, it performs pretty well. Add more tables, and its performance goes downhill fast.

So, if I have fairly limited number of constant values, I select them into pseudo-constant variables ahead of time, and then use those pseudo-constants in my SQL statement. Here's the Optimizer's plan for the preceding SQL INSERT statement:

Explained.

Plan hash value: 3139420850

```
---------------------------------------------------------------------------
| Id  | Operation                   | Name                 | Rows  | Bytes |
---------------------------------------------------------------------------
|   0 | INSERT STATEMENT            |                      |  260K |  4570K|
|   1 |  LOAD TABLE CONVENTIONAL    | WORKERS              |       |       |
|   2 |   SEQUENCE                  | WORKERS_ID           |       |       |
|   3 |    MERGE JOIN CARTESIAN     |                      |  260K |  4570K|
|   4 |     MERGE JOIN CARTESIAN    |                      |  2600 | 23400 |
|   5 |      INDEX FULL SCAN        | A_THRU_Z_PK          |   26  |   52  |
|   6 |      BUFFER SORT            |                      |  100  |  700  |
|   7 |       INDEX FAST FULL SCAN  | TOP_100_LAST_NAMES_PK|  100  |  700  |
|   8 |     BUFFER SORT             |                      |  100  |  900  |
|   9 |      INDEX FAST FULL SCAN   | TOP_100_FIRST_NAMES_PK|  100 |  900  |
---------------------------------------------------------------------------
```

```
-----------------------------
| Cost (%CPU)| Time          |
-----------------------------
|   717   (1)| 00:00:01 |
|            |          |
|            |          |
|   717   (1)| 00:00:01 |
|    10   (0)| 00:00:01 |
|     1   (0)| 00:00:01 |
|     9   (0)| 00:00:01 |
|     0   (0)| 00:00:01 |
|   717   (1)| 00:00:01 |
|     0   (0)| 00:00:01 |
-----------------------------
```

16 rows selected.

So here's your assignment. Rewrite the preceding SQL INSERT statement, which takes 47 seconds on average to execute on my machine, so the ID values for EMPLOYEE, CONTRACTOR, FEMALE, and MALE come from tables in the SQL INSERT statement's SELECT statement. Figure out if my working assumption about the number of tables in a SQL statement was true for this case, too. Follow these steps in order to find out for yourself.

1. Rewrite the SQL INSERT statement from Listing 5-14, adding two more tables to the SELECT statement, so you can get the ID values for corresponding codes from the database in the SQL statement.

2. Do an EXPLAIN PLAN on your SQL INSERT statement to determine what the Optimizer is planning. Is your plan better than the one for the SQL INSERT statement from Listing 5-14?

3. Look up the ID values for EMPLOYEE, CONTRACTOR, FEMALE, and MALE, and then substitute these values into the SQL INSERT statement from Listing 5-14.

4. Delete the contents of table WORKERS, and then execute the SQL INSERT statement from Listing 5-14 that you just modified, keeping track of how long it takes to execute. I suggest you do this at least three times, and then calculate the average value for how long it takes for the INSERT statement to execute.

5. Delete the contents of table WORKERS, and then execute your SQL INSERT statement where you include the GENDER_TYPES and WORKER_TYPES tables in its SELECT statement. Once again, I suggest you do this three times, and then calculate the average response time.

6. Compare the results of your timings between the two SQL INSERT statements. Which one was faster? Which SQL INSERT would you choose?

I'll show you my solution to this exercise. First, here's the SQL INSERT statement from Listing 5-14, modified to include tables GENDER_TYPES and WORKER_TYPES in its SELECT statement:

```
insert into WORKERS (
        id,
        worker_type_id,
        external_id,
        first_name,
        middle_name,
        last_name,
        name,
        birth_date,
        gender_type_id)
select WORKERS_ID.nextval,
        decode(mod(WORKERS_ID.currval, 2),
          0, c1.id, c2.id),
        lpad(to_char(EXTERNAL_ID_SEQ.nextval), 9, '0'),
        first_name,
        letter||'.',
        last_name,
        WORKER.get_formatted_name(
          first_name, letter||'.', last_name),
        DATE_.random(
          to_number(to_char(SYSDATE, 'YYYY')) - 65,
          to_number(to_char(SYSDATE, 'YYYY')) - 18),
        decode(gender_code, 'F', c3.id, c4.id)
from    TOP_100_LAST_NAMES,
        TOP_100_FIRST_NAMES,
        A_THRU_Z,
        WORKER_TYPES c1,
        WORKER_TYPES c2,
        GENDER_TYPES c3,
        GENDER_TYPES c4
where   c1.code = 'E'
and     c2.code = 'C'
and     c3.code = 'F'
and     c4.code = 'M';
```

And here's the Optimizer's plan for this SQL INSERT statement:

Explained.

Plan hash value: 599918850

```
---------------------------------------------------------------------------
| Id  | Operation                               | Name                     |
---------------------------------------------------------------------------
|   0 | INSERT STATEMENT                        |                          |
|   1 |  LOAD TABLE CONVENTIONAL                | WORKERS                  |
|   2 |   SEQUENCE                              | WORKERS_ID               |
|   3 |    MERGE JOIN CARTESIAN                 |                          |
|   4 |     MERGE JOIN CARTESIAN                |                          |
|   5 |      MERGE JOIN CARTESIAN               |                          |
|   6 |       MERGE JOIN CARTESIAN              |                          |
|   7 |        NESTED LOOPS                     |                          |
|   8 |         NESTED LOOPS                    |                          |
|   9 |          TABLE ACCESS BY INDEX ROWID    | GENDER_TYPES             |
|* 10 |           INDEX UNIQUE SCAN             | GENDER_TYPES_UK          |
|  11 |          TABLE ACCESS BY INDEX ROWID    | GENDER_TYPES             |
|* 12 |           INDEX UNIQUE SCAN             | GENDER_TYPES_UK          |
|  13 |         TABLE ACCESS BY INDEX ROWID     | WORKER_TYPES             |
|* 14 |          INDEX RANGE SCAN               | WORKER_TYPES_UK          |
|  15 |        BUFFER SORT                      |                          |
|  16 |         TABLE ACCESS BY INDEX ROWID BATCHED| WORKER_TYPES          |
|* 17 |          INDEX RANGE SCAN               | WORKER_TYPES_UK          |
|  18 |       BUFFER SORT                       |                          |
|  19 |        INDEX FULL SCAN                  | A_THRU_Z_PK              |
|  20 |      BUFFER SORT                        |                          |
|  21 |       INDEX FAST FULL SCAN              | TOP_100_LAST_NAMES_PK    |
|  22 |     BUFFER SORT                         |                          |
|  23 |      INDEX FAST FULL SCAN               | TOP_100_FIRST_NAMES_PK   |
---------------------------------------------------------------------------
```

```
------ --------------------------------------------
| Id    | Rows  | Bytes | Cost (%CPU)| Time        |
------ --------------------------------------------
|    0  |  260K|  9648K|   723   (1)| 00:00:01 |
|    1  |      |       |            |          |
|    2  |      |       |            |          |
|    3  |  260K|  9648K|   723   (1)| 00:00:01 |
|    4  |  2600| 75400 |    16   (0)| 00:00:01 |
|    5  |    26|   572 |     7   (0)| 00:00:01 |
|    6  |     1|    20 |     6   (0)| 00:00:01 |
|    7  |     1|    15 |     4   (0)| 00:00:01 |
|    8  |     1|    10 |     2   (0)| 00:00:01 |
|    9  |     1|     5 |     1   (0)| 00:00:01 |
|*  10  |     1|       |     0   (0)| 00:00:01 |
|   11  |     1|     5 |     1   (0)| 00:00:01 |
|*  12  |     1|       |     0   (0)| 00:00:01 |
|   13  |     1|     5 |     2   (0)| 00:00:01 |
|*  14  |     1|       |     1   (0)| 00:00:01 |
|   15  |     1|     5 |     4   (0)| 00:00:01 |
|   16  |     1|     5 |     2   (0)| 00:00:01 |
|*  17  |     1|       |     1   (0)| 00:00:01 |
|   18  |    26|    52 |     5   (0)| 00:00:01 |
|   19  |    26|    52 |     1   (0)| 00:00:01 |
|   20  |   100|   700 |    15   (0)| 00:00:01 |
|   21  |   100|   700 |     0   (0)| 00:00:01 |
|   22  |   100|   900 |   723   (1)| 00:00:01 |
|   23  |   100|   900 |     0   (0)| 00:00:01 |
------ --------------------------------------------

Predicate Information (identified by operation id):
---------------------------------------------------

  10 - access("C4"."CODE"='M')
  12 - access("C3"."CODE"='F')
  14 - access("C1"."CODE"='E')
  17 - access("C2"."CODE"='C')
```

38 rows selected.

The SQL INSERT statement with the GENDER_TYPES and WORKER_TYPES tables in its SQL SELECT statement is less efficient (cost equal to 723 vs. 717) according to EXPLAIN PLAN. What about how long it actually takes to execute? On my machine, it's actually three seconds faster than the SQL INSERT statement from Listing 5-14! So much for my experience!

The moral of this story is that you can't assume anything. You must always test the actual performance of your SQL statements before and after you've made modifications to the database, or to your SQL statements, in order to improve performance.

If you want a larger view of SQL statement performance, then perhaps you should use TKPROF.

TKPROF

TKPROF is a tool that's normally available only to your DBA. You're nice to your DBA, aren't you? So asking for his or her help in accessing trace files won't be a problem, right?

TKPROF is a utility that you can use in conjunction with session or system tracing to format the output of tracing into plans similar to those generated by EXPLAIN PLAN. The big difference is that you can gather statistics using package SYS.DBMS_MONITOR, which in turn will create trace files. Then you can use the trcsess utility to format the trace information into a format for TKPROF, and use TKPROF to format the output of the trace files into information you can use to examine the efficiency of an application's SQL statements as they were actually executed in a database.

To use TKPROF, follow these steps.

1. Utilize package DBMS_MONITOR to trace your application's use of SQL.

2. Use the trcsess utility to consolidate trace information into a file that can be analyzed using TKPROF.

3. Examine the consolidated trace file using TKPROF, in order to determine high-cost SQL statements in your application.

Using TKPROF, you'll be able to see the following for each SQL statement executed while you're monitoring the database:

- Resources consumed

- Number of times it was called

- Number of rows processed

- Optimizer's execution plan

Once you're armed with this information, you can use EXPLAIN PLAN to determine if there is a better alternative SQL statement, or if you need to come up with an entirely new solution. You may also want to investigate using package SYS.DBMS_SQLTUNE to help you decide how to properly tune a SQL statement.

You can find more information about performance tuning and EXPLAIN PLAN in the *Oracle Database Performance Tuning Guide*. You can find more information about the SYS.DBMS_* PL/SQL packages mentioned in this chapter in the *PL/SQL Packages and Types Reference*.

So what have you learned?

Summary

This chapter was all about troubleshooting. First, I discussed how to reduce the amount of troubleshooting you may have to do by simply preventing trouble in the first place. Second, I talked about adding troubleshooting-enabling code into your PL/SQL program units as you go, in anticipation of and preparation for trouble. Next, I covered four different troubleshooting tools:

- put_line()

- Debug logging

- Remote debugging

- EXPLAIN PLAN

Armed with these tools, you'll be able to handle any PL/SQL problem that comes your way. Now that you know how to fix any defect, how do you go about finding them all? By testing! And that's what I'm going to cover next.

CHAPTER 8

■ ■ ■

Testing

After 30 plus years of enterprise application development, I've found that the actual application development process for programmers consists of three high-level tasks:

- Coding
- Testing
- Documenting

The graph in Figure 8-1 is what I consider the ideal distribution of time for those three tasks. Yes, that's 60% of the development time spent on testing. The first response I get from most developers and project managers is, "Wow, that's an awful lot of time for testing, isn't it?" Not really. All the time you spend testing is time you won't have to spend supporting the application. And it costs a lot more to fix a defect in production than it does to take care of the problem earlier. It's as simple as that.

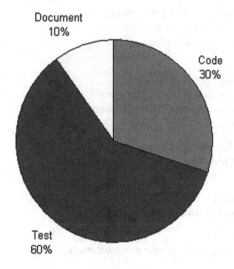

Figure 8-1. *An ideal distribution of development work*

Professional PL/SQL programmers write test units for their PL/SQL program units as they write their program units. I've been having you write them all along, haven't I? These are the only proper ways to reduce the amount of time spent testing:

- Develop with modularity (object orientation) because once a well-encapsulated software component is tested, it's unlikely it will break or need testing if a different unrelated module is modified.

- Automate testing by writing automated test units for every program unit (within reason) and/or by using a testing application suite.

- Write rerunnable test units. You should be able to run test units over and over again until there are no errors, without having to do any extra work to run them again.

- Update test units with additional tests if a defect not caught by the current test unit rears its ugly head.

- Don't lose your test units.

- Document your test units.

In contrast, nowadays it seems that everyone's favorite way to reduce the amount of time spent testing is to not test at all, which means passing testing on to the end user (not a good idea), which in turn means passing it on to support personnel (even worse). Why is passing testing on to support personnel even worse? At least the end users have a good idea how things should work. Support personnel usually know even less. It becomes a case of the proverbial "blind leading the blind."

So just whose responsibility is testing?

1. You are primarily responsible for testing your own code. You need to write test plans and test units to execute those test plans.

2. Your peers on your programming team are also responsible if they run into an error when using one of your components. Their responsibility is to inform you that there is a defect in your code, to ask you to update your test plans, update your test units, and then to test your code again.

3. Your supervisor, whether a technical lead, project manager, or in another position, is responsible for verifying that you have executed your test plans and that there are no errors. Your supervisor is also responsible for verifying that your test plans are updated if someone encounters an error.

4. An application's support personnel are responsible for reporting errors to the development team so defects can be fixed, and then test plans and test units can be updated and rerun.

5. An application's end users are responsible for reporting errors to the support team so defects can be fixed, and then test plans and test units can be updated and rerun.

I used a numbered list for these responsibilities to emphasize that *you are the one most responsible for testing*.

So just what do I mean by "test plan" and "test unit"? A test plan is a document that outlines how an application is to be tested. It should at least answer the following questions:

- How will the persistence layer (database) be tested?

- How will the application layer (middle tier) be tested?

- How will the presentation layer (the various presentation layers: data entry, reporting, interfaces, and so on) be tested?

- What technique will be used to keep track of what needs to be tested?

- What technique will be used to record that something has been tested?

- Who will sign off that the testing has been completed successfully and that there are no errors?

- How many rounds of testing will there be, and who will perform each round of testing?

A test unit is a list of tests to be executed by a tester (a person who tests) or executed by a program, written or scripted, which executes the test steps in an automated fashion. This chapter is about writing test units:

- The commonly executed steps in a PL/SQL test unit for SQL

- The commonly executed steps in a PL/SQL test unit for PL/SQL

- A table to store the tests performed and their results

- A package to aid in writing PL/SQL test units

- A framework for keeping track of what needs to be tested in a persistence layer (database/objectbase)

Let's start by looking at the common tasks involved in testing SQL.

SQL Test Patterns

If you have a PL/SQL method that uses SQL, then you must devise some method to test that the SQL in that program unit works correctly. From an abstract point of view, that boils down to executing some or all of these steps in the following order:

1. DELETE

2. INSERT

3. SELECT

4. UPDATE

5. DELETE

If you're going to test a program unit's ability to INSERT a new entry into a table, you first need to decide on an acceptable set of values to use during the INSERT, and then you must clean up after yourself by removing what you've just added so the test unit can be run again. Since it's entirely possible that an error may have occurred before your INSERT operation, you need to DELETE first. Otherwise, when you rerun your test on INSERT, you may get an error due to a row that was not properly cleaned up or removed during a prior test. That's why I have DELETE as the number one high-level operation for testing any PL/SQL program unit that automates SQL testing.

Next, if you're going to test a PL/SQL program unit's ability to retrieve values from a table, you first need to INSERT those values so they are available. That means you must INSERT before you SELECT, which, in turn, means you need to DELETE, INSERT, SELECT, and then DELETE in your test unit.

Now if you're going to test a program unit's ability to UPDATE, it follows that you must first SELECT to verify that there is something to UPDATE, which requires you to INSERT before you SELECT and DELETE before you INSERT. Then you need to DELETE in order to clean up after yourself.

Last, if you're going to test a program unit's ability to DELETE, you need to perform a DELETE, then an INSERT, followed by a SELECT, (yes, you can skip UPDATE) and then a DELETE. I like to call this abstract pattern *the SQL Circle of Life,* as illustrated in Figure 8-2.

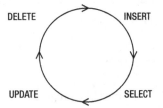

Figure 8-2. *The SQL Circle of Life*

At this moment, this discussion may seem quite silly. But you'll see soon enough, when you start writing test units, you will need to keep the SQL Circle of Life in mind when writing rerunnable SQL test units in PL/SQL.

Let's look at patterns found when testing PL/SQL methods next.

PL/SQL Test Patterns

Just as there is an abstract pattern to testing SQL in PL/SQL, there is also a pattern you'll need to follow to test PL/SQL program units themselves. The PL/SQL testing pattern is "blocking" your test code.

You need to wrap each of your PL/SQL tests in a PL/SQL block so you can programmatically maintain control in your test unit. If you can't maintain control in your test unit, it may end abruptly without performing all your tests. Here's an example:

```
...
begin
  -- Perform your test by calling a method with test data here

  -- Then check to ensure test success here
exception
  when OTHERS then
    -- Catch any PL/SQL exception and report the error here
end;
-- Go on to the next test
...
```

You'll end up testing your PL/SQL methods by calling them with test values in your test unit, and then inspecting the results of the operation to verify it worked correctly. In order to maintain control, you'll need to catch any raised exceptions, hence the when OTHERS then clause in the exception-handling section of the PL/SQL block surrounding your code. From the exception-handling section, you'll report any errors that take place, therefore handling the exception, not raising the exception to the outer (enclosing) PL/SQL block. Then you'll go on to perform your next method test.

How will you report and keep track of success or failure in your test units? You'll do that with a testing tool. Let's look at that next.

A Testing Tool

Humans are very good at creating their own tools. To that end, I've created a "testing tool" that helps me code my PL/SQL test units.

I have two high-level requirements for this testing tool. It needs to

- Provide a set of constants that I can use for column values when testing.

- Provide a set of methods that I can use to save tests and results for later analysis.

Do you recall that in the "SQL Test Patterns" section, I stated that you first need to decide on an acceptable set of values to use during the INSERT? How do you go about that?

Well here's how I do it: I ask the database! Listing 8-1 is a SQL*Plus query I run to determine the varchar2 lengths that are in common use. For the most part, there should only be a few. While in the past, the lengths of a character field may have had some meaning, they no longer do. With the advent of globalization, the lengths of character fields only amount to specifying an upper limit on the amount of storage you're willing to use for a given string value.

Listing 8-1. A Query to Determine Commonly Used Lengths for Varchar2 Columns, data_length_histogram.sql

```
01   rem data_length_histogram.sql
02   rem by Donald J. Bales on 2014-10-20
03   rem Create a histogram of VARCHAR2 data lengths in use
04
05   column column_name format a30;
06
07   set linesize   1000;
08   set newpage    1;
09   set pagesize   32767;
10   set trimspool on;
11
12   spool data_length_histogram.txt;
13
14   select column_name,
15          min(data_length) min,
16          avg(data_length) avg,
17          max(data_length) max,
18          count(1) occurs
19   from   SYS.ALL_TAB_COLUMNS
20   where  owner = USER
21   and    data_type like 'VARCHAR%'
22   and    table_name not in (
23          'AUTHORS',
24          'AUTHOR_PUBLICATIONS',
25          'A_THRU_Z',
26          'DEBUGS',
27          'PLAN_TABLE',
28          'PLSQL_PROFILER_RUNS',
29          'PLSQL_PROFILER_UNITS',
```

```
30              'PLSQL_PROFILER_DATA',
31              'TOP_100_FIRST_NAMES',
32              'TOP_100_LAST_NAMES' )
33  group by column_name
34  order by max(data_length),
35              column_name
36  /
37
38  spool off;
```

And here's the output from the query in Listing 8-1:

```
COLUMN_NAME                           MIN        AVG        MAX      OCCURS
------------------------------   ----------  ----------  ----------  ----------
LOGICAL_INDICATOR                       1          1          1          1
PHYSICAL_INDICATOR                      1          1          1          1
CAS_NUMBER                             30         30         30          1
CODE                                   30         30         30          7
EXTERNAL_ID                            30         30         30          1
FIRST_NAME                             30         30         30          1
LAST_NAME                              30         30         30          1
MIDDLE_NAME                            30         30         30          1
DESCRIPTION                            80         80         80          4
ID_CONTEXT                            100        100        100          2
NAME                                   80  85.7142857        100          7
TITLE                                 100        100        100          1
NARRATIVE                            2000       2000       2000          1
```

```
13 rows selected.
```

Analyzing this output, I have concluded that I will need the following constants for testing:

- A TRUE value for the indicator variables

- A FALSE value for the indicator variables

- A 30-character code value that I can specify any time I test inserting a new code or partial name value into a code or content table

- An 80-character description value that I can specify any time I test inserting a new description into a code or content table

- A 100-character value that I can specify any time I test inserting a new ID context or title into a content or intersection table

- A 2,000-character value that I can specify any time I test inserting a new comment or narrative into a content table

I'll keep this list of requirements in mind when I code my testing tool's package specification, so the constants will be accessible to all other program units, and therefore available when writing their test units.

WHY ARE WE SPECIFYING CHARACTER COLUMN LENGTHS ANYWAY?

After having internationalized a number of enterprise applications, I began to wonder why we have to specify a maximum column length for character columns at all. In the future, I don't think we'll need to do this; the database will handle the length automatically, and why not?

One programmer I know argued that was important and gave me what he thought was a valid example: "It's important to constrain a number column for money. It should be NUMBER(11,2), because dollars have hundredths values (dimes and pennies)." But that's only valid for dollars; other currencies have thousandths.

Consider that characters used in the English language use one byte of storage. Other languages use characters that require two to four bytes of storage. In addition, sentences, even words, in English are quite compact when compared with other languages. For example, an idea expressed in 30 *characters* in English may take four to five times as many words and/or *characters* in German.

So just what are we specifying when we constrain a varchar2's length? I think it's just our expectation that nothing entered into the column will ever need to be larger than what we've specified. So until Oracle gets with my line of thinking, we might as well decide on a standard set of character column lengths and stick to it. Here are the lengths I commonly use for character fields in applications:

- *Code*: 30 English only; 60 internationalized

- *Code context*: 500 English only; 1,000 internationalized

- *Comments*: 2,000 English only; 4,000 internationalized

- *Description*: 80 English only; 160

- *ID context*: 100 English only; 200 internationalized

- *Name*: 80 English only; 160 internationalized

- *Name context*: 1,000 English only; 2,000 internationalized

- *Title*: 80 English only; 160 internationalized

I would like to hear your thoughts: don@donaldbales.com. Now back to testing.

How about some behavior? What will I call the methods that aid me with writing test units? Here's a preliminary set of requirements:

- clear(): To erase the results of a previous test run from table TESTS

- get_id(): To allocate a new primary key value for the table TESTS

- test(): To test the testing tool

- set_test(): To start a new test

- set_result(): To store the results of a test

However, before I write a testing tool package, I need to create a table to permanently store the results of my tests.

A TEST Table

Why store my test results in a table? Because then I can use SQL to query the table to analyze the results of my testing. No tool is more powerful at manipulating data than SQL, so a table is the ideal place to save the results of testing.

What do I need to store? Here's my short list of data to store:

- The name of the package or user-defined TYPE (object name) that contains the method being tested

- The name of the method being tested

- An external identifier for the test being performed on a given method so I can identify a given test if it fails

- A short but meaningful description of the test

- The result of the test

In order to store this data, I've written the DDL script in Listing 8-2. It creates a test table named TESTS. I've also added an ID column for a primary key. This will be a unique session ID, so testing in one session does not collide with testing going on in another session. I've also included insert user and insert date columns, which are standard columns I add to all tables (to add those bread crumbs I talked about in Chapter 7).

Listing 8-2. A DDL Script to Create a Testing Results Table, rps.tests.tab

```
01  rem tests.tab
02  rem by Donald Bales on 2014-10-20
03  rem Create test results
04
05  create table TESTS (
06  id                         number                      not null,
07  object_name                varchar2(30),
08  method_name                varchar2(30),
09  test_number                number,
10  description                varchar2(80),
11  result                     varchar2(256),
12  unique_session_id          varchar2(24)                not null,
13  insert_user                varchar2(30)  default USER      not null,
14  insert_date                date          default SYSDATE  not null );
15
16  alter  table TESTS add
17  constraint   TESTS_PK
18  primary key (
19  id )
20  using index
21  tablespace USERS pctfree 0
22  storage (initial 1M next 1M pctincrease 0);
23
24  create sequence TESTS_ID
25  start with 1 order;
26
27  execute SYS.DBMS_STATS.gather_table_stats(USER, 'TESTS');
28
29  grant all on TESTS to PUBLIC;
31  grant all on TESTS to PUBLIC;
```

Now that I have a table to store results, let's get to writing a testing tool package.

A TEST Package Specification

In my testing tool's package, I define a set of variables or constants that are suitable as insert values for SQL statements. I can then use these predefined values when writing test units. This approach has several advantages. First, global use of these testing values will create an environment where testing is done with consistency. In turn, because of that consistency, everyone involved in testing will know what these predefined values are, and then know that they are looking at test data if they encounter these values while testing.

Listing 8-3 is the package specification for my testing tool. On the top half of the specification, I've added globally accessible constants to be utilized by all programmers when writing their test units. These are followed by methods designed to aid programmers when writing their test units. By using these methods, the test data is consistently formatted and stored for easy analysis.

Listing 8-3. A Testing Tool Package Spec, rps.test.pks

```
001  create or replace package TEST as
002  /*
003  test.pks
004  by Donald J. Bales on 2014-10-20
005  A Testing package
006  */
007
008  -- Result constants
009  v_TEST_ERROR                 constant  varchar2(5) := 'ERROR';
010  v_TEST_OK                    constant  varchar2(2) := 'OK';
011  v_TEST_SUCCESS               constant  varchar2(7) := 'SUCCESS';
012
013  -- Testing constants
014  d_TEST_19000101              constant  date        :=
015    to_date('19000101', 'YYYYMMDD');
016  d_TEST_99991231              constant  date        :=
017    to_date('99991231', 'YYYYMMDD');
018
019  v_TEST_N                     constant  varchar2(1) := 'N';
020
021  v_TEST_Y                     constant  varchar2(1) := 'Y';
022
023  v_TEST_30                    constant  varchar2(30) :=
024    'TEST TEST TEST TEST TEST TESTx';
025
026  v_TEST_30_1                  constant  varchar2(30) :=
027    'TEST1 TEST1 TEST1 TEST1 TEST1x';
028
029  v_TEST_30_2                  constant  varchar2(30) :=
030    'TEST2 TEST2 TEST2 TEST2 TEST2x';
031
032  v_TEST_80                    constant  varchar2(80) :=
033    'Test Test Test Test Test Test Test Test '||
034    'Test Test Test Test Test Test Test Testx';
035
```

```
036   v_TEST_100                    constant  varchar2(100) :=
037      'Test Test Test Test Test Test Test Test Test Test '||
038      'Test Test Test Test Test Test Test Test Test Testx';
039
040   v_TEST_2000                   constant  varchar2(2000) :=
041      'Test Test Test Test Test Test Test Test Test Test '||
042      'Test Test Test Test Test Test Test Test Test Test '||
043      'Test Test Test Test Test Test Test Test Test Test '||
044      'Test Test Test Test Test Test Test Test Test Test '||
045      'Test Test Test Test Test Test Test Test Test Test '||
046      'Test Test Test Test Test Test Test Test Test Test '||
047      'Test Test Test Test Test Test Test Test Test Test '||
048      'Test Test Test Test Test Test Test Test Test Test '||
049      'Test Test Test Test Test Test Test Test Test Test '||
050      'Test Test Test Test Test Test Test Test Test Test '||
051      'Test Test Test Test Test Test Test Test Test Test '||
052      'Test Test Test Test Test Test Test Test Test Test '||
053      'Test Test Test Test Test Test Test Test Test Test '||
054      'Test Test Test Test Test Test Test Test Test Test '||
055      'Test Test Test Test Test Test Test Test Test Test '||
056      'Test Test Test Test Test Test Test Test Test Test '||
057      'Test Test Test Test Test Test Test Test Test Test '||
058      'Test Test Test Test Test Test Test Test Test Test '||
059      'Test Test Test Test Test Test Test Test Test Test '||
060      'Test Test Test Test Test Test Test Test Test Test '||
061      'Test Test Test Test Test Test Test Test Test Test '||
062      'Test Test Test Test Test Test Test Test Test Test '||
063      'Test Test Test Test Test Test Test Test Test Test '||
064      'Test Test Test Test Test Test Test Test Test Test '||
065      'Test Test Test Test Test Test Test Test Test Test '||
066      'Test Test Test Test Test Test Test Test Test Test '||
067      'Test Test Test Test Test Test Test Test Test Test '||
068      'Test Test Test Test Test Test Test Test Test Test '||
069      'Test Test Test Test Test Test Test Test Test Test '||
070      'Test Test Test Test Test Test Test Test Test Test '||
071      'Test Test Test Test Test Test Test Test Test Test '||
072      'Test Test Test Test Test Test Test Test Test Test '||
073      'Test Test Test Test Test Test Test Test Test Test '||
074      'Test Test Test Test Test Test Test Test Test Test '||
075      'Test Test Test Test Test Test Test Test Test Test '||
076      'Test Test Test Test Test Test Test Test Test Test '||
077      'Test Test Test Test Test Test Test Test Test Testx'||
078      'Test Test Test Test Test Test Test Test Test Test '||
079      'Test Test Test Test Test Test Test Test Test Test '||
080      'Test Test Test Test Test Test Test Test Test Testx';
081
082   --          1         2         3         4         5
083   -- 12345678901234567890123456789012345678901234567890
084
085   -- Clear the results of the last test
086   PROCEDURE clear(
```

```
087 aiv_object_name                          TESTS.object_name%TYPE);
088
089
090 -- Set the result of the last test to v_TEST_ERROR
091 PROCEDURE error;
092
093
094 -- Set the result of the last test to the passed Oracle error
095 PROCEDURE error(
096 aiv_result                  in     TESTS.result%TYPE);
097
098
099 -- Display help text
100 PROCEDURE help;
101
102
103 -- Instantiate the package
104 PROCEDURE initialize;
105
106
107 -- Set the result of the last test to v_TEST_OK
108 PROCEDURE ok;
109
110
111 -- Update the test with its results
112 PROCEDURE set_result(
113 aiv_result                  in     TESTS.result%TYPE);
114
115
116 -- Add a test
117 PROCEDURE set_test(
118 aiv_object_name             in     TESTS.object_name%TYPE,
119 aiv_method_name             in     TESTS.method_name%TYPE,
120 ain_test_number             in     TESTS.test_number%TYPE,
121 aiv_description             in     TESTS.description%TYPE);
122
123
124 -- Set the result of the last test to v_TEST_SUCCESS
125 PROCEDURE success;
126
127
128 -- Test unit
129 PROCEDURE test;
130
131
132 end TEST;
133 /
134 @se.sql TEST
```

Let's examine Listing 8-3, line by line:

- Lines 9 through 11 add three character constants, ERROR, OK, and SUCCESS, to be used as values for parameter aiv_result, when calling method result(). OK means the test completed successfully, and ERROR means the test did not complete successfully. Constant SUCCESS is called only at the end of a program unit's test unit after recording a test for the package or user-defined TYPE in question, in order to flag that the package or TYPE's test unit completely successfully, without raising any uncaught exceptions. If an uncaught exception does occur, the programmer should pass the value of SQLERRM as the result.

- Lines 14 through 80 add constants to be used globally for testing inserts into SQL tables. These "testing" values not only self-document their values as test values, but also exercise the maximum column size constraints on the columns for tables for which they are used to test.

- Lines 86 and 87 declare method clear(), which a program should call at the beginning of a test unit in order to clear any previous test results before starting a new round of tests.

- Line 91 declares method error(), which a program should call to record that the test resulted in an error.

- Lines 95 and 96 declare an overridden version of method error(), which takes one argument. A program should call this method if it needs to record an Oracle exception error message.

- Lines 107 and 108 declare method ok(), which a program should call to record that an individual test completed without errors.

- Lines 112 and 113 declare the method set_result(). Methods error(), ok(), and success() call this method to record testing results. This method uses pragma autonomous_transaction so entries are not lost if the test fails in the program unit in question because of an uncaught exception.

- Lines 117 through 121 declare the method set_test(), which a programmer should use to record a test that is about to be executed inside a test unit. This method also uses pragma autonomous_transaction so entries are not lost if the test fails in the program unit in question because of an uncaught exception.

- Line 125 declares method success(), which a program should call at the end of a test unit to flag that the entire test unit completed successfully. That doesn't mean that there weren't errors during the individual tests; it means that the method test() itself was completely executed.

- Line 129 declares the standard test unit method to be used by every package and user-defined TYPE: test(). This is where a programmer codes the test units for every associated PL/SQL program unit. You'll see an example in the testing tool's package body shortly.

The test result constants OK, ERROR, and SUCCESS make it easy to identify errors after tests are run. If you want to know which test unit methods failed, just write a query where you list every object in the table TESTS that doesn't have a row where the object_name can also be found with a result value of SUCCESS. If you want to know which individual tests failed, write a query to list the rows where column result starts with ERR or ORA. I'll show you a couple of sample queries like these in the "Automating Testing" section later in this chapter.

Now let's look at the implementation.

A TEST Package Body

Now that you've seen the specification for my testing tool, let's look at its implementation, including an example of its use. Listing 8-4 is the DDL to create the package body for package TEST.

Listing 8-4. A Testing Tool Package Body, rps.test.pkb

```
001  create or replace package body TEST as
002  /*
003  test.pkb
004  by Donald J. Bales on 2014-10-20
005  A Testing package
006  */
007
008  -- Hold this value across calls to test() and result()
009  n_id                                 TESTS.id%TYPE;
010
011
012  PROCEDURE clear(
013  aiv_object_name                      TESTS.object_name%TYPE) is
014
015  pragma autonomous_transaction;
016
017  begin
018    delete TESTS
019    where  object_name      = aiv_object_name
020    and    unique_session_id = SYS.DBMS_SESSION.unique_session_id;
021
022    commit;
023  end clear;
024
025
026  PROCEDURE error is
027
028  begin
029    set_result(v_TEST_ERROR);
030  end error;
031
032
033  PROCEDURE error(
034  aiv_result                 in      TESTS.result%TYPE) is
035
036  begin
037    set_result(aiv_result);
038  end error;
039
040
041  FUNCTION get_id
042  return                               TESTS.id%TYPE is
043
044  n_id                                 TESTS.id%TYPE;
045
```

269

```
046   begin
047     select TESTS_ID.nextval
048     into   n_id
049     from   SYS.DUAL;
050
051     return n_id;
052   end get_id;
053
054
055   PROCEDURE help is
056   begin
057     pl('You''re on your own buddy.');
058   end help;
059
060
061   PROCEDURE initialize is
062   begin
063     null;
064   end;
065
066
067   PROCEDURE ok is
068
069   begin
070     set_result(v_TEST_OK);
071   end ok;
072
073
074   PROCEDURE set_result(
075   aiv_result                    in      TESTS.result%TYPE) is
076
077   pragma autonomous_transaction;
078
079   begin
080     update TESTS
081     set    result = aiv_result
082     where  id     = n_id;
083
084     if nvl(sql%rowcount, 0) = 0 then
085       raise_application_error(-20000, 'Can''t find test'||
086         to_char(n_id)||
087         ' on update TEST'||
088         ' in TEST.test');
089     end if;
090
091     n_id := NULL;
092
093     commit;
094   end set_result;
095
096
```

```
097  PROCEDURE set_test(
098  aiv_object_name              in        TESTS.object_name%TYPE,
099  aiv_method_name              in        TESTS.method_name%TYPE,
100  ain_test_number              in        TESTS.test_number%TYPE,
101  aiv_description              in        TESTS.description%TYPE) is
102
103  pragma autonomous_transaction;
104
105  begin
106    n_id := get_id();
107
108    begin
109      insert into TESTS (
110              id,
111              object_name,
112              method_name,
113              test_number,
114              description,
115              result,
116              unique_session_id,
117              insert_user,
118              insert_date )
119      values (
120              n_id,
121              upper(aiv_object_name),
122              upper(aiv_method_name),
123              ain_test_number,
124              aiv_description,
125              NULL,
126              SYS.DBMS_SESSION.unique_session_id,
127              USER,
128              SYSDATE );
129    exception
130      when OTHERS then
131        raise_application_error(-20000, SQLERRM||
132          ' on insert TEST'||
133          ' in TEST.test');
134    end;
135    commit;
136  end set_test;
137
138
139  PROCEDURE success is
140
141  begin
142    set_result(v_TEST_SUCCESS);
143  end success;
144
145
146  PROCEDURE test is
147
```

```
148  n_number                                      number;
149
150  begin
151    pl('TESTS.test()');
152    clear('TEST');
153
154    set_test('TEST', NULL, 1,
155      'Is v_TEST_N equal to N?');
156    if v_TEST_N = 'N' then
157      ok();
158    else
159      error();
160    end if;
161
162    set_test('TEST', NULL, 2,
163      'Is the length of v_TEST_N equal to 1?');
164    if nvl(length(v_TEST_N), 0) = 1 then
165      ok();
166    else
167      error();
168    end if;
169
170    set_test('TEST', NULL, 3,
171      'Is v_TEST_Y equal to Y?');
172    if v_TEST_Y = 'Y' then
173      ok();
174    else
175      error();
176    end if;
177
178    set_test('TEST', NULL, 4,
179      'Is the length of v_TEST_Y equal to 1?');
180    if nvl(length(v_TEST_Y), 0) = 1 then
181      ok();
182    else
183      error();
184    end if;
185
186    set_test('TEST', NULL, 5,
187      'Is the length of v_TEST_30 equal to 30?');
188    if nvl(length(v_TEST_30), 0) = 30 then
189      ok();
190    else
191      error();
192    end if;
193
194    set_test('TEST', NULL, 6,
195      'Is the length of v_TEST_30_1 equal to 30?');
196    if nvl(length(v_TEST_30_1), 0) = 30 then
197      ok();
198    else
```

```
199       error();
200     end if;
201
202     set_test('TEST', NULL, 7,
203       'Is the length of v_TEST_30_2 equal to 30?');
204     if nvl(length(v_TEST_30_2), 0) = 30 then
205       ok();
206     else
207       error();
208     end if;
209
210     set_test('TEST', NULL, 8,
211       'Is the length of v_TEST_80 equal to 80?');
212     if nvl(length(v_TEST_80), 0) = 80 then
213       ok();
214     else
215       error();
216     end if;
217
218     set_test('TEST', NULL, 9,
219       'Is the length of v_TEST_100 equal to 100?');
220     if nvl(length(v_TEST_100), 0) = 100 then
221       ok();
222     else
223       error();
224     end if;
225
226     set_test('TEST', NULL, 10,
227       'Is the length of v_TEST_2000 equal to 2000?');
228     if nvl(length(v_TEST_2000), 0) = 2000 then
229       ok();
230     else
231       error();
232     end if;
233
234     set_test('TEST', 'get_id', 11,
235       'Does get_id() work?');
236     begin
237       n_number := get_id();
238       if n_number > 0 then
239         ok();
240       else
241         error();
242       end if;
243     exception
244       when OTHERS then
245         error(SQLERRM);
246     end;
247
248     set_test('TEST', 'help', 12,
249       'Does help() work?');
```

```
250    begin
251       help();
252    --     raise_application_error(-20999, 'Testing test unit report');
253       ok();
254    exception
255       when OTHERS then
256          error(SQLERRM);
257    end;
258
259    set_test('TEST', NULL, NULL, NULL);
260    success();
261  end test;
262
263
264  end TEST;
265  /
266  @be.sql TESTS
```

Let's look at Listing 8-4 in detail:

- Lines 12 through 23 implement procedure clear(), which is called by method test() to remove any previous test for the same unique session ID.

- Lines 26 through 30 implement procedure error(), which is called by method test() to record a generic error.

- Lines 33 through 38 implement procedure error(), which is called by method test() inside an exception handler in order to record an Oracle exception's error message.

■ **Note** Do you find the use of the same method names for more than one purpose disturbing? This is called *overloading* the method names. One error() method is used to record a generic error, while the second is used to record an Oracle error message.

- Lines 41 through 52 implement function get_id(), which returns the next primary key value to be used when inserting a row into table TESTS.

- Lines 67 through 71 implement procedure ok(), which is called by method test() to record the success of an individual test.

- Lines 74 through 94 implement procedure set_result(), which updates the last recorded test with the passed result value. This method uses an instance-level variable, n_id, in coordination with procedure test(). test() saves the last id it allocates to variable n_id in the package's memory, and then set_result() uses that value when saving the result. I do this to reduce the amount of coding required by the test unit writer.

- Lines 97 through 136 implement procedure set_test(), which is used by test unit writers to record that a test is about to take place.

- Lines 139 through 143 implement procedure success(), which is called by method test() to indicate the successful execution of the test unit itself.

- Lines 146 through 260 implement procedure test(), which is the actual test unit for package TEST. Yes, I've used the testing tool to test the testing tool. Neat, huh?

- Line 148, inside the test unit method test(), declares a number variable to temporarily hold the result of one of the tests.

- Line 151 calls pl() to give feedback to the tester that the test has been started.

- Line 152 calls procedure TEST.clear(), passing the name of the object in order to remove any previous test results.

- Lines 154 and 155 call procedure TEST.test(), passing it the information about the test I'm about to perform.

- Line 156 performs my first test, to see if the constant TEST.v_TEST_N has the correct value. Since I'm certain that this test cannot cause an exception, I have not blocked the code for the test.

- Line 157 sets the result for the test to constant TEST.v_TEST_OK by calling procedure ok() if v_TEST_N is indeed the character N; otherwise, on line 159, I set the result to TEST.v_TEST_ERROR by calling procedure error().

- Lines 162 through 232 perform tests on the remaining constants in a similar fashion. With all these tests, I'm confident that an exception cannot possibly be raised, so I don't block the test code. This is not so for the next test.

- Lines 234 and 235 call procedure TEST.test() in order to record that I'm about to perform a test of function get_id().

- Lines 236 through 246 block the call to method get_id() in order to catch any unexpected exception. Next, I execute my actual test, a call to get_id(). If there is no unexpected exception, the next line, 238, tests to see if the ID value was greater than zero. If so, I call method ok(); otherwise, I call error(). If an exception does occur, I call error(), passing the value of SQLERRM.

- Lines 250 through 256 block a call to help() and then test it in a fashion similar to the previous test.

- Line 258 calls test() for the package, therefore passing only the object's name.

- Line 259 calls procedure success(). These last two calls will indicate that the test procedure test() itself completed successfully, instead of possibly aborting somewhere in the midst of the test from an unhandled exception.

Now that I've shown you my relational testing tool, it's your turn to create an object-relational version.

It's Your Turn to Create a Testing Tool

Your assignment is to recreate the testing tool I've just shown you as an object-relational TYPE instead of a package. There's one twist, though. You can't declare constants, pseudo-constants, or variables in a TYPE, as I did in the TEST package specification, so you'll need to declare additional parameterless functions that return the constant values.

To create an object-relational testing tool, follow these steps.

1. Write a DDL script to create a TYPE specification named TEST. This type should have an attribute for every column name in table TESTS. It should also have corresponding methods for each method found in package TEST. In addition, you'll add parameterless functions in the place of the constants in package TEST. Include the method signature for, but skip coding the methods help() and test(). We'll work on coding test() in the next section, and help() in the next chapter.

2. Save your script as ops.test.tps.

3. Log in as username OPS.

4. Compile your script: SQL> @ops.test.tps.

5. Write a DDL script to create the object table TESTS of TEST.

6. Save your script as ops.tests.tab.

7. Compile your script: SQL> @ops.tests.tab.

8. Write a DDL script to create the TYPE BODY for TEST.

9. Save your script as ops.test.tpb.

10. Compile your script: SQL> @ops.test.tpb.

But what about testing your new test tool? I'll devote the entire next section to that task. Do you want to see my solution for this exercise? Listings 8-5, 8-6, and 8-7 are the DDL for the TYPE specification, table, and body, respectively, for my version of TYPE TEST.

Listing 8-5. A DDL Script for TYPE TEST's Spec, ops.test.tps

```
001  drop    type TEST;
002  create type TEST as object (
003  /*
004  test.tps
005  by Donald J. Bales on 2014-10-20
006  A Type for logging test results
007  */
008  -- Type TEST's attributes
009  id                              number,
010  object_name                     varchar2(30),
011  method_name                     varchar2(30),
012  test_number                     number,
013  description                     varchar2(80),
014  result                          varchar2(256),
015  unique_session_id               varchar2(24),
016  insert_user                     varchar2(30),
017  insert_date                     date,
018
019  -- Allocate the next primary key value fir id
020  STATIC FUNCTION get_id
021  return                          number,
022
023  -- Get the test value for January 1, 1900
```

```
024    STATIC FUNCTION get_test_19000101
025    return                               date,
026
027    -- Get the test value for December 31, 1999
028    STATIC FUNCTION get_test_19991231
029    return                               date,
030
031    -- Get the test value N for any indicators
032    STATIC FUNCTION get_test_n
033    return                            varchar2,
034
035    -- Get the test value Y for any indicators
036    STATIC FUNCTION get_test_y
037    return                            varchar2,
038
039    -- Get the 30 character test value
040    STATIC FUNCTION get_test_30
041    return                            varchar2,
042
043    -- Get the first 30 character test value duplicate for LIKE
044    STATIC FUNCTION get_test_30_1
045    return                            varchar2,
046
047    -- Get the second 30 character test value duplicate for LIKE
048    STATIC FUNCTION get_test_30_2
049    return                            varchar2,
050
051    -- Get the 80 character test value
052    STATIC FUNCTION get_test_80
053    return                            varchar2,
054
055    -- Get the 100 character test value
056    STATIC FUNCTION get_test_100
057    return                            varchar2,
058
059    -- Get the 2000 character test value
060    STATIC FUNCTION get_test_2000
061    return                            varchar2,
062
063    -- Clear any previous test run for the specified object name
064    STATIC PROCEDURE clear(
065    aiv_object_name                   varchar2),
066
067    -- Set the result to ERROR
068    MEMBER PROCEDURE error,
069
070    -- Set the result to Oracle ERROR
071    MEMBER PROCEDURE error(
072    aiv_result                 in     varchar2),
073
```

```
074   -- Set the result to the specified result value
075   MEMBER PROCEDURE set_result(
076   aiv_result                         in      varchar2),
077
078   -- Show the help text for this object
079   STATIC PROCEDURE help,
080
081   -- Set the result to OK
082   MEMBER PROCEDURE ok,
083
084   -- Set the result of the execution of test() to SUCCESS
085   MEMBER PROCEDURE success,
086
087   -- Test this object
088   STATIC PROCEDURE "test",
089
090   -- Set the test about to be performed
091   MEMBER PROCEDURE set_test(
092   aiv_object_name                    in      varchar2,
093   aiv_method_name                    in      varchar2,
094   ain_test_number                    in      number,
095   aiv_description                    in      varchar2),
096
097   -- Get the map value
098   MAP MEMBER FUNCTION to_map
099   return                                     number,
100
101   -- Parameter-less constructor
102   CONSTRUCTOR FUNCTION test(
103   self                       in out nocopy test)
104   return                             self as result,
105
106   -- Convenience constructor
107   CONSTRUCTOR FUNCTION test(
108   self                       in out nocopy test,
109   ain_id                     in      number,
110   aiv_object_name            in      varchar2,
111   aiv_method_name            in      varchar2,
112   ain_test_number            in      number,
113   aiv_description            in      varchar2)
114   return                             self as result
115   );
116   /
117   @se.sql
118
119   grant execute on TEST to public;
```

In Listing 8-5, the TYPE specification for TEST, I added the static functions get_test_19000101()
through get_test_2000() to act as and replace the constants d_TEST_19000101 through v_TEST_2000 from
the package TEST specification on lines 14 through 80.

Listing 8-6. The DDL Script for Table TESTS, ops.tests.tab

```
01  rem tests.tab
02  rem by Donald Bales on 2014-10-20
03  rem Create test results
04
05  --drop   table TESTS;
06  create table TESTS of TEST
07  tablespace USERS pctfree 0
08  storage (initial 1M next 1M pctincrease 0);
09
10  alter  table TESTS add
11  constraint    TESTS_PK
12  primary key (
13  id )
14  using index
15  tablespace USERS pctfree 0
16  storage (initial 1M next 1M pctincrease 0);
17
18  --drop   sequence TESTS_ID;
19  create sequence TESTS_ID
20  start with 1 order;  °
21
22  execute SYS.DBMS_STATS.gather_table_stats(USER, 'TESTS');
23
24  grant all on TESTS to PUBLIC;
```

There's nothing really new in Listing 8-6, the script to create a table based on TYPE TEST.

Listing 8-7. A DDL Script for TYPE TEST's BODY, ops.test.tpb

```
001  create or replace type body TEST as
002  /*
003  test.tpb
004  by Donald J. Bales on 2014-10-20
005  A Type for logging test results
006  */
007
008  STATIC PROCEDURE clear(
009  aiv_object_name                       varchar2) is
010
011  pragma autonomous_transaction;
012
013  begin
014    delete TESTS
015    where  object_name       = aiv_object_name
016    and    unique_session_id = SYS.DBMS_SESSION.unique_session_id;
017
018    commit;
019  end clear;
020
021
```

```
022   STATIC FUNCTION get_id
023   return                              number is
024
025   n_id                               number;
026
027   begin
028     select TESTS_ID.nextval
029     into   n_id
030     from   SYS.DUAL;
031
032     return n_id;
033   end get_id;
034
035
036   STATIC FUNCTION get_test_19000101
037   return                                date is
038
039   begin
040     return to_date('19000101', 'YYYYMMDD');
041   end get_test_19000101;
042
043
044   STATIC FUNCTION get_test_19991231
045   return                                date is
046
047   begin
048     return to_date('19991231', 'YYYYMMDD');
049   end get_test_19991231;
050
051
052   STATIC FUNCTION get_test_n
053   return                                varchar2 is
054
055   begin
056     return 'N';
057   end get_test_n;
058
059
060   STATIC FUNCTION get_test_y
061   return                                varchar2 is
062
063   begin
064     return 'Y';
065   end get_test_y;
066
067
068   STATIC FUNCTION get_test_30
069   return                                varchar2 is
070
071   begin
072     return 'TEST TEST TEST TEST TEST TESTx';
073   end get_test_30;
```

```
074
075
076  STATIC FUNCTION get_test_30_1
077  return                              varchar2 is
078
079  begin
080    return 'TEST1 TEST1 TEST1 TEST1 TEST1x';
081  end get_test_30_1;
082
083
084  STATIC FUNCTION get_test_30_2
085  return                              varchar2 is
086
087  begin
088    return 'TEST2 TEST2 TEST2 TEST2 TEST2x';
089  end get_test_30_2;
090
091
092  STATIC FUNCTION get_test_80
093  return                              varchar2 is
094
095  begin
096    return 'Test Test Test Test Test Test Test Test '||
097           'Test Test Test Test Test Test Test Testx';
098  end get_test_80;
099
100
101  STATIC FUNCTION get_test_100
102  return                              varchar2 is
103
104  begin
105    return 'Test Test Test Test Test Test Test Test Test Test '||
106           'Test Test Test Test Test Test Test Test Test Testx';
107  end get_test_100;
108
109
110  STATIC FUNCTION get_test_2000
111  return                              varchar2 is
112  --              1         2         3         4         5
113  --     12345678901234567890123456789012345678901234567890
114  begin
115    return 'Test Test Test Test Test Test Test Test Test Test '||
116           'Test Test Test Test Test Test Test Test Test Test '||
117           'Test Test Test Test Test Test Test Test Test Test '||
118           'Test Test Test Test Test Test Test Test Test Test '||
119           'Test Test Test Test Test Test Test Test Test Test '||
120           'Test Test Test Test Test Test Test Test Test Test '||
121           'Test Test Test Test Test Test Test Test Test Test '||
122           'Test Test Test Test Test Test Test Test Test Test '||
123           'Test Test Test Test Test Test Test Test Test Test '||
```

281

```
124               'Test Test Test Test Test Test Test Test Test Test '||
125               'Test Test Test Test Test Test Test Test Test Test '||
126               'Test Test Test Test Test Test Test Test Test Test '||
127               'Test Test Test Test Test Test Test Test Test Test '||
128               'Test Test Test Test Test Test Test Test Test Test '||
129               'Test Test Test Test Test Test Test Test Test Test '||
130               'Test Test Test Test Test Test Test Test Test Test '||
131               'Test Test Test Test Test Test Test Test Test Test '||
132               'Test Test Test Test Test Test Test Test Test Test '||
133               'Test Test Test Test Test Test Test Test Test Test '||
134               'Test Test Test Test Test Test Test Test Test Test '||
135               'Test Test Test Test Test Test Test Test Test Test '||
136               'Test Test Test Test Test Test Test Test Test Test '||
137               'Test Test Test Test Test Test Test Test Test Test '||
138               'Test Test Test Test Test Test Test Test Test Test '||
139               'Test Test Test Test Test Test Test Test Test Test '||
140               'Test Test Test Test Test Test Test Test Test Test '||
141               'Test Test Test Test Test Test Test Test Test Test '||
142               'Test Test Test Test Test Test Test Test Test Test '||
143               'Test Test Test Test Test Test Test Test Test Test '||
144               'Test Test Test Test Test Test Test Test Test Test '||
145               'Test Test Test Test Test Test Test Test Test Test '||
146               'Test Test Test Test Test Test Test Test Test Test '||
147               'Test Test Test Test Test Test Test Test Test Test '||
148               'Test Test Test Test Test Test Test Test Test Test '||
149               'Test Test Test Test Test Test Test Test Test Test '||
150               'Test Test Test Test Test Test Test Test Test Test '||
151               'Test Test Test Test Test Test Test Test Test Test '||
152               'Test Test Test Test Test Test Test Test Test Test '||
153               'Test Test Test Test Test Test Test Test Test Test '||
154               'Test Test Test Test Test Test Test Test Test Testx';
155   end get_test_2000;
156
157
158   STATIC PROCEDURE help is
159   begin
160     pl('You''re on your own buddy.');
161   end help;
162
163
164   MEMBER PROCEDURE error is
165
166   begin
167     set_result('ERROR');
168   end error;
169
170
171   MEMBER PROCEDURE error(
172   aiv_result                    in      varchar2) is
173
```

```
174  begin
175    set_result(aiv_result);
176  end error;
177
178
179  MEMBER PROCEDURE ok is
180
181  begin
182    set_result('OK');
183  end ok;
184
185
186  MEMBER PROCEDURE set_result(
187  aiv_result                     in      varchar2) is
188
189  pragma autonomous_transaction;
190
191  begin
192    result := aiv_result;
193
194    update TESTS
195    set    result = self.result
196    where  id     = self.id;
197
198    if nvl(sql%rowcount, 0) = 0 then
199      raise_application_error(-20000, 'Can''t find test'||
200        to_char(self.id)||
201        ' on update TEST'||
202        ' in TEST_TS.test');
203    end if;
204
205    self := new test();
206
207    commit;
208  end set_result;
209
210
211  MEMBER PROCEDURE set_test(
212  aiv_object_name                in      varchar2,
213  aiv_method_name                in      varchar2,
214  ain_test_number                in      number,
215  aiv_description                in      varchar2) is
216
217  pragma autonomous_transaction;
218
219  begin
220    self.id                := TEST.get_id();
221    self.object_name       := upper(aiv_object_name);
222    self.method_name       := upper(aiv_method_name);
223    self.test_number       := ain_test_number;
224    self.description        := aiv_description;
225    self.result            := NULL;
```

```
226    self.unique_session_id := SYS.DBMS_SESSION.unique_session_id;
227    self.insert_user        := USER;
228    self.insert_date        := SYSDATE;
229
230    begin
231      insert into TESTS values (self);
232    exception
233      when OTHERS then
234        raise_application_error(-20000, SQLERRM||
235          ' on insert TESTS'||
236          ' in TEST.set_test');
237    end;
238    commit;
239  end set_test;
240
241
242  MEMBER PROCEDURE success is
243
244  begin
245    set_result('SUCCESS');
246  end success;
247
248
249  STATIC PROCEDURE "test" is
250
251  n_number                              number;
252  o_test                                TEST;
253
254  begin
255    pl('TEST.test()');
256
257    -- A defect requires the schema owner
258    &_USER..TEST.clear('TEST');
259
260    o_test := new TEST();
261    o_test.set_test('TEST', NULL, 1,
262      'Is get_test_N equal to N?');
263    if TEST.get_test_N = 'N' then
264      o_test.success();
265    else
266      o_test.error();
267    end if;
268
269    o_test.set_test('TEST', NULL, 2,
270      'Is the length of get_test_N equal to 1?');
271    if nvl(length(TEST.get_test_N), 0) = 1 then
272      o_test.success();
273    else
274      o_test.error();
275    end if;
276
```

```
277     o_test.set_test('TEST', NULL, 3,
278       'Is get_test_Y equal to Y?');
279     if TEST.get_test_Y = 'Y' then
280       o_test.success();
281     else
282       o_test.error();
283     end if;
284
285     o_test.set_test('TEST', NULL, 4,
286       'Is the length of get_test_Y equal to 1?');
287     if nvl(length(TEST.get_test_Y), 0) = 1 then
288       o_test.success();
289     else
290       o_test.error();
291     end if;
292
293     o_test.set_test('TEST', NULL, 5,
294       'Is the length of get_test_30 equal to 30?');
295     if nvl(length(TEST.get_test_30), 0) = 30 then
296       o_test.success();
297     else
298       o_test.error();
299     end if;
300
301     o_test.set_test('TEST', NULL, 6,
302       'Is the length of get_test_30_1 equal to 30?');
303     if nvl(length(TEST.get_test_30_1), 0) = 30 then
304       o_test.success();
305     else
306       o_test.error();
307     end if;
308
309     o_test.set_test('TEST', NULL, 7,
310       'Is the length of get_test_30_2 equal to 30?');
311     if nvl(length(TEST.get_test_30_2), 0) = 30 then
312       o_test.success();
313     else
314       o_test.error();
315     end if;
316
317     o_test.set_test('TEST', NULL, 8,
318       'Is the length of get_test_80 equal to 80?');
319     if nvl(length(TEST.get_test_80), 0) = 80 then
320       o_test.success();
321     else
322       o_test.error();
323     end if;
324
325     o_test.set_test('TEST', NULL, 9,
326       'Is the length of get_test_100 equal to 100?');
327     if nvl(length(TEST.get_test_100), 0) = 100 then
```

```
328       o_test.success();
329    else
330      o_test.error();
331    end if;
332
333    o_test.set_test('TEST', NULL, 10,
334      'Is the length of get_test_2000 equal to 2000?');
335    if nvl(length(TEST.get_test_2000), 0) = 2000 then
336      o_test.success();
337    else
338      o_test.error();
339    end if;
340
341    o_test.set_test('TEST', 'get_id', 11,
342      'Does get_id() work?');
343    begin
344      n_number := TEST.get_id();
345      if n_number > 0 then
346        o_test.success();
347      else
348        o_test.error();
349      end if;
350    exception
351      when OTHERS then
352        o_test.error(SQLERRM);
353    end;
354
355    o_test.set_test('TEST', 'help', 12,
356      'Does help() work?');
357    begin
358      &_USER..TEST.help();
359      raise_application_error(-20999, 'Testing the error routine');
360      o_test.success();
361    exception
362      when OTHERS then
363        o_test.error(SQLERRM);
364    end;
365
366    o_test.set_test('TEST', NULL, NULL, NULL);
367    o_test.success();
368 end "test";
369
370
371 MAP MEMBER FUNCTION to_map
372 return                                  number is
373
374 begin
375    return self.id;
376 end to_map;
377
378
```

```
379  CONSTRUCTOR FUNCTION test(
380  self                          in out nocopy test)
381  return                                self as result is
382
383  begin
384     self.id                 := NULL;
385     self.object_name        := NULL;
386     self.method_name        := NULL;
387     self.test_number        := NULL;
388     self.description        := NULL;
389     self.result             := NULL;
390     self.unique_session_id  := NULL;
391     self.insert_user        := NULL;
392     self.insert_date        := NULL;
393
394     return;
395  end test;
396
397
398  CONSTRUCTOR FUNCTION test(
399  self                          in out nocopy test,
400  ain_id                        in      number,
401  aiv_object_name               in      varchar2,
402  aiv_method_name               in      varchar2,
403  ain_test_number               in      number,
404  aiv_description               in      varchar2)
405  return                                self as result is
406
407  begin
408     self.id                 := ain_id;
409     self.object_name        := aiv_object_name;
410     self.method_name        := aiv_method_name;
411     self.test_number        := ain_test_number;
412     self.description        := aiv_description;
413     self.result             := NULL;
414     self.unique_session_id  := SYS.DBMS_SESSION.unique_session_id;
415     self.insert_user        := USER;
416     self.insert_date        := SYSDATE;
417
418     return;
419  end test;
420
421
422  end;
423  /
424  @be.sql TEST
```

Did you notice in Listing 8-6 that I used the SQL*Plus defined variable &USER in the source listing? This is a work-around to a defect in the Oracle compiler when trying to resolve the name of a method that is part of the same TYPE BODY.

In the sections that follow, I'll use the relational testing tool to test packages and the object-relational tool I just created to test TYPEs. So let's move on to a discussion of testing with these new testing tools.

Testing

Do you recall the discussion about table types early in Chapter 1, where I said that tables fall into one of three categories: content, codes, or intersections? The types of methods and method names used by each of these three categories will follow a pattern. Content table packages (or TYPEs) will all have a similar set of methods and method names. Code table packages (or TYPEs) will also have a similar set of methods and method names. And so will intersection table packages (or TYPEs).

Accordingly, these three categories will have a pattern of tests that follows the set of methods and method names used by each category. Content table packages will generally have methods to insert, update, delete, and select a specified row from a table. In contrast, a code table will have only a method to get the ID value for a specified code, or code and description for a specified ID. Intersection table packages will have methods like content table packages, and additional methods suitable only for intersections.

So the SQL Circle of Life I talked about earlier in this chapter will be fully employed for content and intersection table packages but not for code table packages. Since content tables are usually dependent on one or more code tables, and intersection tables are dependent on two content tables, let's start with a code table package. I'll cover the testing of the WORKER_TYPE table package now, and you'll code and test the GENDER_TYPE table package later in this section.

Testing a Code Table Package

As usual, let's dive right into a code listing. Listings 8-8 and 8-9 are the full-blown, production-ready packages for the WORKER_TYPE table.

The package specification lists methods that are specific to a code table.

- get_code_descr(): Used to retrieve the code and description values for a specified ID.

- get_code_id_descr(): Used to retrieve the code, ID, and description values for a fully or partially specified code. For a partially specified code, the method may return a single matching set of values or raise exception TOO_MANY_ROWS if more than one matching entry exists in the table.

- get_id(): Returns the ID that corresponds to the specified code.

The package specification also lists some methods that are universal to all table packages.

- get_id(): Returns a newly allocated primary key value for the table.

- help(): Displays help text for the package.

- test(): Tests the package.

Listing 8-8. The Specification for Table Package WORKER_TYPE, rps.worker_type.pks

```
01  create or replace PACKAGE WORKER_TYPE as
02  /*
03  worker_type.pks
04  by Don Bales on 2014-10-20
05  Code Table WORKER_TYPES's methods.
06  */
07
```

```
08
09   -- Gets the code and decription values for the specified ain_id.
10   PROCEDURE get_code_descr(
11   ain_id                          in      WORKER_TYPES.id%TYPE,
12   aov_code                        out WORKER_TYPES.code%TYPE,
13   aov_description                 out WORKER_TYPES.description%TYPE );
14
15
16   -- Verifies the passed aiov_code value is an exact or like match on
17   -- the date specified.
18   PROCEDURE get_code_id_descr(
19   aiov_code                       in out WORKER_TYPES.code%TYPE,
20   aon_id                          out WORKER_TYPES.id%TYPE,
21   aov_description                 out WORKER_TYPES.description%TYPE,
22   aid_on                          in      WORKER_TYPES.active_date%TYPE );
23
24
25   -- Verifies the passed aiov_code value is currently an exact or like
26   -- match.
27   PROCEDURE get_code_id_descr(
28   aiov_code                       in out WORKER_TYPES.code%TYPE,
29   aon_id                          out WORKER_TYPES.id%TYPE,
30   aov_description                 out WORKER_TYPES.description%TYPE );
31
32
33   -- Returns a newly allocated id value.
34   FUNCTION get_id
35   return                                  WORKER_TYPES.id%TYPE;
36
37
38   -- Returns the id for the specified code value.
39   FUNCTION get_id(
40   aiv_code                        in      WORKER_TYPES.code%TYPE )
41   return                                  WORKER_TYPES.id%TYPE;
42
43
44   -- Test-based help for this package. "set serveroutput on" in
45   -- SQL*Plus.
46   PROCEDURE help;
47
48
49   -- Test units for this package.
50   PROCEDURE test;
51
52
53   end WORKER_TYPE;
54   /
55   @se.sql WORKER_TYPE
```

Listing 8-9. The Body for Table Package WORKER_TYPE ,rps. worker_type.pkb

```
001  create or replace PACKAGE BODY WORKER_TYPE as
002  /*
003  worker_type.pkb
004  by Don Bales on 2014-10-20
005  Table WORKER_TYPES's methods
006  */
007
008
009  PROCEDURE get_code_descr(
010  ain_id                        in    WORKER_TYPES.id%TYPE,
011  aov_code                          out WORKER_TYPES.code%TYPE,
012  aov_description                   out WORKER_TYPES.description%TYPE ) is
013
014  begin
015    select code,
016           description
017    into   aov_code,
018           aov_description
019    from   WORKER_TYPES
020    where  id = ain_id;
021  end get_code_descr;
022
023
024  PROCEDURE get_code_id_descr(
025  aiov_code                     in out WORKER_TYPES.code%TYPE,
026  aon_id                            out WORKER_TYPES.id%TYPE,
027  aov_description                   out WORKER_TYPES.description%TYPE,
028  aid_on                        in    WORKER_TYPES.active_date%TYPE ) is
029
030  v_code                               WORKER_TYPES.code%TYPE;
031
032  begin
033    select id,
034           description
035    into   aon_id,
036           aov_description
037    from   WORKER_TYPES
038    where  code = aiov_code
039    and    aid_on between active_date and nvl(inactive_date, DATE_.d_MAX);
040  exception
041    when NO_DATA_FOUND then
042      select id,
043             code,
044             description
045      into   aon_id,
046             v_code,
047             aov_description
048      from   WORKER_TYPES
049      where  code like aiov_code||'%'
050      and    aid_on between active_date and nvl(inactive_date, DATE_.d_MAX);
```

```
051
052      aiov_code := v_code;
053  end get_code_id_descr;
054
055
056  PROCEDURE get_code_id_descr(
057  aiov_code                        in out WORKER_TYPES.code%TYPE,
058  aon_id                           out WORKER_TYPES.id%TYPE,
059  aov_description                  out WORKER_TYPES.description%TYPE ) is
060
061  begin
062    get_code_id_descr(
063      aiov_code,
064      aon_id,
065      aov_description,
066      SYSDATE );
067  end get_code_id_descr;
068
069
070  FUNCTION get_id
071  return                           WORKER_TYPES.id%TYPE is
072
073  n_id                             WORKER_TYPES.id%TYPE;
074
075  begin
076    select WORKER_TYPES_ID.nextval
077    into   n_id
078    from   SYS.DUAL;
079
080    return n_id;
081  end get_id;
082
083
084  FUNCTION get_id(
085  aiv_code                    in   WORKER_TYPES.code%TYPE )
086  return                           WORKER_TYPES.id%TYPE is
087
088  n_id                             WORKER_TYPES.id%TYPE;
089
090  begin
091    select id
092    into   n_id
093    from   WORKER_TYPES
094    where  code = aiv_code;
095
096    return n_id;
097  end get_id;
098
099
100  PROCEDURE help is
101
```

```
102    begin
103    --     123456789012345678901234567890123456789012345678901234567890123456789012345678901234567890
104    pl('=================================== PACKAGE ======================================');
105    pl(chr(9));
106    pl('WORKER_TYPE');
107    pl(chr(9));
108    pl('--------------------------------- FUNCTIONS ---------------------------------------');
109    pl(chr(9));
110    pl('WORKER_TYPE.get_id');
111    pl('return                                    WORKER_TYPES.id%TYPE;');
112    pl(chr(9)||'Returns a newly allocated sequence value for id.');
113    pl(chr(9));
114    pl('WORKER_TYPE.get_id(');
115    pl('aiv_code                       in      WORKER_TYPES.code%TYPE )');
116    pl('return                                    WORKER_TYPES.id%TYPE;');
117    pl(chr(9)||'Returns the corresponding id for the specified code.');
118    pl(chr(9));
119    pl('--------------------------------- PROCEDURES --------------------------------------');
120    pl(chr(9));
121    pl('WORKER_TYPE.get_code_descr(');
122    pl('ain_id                         in      WORKER_TYPES.id%TYPE,');
123    pl('aov_code                               out WORKER_TYPES.code%TYPE,');
124    pl('aov_description                        out WORKER_TYPES.description%TYPE );');
125    pl(chr(9)||'Gets the corresponding code and description for the specified');
126    pl(chr(9)||'id.');
127    pl(chr(9));
128    pl('WORKER_TYPE.get_code_id_descr(');
129    pl('aiov_code                      in out WORKER_TYPES.code%TYPE,');
130    pl('aon_id                                 out WORKER_TYPES.id%TYPE,');
131    pl('aov_description                        out WORKER_TYPES.description%TYPE,');
132    pl('aid_on                         in      WORKER_TYPES.active_date%TYPE );');
133    pl(chr(9)||'Gets the corresponding code, id, and description for');
134    pl(chr(9)||'the specified code.  First it trys to find an exact match.  If one');
135    pl(chr(9)||'cannot be found, it trys to find a like match.  It may throw a');
136    pl(chr(9)||'NO_DATA_FOUND or a TOO_MANY_ROWS exception if a match cannot be');
137    pl(chr(9)||'found for the specified code and point in time.');
138    pl(chr(9));
139    pl('WORKER_TYPE.get_code_id_descr(');
140    pl('aiov_code                      in out WORKER_TYPES.code%TYPE,');
141    pl('aon_id                                 out WORKER_TYPES.id%TYPE,');
142    pl('aov_description                        out WORKER_TYPES.description%TYPE );');
143    pl(chr(9)||'Gets the corresponding code, id, and description for');
144    pl(chr(9)||'the specified code.  First it trys to find an exact match.  If one');
145    pl(chr(9)||'cannot be found, it trys to find a like match.  It may throw a');
146    pl(chr(9)||'NO_DATA_FOUND or a TOO_MANY_ROWS exception if a match cannot be');
147    pl(chr(9)||'found for the specified code at the current point in time.');
148    pl(chr(9));
```

```
149    pl('WORKER_TYPE.help( );');
150    pl(chr(9)||'Displays this help text if set serveroutput is on.');
151    pl(chr(9));
152    pl('WORKER_TYPE.test( );');
153    pl(chr(9)||'Built-in test unit.  It will report success or error for each test if
set');
154    pl(chr(9)||'serveroutput is on.');
155    pl(chr(9));
156  end help;
157
158
159  PROCEDURE test is
160
161  n_id                               WORKER_TYPES.id%TYPE;
162  v_code                             WORKER_TYPES.code%TYPE;
163  v_description                      WORKER_TYPES.description%TYPE;
164
165  begin
166    -- Send feedback that the test ran
167    pl('WORKER_TYPE.test()');
168
169    -- Clear the last set of test results
170    &_USER..TEST.clear('WORKER_TYPE');
171
172    -- First, we need some test values
173
174    -- Let's make sure they don't already exist: DELETE
175    &_USER..TEST.set_test('WORKER_TYPE', 'DELETE', 0,
176      'Delete test entries');
177    begin
178      delete WORKER_TYPES
179      where  code in (
180        &_USER..TEST.v_TEST_30,
181        &_USER..TEST.v_TEST_30_1,
182        &_USER..TEST.v_TEST_30_2);
183      &_USER..TEST.ok();
184    exception
185      when OTHERS then
186        &_USER..TEST.error(SQLERRM);
187    end;
188
189    -- Now let's add three test codes: INSERT
190    &_USER..TEST.set_test('WORKER_TYPE', 'INSERT', 1,
191      'Insert 3 test entries');
192    begin
193      insert into WORKER_TYPES (
194              id,
195              code,
196              description,
197              active_date,
198              inactive_date )
```

```
199      values (
200            get_id(),
201            &_USER..TEST.v_TEST_30,
202            &_USER..TEST.v_TEST_80,
203            &_USER..TEST.d_TEST_19000101,
204            &_USER..TEST.d_TEST_99991231 );
205
206      insert into WORKER_TYPES (
207            id,
208            code,
209            description,
210            active_date,
211            inactive_date )
212      values (
213            get_id(),
214            &_USER..TEST.v_TEST_30_1,
215            &_USER..TEST.v_TEST_80,
216            &_USER..TEST.d_TEST_19000101,
217            &_USER..TEST.d_TEST_99991231 );
218
219      insert into WORKER_TYPES (
220            id,
221            code,
222            description,
223            active_date,
224            inactive_date )
225      values (
226            get_id(),
227            &_USER..TEST.v_TEST_30_2,
228            &_USER..TEST.v_TEST_80,
229            &_USER..TEST.d_TEST_19000101,
230            &_USER..TEST.d_TEST_99991231 );
231
232      &_USER..TEST.ok();
233    exception
234      when OTHERS then
235        &_USER..TEST.error(SQLERRM);
236    end;
237
238    -- Now that we have test entries,
239    -- let's test the package methods
240    &_USER..TEST.set_test('WORKER_TYPE', 'get_id()', 2,
241      'Get the ID for the specified code');
242    begin
243      n_id := get_id(&_USER..TEST.v_TEST_30);
244
245      if n_id > 0 then
246        &_USER..TEST.ok();
247      else
248        &_USER..TEST.error();
249      end if;
```

```
250    exception
251      when OTHERS then
252        &_USER..TEST.error(SQLERRM);
253    end;
254
255    &_USER..TEST.set_test('WORKER_TYPE', 'get_code_descr()', 3,
256      'Get the code and description for the specified ID');
257    begin
258      get_code_descr(
259        n_id,
260        v_code,
261        v_description);
262      if v_code        = &_USER..TEST.v_TEST_30 and
263        v_description = &_USER..TEST.v_TEST_80 then
264        &_USER..TEST.ok();
265      else
266        &_USER..TEST.error();
267      end if;
268    exception
269      when OTHERS then
270        &_USER..TEST.error(SQLERRM);
271    end;
272
273    &_USER..TEST.set_test('WORKER_TYPE', 'get_code_id_descr()', 4,
274      'Get the code, ID, and description for the specified code');
275    begin
276      v_code := &_USER..TEST.v_TEST_30;
277      get_code_id_descr(
278        v_code,
279        n_id,
280        v_description);
281      if v_code            = &_USER..TEST.v_TEST_30 and
282        n_id              > 0                       and
283        v_description     = &_USER..TEST.v_TEST_80 then
284        &_USER..TEST.ok();
285      else
286        &_USER..TEST.error();
287      end if;
288    exception
289      when OTHERS then
290        &_USER..TEST.error(SQLERRM);
291    end;
292
293    &_USER..TEST.set_test('WORKER_TYPE', 'get_code_id_descr()', 5,
294      'Get the code, ID, and description for the specified date');
295    begin
296      v_code := 'TEST';
297      -- This test should raise a TOO_MANY_ROWS exception
298      -- because at least three duplicate values will
299      -- on the date specified
300      get_code_id_descr(
```

```
301          v_code,
302          n_id,
303          v_description,
304          &_USER..TEST.d_TEST_99991231);
305      if v_code            = &_USER..TEST.v_TEST_30 and
306         n_id > 0                    and
307         v_description     = &_USER..TEST.v_TEST_80 then
308         &_USER..TEST.ok();
309      else
310         &_USER..TEST.error();
311      end if;
312    exception
313      when TOO_MANY_ROWS then
314         &_USER..TEST.ok();
315      when OTHERS then
316         &_USER..TEST.error(SQLERRM);
317    end;
318
319    &_USER..TEST.set_test('WORKER_TYPE', 'help()', 6,
320      'Display help');
321    begin
322      help();
323      &_USER..TEST.ok();
324    exception
325      when OTHERS then
326         &_USER..TEST.error(SQLERRM);
327    end;
328
329    -- Let's make sure they don't already exist: DELETE
330    &_USER..TEST.set_test('WORKER_TYPE', 'DELETE', 7,
331      'Delete test entries');
332    begin
333      delete WORKER_TYPES
334      where   code in (
335         &_USER..TEST.v_TEST_30,
336         &_USER..TEST.v_TEST_30_1,
337         &_USER..TEST.v_TEST_30_2);
338      &_USER..TEST.ok();
339    exception
340      when OTHERS then
341         &_USER..TEST.error(SQLERRM);
342    end;
343
344    &_USER..TEST.set_test('WORKER_TYPE', NULL, NULL, NULL);
345    &_USER..TEST.success();
346  end test;
347
348
349  end WORKER_TYPE;
350  /
351  @be.sql WORKER_TYPE
```

I'll explain only the test unit method test() in Listing 8-9 this time around.

- Lines 161 through 163 declare a handful of variables that I will need while testing the package's methods.

- Line 167 uses pl() to output some feedback to the tester that the test method did indeed execute.

- Line 170 clears any previous test results for this package.

- Lines 175 through 187 delete any existing "test" entries so they don't cause a problem with the current test. I do this with a SQL DELETE statement because the code table package pattern of methods has no ongoing use for a routine that deletes code values.

- Lines 190 through 236 insert three "test" entries into the code table. The first entry uses the standard 30-character value for the code. I'll try to find an exact match for this value later in testing. The second and third entries exist to cause a TOO_MANY_ROWS exception later in testing. Without explicitly testing the method, get_id(), the method that returns a new primary key value is also tested during the insertion of the three "test" entries.

- Lines 240 through 253 test the second get_id() method, the code table package pattern method, which returns a code's ID value.

- Lines 255 through 271 test method get_code_descr().

- Lines 273 through 291 test the method get_code_id_descr() for an exact match on today's date.

- Lines 293 through 317 test the method get_code_id_descr() to verify it will raise exception TOO_MANY_ROWS when there is no exact match.

- Lines 319 through 327 test method help().

- Lines 330 through 342 delete the "test" entries I added at the beginning of the test. This means I've used DELETE, INSERT, and then DELETE as the SQL Circle of Life for testing this code table package.

- Lines 344 and 345 add the entry to the testing table that indicates the test method itself ran successfully.

I can now query the table TESTS to find the results of the test. Listing 8-10 is a SQL*Plus script to list the results of the last performed test.

Listing 8-10. A Report to Show the Results of the Last Test, rps.last_test_results.sql

```
01  rem last_test_results.sql
02  rem by Donald J. Bales on 2014-10-20
03  rem Display the last test results
04
05  set linesize 1000;
06  set newpage  1;
07  set pagesize 32767;
08  set trimspool on;
09
10  column test            format a34;
11  column t#              format 99;
```

```
12   column description   format a27;
13   column result         format a7;
14
15   spool last_test_results.txt;
16
17   select t.object_name||
18          decode(substr(t.method_name, -1, 1), ')', '.', ' ')||
19          t.method_name test,
20          t.test_number t#,
21          t.description,
22          t.result
23   from   TESTS t
24   where  t.unique_session_id = SYS.DBMS_SESSION.unique_session_id
25   and    t.object_name       = (
26   select e.object_name
27   from   TESTS e
28   where  e.unique_session_id = SYS.DBMS_SESSION.unique_session_id
29   and    e.id                = (
30   select max(x.id)
31   from   TESTS x
32   where  x.unique_session_id = SYS.DBMS_SESSION.unique_session_id))
33   order by t.id;
34
35   spool off;
```

When I run script last_test_results.sql after testing WORKER_TYPE I get the following output from SQL*Plus:

```
TEST                                T# DESCRIPTION                          RESULT
----------------------------------- --- ------------------------------------ -------
WORKER_TYPE DELETE                   0 Delete test entries                  OK
WORKER_TYPE INSERT                   1 Insert 3 test entries                OK
WORKER_TYPE.GET_ID()                 2 Get the ID for the specified code    OK

WORKER_TYPE.GET_CODE_DESCR()         3 Get the code and description          OK
                                       for the specified ID

WORKER_TYPE.GET_CODE_ID_DESCR()      4 Get the code, ID, and                OK
                                       description for the specified code

WORKER_TYPE.GET_CODE_ID_DESCR()      5 Get the code, ID, and descr          OK
                                       iption for the specified date

WORKER_TYPE.HELP()                   6 Display help                         OK
WORKER_TYPE DELETE                   7 Delete test entries                  OK
WORKER_TYPE                                                                 SUCCESS

9 rows selected.
```

If any of the tests failed, the enclosing PL/SQL block caught any raised exception, then the column `result` would list the word `ERROR` or the reported Oracle error message from any raised exception. If the enclosing PL/SQL block around a test failed to catch a raised exception, then the test unit itself would not complete, and the last entry in the report, `SUCCESS`, would not exist. Now that you've seen me do it, it's your turn.

It's Your Turn to Test a Code Table Package

I tested the `WORKER_TYPE` code table package, and you'll test the `GENDER_TYPE` code table package. The two tests should be very similar. You can find a full-blown, production-ready version of package `GENDER_TYPE` in the downloaded code directory for Chapter 8. I suggest you proceed as follows.

1. Copy the method `WORKER_TYPE.test()` and paste it into package body `GENDER_TYPE`.

2. Modify the method for any column name and other changes.

3. Save and compile the package body.

4. Execute the test against `GENDER_TYPE` by executing method `test()`.

5. Use report `last_test_results.sql` to see the results of your test.

No, I'm not going to show you my solution because it follows the same pattern as any other code table package's `test()` method. Instead, let's move on to testing a content table's package.

Testing a Content Table Package

This time, for an example of a content table test unit, I'm going to show you only a partial code listing. Listing 8-11 is the test unit from the full-blown, production-ready package for the `LOGICAL_WORKPLACES` table. Its package specification (not shown) lists the following methods that are specific to a content table package (or `TYPE`):

- `get_name()` or `get_name_context()`: Actually, in this case, since table `LOGICAL_WORKPLACES` has a hierarchal relationship with itself, the method is `get_name_context()`, which shows all the names in the hierarchy separated by periods (`.`).

- `get_external_id()` or `get_code_context()`: Once again, since table `LOGICAL_WORKPLACES` has a hierarchal relationship with itself, the method is named `get_code_context()`, which shows all the external IDs in the hierarchy separated by periods (`.`).

- `get_row()`: Returns a matching row depending on primary key column or unique key column value(s) set in the record passed to the method.

- `set_row()`: Updates an existing matching row, using the same rules implemented by `get_row()` to find a matching row, or inserts a new row if a match is not found.

The package specification has one method that is unique to a hierarchal table:

- `create_id_context()`: Creates a hierarchal unique key that represents the hierarchal relationship between rows in the same table as a character value separated by periods (`.`)

And it also has some methods that are universal to all table packages:

- get_id()Returns a newly allocated primary key value for the table
- help()help text for the package
- test()package

Listing 8-11. The test( ) Method from Table Package Body LOGICAL_WORKPLACE, rps.logical_workplace.pkb

```
264  PROCEDURE test is
265
266  /*
267  LOGICAL_WORKPLACES
268   Name                                          Null?     Type
269   ------------------------------------------    --------  -------------
270   LOGICAL_WORKPLACE_ID                          NOT NULL  NUMBER
271   PARENT_ID                                               NUMBER
272   ID_CONTEXT                                    NOT NULL  VARCHAR2(100)
273   WORKPLACE_TYPE_ID                             NOT NULL  NUMBER
274   CODE                                          NOT NULL  VARCHAR2(30)
275   NAME                                          NOT NULL  VARCHAR2(80)
276   ACTIVE_DATE                                   NOT NULL  DATE
277   INACTIVE_DATE                                           DATE
278  */
279
280  v_id_context
281    LOGICAL_WORKPLACES.id_context%TYPE;
282  r_logical_workplace                    LOGICAL_WORKPLACES%ROWTYPE;
283
284  begin
285    pl('LOGICAL_WORKPLACE.test()');
286
287    &_USER..TEST.clear('LOGICAL_WORKPLACE');
288
289    &_USER..TEST.set_test('LOGICAL_WORKPLACE', 'DELETE', 0,
290      'Delete existing test entries');
291    begin
292      delete LOGICAL_WORKPLACES
293      where   code in (
294        &_USER..TEST.v_TEST_30_1,
295        &_USER..TEST.v_TEST_30_2);
296
297      delete LOGICAL_WORKPLACES
298      where   code = &_USER..TEST.v_TEST_30;
299
300      &_USER..TEST.ok();
301    exception
302      when OTHERS then
303        &_USER..TEST.error(SQLERRM);
304    end;
305
```

```
306    &_USER..TEST.set_test('LOGICAL_WORKPLACE', 'get_id()', 1,
307      'Allocate the next primary key value');
308    begin
309      r_logical_workplace.id := get_id();
310
311      if r_logical_workplace.id > 0 then
312        &_USER..TEST.ok();
313      else
314        &_USER..TEST.error();
315      end if;
316    exception
317      when OTHERS then
318        &_USER..TEST.error(SQLERRM);
319    end;
320
321    &_USER..TEST.set_test('LOGICAL_WORKPLACE',
322      'create_id_context()', 2, 'Create an ID context value');
323    begin
324      r_logical_workplace.parent_id            := NULL;
325      r_logical_workplace.id_context           :=
326        create_id_context(
327          r_logical_workplace.parent_id,
328          r_logical_workplace.id);
329
330      if r_logical_workplace.id_context =
331        to_char(r_logical_workplace.id) then
332        &_USER..TEST.ok();
333      else
334        &_USER..TEST.error();
335      end if;
336    exception
337      when OTHERS then
338        &_USER..TEST.error(SQLERRM);
339    end;
340
341    &_USER..TEST.set_test('LOGICAL_WORKPLACE', 'set_row()', 3,
342      'Insert parent test entry');
343    begin
344      r_logical_workplace.workplace_type_id    :=
345        WORKPLACE_TYPE.get_id('C');
346      r_logical_workplace.code                 :=
347        &_USER..TEST.v_TEST_30;
348      r_logical_workplace.name                 :=
349        &_USER..TEST.v_TEST_80;
350      r_logical_workplace.active_date          :=
351        &_USER..TEST.d_TEST_19000101;
352      r_logical_workplace.inactive_date        :=
353        &_USER..TEST.d_TEST_99991231;
354      set_row(r_logical_workplace);
355
356      &_USER..TEST.ok();
357    exception
```

```
358        when OTHERS then
359          &_USER..TEST.error(SQLERRM);
360      end;
361
362      &_USER..TEST.set_test('LOGICAL_WORKPLACE', 'set_row()', 4,
363        'Insert child entries');
364      begin
365        r_logical_workplace.parent_id              :=
366          r_logical_workplace.id;
367        r_logical_workplace.id                     := get_id();
368        r_logical_workplace.id_context             :=
369          create_id_context(
370            r_logical_workplace.parent_id,
371            r_logical_workplace.id);
372        -- save this value for testing get_row()
373        v_id_context                               :=
374          r_logical_workplace.id_context;
375        r_logical_workplace.workplace_type_id      :=
376          WORKPLACE_TYPE.get_id('B');
377        r_logical_workplace.code                   :=
378          &_USER..TEST.v_TEST_30_1;
379        r_logical_workplace.name                   :=
380          &_USER..TEST.v_TEST_80;
381        set_row(r_logical_workplace);
382
383        r_logical_workplace.id                     := get_id();
384        r_logical_workplace.id_context             :=
385          create_id_context(
386            r_logical_workplace.parent_id,
387            r_logical_workplace.id);
388        r_logical_workplace.code                   :=
389          &_USER..TEST.v_TEST_30_2;
390        set_row(r_logical_workplace);
391
392        &_USER..TEST.ok();
393      exception
394        when OTHERS then
395          &_USER..TEST.error(SQLERRM);
396      end;
397
398      &_USER..TEST.set_test('LOGICAL_WORKPLACE', 'get_code_context()', 5,
399        'Get the code context for v_TEST_30_2');
400      begin
401        pl(get_code_context(
402          r_logical_workplace.id));
403
404        &_USER..TEST.ok();
405      exception
406        when OTHERS then
407          &_USER..TEST.error(SQLERRM);
408      end;
409
```

```
410     &_USER..TEST.set_test('LOGICAL_WORKPLACE', 'get_name_context()', 6,
411       'Get the name context for v_TEST_30_2');
412     begin
413       pl(get_name_context(
414         r_logical_workplace.id));
415
416       &_USER..TEST.ok();
417     exception
418       when OTHERS then
419         &_USER..TEST.error(SQLERRM);
420     end;
421
422     &_USER..TEST.set_test('LOGICAL_WORKPLACE', 'get_row()', 7,
423       'Get the row using the id for v_TEST_30_2');
424     begin
425 --    r_logical_workplace.id                  := NULL;
426       r_logical_workplace.parent_id           := NULL;
427       r_logical_workplace.id_context          := NULL;
428       r_logical_workplace.workplace_type_id   := NULL;
429       r_logical_workplace.code                := NULL;
430       r_logical_workplace.name                := NULL;
431       r_logical_workplace.active_date         := NULL;
432       r_logical_workplace.inactive_date       := NULL;
433
434       r_logical_workplace := get_row(r_logical_workplace);
435
436       if r_logical_workplace.id_context is not NULL then
437         &_USER..TEST.ok();
438       else
439         &_USER..TEST.error();
440       end if;
441     exception
442       when OTHERS then
443         &_USER..TEST.error(SQLERRM);
444     end;
445
446     &_USER..TEST.set_test('LOGICAL_WORKPLACE', 'get_row()', 8,
447       'Get the row using the id_context for v_TEST_30_1');
448     begin
449       r_logical_workplace.id                  := NULL;
450       r_logical_workplace.parent_id           := NULL;
451       r_logical_workplace.id_context          :=
452         v_id_context;
453       r_logical_workplace.workplace_type_id   := NULL;
454       r_logical_workplace.code                := NULL;
455       r_logical_workplace.name                := NULL;
456       r_logical_workplace.active_date         := NULL;
457       r_logical_workplace.inactive_date       := NULL;
458
459       r_logical_workplace := get_row(r_logical_workplace);
460
```

```
461       if r_logical_workplace.id is not NULL then
462          &_USER..TEST.ok();
463       else
464          &_USER..TEST.error();
465       end if;
466    exception
467      when OTHERS then
468         pl('v_id_context="'||v_id_context||'"');
469         &_USER..TEST.error(SQLERRM);
470    end;
471
472    &_USER..TEST.set_test('LOGICAL_WORKPLACE', 'get_row()', 9,
473      'Get the row using the code for v_TEST_30');
474    begin
475      r_logical_workplace.id                   := NULL;
476      r_logical_workplace.parent_id            := NULL;
477      r_logical_workplace.id_context           := NULL;
478      r_logical_workplace.workplace_type_id    := NULL;
479      r_logical_workplace.code                 :=
480         &_USER..TEST.v_TEST_30;
481      r_logical_workplace.name                 :=
482         &_USER..TEST.v_TEST_80;
483      r_logical_workplace.active_date          :=
484         &_USER..TEST.d_TEST_19000101;
485      r_logical_workplace.inactive_date        := NULL;
486
487      r_logical_workplace := get_row(r_logical_workplace);
488
489      if r_logical_workplace.id is not NULL then
490         &_USER..TEST.ok();
491      else
492         &_USER..TEST.error();
493      end if;
494    exception
495      when OTHERS then
496         &_USER..TEST.error(SQLERRM);
497    end;
498
499    &_USER..TEST.set_test('LOGICAL_WORKPLACE', 'help()', 10,
500      'Display the help text');
501    begin
502      help();
503
504      &_USER..TEST.ok();
505    exception
506      when OTHERS then
507         &_USER..TEST.error(SQLERRM);
508    end;
509
510    &_USER..TEST.set_test('LOGICAL_WORKPLACE', 'DELETE', 11,
511      'Delete test entries');
```

```
512     begin
513       delete LOGICAL_WORKPLACES
514       where   code in (
515         &_USER..TEST.v_TEST_30_1,
516         &_USER..TEST.v_TEST_30_2);
517
518       delete LOGICAL_WORKPLACES
519       where   code = &_USER..TEST.v_TEST_30;
520
521       &_USER..TEST.ok();
522     exception
523       when OTHERS then
524           &_USER..TEST.error(SQLERRM);
525     end;
526
527     commit;
528     &_USER..TEST.set_test('LOGICAL_WORKPLACE', NULL, NULL, NULL);
529     &_USER..TEST.success();
530   end test;
```

The test unit for package LOGICAL_WORKPLACE is quite lengthy, so that's why I'm using a partial listing in Listing 8-11. You can find the entire listing in the download directory for Chapter 8.

Let's examine this content table package's test unit line by line:

- Lines 280 through 282 declare two variables that I use during the test.

- Line 285 outputs some feedback so the tester knows the test has actually executed.

- Line 287 clears any previous test data.

- Lines 287 through 304 start the SQL Circle of Life for my test entries by pre-deleting any that may still exist.

- Lines 306 through 319 test method get_id().

- Lines 321 through 339 test method create_id_context().

- Lines 341 through 360 test method set_row() by inserting a parent company row based on TEST.v_TEST_30. This begins the INSERT portion of the SQL Circle of Life.

- Lines 362 through 396 test method set_row() again, this time inserting two child rows, business units, based on TEST.v_TEST_30_1 and TEST.v_TEST_30_2. This begins the INSERT or UPDATE portion of the SQL Circle of Life.

- Lines 398 through 408 test method get_code_context(). This starts the SELECT portion of the SQL Circle of Life.

- Lines 410 through 420 test method get_name_context().

- Lines 422 through 444 test method get_row() using the primary key column.

- Lines 446 through 470 test method get_row() a second time, using the unique id_context column.

- Lines 472 through 497 test method get_row() a third time, this time using unique columns code, name, and active_date.

- Lines 499 through 508 test method help().

- Lines 510 through 525 delete my test entries from the table. This brings me full circle on my SQL Circle of Life, from DELETE to INSERT to UPDATE to SELECT, and then back to DELETE.

- Finally, on lines 528 through 529, I record that the test unit executed successfully.

Did you notice that in this example, a content table package's test unit used the full SQL Circle of Life, whereas the code table package used only a portion of it? And did you see that every test was blocked—executed in its own PL/SQL block in order to catch any raised exceptions, rather than abort the test unit? Now it's your turn.

It's Your Turn to Test a Content Table Package

Now you will create a test unit for content table package PHYSICAL_WORKPLACE. In case you haven't noticed yet, table PHYSICAL_WORKPLACES is extremely similar to table LOGICAL_WORKPLACES, so you should be able to do some "code borrowing" to create a table package for PHYSICAL_WORKPLACES, including its test unit method test(). Please follow these steps.

1. Write the DDL scripts to create a table package for table PHYSICAL_WORKPLACES by borrowing the code from LOGICAL_WORKPLACE. This means you'll need to do some thinking about the differences between the two tables, and the resulting differences between the two packages, and then make the appropriate changes.

2. Save your specification script as rps.physical_workplace.pks, and your body script as rp.physical_workplace.pkb.

3. Compile the WORKER package because your solution may require it as a dependency: rps.worker.pks and rps.worker.pkb.

4. Compile your package.

5. Execute the test unit: SQL> execute physical_workplace.test();.

6. Use script last_test_results.sql to view the outcome of your test unit.

7. Add a test to your test unit to change the inactive date for business unit TEST_TS.v_TEST_CODE_30_2 to TEST_TS.d_TEST_19991231.

8. Execute the test unit again: SQL> execute physical_workplace.test();.

9. Use script last_test_results.sql to view the outcome of your test unit.

Once again, I'm not going to show you my solution. But you can find it in the solutions download directory for Chapter 8.

Next, let's test an intersection table package.

Testing an Intersection Table Package

It's time to test the third category of the dynamic trio: an intersection table package. As in the previous example, Listing 8-12 is a partial code listing, showing the test unit from the full-blown, production-ready package for the LOGICAL_ASSIGNMENTS table. In case you've forgotten, LOGICAL_ASSIGNMENTS holds a list (a history) of logical assignments for a worker, such as which department the person worked for from one point in time to another. Its package specification lists the following methods that are specific to an intersection table package (or TYPE):

- get_logical_workplace(): Returns the LOGICAL_WORKPLACES assigned at the specified point in time

- is_active(): Returns TRUE if the specified worker has a logical assignment at the specified point in time

The package specification contains several methods in common with a content table package:

- get_row(): Returns a matching row depending on primary key column or unique key column value(s) set in the record passed to the method

- set_row(): Updates an existing matching row, using the same rules implemented by get_row() to find a matching row, or inserts a new row if a match is not found

And the package specification also has some methods that are universal to all table packages:

- get_id()Returns a newly allocated primary key value for the table

- help()Display help text for the package

- test()the package

Listing 8-12. The test( ) Method from Table Package Body LOGICAL_ASSIGNMENT,rps. logical_assignment.pkb

```
195  PROCEDURE test is
196
197  n_logical_workplace_id              LOGICAL_WORKPLACES.id%TYPE;
198  n_logical_workplace_id_1            LOGICAL_WORKPLACES.id%TYPE;
199  n_logical_workplace_id_2            LOGICAL_WORKPLACES.id%TYPE;
200  n_worker_id                         WORKERS.id%TYPE;
201  n_worker_id_1                       WORKERS.id%TYPE;
202  n_worker_id_2                       WORKERS.id%TYPE;
203  r_worker                            WORKERS%ROWTYPE;
204  r_logical_workplace                 LOGICAL_WORKPLACES%ROWTYPE;
205  r_logical_assignment                LOGICAL_ASSIGNMENTS%ROWTYPE;
206
207  begin
208    pl('LOGICAL_ASSIGNMENT.test()');
209
210    &_USER..TEST.clear('LOGICAL_ASSIGNMENT');
211
212    -- In order to make entries into an Intersection table
213    -- you first have to have entries in the two tables
214    -- for which an entry will create an intersection
215    &_USER..TEST.set_test('LOGICAL_ASSIGNMENT', 'DELETE', 0,
216      'Delete existing test entries from LOGICAL_ASSIGNMENTS');
217    begin
218      delete LOGICAL_ASSIGNMENTS
219      where  logical_workplace_id in (
220      select logical_workplace_id
221      from   LOGICAL_WORKPLACES
222      where  code in (
```

```
223        &_USER..TEST.v_TEST_30,
224        &_USER..TEST.v_TEST_30_1,
225        &_USER..TEST.v_TEST_30_2 ) );
226
227      delete LOGICAL_ASSIGNMENTS
228      where  worker_id in (
229      select worker_id
230      from   WORKERS
231      where  external_id in (
232        &_USER..TEST.v_TEST_30,
233        &_USER..TEST.v_TEST_30_1,
234        &_USER..TEST.v_TEST_30_2 ) );
235
236      &_USER..TEST.ok();
237    exception
238      when OTHERS then
239        &_USER..TEST.error(SQLERRM);
240    end;
241
242    &_USER..TEST.set_test('LOGICAL_ASSIGNMENT', 'DELETE', 1,
243      'Delete existing test entries from LOGICAL_WORKPLACES');
244    begin
245      delete LOGICAL_WORKPLACES
246      where  code in (
247        &_USER..TEST.v_TEST_30_1,
248        &_USER..TEST.v_TEST_30_2 );
249
250      delete LOGICAL_WORKPLACES
251      where  code in (
252        &_USER..TEST.v_TEST_30 );
253
254      &_USER..TEST.ok;
255    exception
256      when OTHERS then
257        &_USER..TEST.error(SQLERRM);
258    end;
259
260    &_USER..TEST.set_test('LOGICAL_ASSIGNMENT', 'DELETE', 2,
261      'Delete existing test entries from WORKERS');
262    begin
263      delete WORKERS
264      where  external_id in (
265        &_USER..TEST.v_TEST_30,
266        &_USER..TEST.v_TEST_30_1,
267        &_USER..TEST.v_TEST_30_2 );
268
269      &_USER..TEST.ok();
270    exception
271      when OTHERS then
272        &_USER..TEST.error(SQLERRM);
273    end;
274
```

```
275    &_USER..TEST.set_test('LOGICAL_ASSIGNMENT', 'INSERT', 3,
276      'Insert WORKERS test entries using set_row()');
277    begin
278      r_worker.id             := WORKER.get_id();
279      r_worker.worker_type_id := WORKER_TYPE.get_id('E');
280      r_worker.external_id    := &_USER..TEST.v_TEST_30;
281      r_worker.first_name     := &_USER..TEST.v_TEST_30;
282      r_worker.middle_name    := &_USER..TEST.v_TEST_30;
283      r_worker.last_name      := &_USER..TEST.v_TEST_30;
284      r_worker.name           := WORKER.get_formatted_name(
285        r_worker.first_name,
286        r_worker.middle_name,
287        r_worker.last_name);
288      r_worker.birth_date     := to_date('19800101', 'YYYYMMDD');
289      r_worker.gender_type_id := GENDER_TYPE.get_id('M');
290      WORKER.set_row(r_worker);
291      n_worker_id             := r_worker.id;
292
293      r_worker.id             := WORKER.get_id();
294      r_worker.worker_type_id := WORKER_TYPE.get_id('E');
295      r_worker.external_id    := &_USER..TEST.v_TEST_30_1;
296      r_worker.first_name     := &_USER..TEST.v_TEST_30_1;
297      r_worker.middle_name    := &_USER..TEST.v_TEST_30_1;
298      r_worker.last_name      := &_USER..TEST.v_TEST_30_1;
299      r_worker.name           := WORKER.get_formatted_name(
300        r_worker.first_name,
301        r_worker.middle_name,
302        r_worker.last_name);
303      r_worker.birth_date     := to_date('19700101', 'YYYYMMDD');
304      r_worker.gender_type_id := GENDER_TYPE.get_id('F');
305      WORKER.set_row(r_worker);
306      n_worker_id_1           := r_worker.id;
307
308      r_worker.id             := WORKER.get_id();
309      r_worker.worker_type_id := WORKER_TYPE.get_id('C');
310      r_worker.external_id    := &_USER..TEST.v_TEST_30_2;
311      r_worker.first_name     := &_USER..TEST.v_TEST_30_2;
312      r_worker.middle_name    := &_USER..TEST.v_TEST_30_2;
313      r_worker.last_name      := &_USER..TEST.v_TEST_30_2;
314      r_worker.name           := WORKER.get_formatted_name(
315        r_worker.first_name,
316        r_worker.middle_name,
317        r_worker.last_name);
318      r_worker.birth_date     := to_date('19600101', 'YYYYMMDD');
319      r_worker.gender_type_id := GENDER_TYPE.get_id('M');
320      WORKER.set_row(r_worker);
321      n_worker_id_2           := r_worker.id;
322
```

```
323     & USER..TEST.ok();
324   exception
325     when OTHERS then
326         & USER..TEST.error(SQLERRM);
327   end;
328
329   & USER..TEST.set_test('LOGICAL_ASSIGNMENT', 'INSERT', 4,
330     'Insert LOGICAL_WORKPLACES test entries using set_row()');
331   begin
332     r_logical_workplace.id                      :=
333         LOGICAL_WORKPLACESS.get_id();
334     r_logical_workplace.parent_id               := NULL;
335     r_logical_workplace.id_context              :=
336         LOGICAL_WORKPLACESS.create_id_context(
337             r_logical_workplace.parent_id,
338             r_logical_workplace.id);
339     r_logical_workplace.workplace_type_id       :=
340         WORKPLACE_TYPE_TS.get_id('C');
341     r_logical_workplace.code                    := & USER..TEST.v_TEST_30;
342     r_logical_workplace.name                    := & USER..TEST.v_TEST_80;
343     r_logical_workplace.active_date             := & USER..TEST.d_TEST_19000101;
344     r_logical_workplace.inactive_date           := & USER..TEST.d_TEST_99991231;
345     LOGICAL_WORKPLACESS.set_row(r_logical_workplace);
346     n_logical_workplace_id                      :=
347         r_logical_workplace.id;
348
349     r_logical_workplace.id                      :=
350         LOGICAL_WORKPLACESS.get_id();
351     r_logical_workplace.parent_id               :=
352         n_logical_workplace_id;
353     r_logical_workplace.id_context              :=
354         LOGICAL_WORKPLACESS.create_id_context(
355             r_logical_workplace.parent_id,
356             r_logical_workplace.id);
357     r_logical_workplace.workplace_type_id       :=
358         WORKPLACE_TYPE_TS.get_id('B');
359     r_logical_workplace.code                    := & USER..TEST.v_TEST_30_1;
360     r_logical_workplace.name                    := & USER..TEST.v_TEST_80;
361     r_logical_workplace.active_date             := & USER..TEST.d_TEST_19000101;
362     r_logical_workplace.inactive_date           := & USER..TEST.d_TEST_99991231;
363     LOGICAL_WORKPLACESS.set_row(r_logical_workplace);
364     n_logical_workplace_id_1                     :=
365         r_logical_workplace.id;
366
367     r_logical_workplace.id :=
368         LOGICAL_WORKPLACESS.get_id();
369     r_logical_workplace.parent_id               :=
370         n_logical_workplace_id;
371     r_logical_workplace.id_context              :=
372         LOGICAL_WORKPLACESS.create_id_context(
373             r_logical_workplace.parent_id,
```

```
374           r_logical_workplace.id);
375       r_logical_workplace.workplace_type_id    :=
376         WORKPLACE_TYPE_TS.get_id('B');
377       r_logical_workplace.code                        := &_USER..TEST.v_TEST_30_2;
378       r_logical_workplace.name                        := &_USER..TEST.v_TEST_80;
379       r_logical_workplace.active_date            := &_USER..TEST.d_TEST_19000101;
380       r_logical_workplace.inactive_date          := &_USER..TEST.d_TEST_99991231;
381       LOGICAL_WORKPLACESS.set_row(r_logical_workplace);
382       n_logical_workplace_id_2                    :=
383         r_logical_workplace.id;
384
385       &_USER..TEST.ok();
386     exception
387       when OTHERS then
388         &_USER..TEST.error(SQLERRM);
389     end;
390
391     -- Now that I have entries in the two tables being intersected
392     -- I can now start testing this package...
393     &_USER..TEST.set_test('LOGICAL_ASSIGNMENT', 'get_id()', 5,
394       'Allocate the next primary key value using get_id()');
395     begin
396       r_logical_assignment.id :=
397         LOGICAL_ASSIGNMENT.get_id();
398
399       if nvl(r_logical_assignment.id, 0) > 0 then
400         &_USER..TEST.ok();
401       else
402         &_USER..TEST.error();
403       end if;
404     exception
405       when OTHERS then
406         &_USER..TEST.error(SQLERRM);
407     end;
408
409     &_USER..TEST.set_test('LOGICAL_ASSIGNMENT', 'set_row()', 6,
410       'Insert history for v_TEST_30 using set_row()');
411     begin
412       r_logical_assignment.worker_id                := n_worker_id;
413       r_logical_assignment.logical_workplace_id :=
414         n_logical_workplace_id_2;
415       r_logical_assignment.active_date          :=
416         to_date('20000101', 'YYYYMMDD');
417       r_logical_assignment.inactive_date        := NULL;
418       LOGICAL_ASSIGNMENT.set_row(r_logical_assignment);
419
420       &_USER..TEST.ok;
421     exception
422       when OTHERS then
423         &_USER..TEST.error(SQLERRM);
424     end;
425
```

```
426     &_USER..TEST.set_test('LOGICAL_ASSIGNMENT', 'set_row()', 7,
427       'Insert history for V_TEST_30_1 using set_row()');
428     begin
429       r_logical_assignment.id :=
430         LOGICAL_ASSIGNMENT.get_id();
431       r_logical_assignment.worker_id            := n_worker_id_1;
432       r_logical_assignment.logical_workplace_id :=
433         n_logical_workplace_id_1;
434       r_logical_assignment.active_date          :=
435         to_date('19900101', 'YYYYMMDD');
436       r_logical_assignment.inactive_date        :=
437         to_date('19991231', 'YYYYMMDD');
438       LOGICAL_ASSIGNMENT.set_row(r_logical_assignment);
439
440       r_logical_assignment.id :=
441         LOGICAL_ASSIGNMENT.get_id();
442       r_logical_assignment.worker_id            := n_worker_id_1;
443       r_logical_assignment.logical_workplace_id :=
444         n_logical_workplace_id_2;
445       r_logical_assignment.active_date          :=
446         to_date('20000101', 'YYYYMMDD');
447       r_logical_assignment.inactive_date        := NULL;
448       LOGICAL_ASSIGNMENT.set_row(r_logical_assignment);
449
450       &_USER..TEST.ok;
451     exception
452       when OTHERS then
453         &_USER..TEST.error(SQLERRM);
454     end;
455
456     &_USER..TEST.set_test('LOGICAL_ASSIGNMENT', 'set_row()', 8,
457       'Insert history for V_TEST_30_2 using set_row()');
458     begin
459       r_logical_assignment.id :=
460         LOGICAL_ASSIGNMENT.get_id();
461       r_logical_assignment.worker_id            := n_worker_id_2;
462       r_logical_assignment.logical_workplace_id :=
463         n_logical_workplace_id_1;
464       r_logical_assignment.active_date          :=
465         to_date('19800101', 'YYYYMMDD');
466       r_logical_assignment.inactive_date        :=
467         to_date('19891231', 'YYYYMMDD');
468       LOGICAL_ASSIGNMENT.set_row(r_logical_assignment);
469
470       r_logical_assignment.id :=
471         LOGICAL_ASSIGNMENT.get_id();
472       r_logical_assignment.worker_id            := n_worker_id_2;
473       r_logical_assignment.logical_workplace_id :=
474         n_logical_workplace_id_2;
475       r_logical_assignment.active_date          :=
476         to_date('19900101', 'YYYYMMDD');
```

```
477     r_logical_assignment.inactive_date     :=
478        to_date('19901231', 'YYYYMMDD');
479     LOGICAL_ASSIGNMENT.set_row(r_logical_assignment);
480
481     &_USER..TEST.ok;
482   exception
483     when OTHERS then
484        &_USER..TEST.error(SQLERRM);
485   end;
486
487   -- Commit the deletes and inserts
488   commit;
489
490   &_USER..TEST.set_test('LOGICAL_ASSIGNMENT',
491     'get_logical_workplace()', 9,
492     'Get the current logical workplace for v_TEST_30');
493   begin
494     r_logical_workplace := NULL;
495     r_logical_workplace := get_logical_workplace(n_worker_id);
496
497     if nvl(r_logical_workplace.id, 0) > 0 then
498        &_USER..TEST.ok();
499     else
500        &_USER..TEST.error();
501     end if;
502   exception
503     when OTHERS then
504        &_USER..TEST.error(SQLERRM);
505   end;
506
507   &_USER..TEST.set_test('LOGICAL_ASSIGNMENT',
508     'get_logical_workplace()', 10,
509     'Get the logical workplace on 6/30/1995 for v_TEST_30_1');
510   begin
511     r_logical_workplace := NULL;
512     r_logical_workplace := get_logical_workplace(
513       n_worker_id_1,
514       to_date('19950630', 'YYYYMMDD'));
515
516     if nvl(r_logical_workplace.id, 0) > 0 then
517        &_USER..TEST.ok();
518     else
519        &_USER..TEST.error();
520     end if;
521   exception
522     when OTHERS then
523        &_USER..TEST.error(SQLERRM);
524   end;
525
526   &_USER..TEST.set_test('LOGICAL_ASSIGNMENT',
527     'get_logical_workplace()', 11,
```

```
528          'Get the logical workplace on 6/30/1995 for v_TEST_30_2');
529       begin
530         -- this should fail
531         r_logical_workplace := NULL;
532         r_logical_workplace := get_logical_workplace(
533           n_worker_id_2,
534           to_date('19950630', 'YYYYMMDD'));
535
536         if nvl(r_logical_workplace.id, 0) > 0 then
537           &_USER..TEST.error();
538         else
539           &_USER..TEST.ok();
540         end if;
541       exception
542         when NO_DATA_FOUND then
543           &_USER..TEST.ok();
544         when OTHERS then
545           &_USER..TEST.error(SQLERRM);
546       end;
547
548       &_USER..TEST.set_test('LOGICAL_ASSIGNMENT', 'help()', 12,
549         'Test help()');
550       begin
551         help();
552
553         &_USER..TEST.ok;
554       exception
555         when OTHERS then
556           &_USER..TEST.error(SQLERRM);
557       end;
558
559       &_USER..TEST.set_test('LOGICAL_ASSIGNMENT', 'is_active()', 13,
560         'Is there an active assignment on 6/30/1995 for v_TEST_30?');
561         -- No
562       begin
563         if is_active(n_worker_id, to_date('19950630', 'YYYYMMDD')) then
564           &_USER..TEST.error();
565         else
566           &_USER..TEST.ok();
567         end if;
568       exception
569         when OTHERS then
570           &_USER..TEST.error(SQLERRM);
571       end;
572
573       &_USER..TEST.set_test('LOGICAL_ASSIGNMENT', 'is_active()', 14,
574         'Is there an active assignment on 6/30/1995 for v_TEST_30_1?');
575         -- Yes
576       begin
577         if is_active(n_worker_id_1, to_date('19950630', 'YYYYMMDD')) then
578           &_USER..TEST.ok();
```

```
579        else
580          &_USER..TEST.error();
581        end if;
582    exception
583      when OTHERS then
584          &_USER..TEST.error(SQLERRM);
585    end;
586
587    &_USER..TEST.set_test('LOGICAL_ASSIGNMENT', 'is_active()', 15,
588      'Is there currently an active assignment for v_TEST_30_2?');
589      -- No
590    begin
591      if is_active(n_worker_id_2) then
592          &_USER..TEST.error();
593      else
594          &_USER..TEST.ok();
595      end if;
596    exception
597      when OTHERS then
598          &_USER..TEST.error(SQLERRM);
599    end;
600
601    -- Now clean up after the tests by deleting the test entries
602    &_USER..TEST.set_test('LOGICAL_ASSIGNMENT', 'DELETE', 16,
603      'Delete existing test entries from LOGICAL_ASSIGNMENTS');
604    begin
605      delete LOGICAL_ASSIGNMENTS
606      where  logical_workplace_id in (
607      select logical_workplace_id
608      from   LOGICAL_WORKPLACES
609      where  code in (
610        &_USER..TEST.v_TEST_30,
611        &_USER..TEST.v_TEST_30_1,
612        &_USER..TEST.v_TEST_30_2 ) );
613
614      delete LOGICAL_ASSIGNMENTS
615      where  worker_id in (
616      select worker_id
617      from   WORKER_T
618      where  external_id in (
619        &_USER..TEST.v_TEST_30,
620        &_USER..TEST.v_TEST_30_1,
621        &_USER..TEST.v_TEST_30_2 ) );
622
623      &_USER..TEST.ok();
624    exception
625      when OTHERS then
626          &_USER..TEST.error(SQLERRM);
627    end;
628
```

315

```
629    & USER..TEST.set_test('LOGICAL_ASSIGNMENT', 'DELETE', 17,
630      'Delete existing test entries from LOGICAL_WORKPLACES');
631    begin
632      delete LOGICAL_WORKPLACES
633      where  code in (
634        & USER..TEST.v_TEST_30_1,
635        & USER..TEST.v_TEST_30_2 );
636
637      delete LOGICAL_WORKPLACES
638      where  code in (
639        & USER..TEST.v_TEST_30 );
640
641      & USER..TEST.ok;
642    exception
643      when OTHERS then
644        & USER..TEST.error(SQLERRM);
645    end;
646
647    & USER..TEST.set_test('LOGICAL_ASSIGNMENT', 'DELETE', 18,
648      'Delete existing test entries from WORKERS');
649    begin
650      delete WORKERS
651      where  external_id in (
652        & USER..TEST.v_TEST_30,
653        & USER..TEST.v_TEST_30_1,
654        & USER..TEST.v_TEST_30_2 );
655
656      & USER..TEST.ok();
657    exception
658      when OTHERS then
659        & USER..TEST.error(SQLERRM);
660    end;
661
662    commit;
663    & USER..TEST.set_test('LOGICAL_ASSIGNMENT', NULL, NULL, NULL);
664    & USER..TEST.success();
665  end test;
```

The important point about an intersection table package is that it is dependent on test entries in the two tables it intersects. So you'll see that on lines 215 through 392, I must start out by deleting any test entries in the "intersected" tables, WORKERS and LOGICAL_WORKPLACES, and then I must add entries to these tables in order to have entries from which to establish an intersection entry. So every intersection table package must also insert and delete entries from the tables on which is depends. Now it's your turn to work on an intersection table package.

It's Your Turn to Test an Intersection Table Package

You will now create a test unit for intersection table package PHYSICAL_ASSIGNMENT. Just as in the last exercise, the corresponding table for this exercise, PHYSICAL_ASSIGNMENTS, is extremely similar to table LOGICAL_ASSIGNMENTS, so you should once again be able to do some "code borrowing" to create a table package for PHYSICAL_ASSIGNMENTS, including its test unit method test(). Follow these steps.

1. Write the DDL scripts to create a table package for table PHYSICAL_ASSIGNMENTS by borrowing the code from LOGICAL_ASSIGNMENT.

2. Save your specification script as rps.physical_assignment.pks, and your body script as rps.physical_assignment.pkb.

3. Compile your package.

4. Execute the test unit: SQL> execute physical_assignment.test();.

5. Use script last_test_results.sql to view the outcome of your test unit.

Once again, I'm not going to show you my solution. But you can find it in the solutions download directory for Chapter 8.

So just how different can it be to test a TYPE instead of a package? Let's find out.

Testing a Type

Testing a TYPE is not all that different from testing a package. The only significant difference is that when you declare the test() method in a TYPE, it must be declared as a STATIC method. And when you code the method, you must remember that you'll need to work with a variable of that TYPE, and instance, as well as the TYPE when performing your testing. If you don't have an instance of the TYPE, you won't be able to access and test all its methods.

Listing 8-13 is a partial listing of the TYPE TEST, an object-relational testing tool. This listing shows only the test unit for the TYPE itself.

Listing 8-13. The Test Unit from TYPE TEST, ops.test.tpb

```
416  STATIC PROCEDURE "test" is
417
418  n_number                              number;
419  o_test                                TEST;
420
421  begin
422    pl('TEST.test()');
423
424    -- A defect requires the schema owner
425    &_USER..TEST.clear('TEST');
426
427    o_test := new TEST();
428    o_test.set_test('TEST', NULL, 1,
429      'Is get_test_N equal to N?');
430    if TEST.get_test_N = 'N' then
431      o_test.success();
432    else
433      o_test.error();
434    end if;
435
436    o_test.set_test('TEST', NULL, 2,
437      'Is the length of get_test_N equal to 1?');
438    if nvl(length(TEST.get_test_N), 0) = 1 then
439      o_test.success();
```

```
440    else
441      o_test.error();
442    end if;
443
444    o_test.set_test('TEST', NULL, 3,
445      'Is get_test_Y equal to Y?');
446    if TEST.get_test_Y = 'Y' then
447      o_test.success();
448    else
449      o_test.error();
450    end if;
451
452    o_test.set_test('TEST', NULL, 4,
453      'Is the length of get_test_Y equal to 1?');
454    if nvl(length(TEST.get_test_Y), 0) = 1 then
455      o_test.success();
456    else
457      o_test.error();
458    end if;
459
460    o_test.set_test('TEST', NULL, 5,
461      'Is the length of get_test_30 equal to 30?');
462    if nvl(length(TEST.get_test_30), 0) = 30 then
463      o_test.success();
464    else
465      o_test.error();
466    end if;
467
468    o_test.set_test('TEST', NULL, 6,
469      'Is the length of get_test_30_1 equal to 30?');
470    if nvl(length(TEST.get_test_30_1), 0) = 30 then
471      o_test.success();
472    else
473      o_test.error();
474    end if;
475
476    o_test.set_test('TEST', NULL, 7,
477      'Is the length of get_test_30_2 equal to 30?');
478    if nvl(length(TEST.get_test_30_2), 0) = 30 then
479      o_test.success();
480    else
481      o_test.error();
482    end if;
483
484    o_test.set_test('TEST', NULL, 8,
485      'Is the length of get_test_80 equal to 80?');
486    if nvl(length(TEST.get_test_80), 0) = 80 then
487      o_test.success();
488    else
489      o_test.error();
490    end if;
491
```

```
492    o_test.set_test('TEST', NULL, 9,
493      'Is the length of get_test_100 equal to 100?');
494    if nvl(length(TEST.get_test_100), 0) = 100 then
495      o_test.success();
496    else
497      o_test.error();
498    end if;
499
500    o_test.set_test('TEST', NULL, 10,
501      'Is the length of get_test_2000 equal to 2000?');
502    if nvl(length(TEST.get_test_2000), 0) = 2000 then
503      o_test.success();
504    else
505      o_test.error();
506    end if;
507
508    o_test.set_test('TEST', 'get_id', 11,
509      'Does get_id() work?');
510    begin
511      n_number := TEST.get_id();
512      if n_number > 0 then
513        o_test.success();
514      else
515        o_test.error();
516      end if;
517    exception
518      when OTHERS then
519        o_test.error(SQLERRM);
520    end;
521
522    o_test.set_test('TEST', 'help', 12,
523      'Does help() work?');
524    begin
525      & USER..TEST.help();
526      raise_application_error(-20999, 'Testing the error routine');
527      o_test.success();
528    exception
529      when OTHERS then
530        o_test.error(SQLERRM);
531    end;
532
533    o_test.set_test('TEST', NULL, NULL, NULL);
534    o_test.success();
535  end "test";...
```

First, notice that I've declared the method as a STATIC procedure. This means it will be accessible from the TYPE itself, not through an instance of the type.

Second, on line 419, I declare a variable of the TYPE and then on line 427, I set the variable to a new instance of the TYPE. Then I use this instance when calling MEMBER methods in the test unit. Beyond those two major changes, the differences in methods test() in package TEST and TYPE TEST are only semantic (as in the variations in the programmer-created language). One last detail! I had to test the method "test" in order to get around a name space error. I could have named it test_ or TEST_ or anything other than the name of the TYPE itself, but I like to keep things obvious, so I forced Oracle to name it test in lower case.

Now that you have seen an example of testing a TYPE, it's your turn.

It's Your Turn to Test a Type

Now you'll select any TYPE that you've created so far, and code its test unit method test(). However, you'll use your object-relational testing tool. This means you'll also need to modify the SQL*Plus report last_test_results.sql so it queries your testing tool's object table TESTS. This time, I'm not even going to give you any steps. You've seen enough examples that you should be able to list the steps you need to complete in order to do this exercise. Good skill!

Now, it's time we move on to the automation of testing.

Automating Testing

Do you remember that in the beginning of this chapter I promised you a framework for automating your testing? Well, by utilizing information from Oracle's data dictionary and writing another program unit that calls all your test units, you can execute one PL/SQL method that will in turn execute every test() method you've written, and then report on the test results.

There are several data dictionary views that have information about packages, TYPEs, and their methods. The three best suited to my needs of identifying every package and TYPE that does and does not have a test() method are SYS.ALL_ARGUMENTS, SYS.USER_PROCDURES, and SYS.USER_TYPE_METHODS. The following are SQL*Plus descriptions of the views:

```
SYS.USER_ARGUMENTS
 Name                                     Null?    Type
 ---------------------------------------- -------- ----------------------------
 OBJECT_NAME                                       VARCHAR2(128)
 PACKAGE_NAME                                      VARCHAR2(128)
 OBJECT_ID                                NOT NULL NUMBER
 OVERLOAD                                          VARCHAR2(40)
 SUBPROGRAM_ID                                     NUMBER
 ARGUMENT_NAME                                     VARCHAR2(128)
 ...
SYS.USER_TYPE_METHODS
 Name                                     Null?    Type
 ---------------------------------------- -------- ----------------------------
 TYPE_NAME                                NOT NULL VARCHAR2(128)
 METHOD_NAME                              NOT NULL VARCHAR2(128)
 METHOD_NO                                NOT NULL NUMBER
 METHOD_TYPE                                       VARCHAR2(6)
 PARAMETERS                               NOT NULL NUMBER
 ...
```

```
SYS.USER_PROCEDURES
Name                                        Null?      Type
--------------------------------------      --------   -------------
OBJECT_NAME                                            VARCHAR2(128)
PROCEDURE_NAME                                         VARCHAR2(128)
OBJECT_ID                                              NUMBER
SUBPROGRAM_ID                                          NUMBER
OVERLOAD                                               VARCHAR2(40)
OBJECT_TYPE                                            VARCHAR2(13)
...
```

Using the information provided by these views, I can write a query that does the following:

- Lists the name of every package and TYPE that has a test() method

- Lists the name of every package and TYPE that does not have a test() method

If I couple that information with the output of the test units that is stored in table TESTS, I can write a query that does the following:

- Lists information about every test that failed

- Lists the name of every package or TYPE where its test method failed

So the information provided by the data dictionary views and the testing tool's table TESTS arms me with all the information I need to automate the testing of the PL/SQL program units and to report on the test results. Therefore, to automate the testing of the PL/SQL program units, all I need to do is follow these two simple steps.

1. Add a test unit method test() to every PL/SQL package or TYPE definition.

2. Execute a process to execute each test unit method and report the results.

You already know how to do the first step, so let's see an example of how to do the second step.

Automate Test Processing

Listing 8-14 is an example of a PL/SQL program unit that executes all coded test() methods for the current schema, and then reports on the results. It queries view SYS.ALL_ARGUMENTS to get a list of packages and TYPEs that do and do not have test() methods. It executes each test() method, recording the results of execution, as the test method itself records the results of each of its tests. Finally, it reports the results of the tests.

Listing 8-14. An Example of a Test Unit Processing, test.sql

```
001  rem test.sql
002  rem by Donald J. Bales on 2014-10-20
003  rem An anonymous PL/SQL procedure to execute all test units
004  rem and to report on the results of each test.
005
006  declare
007
008  -- Get the names of all packages and types that have a test unit
009  cursor c_test is
010  select p.object_name package_name
011  from   SYS.USER_PROCEDURES p
```

```
012   where   p.object_type               = 'PACKAGE'
013   and     upper(p.procedure_name) = 'TEST'
014   and not exists (
015   select 1
016   from    SYS.USER_ARGUMENTS x
017   where   x.package_name              = p.object_name
018   and     x.object_name               = p.procedure_name)
019   UNION
020   select m.type_name package_name
021   from    SYS.USER_TYPE_METHODS m
022   where   upper(m.method_name)    = 'TEST'
023   and     m.parameters            = 0
024   order by 1;
025
026   -- Get the names of all packages and types that don't have a test unit
027   cursor c_missing is
028   (select p.object_name package_name
029   from    SYS.USER_PROCEDURES p
030   where   p.object_type               = 'PACKAGE'
031   UNION
032   select m.type_name package_name
033   from    SYS.USER_TYPE_METHODS m )
034   MINUS
035   (select p.object_name package_name
036   from    SYS.USER_PROCEDURES p
037   where   upper(p.procedure_name) = 'TEST'
038   and not exists (
039   select 1
040   from    SYS.USER_ARGUMENTS x
041   where   x.package_name              = p.object_name
042   and     x.object_name               = p.procedure_name)
043   UNION
044   select m.type_name package_name
045   from    SYS.USER_TYPE_METHODS m
046   where   upper(m.method_name)    = 'TEST'
047   and     m.parameters            = 0)
048   order by 1;
049
050   -- Get the names of all packages and types that have test unit errors
051   cursor c_error is
052   select object_name||
053           decode(substr(method_name, -1, 1), ')', '.', ' ')||
054           method_name object_method,
055          test_number,
056          result
057   from    TESTS
058   where   result <> 'OK'
059   and     result <> 'SUCCESS'
060   order by 1;
061
```

```
062   TYPE error_message_table is table of varchar2(32767)
063   index by binary_integer;
064
065   n_error_message                          number := 0;
066   n_object_method_width                    number := 39;
067   n_result_width                           number := 29;
068   n_status                                 number;
069   n_test_number_width                      number := 5;
070
071   t_error_message                          error_message_table;
072
073   v_line                                   varchar2(32767);
074
075   begin
076     -- execute the test units
077     for r_test in c_test loop
078       begin
079         execute immediate 'begin '||r_test.package_name||'.test(); end;';
080       exception
081         when OTHERS then
082           n_error_message := n_error_message + 1;
083           t_error_message(n_error_message) :=
084             r_test.package_name||'.test() '||SQLERRM;
085       end;
086     end loop;
087     -- Empty the output buffer
088     loop
089       SYS.DBMS_OUTPUT.get_line(v_line, n_status);
090       if nvl(n_status, 0) < 1 then
091         exit;
092       end if;
093     end loop;
094     -- Show the test units that had errors
095     for r_error in c_error loop
096       if c_error%rowcount = 1 then
097         pl(chr(9));
098         pl('THE FOLLOWING OBJECT''S TEST UNITS HAD ERRORS:');
099         pl(chr(9));
100         pl(
101           rpad(
102             substr('OBJECT/METHOD',
103               1, n_object_method_width),
104             n_object_method_width, ' ')||
105           ' '||
106           lpad(
107             substr('TEST#',
108               1, n_test_number_width),
109             n_test_number_width, ' ')||
110           ' '||
111           rpad(
112             substr('ERROR',
113               1, n_result_width),
```

```
114              n_result_width, ' ')
115            );
116        pl(
117          rpad(
118            substr('-------------',
119              1, n_object_method_width),
120            n_object_method_width, '-')||
121          ' '||
122          lpad(
123            substr('-----',
124              1, n_test_number_width),
125            n_test_number_width, '-')||
126          ' '||
127          rpad(
128            substr('-----',
129              1, n_result_width),
130            n_result_width, '-')
131          );
132      end if;
133      pl(
134        rpad(
135          substr(r_error.object_method,
136            1, n_object_method_width),
137          n_object_method_width, ' ')||
138        ' '||
139        lpad(
140          substr(ltrim(to_char(r_error.test_number)),
141            1, n_test_number_width),
142          n_test_number_width, ' ')||
143        ' '||
144        rpad(
145          substr(r_error.result,
146            1, n_result_width),
147          n_result_width, ' ')
148        );
149    end loop;
150    -- Show the test units that failed to run
151    if t_error_message.count > 0 then
152      for i in t_error_message.first..t_error_message.last loop
153        if i = t_error_message.first then
154          pl(chr(9));
155          pl('THE FOLLOWING OBJECT''S TEST UNITS FAILED:');
156        end if;
157        pl(chr(9));
158        pl(t_error_message(i));
159      end loop;
160    end if;
161    -- Show the object that missing test units
162    for r_missing in c_missing loop
163      if c_missing%rowcount = 1 then
164        pl(chr(9));
```

```
165          pl('THE FOLLOWING OBJECTS ARE MISSING TEST UNITS:');
166          pl(chr(9));
167        end if;
168        pl(r_missing.package_name);
169      end loop;
170    end;
171    /
```

Let's break this listing down line by line:

- Lines 9 through 24 declare a cursor, c_test, against data dictionary views
  SYS.USER_ARGUMENTS, SYS.USER_PROCEDURES, and SYS.USER_TYPE_METHODS,
  which gives me a list of packages and TYPEs that have a method test().

- Lines 27 through 48 declare second cursor, c_missing, against SYS.USER_ARGUMENTS,
  SYS.USER_PROCEDURES, and SYS.USER_TYPE_METHODSwhich gives me a list of
  packages and TYPEs that do not have a test() method.

- Lines 51 through 60 declare a cursor, c_error, against table TESTS that lists all the
  individual tests that failed during the current test run.

- Lines 62 and 63 declare a PL/SQL table TYPE, error_message_table, which I will use
  to declare an array of exceptions raised during the execution of each test() method.

- Lines 77 through 86 execute a cursor for loop, where I call each package and TYPE's
  test() method. I've blocked the dynamic call to each method, so I can capture and
  later report on any raised exceptions (test() method failures).

- Lines 88 through 93 use a manual for loop to empty the SYS.DBMS_OUTPUT.put_
  line() buffer after having executed every test unit method. I do this to throw out any
  put_line() messages generated by each test unit.

- Lines 95 through 149 report, using put_line(), about any test failures during the test run.

- Lines 151 through 160 report any test() method failures during the test run. I could
  have created a fourth cursor to show me the test() methods that failed during
  execution, but I'm already getting this information from the blocked dynamic PL/
  SQL call to each method on lines 77 through 86.

- Lines 162 through 169 list any packages or TYPEs that do not have a test unit method
  test().

The only thing this procedure cannot do is determine whether or not a programmer has actually taken
the time to code the test unit. The following is sample output from this procedure while I was coding in my
environment:

```
SQL> @test.sql

THE FOLLOWING OBJECT'S TEST UNITS HAD ERRORS:

OBJECT/METHOD                            TEST# ERROR
---------------------------------------- ----- ------------------------------
LOGICAL_WORKPLACE.GET_ROW()                  7 ORA-01403: no data found
LOGICAL_WORKPLACE.GET_ROW()                  8 ORA-01403: no data found
LOGICAL_WORKPLACE.GET_ROW()                  9 ORA-01403: no data found
LOGICAL_WORKPLACE.SET_ROW()                  4 ORA-01403: no data found
LOGICAL_WORKPLACE.SET_ROW()                  3 ORA-20003: ORA-01400: cannot
```

```
THE FOLLOWING OBJECTS ARE MISSING TEST UNITS:

DEBUG
PARAMETER
SCOPE

PL/SQL procedure successfully completed.
```

The first part of the report, test unit errors, shows that exception ORA-20003 was raised while testing method LOGICAL_WORKPLACE.SET_ROW(). This information tells me to go directly to package LOGICAL_WORKPLACE to examine what might be wrong with the test or the method set_row().

The second part of the report, missing test units, lists the packages and TYPEs that are missing a test unit method. With this information, I can add the task of coding test units for these to my to-do list. Don't ignore this list. Anything not tested is something that can and probably will produce errors.

In practice, on an enterprise application, I've seen a test unit process like this take two to three hours to execute. In addition, it always finds one to three errors in each newly coded package. As time goes by, and new defects are detected by end users and others, it's your responsibility to go back and update the test unit method to test for any newly reported defect. Using this kind of automated testing, combined with consistently adding any new test cases, you can make your persistence layer statistically error-free.

I don't think that the "processing" procedure just described should be external (losable) to the database/objectbase. Instead, it should be added to package TEST as method process(). That way, you will be able to test any package or procedure by calling its test() method, and you can test the entire persistence layer by calling TEST.process(). Now that's a powerful testing tool!

It's Your Turn to Automate Test Processing

For your final assignment in this chapter, modify your object-relational testing tool to add STATIC procedure process(), which will execute a program unit similar to test.sql using your testing tool's result table TESTS. Then execute TEST.process() to see the results of testing your object-relational persistence layer.

Summary

My hope is that you now realize how important, and easy, it is to properly test your PL/SQL program units. A couple of hours of extra coding up front for each program unit can save your hundreds of hours of troubleshooting later on. More important, it will save your end users from hundreds of hours of lost productivity and frustration.

I've shown you the coding patterns involved when coding test units for SQL and PL/SQL. I've shown you how to create a relational and object-relational testing tool that can automatically test every program unit and access to their associated tables in your database by executing one procedure: process().

My final suggestion is that you decide on the use of a relational or an object-relation testing tool and then add the required test units that access that tool to each and every program unit you write. As a developer of enterprise applications, I have historically had low error rates. I've achieved them by incorporating testing into the process of developing. Assume nothing. Test everything.

Just how important is it to test everything? During the coding of the examples for this book, this testing framework found an average of two errors for each package or TYPE. And I've been coding in PL/SQL for more than 20 years!

There's one last tactic you can employ to help prevent errors: provide access to good documentation to your developers. And that's what I'm going to cover in the next chapter.

CHAPTER 9

■ ■ ■

Documenting

Once, when I was a young executive, I reported to the chief financial officer (CFO). Upon arriving at the new organization, I formulated a strategy to bring the company's computer technology up to date. Part of that plan was to provide each computer user in the organization with a computer that best suited that user's needs. This meant that executive administrators got high-powered desktop computers, while executives and consultants were armed with top-of-the-line notebooks. Not only did we make sure everyone was using the latest office automation software and groupware, we also built a state-of-the-art Executive Information System (EIS) that was tightly integrated with the accounting system.

The management team had no issues with authorizing capital expenditures for the computer hardware. Nor did the team balk about the investment in software. But when it came to spending money to provide personnel with training so they could take advantage of the new hardware and software, I could not get approval from the CFO. Why? He explained to me that any time you train people, they just move on to a better-paying job, so training was counterproductive.

To say the least, I was amazed and dismayed at the same time. I thought to myself, and further argued with the management team, "Why did you invest in hardware and software if you never had any intention of training people how to use it?" No amount of arguing could move them on this issue. So from my perspective, they attained minimal gains from their investment in hardware and software. Do you find this attitude as strange as I do?

If you do, then you'll logically also have to agree with me that the development of any reusable software component has no value if you don't inform your programming staff members that the reusable component exists, and then educate them on how to use the component. At the very least, you should have some documentation they can refer to in order to find out what is available and how to use it!

Here's a second story. I once worked on a project for a major retailer to package some of its software for distribution to regional offices in the company. As part of that work, I wrote the (missing) technical reference and end-user tutorial documentation so the support staff could figure out how to support the software, and the end users would know how to use the software. A novel idea, don't you think? When it came time to send the software to each regional office, I was told that I first had to remove the documentation from the distribution. Why? Because the documentation held trade secrets that the personnel of the firm could not be trusted with. Argh!

If I ran a tool and die company that made nuts and bolts, created a catalog of available parts, but then never distributed it to perspective customers, I would be out of business in no time at all. If I ran an integrated circuit manufacturing firm, but didn't let anyone know that the firm existed and what electronic components it manufactured, once again, I would be filing for bankruptcy in less than a month.

What's my point? The day and age of software components has been here for more than 30 years, but reuse depends on the distribution of documentation. Since the first machine language subroutine was written, that subroutine has been available as a reusable component. Since the first procedure programming language library was created, that library has been available as a reusable component. Since object-oriented languages first appeared on the scene, the creation of software components was made simple.

If you've created a web application using PHP, Python Django, or Ruby on Rails, you know how important API documentation is in order to use those programming languages or frameworks. If you've programmed in Java, you've used the Java Foundation Classes (JFC) or Java Enterprise Edition (JEE) framework. If you've programmed in PL/SQL, you've at least used the standard library. I could go on and on. These are all reusable software components.

If you're developing a solution to a business problem, you should have use-case narratives, use-case diagrams, process-flow diagrams, and so on to use a set of requirements for doing your programming work. During the creation of these documents, it should have become obvious what higher-level abstractions and patterns could be discerned from the end user's requirements. Using these abstractions and patterns, you can create components that are reusable through inheritance.

Furthermore, while developing, if you find yourself writing the same SQL statement or PL/SQL routine more than once, it's time to abstract that repeated pattern into a reusable component that can then be used by other components in your solution. If you do this, great! But if you don't document the existence of each and every component, what it does, and how to use it, it doesn't exist outside the realm of your own mind. So you must—I mean *must*—document as you go. And second, you must provide other possible users a means to know that reusable (even non-reusable) components exist, what they can do, and how to use them. And that is what this chapter is all about.

In this chapter, I'll cover the following:

- Documentation that cannot be lost or thrown away

- Documentation that is available on demand

- Distributable documentation

Let's start with documentation that cannot be lost or thrown away.

Indestructible Documentation

What a silly notion—indestructible documentation. Or perhaps not? You know of Murphy's Law, don't you? "Anything that can go wrong will go wrong." It's easy to lose your documentation if it's stored on a file system that is not part of the ongoing application.

One beautiful thing about PL/SQL is that the source code is permanently stored in the database. The only way to lose it is to lose the database, and at that point, who needs the source code?

Another beautiful thing about PL/SQL is that most executable code resides in either a package or TYPE specification. And these specifications allow you to comment the code. So the easiest way to document your packages and TYPEs is to put meaningful and properly formatted comments in each object's specification. At the very least, the text of the specification will then be available via the SYS.USER_SOURCE view.

But before you make up your mind on what to document, how to document it, and where to put any documentation you do create, let's look at what SQL*Plus provides for package and TYPE documentation.

SQL*Plus Documentation Tools

In SQL*Plus, you can use the describe command to determine the format of a table or the call specifications of a function, procedure, package, or TYPE. Here's an example of using describe on the table WORKER_TYPE_T:

```
SQL> desc WORKER_TYPES

WORKER_TYPES
```

```
Name                                        Null?     Type
------------------------------------------- --------  -------------
ID                                          NOT NULL  NUMBER(38)
CODE                                        NOT NULL  VARCHAR2(30)
DESCRIPTION                                 NOT NULL  VARCHAR2(80)
ACTIVE_DATE                                 NOT NULL  DATE
INACTIVE_DATE                               NOT NULL  DATE
```

And here's an example of using the describe command on the package WORKER_TYPE:

```
SQL> desc WORKER_TYPES
```

```
WORKER_TYPES
  Name                                      Null?     Type
  ----------------------------------------- --------  -------------
  ID                                        NOT NULL  NUMBER(38)
  CODE                                      NOT NULL  VARCHAR2(30)
  DESCRIPTION                               NOT NULL  VARCHAR2(80)
  ACTIVE_DATE                               NOT NULL  DATE
  INACTIVE_DATE                             NOT NULL  DATE

SQL> @desc WORKER_TYPE
WORKER_TYPE
PROCEDURE GET_CODE_DESCR
  Argument Name               Type                     In/Out Default?
  --------------------------- ------------------------ ------ --------
  AIN_ID                      NUMBER(38)               IN
  AOV_CODE                    VARCHAR2(30)             OUT
  AOV_DESCRIPTION             VARCHAR2(80)             OUT
PROCEDURE GET_CODE_ID_DESCR
  Argument Name               Type                     In/Out Default?
  --------------------------- ------------------------ ------ --------
  AIOV_CODE                   VARCHAR2(30)             IN/OUT
  AON_ID                      NUMBER(38)               OUT
  AOV_DESCRIPTION             VARCHAR2(80)             OUT
  AID_ON                      DATE                     IN
PROCEDURE GET_CODE_ID_DESCR
  Argument Name               Type                     In/Out Default?
  --------------------------- ------------------------ ------ --------
  AIOV_CODE                   VARCHAR2(30)             IN/OUT
  AON_ID                      NUMBER(38)               OUT
  AOV_DESCRIPTION             VARCHAR2(80)             OUT
FUNCTION GET_ID RETURNS NUMBER(38)
FUNCTION GET_ID RETURNS NUMBER(38)
  Argument Name               Type                     In/Out Default?
  --------------------------- ------------------------ ------ --------
  AIV_CODE                    VARCHAR2(30)             IN
PROCEDURE HELP
PROCEDURE TEST
```

The describe command shows the format of the table, or the signature of the methods, but nothing else. It doesn't provide an explanation as to what the column names in the table are supposed to store, nor what the methods may actually do.

Sometimes, you'll already know what a method can do, and you're just looking for its method signature. In that case, describe will suit your purpose. But describe will never be a suitable means of looking up documentation on how something works.

Let's see what GUI development environment tools can provide.

GUI Development Environment Tools

Tools like Oracle SQL Developer and TOAD for Oracle also show table formats and method signatures in much the same manner as SQL*Plus does. In Figures 9-1 and 9-2, you can see how Oracle SQL Developer presents information about table and package methods. When it comes to help with a package or TYPE definition, Oracle SQL Developer simply displays the source for the package specification.

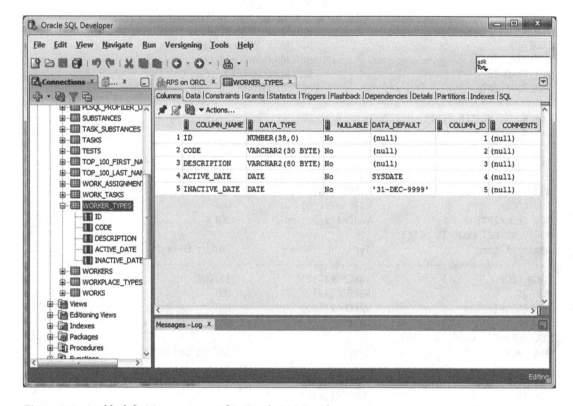

Figure 9-1. A table definition as presented in Oracle SQL Developer

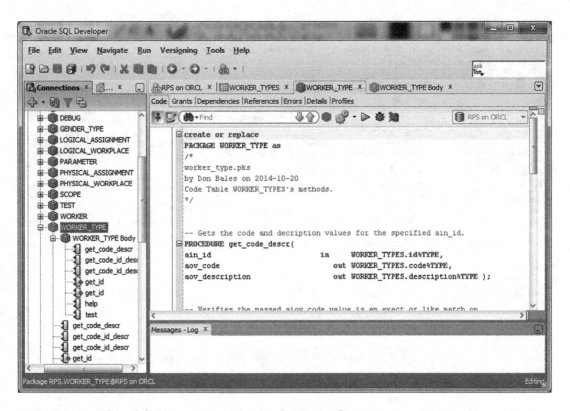

Figure 9-2. *A package definition as presented in Oracle SQL Developer*

So how does TOAD present the same information? Look in Figures 9-3 and 9-4 for the answer. When it comes to package or TYPE information, TOAD also presents the source code of the package specification, just as Oracle SQL Developer does.

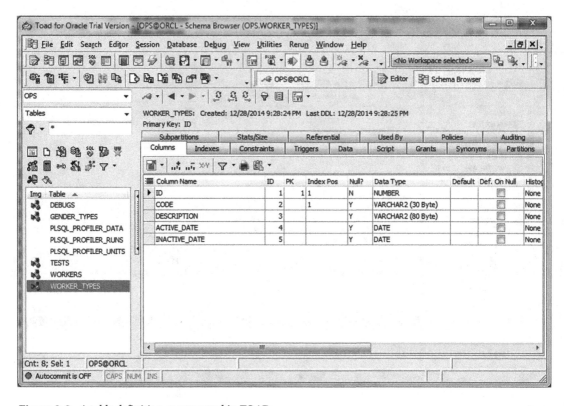

Figure 9-3. A table definition as presented in TOAD

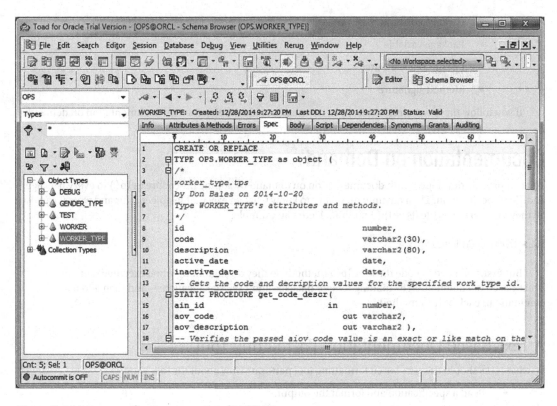

Figure 9-4. *A type specification as presented in TOAD*

Looking at the examples from these two IDEs, it occurs to me, once again, that the best place for documentation on what methods are for and how they actually work is right there in the specification source code itself, as properly formatted comments.

So if you properly format comments in a package or TYPE specification, you should be able to create a tool to display those comments, along with method call specifications as text or in any format. But first, you'll need to follow some commenting rules.

Rules for Documentation Comments

In order to be able to do any level of manipulation with the comments placed in the specifications for a package or TYPE, the use of the comments needs to be consistent from one specification to the next. To that end, following a minimal set of rules for adding comments to a specification will enable you to later display that information in various formats. The rules consist of the following:

- Place a multiline descriptive comment at the very beginning of each package and TYPE specification. This comment includes the object name, author, date written, and modification history.

- Place a single or multiline comment before every

- Package constant

- Package variable

- List of TYPE attributes

- Method signature

If you follow these two simple rules, you can next provide developers with documentation on demand.

Documentation on Demand

You can provide developers with documentation on demand by adding procedure help() to every package and TYPE specification. Then anytime they want to know what an executable object is for and what it can do, all they need to is execute its help() method. Here's an example:

```
SQL> WORKER_TYPE.help();
```

But first, you need to code those help() methods so they do something when executed! Let's build a text-based documentation formatting tool for package and TYPE specifications—and then add it as a command in each help() method.

A Text-Based Documentation Formatting Tool

So what tasks should this text-based formatting tool perform? How about the following?

- Read a specification and format the output.

- Remove any single-line or multiline comment delimiters.

- Preserve any hard carriage returns in order to maintain vertical spacing.

- Preserve any space or tab indentation in order to maintain horizontal spacing.

Using PL/SQL, I can accomplish the following tasks:

- Read through the source code of a specification by accessing view SYS.USER_SOURCE.

- Parse out and replace any single-line or multiline comment delimiters.

- Identify a hard carriage return and forward it to put_line().

But the last requirement will be difficult. put_line(), the only means of displaying text from PL/SQL, will just truncate any leading spaces, so the best I can do is provide a hack where I send put_line() a tab character any time I have a source line that starts with a space character.

Now that I have some requirements to work with, I can build the text-based help tool. Listing 9-1 is the package specification for a text-based documentation formatting tool, or "text-help" tool appropriately named TEXT_HELP.

Listing 9-1. A Package Spec to Create Text-Based Help, text_help.pks

```
01  create or replace PACKAGE TEXT_HELP as
02  /*
03  test_help.pkb
04  by Donald J. Bales on 2014-10-20
05  A package to produce text based help
```

```
06  */
07
08  /*
09  The help text for this package.
10  */
11  PROCEDURE help;
12
13
14  /*
15  Generate help text for the specified object using its specification.
16  */
17  PROCEDURE process(
18  aiv_object_name                in       varchar2);
19
20
21  /*
22  The test unit for this package.
23  */
24  PROCEDURE test;
25
26
27  end text_help;
28  /
29  @se.sql
```

TEXT_HELP has three methods:

- help() displays on-demand help for this package by utilizing its second method process().

- process() retrieves the specified specification from view SYS.USER_SOURCE, and then displays the specification as nicely formatted text.

- test() is the test unit for this package.

Also notice that in Listing 9-1, I followed the commenting rules outlined earlier. Do as I say, *and* as I do!

Listing 9-2 is the implementation for TEXT_HELP. The only "new" method is process(). It's an ugly combination of parsing with substr() and an if-then-elsif-then-else tree that implements the requirements outlined earlier in this section.

Listing 9-2. A Package Body to Create Text-Based Help, text_help.pkb

```
001  create or replace PACKAGE BODY TEXT_HELP as
002  /*
003  test_help.pkb
004  by Donald J. Bales on 2014-10-20
005  A package to produce text based help
006  */
007
008  PROCEDURE help is
009
010  begin
011    TEXT_HELP.process('TEXT_HELP');
012  end help;
```

```
013
014
015    /*
016    A procedure to output formatted package or TYPE text
017    */
018    PROCEDURE out(
019    aiv_text                          in      varchar2) is
020
021    v_text                                    varchar(255);
022    n_text                                    number := 1;
023
024    begin
025      if nvl(length(aiv_text), 0) < 256 then
026        v_text := aiv_text;
027      else
028        v_text := substr(aiv_text, 1, 252)||'...';
029      end if;
030      if nvl(substr(v_text, 1, 1), chr(32)) = chr(32) then
031        if length(v_text) > 0 then
032          for i in 1..length(v_text) loop
033            if nvl(substr(v_text, i, 1), chr(32)) <> chr(32) then
034              n_text := i;
035              exit;
036            end if;
037          end loop;
038        end if;
039        SYS.DBMS_OUTPUT.put_line(chr(9)||substr(v_text, n_text));
040      else
041        SYS.DBMS_OUTPUT.put_line(v_text);
042      end if;
043    end out;
044
045
046    PROCEDURE process(
047    aiv_object_name               in      varchar2) is
048
049    cursor c1(
050    aiv_object_name               in      varchar2) is
051    select text
052    from    SYS.USER_SOURCE
053    where   name = upper(aiv_object_name)
054    and     type in ('PACKAGE', 'TYPE')
055    order by line;
056
057    b_method                              boolean := FALSE;
058    b_comment                             boolean := FALSE;
059    v_text                                SYS.USER_SOURCE.text%TYPE;
060
061    begin
062      for r1 in c1(aiv_object_name) loop
063        v_text := replace(replace(r1.text, chr(13), NULL), chr(10), NULL);
```

```
064     if     substr(ltrim(v_text), 1, 3) = '/* '                          then
065       if nvl(instr(v_text, '*/'), 0) = 0 then
066         b_comment := TRUE;
067       end if;
068       out(substr(ltrim(v_text), 4));
069     elsif substr(ltrim(v_text), 1, 2) = '/*'                            then
070       if nvl(instr(v_text, '*/'), 0) = 0 then
071         b_comment := TRUE;
072       end if;
073       out(substr(ltrim(v_text), 3));
074     elsif b_comment                                                     and
075          substr(rtrim(v_text), -2, 2) = '*/'                            then
076       b_comment := FALSE;
077       out(substr(rtrim(v_text), 1, length(rtrim(v_text)) - 2));
078     elsif b_comment                                                     then
079       out(v_text);
080     elsif substr(ltrim(v_text), 1, 3) = '-- '                           then
081       out(substr(ltrim(v_text), 4));
082     elsif substr(ltrim(v_text), 1, 2) = '--'                            then
083       out(substr(ltrim(v_text), 3));
084     elsif upper(substr(ltrim(v_text), 1,  8)) = 'FUNCTION'            or
085          upper(substr(ltrim(v_text), 1,  9)) = 'PROCEDURE'           or
086          upper(substr(ltrim(v_text), 1, 15)) = 'MEMBER FUNCTION'     or
087          upper(substr(ltrim(v_text), 1, 16)) = 'MEMBER PROCEDURE'    or
088          upper(substr(ltrim(v_text), 1, 16)) = 'STATIC FUNCTION'     or
089          upper(substr(ltrim(v_text), 1, 16)) = 'STATIC PROCEDURE'    then
090       if nvl(instr(v_text, ';'), 0) = 0 then
091         b_method := TRUE;
092       end if;
093       out(v_text);
094     elsif b_method                                                      and
095          substr(rtrim(v_text), -1, 1) = ';'                            then
096       b_method := FALSE;
097       out(v_text);
098     elsif b_method                                                      then
099       out(v_text);
100     elsif c1%rowcount = 1                                               then
101       out(v_text);
102     elsif upper(substr(ltrim(v_text), 1, 3)) = 'END'                   then
103       out(chr(12)); -- form feed
104       exit;
105     else
106       out(v_text);
107     end if;
108   end loop;
109   SYS.DBMS_OUTPUT.new_line();
110 end process;
111
112
113 PROCEDURE test is
114
```

337

```
115  begin
116    pl('TEXT_HELP.test()');
117
118    &_USER..TEST.clear('TEXT_HELP');
119
120    &_USER..TEST.set_test('TEXT_HELP', 'help()', 1,
121      'Test method help()' );
122    begin
123      help();
124
125      &_USER..TEST.ok();
126    exception
127      when OTHERS then
128        &_USER..TEST.error(SQLERRM);
129    end;
130
131    &_USER..TEST.set_test('TEXT_HELP', 'process()', 2,
132      'Test method help()' );
133    begin
134      process('TEXT_HELP');
135
136      &_USER..TEST.ok();
137    exception
138      when OTHERS then
139        &_USER..TEST.error(SQLERRM);
140    end;
141
142    &_USER..TEST.set_test('TEXT_HELP', NULL, NULL, NULL);
143    &_USER..TEST.success();
144  end test;
145
146
147  end text_help;
148  /
149  @be.sql
```

The code in this package body is not all that impressive, nor important. It's its use that is important, so let's see how to use it.

On lines 8 through 12 in Listing 9-2, I've coded the help() method for TEXT_HELP. In order to produce the text-based help for the package, all I need to do is pass the name of the package or TYPE to method TEXT_HELP.process().

Now, let's see what it produces.

Accessing Documentation on Demand

As I mentioned earlier, now all I need do to get documentation on demand is to execute a package or TYPE's help() method, assuming that the help() method in turn calls TEXT_HELP.process() to produce the output.

Figure 9-5 is an example of executing the help() method for package WORKER_TYPE. As you can see in Figure 9-5, the output is much more significant than the result from using describe in SQL*Plus or what the IDEs had to offer.

```
RPS on ORCL                                                              □    X
SQL> execute WORKER_TYPE.help();
PACKAGE WORKER_TYPE as

worker_type.pks
by Don Bales on 2014-10-20
Code Table WORKER_TYPES's methods.


Gets the code and decription values for the specified ain_id.
PROCEDURE get_code_descr(
ain_id                        in      WORKER_TYPES.id%TYPE,
aov_code                              out WORKER_TYPES.code%TYPE,
aov_description                       out WORKER_TYPES.description%TYPE );


Verifies the passed aiov_code value is an exact or like match on
the date specified.
PROCEDURE get_code_id_descr(
aiov_code                     in out WORKER_TYPES.code%TYPE,
aon_id                               out WORKER_TYPES.id%TYPE,
aov_description                      out WORKER_TYPES.description%TYPE,
aid_on                        in      WORKER_TYPES.active_date%TYPE );


Verifies the passed aiov_code value is currently an exact or like
match.
PROCEDURE get_code_id_descr(
aiov_code                     in out WORKER_TYPES.code%TYPE,
aon_id                               out WORKER_TYPES.id%TYPE,
aov_description                      out WORKER_TYPES.description%TYPE );


Returns a newly allocated id value.
FUNCTION get_id
return                                WORKER_TYPES.id%TYPE;
```

Figure 9-5. *Sample output from TEXT_HELP.process()*

The only limit to the depth of the documentation is the amount of time you're willing to spend writing it as you code each specification. Yes, once again, *you* are responsible for the quality of the outcome of *your* activities. But that's what it means to be a "professional." You're responsible, you know it, and you live up to that responsibility.

Now that you have access to TEXT_HELP, it's your turn to put it to work.

It's Your Turn to Access Documentation on Demand

Here are your tasks for this assignment.

1.   Go back to every package and TYPE specification you've written, and add properly formatted comments (come on, at least do a couple).

2.   Add the specification for procedure help() to each of those specifications, if you haven't already.

3.   Access your help text by executing the help() command on each of your PL/SQL executables.

What do you think? Wouldn't you find immediate and easy access to documentation on what an object is for and how to use it invaluable? In practice, I've found that programmers are twice as likely to reuse a component if they have easy access to its documentation. But you can do even better.

Programmers are four times as likely to use a component if they know it exists beforehand and they also know how to use it. That sounds like training, doesn't it? Will your CFO or project manager tell you that you may not provide training; in other words, that you may not reuse your components? If not, then you'll need documentation you can distribute freely. To that end, let's look at the ability to create distributable documentation from a package or TYPE specification next.

Distributable Documentation

All that's necessary to create a set of distributable documentation for every specification in the database is to query the database's data dictionary for a list of those specifications, and then save each document to an operating system file. And that can be done by calling the help() method for each executable object. But let's do better than that. Text-based documentation can look quite boring and be quite unfriendly.

I know, let's use HTML instead! Let's create an HTML-based documentation formatting tool, or "HTML-help" tool. I'll even go so far as to call it HTML_HELP!

An HTML-Based Documentation Formatting Tool

Listing 9-3 is the package specification for an HTML-based help tool. Working with the capabilities of SQL*Plus, I can use it to produce an HTML help file for each executable object, and then an index to all those documents.

Listing 9-3. A Package Spec to Create HTML-Based Help, html_help.pks

```
01  create or replace PACKAGE HTML_HELP as
02  /*
03  html_help.pks
04  by Donald J. Bales on 2014-10-20
05  Package to create HTML-based help files for packages.
06  */
07
08  -- Creates a "object_index" html file for the current USER.
09
10  PROCEDURE create_index;
11
12
13  -- Creates a "<object_name>" html for each package for the current USER.
14
15  PROCEDURE create_help(
16  aiv_object_name             in     varchar2);
17
18
19  -- Text-based help for this package.  "set serveroutput on" in SQL*Plus.
20
21  PROCEDURE help;
22
23
24  PROCEDURE test;
25
26
```

```
27    end HTML_HELP;
28    /
29    @se.sql HTML_HELP
```

HTML_HELP has four methods:

- create_index() creates an index to all the documents created using the next method, create_help().

- create_help() creates an HTML-based document from the comments and method signatures in a specification.

- help() produces on-demand help for this package.

- test() is the test unit for this package.

Methods create_index() and create_help() require the use of a SQL*Plus script in order to write the output to operating system files.

Listing 9-4 is the implementation for HTML_HELP. In this case, I'm showing only a partial listing; you will find the full listing in the chapter's download directory. What's important here is the outcome of this package: documentation. And that outcome can be distributable if I save it as individual files on a file system.

Listing 9-4. A Package Body to Create HTML-Based Help, html_help.pkb

```
001   create or replace PACKAGE BODY HTML_HELP as
002   /*
003   html_help.pkb
004   by Donald J. Bales on 2014-10-20
005   Package to create HTML-based help files for packages
006   */
007
008   -- TYPES
009
010   TYPE spec_record is record (
011   line_type                      varchar2(1),
012   line_number                    number,
013   line_text                      varchar2(2000),
014   method_name                    varchar2(2000),
015   first_sentence                 varchar2(2000));
016
017   TYPE spec_table is table of spec_record index by binary_integer;
018
019   TYPE buffer_table is table of varchar2(2000) index by binary_integer;
020
021   -- CONSTANTS
022
023   v_LT_COMMENT             constant  varchar2(1) := 'C';
024   v_LT_METHOD              constant  varchar2(1) := 'M';
025   v_LT_OTHER               constant  varchar2(1) := 'O';
026
027   -- FORWARD DECLARATIONS
028
```

```
029    FUNCTION get_comment_start(
030    aiv_text                       in      varchar2)
031    return                                 number;
032
033
034    FUNCTION get_comment_end(
035    aiv_text                       in      varchar2)
036    return                                 number;
037
038
039    FUNCTION get_method_end(
040    aiv_text                       in      varchar2)
041    return                                 number;
042
043
044    FUNCTION get_method_name_start(
045    aiv_text                       in      varchar2)
046    return                                 number;
047
048
049    FUNCTION get_method_name_end(
050    aiv_text                       in      varchar2)
051    return                                 number;
052
053
054    FUNCTION is_comment_start(
055    aiv_text                       in      varchar2)
056    return                                 boolean;
057
058
059    FUNCTION is_comment_end(
060    aiv_text                       in      varchar2)
061    return                                 boolean;
062
063
064    FUNCTION is_method_end(
065    aiv_text                       in      varchar2)
066    return                                 boolean;
067
068
069    PROCEDURE out(
070    aiv_text                       in      varchar2);
071
072
073    PROCEDURE open_html(
074    aiv_title                      in      varchar2);
075
076
077    PROCEDURE close_html;
078
079
```

```
080   -- FUNCTIONS
081
082   FUNCTION get_comment_line_text(
083   aiv_text                        in      varchar2)
084   return                                  varchar2 is
085
086   n_start                                 number := 1;
087   n_end                                   number;
088
089   begin
090     if is_comment_start(aiv_text) then
091       n_start := get_comment_start(aiv_text);
092     end if;
093     if is_comment_end(aiv_text) then
094       n_end := get_comment_end(aiv_text);
095     else
096       n_end := nvl(length(aiv_text), 0);
097     end if;
098     if n_end > n_start then
099       return substr(aiv_text, n_start, (n_end + 1) - n_start);
100     else
101       return NULL;
102     end if;
103   end get_comment_line_text;
104
105
106   FUNCTION get_comment_end(
107   aiv_text                        in      varchar2)
108   return                                  number is
109
110   n_position                              number;
111
112   begin
113     n_position := nvl(instr(upper(aiv_text), '*/'), 0);
114     if n_position > 0 then
115       return n_position - 1;
116     else
117       n_position := nvl(instr(upper(aiv_text), '--'), 0);
118       if n_position > 0 then
119         return nvl(length(aiv_text), 0);
120       else
121         return -1;
122       end if;
123     end if;
124   end get_comment_end;
125
126
127   FUNCTION get_comment_start(
128   aiv_text                        in      varchar2)
129   return                                  number is
130
```

```
131  n_position                              number;
132
133  begin
134    n_position := nvl(instr(upper(aiv_text), '/*'), 0);
135    if n_position > 0 then
136      return n_position + 2;
137    else
138      n_position := nvl(instr(upper(aiv_text), '--'), 0);
139      if n_position > 0 then
140        return n_position + 2;
141      else
142        return -1;
143      end if;
144    end if;
145  end get_comment_start;
146
147
148  FUNCTION get_first_sentence(
149  aiv_text                    in      varchar2)
150  return                              varchar2 is
151
152  n_start                             number := 1;
153  n_end                               number;
154
155  begin
156    if is_comment_start(aiv_text) then
157      n_start := get_comment_start(aiv_text);
158    end if;
159    n_end := nvl(instr(aiv_text, '.') - 1, -1);
160    if n_end = -1 then
161      n_end := nvl(length(aiv_text), 0);
162    end if;
163    if n_end > n_start then
164      return substr(aiv_text, n_start, (n_end + 1) - n_start);
165    else
166      return NULL;
167    end if;
168  end get_first_sentence;
169
170
171  FUNCTION get_method_end(
172  aiv_text                    in      varchar2)
173  return                              number is
174
175  n_position                          number;
176
177  begin
178    n_position := nvl(instr(upper(aiv_text), ';'), 0);
179    if n_position > 0 then
180      return n_position - 1;
181    else
```

```
182       return length(aiv_text);
183     end if;
184 end get_method_end;
185
186
187 FUNCTION get_method_line_text(
188 aiv_text                          in        varchar2)
189 return                                      varchar2 is
190
191 n_start                                     number := 1;
192 n_end                                       number;
193
194 begin
195   if is_method_end(aiv_text) then
196     n_end := get_method_end(aiv_text);
197   else
198     n_end := nvl(length(aiv_text), 0);
199   end if;
200   if n_end > 0 then
201     return substr(aiv_text, n_start, (n_end + 1) - n_start);
202   else
203     return NULL;
204   end if;
205 end get_method_line_text;
206
207
208 FUNCTION get_method_name(
209 aiv_text                          in        varchar2)
210 return                                      varchar2 is
211
212 n_first                                     number;
213 n_end                                       number;
214
215 begin
216   n_first := get_method_name_start(aiv_text);
217   n_end   := get_method_name_end(aiv_text);
218   if n_end > n_first then
219     return substr(aiv_text, n_first, (n_end + 1) - n_first);
220   else
221     return NULL;
222   end if;
223 end get_method_name;
224
225
226 FUNCTION get_method_name_start(
227 aiv_text                          in        varchar2)
228 return                                      number is
229
230 n_position                                  number;
231
```

```
232   begin
233     n_position := nvl(instr(upper(aiv_text), 'FUNCTION '), 0);
234     if n_position > 0 then
235       return n_position + 9;
236     else
237       n_position := nvl(instr(upper(aiv_text), 'PROCEDURE '), 0);
238       if n_position > 0 then
239         return n_position + 10;
240       else
241         return 0;
242       end if;
243     end if;
244   end get_method_name_start;
245
246
247   FUNCTION get_method_name_end(
248   aiv_text                      in      varchar2)
249   return                                number is
250
251   n_position                            number;
252
253   begin
254     n_position := nvl(instr(upper(aiv_text), '('), 0);
255     if n_position > 0 then
256       return n_position - 1;
257     else
258       n_position := get_method_end(aiv_text);
259       if n_position > 0 then
260         return n_position;
261       else
262         return nvl(length(aiv_text), 0);
263       end if;
264     end if;
265   end get_method_name_end;
266
267
268   FUNCTION is_comment_end(
269   aiv_text                      in      varchar2)
270   return                                boolean is
271
272   n_position                            number;
273
274   begin
275     if get_comment_end(aiv_text) >= 0 then
276       return TRUE;
277     else
278       return FALSE;
279     end if;
280   end is_comment_end;
281
282
```

```
283  FUNCTION is_comment_start(
284  aiv_text                      in      varchar2)
285  return                                boolean is
286
287  n_position                            number;
288
289  begin
290    if get_comment_start(aiv_text) >= 0 then
291      return TRUE;
292    else
293      return FALSE;
294    end if;
295  end is_comment_start;
296
297
298  FUNCTION is_method_end(
299  aiv_text                      in      varchar2)
300  return                                boolean is
301
302  n_position                            number;
303
304  begin
305    if nvl(instr(aiv_text, ';'), 0) > 0 then
306      return TRUE;
307    else
308      return FALSE;
309    end if;
310  end is_method_end;
311
312
313  FUNCTION is_method_start(
314  aiv_text                      in      varchar2)
315  return                                boolean is
316
317  n_position                            number;
318
319  begin
320    if get_method_name_start(aiv_text) > 0 then
321      return TRUE;
322    else
323      return FALSE;
324    end if;
325  end is_method_start;
326
327
328  FUNCTION comments_span(
329  aiv_text                      in      varchar2)
330  return                                varchar2 is
331  begin
332    return '<span class="comments_span">'||aiv_text||'</span>';
333  end comments_span;
334
335
```

```
336   FUNCTION first_sentence_span(
337   aiv_text                        in      varchar2)
338   return                          varchar2 is
339   begin
340     return '<span class="first_sentence_span">'||aiv_text||'</span>';
341   end first_sentence_span;
342
343
344   FUNCTION method_span(
345   aiv_text                        in      varchar2)
346   return                          varchar2 is
347   begin
348     return '<span class="method_span">'||aiv_text||'</span>';
349   end method_span;
350
351
352   FUNCTION method_name_span(
353   aiv_text                        in      varchar2)
354   return                          varchar2 is
355   begin
356     return '<span class="method_name_span">'||aiv_text||'</span>';
357   end method_name_span;
358
359
360   FUNCTION package_name_span(
361   aiv_text                        in      varchar2)
362   return                          varchar2 is
363   begin
364     return '<span class="package_name_span">'||aiv_text||'</span>';
365   end package_name_span;
366
367
368   PROCEDURE create_index is
369
370   cursor c1 is
371   select distinct name
372   from    SYS.USER_SOURCE
373   where   type in ('PACKAGE', 'TYPE')
374   order by 1;
375
376   cursor c2(
377   aiv_name                        in      varchar2) is
378   select text
379   from    SYS.USER_SOURCE
380   where   type in ('PACKAGE', 'TYPE')
381   and     name = aiv_name
382   order by line;
383
384   b_comment                       boolean;
385   n_period                        number;
386
```

```
387   begin
388     open_html('Package/Type index');
389     out('<h2>Owner '||user||'</h2>');
390     out('<table>');
391     for r1 in c1 loop
392       if c1%rowcount = 1 then
393         out('<tr><th colspan="2">Packages/Types</th></tr>');
394       end if;
395       b_comment := FALSE;
396       for r2 in c2(r1.name) loop
397         if nvl(instr(r2.text, '/*'), 0) > 0 or
398            nvl(instr(r2.text, '--'), 0) > 0 then
399           b_comment := TRUE;
400         end if;
401         if b_comment                                        and
402            nvl(instr(upper(r2.text), '.PKS'), 0) = 0         and
403            substr(upper(ltrim(r2.text)), 1, 3) <> 'BY '      and
404            substr(upper(ltrim(r2.text)), 1, 13) <> 'COPYRIGHT BY ' then
405           n_period := nvl(instr(ltrim(r2.text), '.'), 0);
406           if n_period > 0 then
407             out('<tr><td class="package_name_td"><a href="'||lower(r1.name)||
                  '.html">'||package_name_span(r1.name)||'</a></td><td class="comments_
                  td">'||comments_span(substr(ltrim(r2.text), 1, n_period))||'</td></tr>');
408             exit;
409           end if;
410         end if;
411       end loop;
412     end loop;
413     out('</table>');
414     close_html();
415   end create_index;
416
417
418   PROCEDURE create_help(
419   aiv_object_name                 in      varchar2) is
420
421   cursor c1(
422   aiv_object_name                 in      varchar2) is
423   select text,
424          type
425   from   SYS.USER_SOURCE
426   where  name = upper(aiv_object_name)
427   and    type in ('PACKAGE', 'TYPE')
428   and    line > 1
429   order by line;
430
431   b_comment                       boolean := FALSE;
432   b_first_sentence                boolean := FALSE;
433   b_method                        boolean := FALSE;
434   b_method_name                   boolean := FALSE;
435   b_other                         boolean := FALSE;
```

```
436   n_backward                              number;
437   n_line_number                           number;
438   n_spec                                  number := 0;
439   t_spec                                  spec_table;
440   v_comment                               varchar2(2000);
441   v_first_sentence                        varchar2(2000);
442   v_method                                varchar2(2000);
443   v_method_name                           varchar2(2000);
444   v_text                                  varchar2(2000);
445   v_type                                  varchar2(30);
446
447   begin
448     for r1 in c1(aiv_object_name) loop
449       if c1%rowcount = 1 then
450         v_type := r1.type;
451       end if;
452
453       -- strip away any carriage-returns and line-feeds
454       v_text := replace(replace(r1.text, chr(13), NULL), chr(10), NULL);
455       -- detect comments and methods
456       if   is_comment_start(v_text) then
457         b_comment                         := TRUE;
458         b_first_sentence                  := FALSE;
459         if not b_first_sentence then
460           v_first_sentence                := get_first_sentence(v_text);
461           if v_first_sentence is not NULL then
462             b_first_sentence              := TRUE;
463             n_line_number                 := 1;
464             n_spec                        := n_spec + 1;
465             t_spec(n_spec).line_type      := v_LT_COMMENT;
466             t_spec(n_spec).line_number    := n_line_number;
467             t_spec(n_spec).line_text      := get_comment_line_text(v_text);
468             t_spec(n_spec).first_sentence := v_first_sentence;
469           end if;
470         else
471           v_comment                       := get_comment_line_text(v_text);
472           if v_comment is not NULL then
473             n_line_number                 := 1;
474             n_spec                        := n_spec + 1;
475             t_spec(n_spec).line_type      := v_LT_COMMENT;
476             t_spec(n_spec).line_number    := n_line_number;
477             t_spec(n_spec).line_text      := get_comment_line_text(v_text);
478             t_spec(n_spec).first_sentence := NULL;
479           end if;
480         end if;
481         if is_comment_end(v_text) then
482           b_comment                       := FALSE;
483           b_first_sentence                := FALSE;
484         end if;
485       elsif b_comment                and
486             is_comment_end(v_text) then
```

```
487        if not b_first_sentence then
488          v_first_sentence                 := get_first_sentence(v_text);
489          if v_first_sentence is not NULL then
490            b_first_sentence               := TRUE;
491            n_line_number                  := 1;
492            n_spec                         := n_spec + 1;
493            t_spec(n_spec).line_type       := v_LT_COMMENT;
494            t_spec(n_spec).line_number     := n_line_number;
495            t_spec(n_spec).line_text       := get_comment_line_text(v_text);
496            t_spec(n_spec).first_sentence  := v_first_sentence;
497          end if;
498        else
499          v_comment                        := get_comment_line_text(v_text);
500          if v_comment is not NULL then
501            n_line_number                  := n_line_number + 1;
502            n_spec                         := n_spec + 1;
503            t_spec(n_spec).line_type       := v_LT_COMMENT;
504            t_spec(n_spec).line_number     := n_line_number;
505            t_spec(n_spec).line_text       := get_comment_line_text(v_text);
506            t_spec(n_spec).first_sentence  := NULL;
507          end if;
508        end if;
509        b_comment                          := FALSE;
510        b_first_sentence                   := FALSE;
511      elsif b_comment                                              then
512        if not b_first_sentence then
513          v_first_sentence                 := get_first_sentence(v_text);
514          if v_first_sentence is not NULL then
515            b_first_sentence               := TRUE;
516            n_line_number                  := 1;
517            n_spec                         := n_spec + 1;
518            t_spec(n_spec).line_type       := v_LT_COMMENT;
519            t_spec(n_spec).line_number     := n_line_number;
520            t_spec(n_spec).line_text       := get_comment_line_text(v_text);
521            t_spec(n_spec).first_sentence  := v_first_sentence;
522          end if;
523        else
524          v_comment                        := get_comment_line_text(v_text);
525          if v_comment is not NULL then
526            n_line_number                  := n_line_number + 1;
527            n_spec                         := n_spec + 1;
528            t_spec(n_spec).line_type       := v_LT_COMMENT;
529            t_spec(n_spec).line_number     := n_line_number;
530            t_spec(n_spec).line_text       := get_comment_line_text(v_text);
531            t_spec(n_spec).first_sentence  := NULL;
532          end if;
533        end if;
534      elsif is_method_start(v_text) then
535        b_method                           := TRUE;
536        b_method_name                      := FALSE;
537        if not b_method_name then
```

351

```
538            v_method_name                        := get_method_name(v_text);
539         if v_method_name is not NULL then
540            b_method_name                      := TRUE;
541            n_line_number                      := 1;
542            n_spec                             := n_spec + 1;
543            t_spec(n_spec).line_type           := v_LT_METHOD;
544            t_spec(n_spec).line_number         := n_line_number;
545            t_spec(n_spec).line_text           := get_method_line_text(v_text);
546            t_spec(n_spec).method_name         := v_method_name;
547         else
548            n_line_number                      := 1;
549            n_spec                             := n_spec + 1;
550            t_spec(n_spec).line_type           := v_LT_METHOD;
551            t_spec(n_spec).line_number         := n_line_number;
552            t_spec(n_spec).line_text           := get_method_line_text(v_text);
553            t_spec(n_spec).method_name         := NULL;
554         end if;
555      else
556         v_method                             := get_method_line_text(v_text);
557         if v_method is not NULL then
558            n_line_number                      := n_line_number + 1;
559            n_spec                             := n_spec + 1;
560            t_spec(n_spec).line_type           := v_LT_METHOD;
561            t_spec(n_spec).line_number         := n_line_number;
562            t_spec(n_spec).line_text           := v_method;
563            t_spec(n_spec).method_name         := NULL;
564         end if;
565      end if;
566      if is_method_end(v_text) then
567         b_method                           := FALSE;
568         b_method_name                      := FALSE;
569      end if;
570   elsif b_method                 and
571         is_method_end(v_text) then
572      if not b_method_name then
573         v_method_name                        := get_method_name(v_text);
574         if v_method_name is not NULL then
575            b_method_name                      := TRUE;
576            n_line_number                      := 1;
577            n_spec                             := n_spec + 1;
578            t_spec(n_spec).line_type           := v_LT_METHOD;
579            t_spec(n_spec).line_number         := n_line_number;
580            t_spec(n_spec).line_text           := get_method_line_text(v_text);
581            t_spec(n_spec).method_name         := v_method_name;
582         else
583            n_line_number                      := 1;
584            n_spec                             := n_spec + 1;
585            t_spec(n_spec).line_type           := v_LT_METHOD;
586            t_spec(n_spec).line_number         := n_line_number;
587            t_spec(n_spec).line_text           := get_method_line_text(v_text);
588            t_spec(n_spec).method_name         := NULL;
```

```
589            end if;
590          else
591            v_method                        := get_method_line_text(v_text);
592            if v_method is not NULL then
593              n_line_number                 := n_line_number + 1;
594              n_spec                        := n_spec + 1;
595              t_spec(n_spec).line_type      := v_LT_METHOD;
596              t_spec(n_spec).line_number    := n_line_number;
597              t_spec(n_spec).line_text      := v_method;
598              t_spec(n_spec).method_name    := NULL;
599            end if;
600          end if;
601          b_method                          := FALSE;
602          b_method_name                     := FALSE;
603        elsif b_method                                            then
604          v_method                          := get_method_line_text(v_text);
605          if v_method is not NULL then
606            n_line_number                   := n_line_number + 1;
607            n_spec                          := n_spec + 1;
608            t_spec(n_spec).line_type        := v_LT_METHOD;
609            t_spec(n_spec).line_number      := n_line_number;
610            t_spec(n_spec).line_text        := v_method;
611            t_spec(n_spec).method_name      := NULL;
612          end if;
613        elsif upper(substr(ltrim(v_text), 1, 3)) = 'END'        then
614          exit;
615        elsif nvl(length(rtrim(v_text)), 0) > 0 then
616          n_line_number                     := 1;
617          n_spec                            := n_spec + 1;
618          t_spec(n_spec).line_type          := v_LT_OTHER;
619          t_spec(n_spec).line_number        := n_line_number;
620          t_spec(n_spec).line_text          := v_text;
621        end if;
622      end loop;
623
624      -- Now create the HTML
625      open_html(aiv_object_name);
626      -- Package name and comments
627      if v_type = 'PACKAGE' then
628        out('<h2>Package '||upper(aiv_object_name)||'</h2>');
629      else
630        out('<h2>Type '||upper(aiv_object_name)||'</h2>');
631      end if;
632      if n_spec > 0 then
633        for i in 1..n_spec loop
634          if t_spec(i).first_sentence is not NULL then
635            out('<p class="comments_p">');
636            n_line_number := t_spec(i).line_number;
637            for j in i..n_spec loop
638              if j                   > 1                and
639                 t_spec(j).line_number <= n_line_number then
```

```
640                 exit;
641               end if;
642             out(t_spec(j).line_text);
643           end loop;
644         out('</p>');
645         exit;
646       end if;
647     end loop;
648     out('<hr/><br/>');
649     -- Other
650     for i in 1..n_spec loop
651       if t_spec(i).line_type = v_LT_OTHER then
652         if not b_other then
653           out('<table>');
654           if v_type = 'PACKAGE' then
655             out('<tr><th colspan="2">Global Constants and Variables</th></tr>');
656           else
657             out('<tr><th colspan="2">Attributes</th></tr>');
658           end if;
659           out('</table>');
660           out('<pre class="other_pre">');
661           b_other := TRUE;
662         end if;
663         if i > 1                                    and
664           t_spec(i - 1).line_type = v_LT_COMMENT then
665           n_backward := i - t_spec(i - 1).line_number;
666           if n_backward > 0 then
667             out('</pre><p class="comments_p">');
668             for j in n_backward..(i - 1) loop
669               out(t_spec(j).line_text);
670             end loop;
671             out('</p><pre class="other_pre">');
672           end if;
673         end if;
674         out(t_spec(i).line_text);
675       end if;
676     end loop;
677     if b_other then
678       out('</pre>');
679     out('<hr/><br/>');
680     end if;
681 /*    -- Debug Output
682     out('<!--');
683     out('<h2>Debug Output</h2>');
684     for i in 1..n_spec loop
685       if i = 1 then
686         out('<table>');
687         out('<tr><th>line_type</th><th>line_number</th><th>line_text</th>
            <th>first_sentence</th><th>method_name</th></tr>');
688       end if;
```

```
689        out('<tr><td>'||t_spec(i).line_type||'</td><td>'||t_spec(i).line_number||
           '</td><td>'||t_spec(i).line_text||'</td><td>'||t_spec(i).first_sentence||
           '</td><td>'||t_spec(i).method_name||'</td></tr>');
690        if i = n_spec then
691          out('</table>');
692          out('<hr/>');
693        end if;
694      end loop;
695      out('<hr/><br/>');
696      out('-->');  */
697      -- Method Summary
698      out('<table>');
699      out('<tr><th colspan="2">Method Summary</th></tr>');
700      for i in 1..n_spec loop
701        if t_spec(i).method_name is not NULL then
702          v_first_sentence := '<br/>';
703          n_backward := i - 1;
704          if n_backward > 0 then
705            loop
706              if t_spec(n_backward).method_name is not NULL then
707                exit;
708              end if;
709              if t_spec(n_backward).first_sentence is not NULL then
710                v_first_sentence := t_spec(n_backward).first_sentence;
711                exit;
712              end if;
713              n_backward := n_backward - 1;
714              if n_backward < 1 then
715                exit;
716              end if;
717            end loop;
718          end if;
719          out('<tr><td class="method_name_td"><a href="#'||t_spec(i).method_name||'_'
             ||to_char(i)||'">'||method_name_span(t_spec(i).method_name)||'</a></td>');
720          out(' <td class="first_sentence_td">'||first_sentence_span(nvl(v_first_
             sentence, '<br/>'))||'</td></tr>');
721        end if;
722      end loop;
723      out('</table>');
724      out('<br/><hr/><br/>');
725      -- Method Details
726      out('<table>');
727      out('<tr><th colspan="2">Method Detail</th></tr>');
728      out('</table>');
729      for i in 1..n_spec loop
730        if t_spec(i).method_name is not NULL then
731          out('<h3><a name="#'||t_spec(i).method_name||'_'||to_char(i)||'">'||
             t_spec(i).method_name||'</a></h3>');
732          out('<pre class="method_pre">');
733          for j in i..n_spec loop
734            if t_spec(j).line_type <> v_LT_METHOD or
735              (j > i                                 and
```

```
736                  t_spec(j).method_name is not NULL) then
737              exit;
738            end if;
739            out(t_spec(j).line_text);
740          end loop;
741          out('</pre>');
742          if i > 1                                          and
743            t_spec(i - 1).line_type = v_LT_COMMENT then
744            n_backward := i - t_spec(i - 1).line_number;
745            if n_backward > 0 then
746              out('<p class="comments_p">');
747              for j in n_backward..(i - 1) loop
748                out(t_spec(j).line_text);
749              end loop;
750              out('</p>');
751            end if;
752          end if;
753          out('<hr/>');
754        end if;
755      end loop;
756    end if;
757    close_html();
758  end create_help;
759
760
761  PROCEDURE help is
762
763  begin
764    TEXT_HELP.process('HTML_HELP');
765  end help;
766
767
768  PROCEDURE out(
769  aiv_text                          in      varchar2) is
770
771  TYPE split_table is table of varchar2(255)
772  index by binary_integer;
773
774  n_length                          number;
775  n_split                           number := 255;
776  n_start                           number := 1;
777  n_stop                            number;
778  n_text                            number := 0;
779
780  t_text                            split_table;
781
782  n_limit_1                         number := 0;
783  n_limit_2                         number := 0;
784
785  begin
786    n_length := nvl(length(aiv_text), 0);
787
```

```
788    if n_length > 255 then
789      loop
790        n_limit_1 := n_limit_1 + 1;
791        n_stop := least(n_start + n_split, n_length);
792        loop
793          n_limit_2 := n_limit_2 + 1;
794
795          if   n_stop = n_start then
796            n_stop := n_length;
797            exit;
798          elsif substr(aiv_text, n_stop, 1) = chr(32) then
799            exit;
800          else
801            n_stop := n_stop - 1;
802          end if;
803        end loop;
804        n_text := n_text + 1;
805        t_text(n_text) := substr(aiv_text, n_start, n_stop - n_start);
806        n_start := n_stop;
807        if n_start >= n_length then
808          exit;
809        end if;
810      end loop;
811      for i in t_text.first..t_text.last loop
812        SYS.DBMS_OUTPUT.put_line(t_text(i));
813      end loop;
814    else
815      SYS.DBMS_OUTPUT.put_line(aiv_text);
816    end if;
817  end out;
818
819
820  PROCEDURE open_html(
821  aiv_title                        in      varchar2) is
822
823  begin
824    out('<html>
825  <head>
826  <title>'||aiv_title||'</title>
827  <link rel="stylesheet" type="text/css" href="stylesheet.css"/>
828  </head>
829  <body>');
830  end open_html;
831
832
833  PROCEDURE close_html is
834
835  begin
836    out('</body>
837  </html>');
838  end close_html;
```

```
839
840
841   PROCEDURE test is
842
843   begin
844     pl('HTML_HELP.test()');
845
846     &_USER..TEST.clear('HTML_HELP');
847
848     &_USER..TEST.set_test('HTML_HELP', 'create_package_index()', 1,
849       'Test method create_package_index()' );
850     begin
851       create_index();
852
853       &_USER..TEST.ok();
854     exception
855       when OTHERS then
856         &_USER..TEST.error(SQLERRM);
857     end;
858
859     &_USER..TEST.set_test('HTML_HELP', 'create_package_help()', 2,
860       'Test method create_package_help()' );
861     begin
862       create_help('HTML_HELP');
863
864       &_USER..TEST.ok();
865     exception
866       when OTHERS then
867         &_USER..TEST.error(SQLERRM);
868     end;
869
870     &_USER..TEST.set_test('HTML_HELP', 'help()', 3,
871       'Test method help()' );
872     begin
873       help();
874
875       &_USER..TEST.ok();
876     exception
877       when OTHERS then
878         &_USER..TEST.error(SQLERRM);
879     end;
880
881     &_USER..TEST.set_test('HTML_HELP', NULL, NULL, NULL);
882     &_USER..TEST.success();
883   end test;
884
885
886   end HTML_HELP;
887   /
888   @be.sql HTML_HELP
```

Listing 9-5 is a SQL*Plus script, `create_html_help.sql`, which in turn writes and executes a SQL*Plus script, `html_help.sql`, in order to generate distributable HTML-based documentation for the executable objects in a schema, as files in a file system.

Listing 9-5. A SQL*Plus Script to Create HTML-Based Help, create_html_help.sql

```
01  rem create_html_help.sql
02  rem by Don Bales on 2014-10-20
03  rem SQL*Plus script to create a SQL*Plus script to create html help for
04  rem the current user.
05
06  set feedback off;
07  set linesize 1000;
08  set newpage  1;
09  set pagesize 0;
10  set trimspool on;
11  set serveroutput on size 1000000;
12
13  spool html_help.sql;
14
15  prompt rem html_help.sql
16  prompt rem by Don Bales on 2014-10-20
17  prompt rem Created by SQL*Plus script create_html_help.sql
18  prompt;
19  prompt set feedback off;;
20  prompt set linesize 1000;;
21  prompt set newpage  1;;
22  prompt set pagesize 32767;;
23  prompt set trimspool on;;
24  prompt;
25  select 'spool '||lower(name)||'.html;'||
26    chr(10)||'execute HTML_HELP.create_help('''||name||''');'||
27    chr(10)||'spool off;'||chr(10)
28  from    SYS.USER_SOURCE
29  where   type in ('PACKAGE', 'TYPE')
30  group by name
31  order by name;
32
33  prompt spool object_index.html;;
34  prompt execute HTML_HELP.create_index();;
35  prompt spool off;;
36  prompt;
37  prompt set feedback on;;
38  prompt set linesize 1000;;
39  prompt set newpage  1;;
40  prompt set pagesize 32767;;
41  prompt set trimspool on;;
42
43  spool off;
44
45  @html_help.sql
```

Now that the HTML-help tool has been built, let's see how easy it is to generate distributable documentation.

Generating Distributable Documentation

All I need to do to generate distributable documentation is compile package HTML_HELP, and then execute SQL*Plus script create_html_help.sql, as in the following example:

```
SQL> @create_html_help.sql
```

Doing so will create an HTML file with the same name as the executable PL/SQL object, but with an .html suffix. It will also create an index named index.html, which you can open from your browser. Figure 9-6 is an example of what index.html looks like in a browser. The format of this, as well as the rest of the documentation files, is controlled by a CSS style sheet named stylesheet.css, which is placed in the same directory as the HTML files.

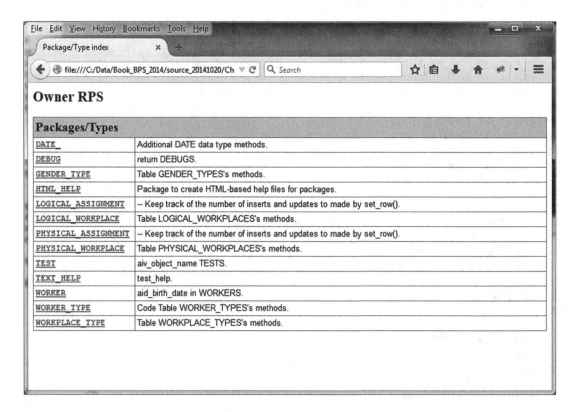

Figure 9-6. *Sample output from HTML_HELP.create_index()*

When I select the DATE_ package from the index in Figure 9-6, my browser opens the generated documentation for the DATE_ specification, as shown in Figure 9-7. When I select method end_of_day() from the method summary, my browser forwards me to another location in the same document where the detail about the method is listed, as shown in Figure 9-8.

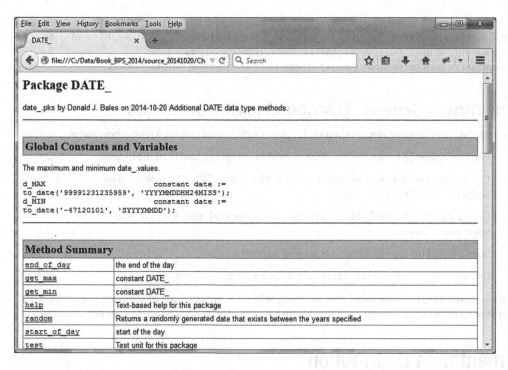

Figure 9-7. *Page 1 of sample output from HTML_HELP.create_help()*

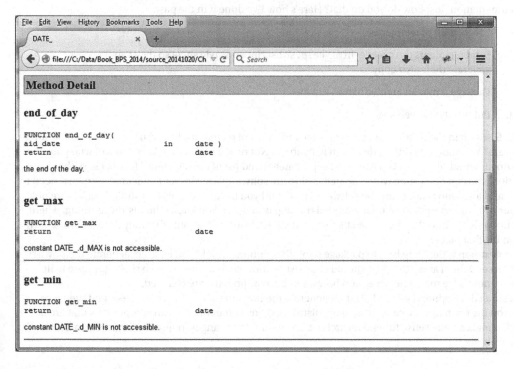

Figure 9-8. *Page 2 of sample output from HTML_HELP.create_help()*

Once again, the depth of the information is bounded only by your imagination and effort. By zipping these HTML files into an archive along with the style sheet, you now have freely distributable, and quite handsome, documentation about your reusable (and non-reusable) components.

Now that you've seen me do it, it's your turn to generate distributable documentation.

It's Your Turn to Generate Distributable Documentation

It's time to generate distributable documentation for your PL/SQL executables. Follow these steps.

1. Find and compile package HTML_HELP, files html_help.pks and html_help.pkb.

2. Create a staging directory where you wish to place the HTML files produced by script create_html_files.sql.

3. Copy script create_html_files.sql and style sheet stylesheet.css to your staging directory.

4. Start a SQL*Plus session from your staging directory.

5. Execute script create_html_files.sql from your staging directory.

You should now have as many .html files as you have PL/SQL executables, plus one for the index.html file in your staging directory. Now you need to take the last step, which is to distribute your documentation.

Documentation Distribution

You're almost finished. You're on the home stretch. But the job is not complete until you actually distribute your documentation. Just how do you do that? Here's how I've done it in the past.

1. Create a list of recipients.

2. Send recipients the create_html_help.sql script and style sheet so they can generate their own copy.

3. Package it into an archive like a .zip file.

4. Publish it on a web site.

Your first step in the distribution process is creating a list of recipients. Just who needs to know about this software? You should maintain this list in a database. Not only can you then keep track of who you sent the documentation to, but you can also keep a categorized list of the recipients' feedback. With this information, you can determine who is actually using the software, what incremental improvements need to be made, and also who is not using the software. If you find you have recipients that should be, but are not, using your software components, then remedial training is in order. You know, "hands-on" training, where you can not only see how they have tried using it in the past, but also find out what they think is wrong with using it in the first place!

Your next step is deciding how to package it for distribution. Should you let users generate their own? Should you send them an archive? Or should you host the documentation on a web site? I suppose it all depends on how large the audience is, and how often the components are changed.

In a small development group, I like to regenerate the documentation on a daily basis and then have everyone on the team make a copy. In a highly distributed environment and with components that are not modified, it makes more sense to send an archive. If the software changes frequently, it's easier to host the files on a web site.

Regardless of how you distribute the documentation, you should also write some summary documentation about how the components can be used together or about the patterns employed in the use of polymorphic names in the components. I'll talk about the latter in the next chapter.

Keep in mind that just as software development is cyclical and recursive, so is the creation and distribution of any documentation for said software. So you must continually maintain your list of recipients and then redistribute your documentation as needed. Don't stop short of this last step. Otherwise, someone will tell a story about your weird behavior in a book someday.

Summary

I started out this chapter trying to impress upon you how important it is to have documentation for your software components. There is no reuse without proper documentation. Second, I showed you how following a small set of commenting rules can turn your package and TYPE specification source into self-documenting source, which also makes losing the documentation impossible.

Next, I showed you how to build and employ a text-based help tool so programmers have access to text-based documentation for any component on demand. Then I showed you how to build and employ an HTML-based help tool so you can generate a distributable form of the documentation embedded in your package and TYPE specifications.

Finally, I gave you some pointers on distributing your software. One last suggestion is that you consider actually training your programmers on how to create new software components and use existing components.

Next, I'm going to share with you some stories of my successful use of PL/SQL, and why they were successful. So grab a cup of joe and let's go.

CHAPTER 10

■ ■ ■

Examples

One could argue that polymorphism is the subject of this chapter. Polymorphism is about using the same message (or command) in order to get the same result, but for different kinds of objects. Let's look at a simple example. Figure 10-1 shows the use of the command draw() for three different geometric shapes: a square, a triangle, and a circle.

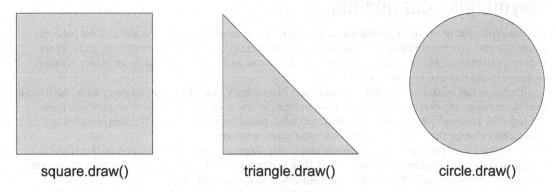

square.draw()   triangle.draw()   circle.draw()

Figure 10-1. *An example of polymorphic command use with different objects*

Although the three geometric shapes in Figure 10-1 are different objects, using the same command, you can communicate what you want each object to do, and the object knows how to do it.

The polymorphic use of commands or messages reduces the use of synonyms in a programming language. If you're a writer, synonyms are wonderful things. They allow you to use words that have similar meanings but sound different, so that your resulting prose can have a somewhat rhythmic cadence. It can sound beautiful.

If you're a programmer, synonyms are awful things. They cause ambiguity because you can't know from "the sound" of the synonym if it means something similar (LIKE) or if it means exactly the same thing (=). And in programming, ambiguity is a really bad thing. Furthermore, synonyms expand the size of a language and make it harder to learn and use. The harder the language is to use, the more defects will be created when using it, and that too is bad.

Let's go back to Figure 10-1 for a second. I could have named the command to draw each geometric shape in the figure draw_square(), draw_triangle(), and draw_circle(). That's the procedural programming paradigm. But by doing so, I would have made the programming language three times larger than when I simply used the same command, draw(), in the context of the object to which it belongs.

Even if you're not using an object-oriented language, you can still use an object-oriented approach by employing modularity and polymorphism. Employing modularity means abstracting large program units into smaller components that can then be reused and assembled to accomplish a larger purpose. Employing polymorphism means abstracting out a set of commands that communicate the same action; however, the action taken will be appropriate for the object executing the command. And that's what I'm going to cover in this chapter, by doing the following:

- Show you a list of polymorphic commands that I have used repeatedly, project after project, always with the same meaning and to take the same action, but an action appropriate to each object.

- Tell you a handful of stories in which I use each polymorphic command, so you'll have some real-world examples to draw from when you employ polymorphism in your next project.

- Leave you with some advice about what you should do next.

I'll get you jump-started with a list of time-tempered polymorphic commands.

Polymorphic Commands

Any time you write or rewrite a program or application, you have an opportunity to abstract out patterns of use that you have experienced beforehand, and employ that experience as the intelligent and wise use of object-orientation. As I've already stated several times, you do not need to be using an object-oriented language in order to employ object-orientation.

Earlier in this book, I introduced you to the idea of creating a "table package" for every table. Each table package contains any executable behavior that "belongs to" the data held in the table in question. Then, in Chapter 6, I showed you how to create an object table, based on a new object TYPE, that contains any executable behavior that "belongs to" its associated object attributes.

Creating a table package is an example of employing object-orientation in a procedural language setting, and creating an object table with a TYPE is an example of employing object-orientation in an object-oriented language setting. Both examples take advantage of polymorphism.

After more than 20 years of coding in PL/SQL, I've created a list of 50 polymorphic commands that can be employed to name most, if not all, of the methods you will use while developing components (and applications) with PL/SQL. Table 10-1 is a list of the top 20 polymorphic commands I commonly use for table packages and TYPEs The first column of the table lists the method name, including whether it is a FUNCTION or PROCEDURE. If a method name is not followed by parentheses, it means that there is a form of the method that takes no parameters. In columns two through four, I indicate whether a method is used for each "kind" of table: a code table, a content table, or an intersection table. Finally, in column five, I indicate whether the method is used in a hierarchical version of one of the three previous table types.

Table 10-1. *Polymorphic Commands for Package Tables and TYPEs*

Method Name	Code	Content	Intersect	Hierarchical
FUNCTION create_id_context()				X
FUNCTION get_code()	X			
FUNCTION get_code_context()				X
FUNCTION get_descr()	X			
FUNCTION get_id	X	X	X	
FUNCTION get_id()	X			
FUNCTION get_id_context()				X
FUNCTION get_name()		X	X	
FUNCTION get_name_context()				X
FUNCTION get_row()		X	X	
FUNCTION is_active()	X	X	X	
FUNCTION is_duplicate()		X	X	
FUNCTION is_history()			X	
PROCEDURE get_code_descr()	X			
PROCEDURE get_code_id_descr()	X			
PROCEDURE get_code_id_name()		X		
PROCEDURE help	X	X	X	
PROCEDURE inactivate()		X	X	
PROCEDURE set_row()		X	X	
PROCEDURE test	X	X	X	

Table 10-2 is a list of polymorphic commands employed by packages and TYPEs that play a particular role in a process, rather than act as merely a persistence entity like a table and table package or object table. The first column of Table 10-2 lists method names along with the type of method. Columns two through six indicate the use of the method name by each of the roles listed in the headings:

- *Data migration*: A one-time process where data is moved and/or transformed from one location to another, typically from a "staging table" to an "application table."

- *On-demand data processing*: A process that manipulates data in the database, on demand, for the purpose of completing some ongoing business-related task.

- *Polling data processing*: A process that manipulates data in the database by managing tasks in a queue or simply sleeping between invocations of the process in question, once again for the purpose of completing some ongoing business-related processing.

- *Data entry*: In support of a presentation layer process of entering data into the database for some ongoing business related task.

- *Reporting*: In support of a presentation layer process of viewing data in the database for some ongoing or ad hoc business-related task.

Table 10-2. *Polymorphic Commands for Roles*

Method Name	Data Migration	Demand Process	Polling Process	Data Entry	Report
FUNCTION calculate()		X	X	X	X
FUNCTION get_next()			X		
FUNCTION get_report					X
FUNCTION get_report()					X
FUNCTION get_status		X	X		
FUNCTION is_authorized()				X	
FUNCTION is_downloaded		X	X		
FUNCTION is_uploaded		X	X		
FUNCTION process	X	X	X		
FUNCTION process()	X	X	X		
PROCEDURE calculate()		X	X	X	X
PROCEDURE disable		X	X		
PROCEDURE download		X	X		
PROCEDURE enable		X	X		
PROCEDURE help	X	X	X	X	X
PROCEDURE initialize	X	X	X	X	X
PROCEDURE load		X	X		
PROCEDURE post_query()				X	
PROCEDURE process	X	X	X		
PROCEDURE process()	X	X	X		
PROCEDURE quit		X	X		
PROCEDURE report					X
PROCEDURE report()					X
PROCEDURE set_downloaded		X	X		
PROCEDURE set_processed	X	X	X		
PROCEDURE set_report()					X
PROCEDURE set_status()		X	X		
PROCEDURE set_uploaded	X	X	X		
PROCEDURE start_logging()		X	X		X
PROCEDURE status		X	X		
PROCEDURE stop_logging()		X	X		X
PROCEDURE test	X	X	X	X	X
PROCEDURE upload		X			

There is some overlap between these five role definitions. For example, a service-oriented interface between two systems will employ data migration, data processing, and table package routines. But that's OK. What I'm trying to do is to get you to think in polymorphic terms.

If you learn to think in polymorphic terms, and then employ polymorphism, once you know what a polymorphic command does on one object, you'll already have a good idea of what it does on the next. And that's quite similar to how we think about the real world. If you tell me you ride a bike, I might respond that I ride a horse. We both know what the other means, even if we've never done the other activity, simply because we apply the word *ride* polymorphically to the context—in your case, a bicycle; in my case, a horse.

In the sections that follow, I'm going to tell you how I've used some (it would take another book to explain them all) of these commands in a particular setting.

Let's start with table packages and TYPEs.

Parametric SQL

I could call this story "The Man Who Hated SQL." The programmer in question was unhappy because he had to break the rhythm of his coding from a procedure language (PL/SQL) to a nonprocedural language (SQL) and back again—back and forth, back and forth, PL/SQL and SQL, PL/SQL and SQL.

While our unhappy programmer was complaining about the nonprocedural nature of SQL and how bad SQL is, he should have been more concerned about reducing the number of different SQL statements used against the database, because reducing the number of SQL statements used against an Oracle database can improve the database's overall performance.

I find it surprising, and at the same time somewhat amusing, how many people hate SQL. You would think its creation was the work of the devil. In contrast, my opinion is that SQL is very effective. You can accomplish a lot of data processing work with very little actual programming effort using SQL. OK, I agree, some things don't work consistently from one implementation to the next, but all in all, no viable alternative has taken its place yet, nor does it appear one will any time soon.

It's really amazing how easy data processing is with SQL. Regardless, *one goal during the development of an application should be to write a particular SQL statement once and only once, just as it should be a goal to write the same code routine once and only once, and then use it as a subroutine.* To that end, I create table packages or TYPEs that employ the same set of polymorphic commands to provide a PL/SQL method in place of writing many of the same SQL statements over and over again.

Code Table Methods

As you saw earlier in the book, I use a database architecture where I always store the primary key, which is a sequence-generated ID value that points to a code, into a content or intersection table. I never store the code or description value. Why?

First, modifying the code or description of a given code table entry will require only an UPDATE against the code table. The next time the code and description values are retrieved for a particular ID value, they will then be the "new" values. The primary key, the ID, will always be the same value, but the code and description values can change without impacting the content and intersection tables that have stored the ID value in question.

Second, in an internationalized application, I can transparently switch the code and description values to those with the same meaning in another language, because the only value that is immutable is the ID. With that in mind, think about this. We code programs in English, therefore we should be able to program access to codes in English, and that's why the first method I'm going to talk about exists.

get_id()

Since we code our programs in English, we should be able to specify our code entries as constant values in our programs in English. So any time you need to get the ID value for a particular code value in English, you call FUNCTION get_id(aiv_code), passing it a code value in English, and it returns the corresponding ID value. If the code you specify does not exist, the underlying singleton SQL SELECT statement raises a NO_DATA_FOUND exception, which you must handle in your calling program unit. Here's an example of the method from code table package WORKER_TYPE:

```
FUNCTION get_id(
aiv_code                    in     WORKER_TYPES.code%TYPE )
return                             WORKER_TYPES.id%TYPE is

n_id                              WORKER_TYPES.id%TYPE;

begin
  select id
  into   n_id
  from   WORKER_TYPES
  where  code = aiv_code;

  return n_id;
end get_id;
```

Once this method is written and in use, one and only one SQL statement need ever be written to retrieve an ID for a specified code value. You will see me use this method quite often in a data migration, data processing, and reporting program units. First, I get the ID values as pseudo-constants in the initialization section of a package whenever there is a small number codes in scope. Next, I reduce the number of tables used in a corresponding cursor's SQL SELECT statement. Instead, I use an IF statement to assign the code entry's code and description values inside the cursor's FOR LOOP. You'll see some examples of this practice later in this chapter, in the "Reporting" section.

get_code_descr()

Once you've decided to use a database architecture where every assigned code value is stored as an ID value, you'll need some way to retrieve the code and description values so they can be displayed in the presentation layer, whether it is for data entry or reporting. And that's the purpose of this method. If you need the code and description values for a specific ID value, you simply call PROCEDURE get_code_descr(ain_id, aov_code, aov_descr), passing it the corresponding ID value. The method returns the code and description values as OUT parameter values If the ID you specify does not exist, the underlying singleton SQL SELECT statement raises a NO_DATA_FOUND exception, which you must handle in your calling program unit. Here's an example of the method from code table package WORKER_TYPE:

```
PROCEDURE get_code_descr(
ain_id                      in     WORKER_TYPES.id%TYPE,
aov_code                           out WORKER_TYPES.code%TYPE,
aov_description                    out WORKER_TYPES.description%TYPE ) is
```

```
begin
  select code,
         description
  into   aov_code,
         aov_description
  from   WORKER_TYPES
  where  id = ain_id;
end get_code_descr;
```

Once again, after this method is written and in use, one and only one SQL statement need ever be written to retrieve a code and description for a specified code ID value. Similar functions can be written to get just the code value or description value, and they would be appropriately named get_code() and get_descr().

get_code_id_descr()

If an application is written for a high volume of data entry, the GUI in question will present a field for the entry of a code value and a second field to display the specified code's description value. The users may also have an icon they can click to see a pop-up list of code values from which to select.

The typical end-user action in this design is for the end user to specify all or part of a code value, and then to tab into the next modifiable field, at which point the presentation layer validates the user's code value entry. That's what this method is for: validation.

In order to validate a code value, simply pass the code value to PROCEDURE get_code_id_descr(aiov_code, aon_id, aov_description, aid_on). This procedure first tries to find an exact code value match for the specified point in time. If it does not find a match, the procedure tries to find a single LIKE match. If it does not find a single LIKE match, it may return a NO_DATA_FOUND or TOO_MANY_ROWS exception, which the presentation layer will need to handle. Both exceptions mean that the user has specified an invalid code value. Here's an example from code table package WORKER_TYPE:

```
PROCEDURE get_code_id_descr(
aiov_code                     in out WORKER_TYPES.code%TYPE,
aon_id                        out WORKER_TYPES.id%TYPE,
aov_description               out WORKER_TYPES.description%TYPE,
aid_on                        in     WORKER_TYPES.active_date%TYPE ) is

v_code                               WORKER_TYPES.code%TYPE;

begin
  select id,
         description
  into   aon_id,
         aov_description
  from   WORKER_TYPES
  where  code = aiov_code
  and    aid_on between active_date and nvl(inactive_date, DATE_.d_MAX);
exception
  when NO_DATA_FOUND then
    select id,
           code,
           description
```

```
    into    aon_id,
            v_code,
            aov_description
    from    WORKER_TYPES
    where   code like aiov_code||'%'
    and     aid_on between active_date and nvl(inactive_date, DATE_.d_MAX);

    aiov_code := v_code;
end get_code_id_descr;
```

Variable v_code is used in the second half of the method, during the LIKE match, to capture the full-length code value from the database and return it to the presentation layer. You can call this method from the WHEN-VALIDATE-ITEM event in Developer/2000 forms, from the item_changed() event in PowerBuilder, from JavaScript (through a servlet) in the onChange event of an AJAX-based web page, and so on.

Now let's look at methods used with content tables.

Content Table Methods

What's the difference between a code table and a content table? In most cases, code tables have a very limited number of entries—values agreed upon by the consensus of users or dictation of management. These "agreed-upon" values are used to categorize the input of content and sometimes intersection entries. In contrast, content tables have an unlimited number of entries, where end users select or specify code values, enter numeric values, or enter textual values as part of doing business.

In response to the unlimited number of entries possible in content tables, it's not uncommon to take the effort to code methods to eliminate the repeated coding of the SQL singleton SELECT, INSERT, and UPDATE statements with parametric method calls. Let's start out by looking at one such method.

get_row()

Method get_row returns a PL/SQL record (a row) from a relational table or an instance of an object TYPE (a row) from an object table, based on the criteria specified in the record or object passed to the method. As the programmer, it's your responsibility to code the method to retrieve by the primary key and any other unique keys defined for the table in question. Then, to use this method, follow these steps.

1. Set column or attribute values in a corresponding PL/SQL record or object instance for only those columns or attributes that are used in a particular primary or unique key constraint.

2. Pass the PL/SQL record or object instance to the method.

get_row() then returns a matching row from the database if a matching row exists; otherwise, it returns a NULL PL/SQL record or object instance.

This method replaces a singleton SQL SELECT statement with a parametric method call based on a set of primary or unique key values. We never need to code that SQL statement ever again. Where's that unhappy SQL programmer now?

The following is an example of the get_row method from content table package LOGICAL_WORKPLACE:

```
FUNCTION get_row(
air_logical_workplace          in      LOGICAL_WORKPLACES%ROWTYPE)
return                                 LOGICAL_WORKPLACES%ROWTYPE is

r_logical_workplace                    LOGICAL_WORKPLACES%ROWTYPE;
```

```
begin
   if    air_logical_workplace.id is not NULL then
      --pl('retrieve the row by the primary key');
      select *
      into   r_logical_workplace
      from   LOGICAL_WORKPLACES
      where  id = air_logical_workplace.id;
   elsif air_logical_workplace.id_context is not NULL then
      --pl('retrieve the row by the id_context unique key');
      select *
      into   r_logical_workplace
      from   LOGICAL_WORKPLACES
      where  id_context = air_logical_workplace.id_context;
   else
      --pl('retrieve the row by the code, name, and active_date');
      select *
      into   r_logical_workplace
      from   LOGICAL_WORKPLACES
      where  code        = air_logical_workplace.code
      and    name        = air_logical_workplace.name
      and    active_date = air_logical_workplace.active_date;
   end if;
   return r_logical_workplace;
exception
   when NO_DATA_FOUND then
      raise;
   when OTHERS then
      raise_application_error(-20001, SQLERRM||
         ' on select LOGICAL_WORKPLACES'||
         ' in LOGICAL_WORKPLACE.get_row()');
end get_row;
```

As you will see shortly, get_row() is called by set_row() in order to determine whether to insert or update.

get_code_id_name(), get_code(), and get_name()

The methods get_code_id_name(), get_code(), and get_name() serve the same purpose as their counterparts in code table packages. See the section about get_code_id_descr() earlier in the chapter for an explanation.

is_duplicate()

In a database design where you use sequence-generated ID values for primary keys, every table will have a primary key that is an ID value, and at least one unique key that acts as a "primary key" made up of real-world values. Method is_duplicate() allows the presentation layer to verify that the values specified in fields on a screen are not going to create a row with duplicate values when an entry is saved to the database.

Here's an example of FUNCTION is_duplicate(aiv_code, aiv_name, aid_active_date) from content table package LOGICAL_WORKPLACE:

```
FUNCTION is_duplicate(
aiv_code                         in      LOGICAL_WORKPLACES.code%TYPE,
aiv_name                         in      LOGICAL_WORKPLACES.name%TYPE,
aid_active_date                  in      LOGICAL_WORKPLACES.active_date%TYPE)
return                                   boolean is

n_count                                  number;

begin
  --pl('retrieve the row by the code, name, and active_date');
  select count(1)
  into    n_count
  from    LOGICAL_WORKPLACES
  where   code              = aiv_code
  and     name              = aiv_name
  and     trunc(active_date) = trunc(aid_active_date);

  if nvl(n_count, 0) > 0 then
    return TRUE;
  else
    return FALSE;
  end if;
end is_duplicate;
```

Like its presentation layer counterpart get_code_id_name(), is_duplicate() can be called from any presentation layer This time, however, in order to provide immediate feedback to users that they are specifying duplicate values, before they try to save an entry to the database, because it will return TRUE if the values already exist in the database. If you're working with a programming language in the presentation layer that does not support a Boolean value from SQL, such as Java, you can simply wrap your call to this function in a stand-alone database function like the following:

```
create or replace FUNCTION to_boolean_number(
aib_boolean                      in      boolean )
return                                   number is
/*
to_boolean_number.fun
by Donald J. Bales on 2014-10-20
A method to return a numeric value for false (0) and true (1).
This is very handy for calling functions that return boolean
values from JDBC, which can't handle boolean database values.
*/
begin
  if aib_boolean is not null then
    if aib_boolean then
      return 1;
    else
      return 0;
    end if;
```

```
else
   return NULL;
   end if;
end to_boolean_number;
```

FUNCTION to_boolean_number() takes a Boolean value as a parameter, and then returns a 1 for TRUE or 0 for FALSE. If you call is_duplicate() from a Java program, you'll need to wrap is_duplicate() with to_boolean_number() so you'll get a numeric value 1 for TRUE and 0 for FALSE. For example, you would code your JDBC stored procedure call as follows:

```
...
int                 duplicate = 0;
CallableStatement cstmt      = null;

try {
  // Create the callable statement
  cstmt = conn.prepareCall(
    "{ ? = call to_boolean_number(is_duplicate(?, ?, ?)) }");

  // Register the OUT parameter
  cstmt.registerOutParameter(1, Types.INTEGER);

  // Set the IN parameters
  cstmt.setString(2, code);
  cstmt.setString(3, name);
  cstmt.setTimestamp(4, activeDate);

  // Execute the stored procedure
  cstmt.execute();

  duplicate = cstmt.getInt(1);
}
catch (SQLException e) {
  System.err.println("SQL Error: " + e.getMessage());
}
finally {
  if (cstmt != null)
    try { cstmt.close(); } catch (SQLException ignore) { }
}
...
```

Enough JDBC, let's get back to PL/SQL.

set_row()

Method set_row is the ultimate parametric method replacement for SQL—that is, as far as our unhappy SQL programmer is concerned! To INSERT or UPDATE the database with the row you desire, you simply pass the row in question, a PL/SQL record or object instance, to PROCEDURE set_row(air_row). When you do, here's what set_row() does.

1. It calls get_row( ) to determine if a row with the specified primary or unique key values already exists in the database. If it does, get_row( ) returns the matching row. Otherwise, get_row( ) returns a NULL row.

2. If the desired row already exists in the database, set_row( ) will compare the non-primary key columns. If any non-primary key column values are different, set_row( ) will UPDATE the database with the modified values.

3. If the desired row doesn't exist in the database, set_row( ) will allocate a primary key value if necessary, and then INSERT the desired row into the database. The row passed to set_row( ) is an IN OUT parameter, so the value of any allocated primary key will be updated in the passed row if a new row is inserted into the database.

This is a very handy method when you're coding a data migration program. You can call set_row( ) as many times as you like with the same values, and it will insert a row only once, and update it only if values have changed. This allows you to code data migration programs that can be rerun as needed until you get the "correct" results.

The following is an example of method set_row( ) from content table package LOGICAL_WORKPLACE:

```
PROCEDURE set_row(
aior_logical_workplace           in out LOGICAL_WORKPLACES%ROWTYPE) is

d_null                       constant date       := DATES.d_MIN;
n_null                       constant number     := 0;
v_null                       constant varchar2(1) := ' ';
r_logical_workplace                  LOGICAL_WORKPLACES%ROWTYPE;

begin
  -- get the existing row
  begin
    r_logical_workplace := get_row(aior_logical_workplace);
  exception
    when NO_DATA_FOUND then
      r_logical_workplace := NULL;
  end;
  -- if a row exists, update it if needed
  if r_logical_workplace.id is not NULL then
    aior_logical_workplace.id         := r_logical_workplace.id;
    aior_logical_workplace.parent_id  := r_logical_workplace.parent_id;
    aior_logical_workplace.id_context := r_logical_workplace.id_context;
    if nvl(r_logical_workplace.workplace_type_id, n_null) <>
       nvl(aior_logical_workplace.workplace_type_id, n_null) or
       nvl(r_logical_workplace.code,              v_null) <>
       nvl(aior_logical_workplace.code,            v_null) or
       nvl(r_logical_workplace.name,              v_null) <>
       nvl(aior_logical_workplace.name,            v_null) or
       nvl(r_logical_workplace.active_date,       d_null) <>
       nvl(aior_logical_workplace.active_date,     d_null) or
       nvl(r_logical_workplace.inactive_date,     d_null) <>
       nvl(aior_logical_workplace.inactive_date,    d_null) then
```

```
      begin
        update LOGICAL_WORKPLACES
        set     workplace_type_id      = aior_logical_workplace.workplace_type_id,
                code                    = aior_logical_workplace.code,
                name                    = aior_logical_workplace.name,
                active_date             = aior_logical_workplace.active_date,
                inactive_date           = aior_logical_workplace.inactive_date
        where   id = aior_logical_workplace.id;

        n_updated := nvl(n_updated, 0) + nvl(sql%rowcount, 0);
      exception
        when OTHERS then
          raise_application_error( -20002, SQLERRM||
            ' on update LOGICAL_WORKPLACES'||
            ' in LOGICAL_WORKPLACE.set_row()' );
      end;
    end if;
  else
  -- add the row if it does not exist
    begin
      if aior_logical_workplace.id is NULL then
        aior_logical_workplace.id := get_id();
      end if;
      aior_logical_workplace.id_context :=
        create_id_context(
          aior_logical_workplace.parent_id,
          aior_logical_workplace.id );
      insert into LOGICAL_WORKPLACES (
            id,
            parent_id,
            id_context,
            workplace_type_id,
            code,
            name,
            active_date,
            inactive_date )
      values (
            aior_logical_workplace.id,
            aior_logical_workplace.parent_id,
            aior_logical_workplace.id_context,
            aior_logical_workplace.workplace_type_id,
            aior_logical_workplace.code,
            aior_logical_workplace.name,
            aior_logical_workplace.active_date,
            aior_logical_workplace.inactive_date );

      n_inserted := nvl(n_inserted, 0) + nvl(sql%rowcount, 0);
    exception
```

```
      when OTHERS then
        raise_application_error( -20003, SQLERRM||
          ' on insert LOGICAL_WORKPLACES'||
          ' in LOGICAL_WORKPLACE.set_row()' );
    end;
  end if;
end set_row;
```

You have to admit that that is a pretty cool method—that is, if you hate to code SQL.

WHAT? NO METHODS TO REPLACE CURSORS?

Have you noticed that I have all kinds of table package methods that wrap singleton SQL statements with a method, yet I have none to wrap a cursor with a method call? An esteemed peer of mine, Steven Feuerstein, has written about doing just that: wrapping a cursor with a method that returns a collection. A program is then written to loop through the rows of a collection instead of the rows of a cursor.

Used judiciously—that is, with cursors that return a small number of rows—Steven's method can be quite effective. However, in practice, I don't find much use for this technique. Remember that I advocate the use of PL/SQL methods in order to eliminate "duplicate" code. In contrast, I find that most stored procedures that use cursors use a rather unique cursor. So, because of that, I see very little opportunity for reuse.

At the same time, misuse of wrapping cursors with methods that return collections can lead to inordinately large amounts of shared memory use in an Oracle database. This in turn leads to poor performance. Regardless, at some point in time, I suggest you check out Steven's ideas. Every good idea has its place.

Intersection Table Methods

Tables that act as the intersection between two content tables (commonly called a *many-to-many relationship/entity*) use all the same methods as a content tables and a few more. So let's start by listing the methods that an intersection table has in common with a content table:

- get_row(): Used to detect and retrieve an existing row based on primary key or unique key data.

- is_duplicate(): Used to detect a duplicate entry before a presentation layer program tries to insert the values in question into the database.

- set_row(): Used to conditionally insert or update a row in the database, based on use of get_row() to detect an existing entry.

An intersection table has two additional methods that are concerned about the existence of intersection history: is_active() and is_history(). Let's look at is_active() first.

is_active()

Method is_active() returns a Boolean value based on whether or not an "active" entry exists in an intersection table for the specified "primary" content entity at the specified point in time. By "primary" content entity, I mean the content entity that is the subject of the query.

For example, the three intersection entities in the example's ERD from Chapter 1—LOGICAL_ASSIGNMENTS, PHYSICAL_ASSIGNMENTS, and WORK_ASSIGNMENTS—have a primary content entity, WORKERS, that is the subject of the relationship. And they have a secondary content entity—LOGICAL_WORKPLACES, PHYSICAL_WORKPLACES, and WORKS, respectively—that is the object of the relationship.

By "active," I mean that the specified point in time is between an entry's active date and inactive date. Figure 10-2 illustrates the method's use.

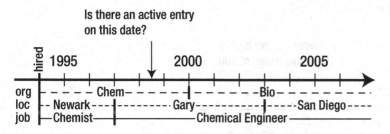

Figure 10-2. *An illustration of method is_active()'s use*

If an active entry exists, FUNCTION is_active(ain_primary_id, aid_on) returns TRUE; otherwise, it returns FALSE. The following is an example of the method from intersection table package LOGICAL_ASSIGNMENT:

```
FUNCTION is_active(
ain_worker_id                    in       LOGICAL_ASSIGNMENTS.worker_id%TYPE,
aid_on                           in       date)
return                                    boolean is

pragma AUTONOMOUS_TRANSACTION;

n_count                                   number;

begin
 select count(1)
 into   n_count
 from   LOGICAL_ASSIGNMENTS
 where  worker_id     = ain_worker_id
 and    aid_on    between active_date
                     and nvl(inactive_date, DATE_.d_MAX);

 if nvl(n_count,0) > 0 then
  return TRUE;
 else
  return FALSE;
 end if;

 commit;
end is_active;
```

In the example above and below, for functions is_inactive() and is_history(), I am judiciously using pragma AUTONOMOUS_TRANSACTION so these methods can "see" outside of the current transaction context. That's a bit of an advanced topic. So until you're ready to study up on that topic, make sure you use that pragma extremely carefully, or not at all.

is_history()

The second intersection table package method, is_history(), exists for a whole different reason. It determines whether there is any history of an active entry over a specified period of time. FUNCTION is_history(ain_primary_id, aid_active_date, aid_inactive_date) is designed to return TRUE if history does exist; otherwise, it returns FALSE. It also uses pragma autonomous transaction, so it can be used in a before insert for each row (BIR) trigger on an intersection table, to prevent overlapping historical entries. Figure 10-3 illustrates the use of is_history().

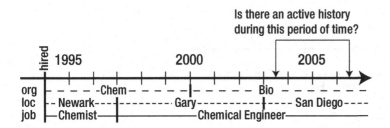

Figure 10-3. *An illustration of method is_history()'s use*

The following is an example of method is_history() from intersection table package LOGICAL_ASSIGNMENT:

```
kFUNCTION is_history(
ain_worker_id                    in        LOGICAL_ASSIGNMENTS.worker_id%TYPE,
aid_active_date                  in        LOGICAL_ASSIGNMENTS.active_date%TYPE,
aid_inactive_date                in        LOGICAL_ASSIGNMENTS.inactive_date%TYPE)
return                                     boolean is

pragma AUTONOMOUS_TRANSACTION;

n_count                                    number;

begin
  select count(1)
  into   n_count
  from   LOGICAL_ASSIGNMENTS
  where  worker_id                         = ain_worker_id
  and    active_date                 <=
         nvl(aid_inactive_date, DATE_.d_MAX)
  and    nvl(inactive_date, DATE_.d_MAX) >= aid_active_date;
  commit;

  if nvl(n_count,0) > 0 then
    return TRUE;
  else
    return FALSE;
  end if;
end is_history;
```

At first glance, most programmers think I've coded the comparisons between the dates in this method incorrectly, but examine Figure 10-4. What I'm asking the database in the query is, "Are there any entries where the active date takes place before the end of the range (inactive date) I'm specifying and at the same time the inactive date takes place after the start of the range (active_date) I'm specifying?" If there are, then these entries are active at some point (or points) in time during the range I've specified.

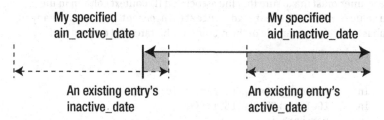

Is there an active history during this period of time?

My specified
ain_active_date

My specified
aid_inactive_date

An existing entry's
inactive_date

An existing entry's
active_date

Figure 10-4. *An illustration of overlapping historical entries*

The use of an autonomous transaction in this method allows it to be used to verify that no existing entries overlap the history of the new entry, without generating a mutating table error.

Hierarchical Table Methods

Hierarchical entities—those that have a relationship with themselves—have three additional methods, which are centered on the hierarchy. A common example of a hierarchical entity is one that stores organization information, as the LOGICAL_WORKPLACE entity does in the example schema from Chapter 1. From data in this entity, we can build an organization chart, as in Figure 10-5.

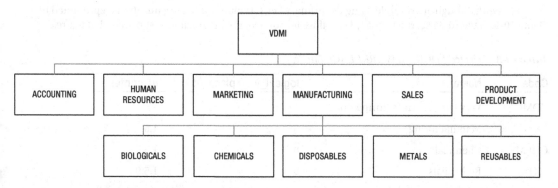

Figure 10-5. *An example of a hierarchical relationship*

Determining who reports to an intermediate organization, like Manufacturing in Figure 10-5, can be quite complex and time-consuming. One option is to use Oracle's CONNECT BY clause in a SQL SELECT statement, but the retrieval times can be onerous. So as a performance work-around, I create what I call a "contextual primary key string," which is made up of a list of primary keys in the hierarchy separated by some predetermined separator character. I prefer to use a period (.).

When I want to identify everyone who works for Manufacturing, I look up the ID context for Manufacturing, and then ask for any entry that is LIKE it. Let's investigate this design further by looking at a method to create the ID context.

create_id_context()

Method create_id_context() returns an ID context string for the specified parent entry and new logical workplace ID. An application programmer must make sure that the associated ID context column in the associated table is set to the return value of FUNCTION create_id_context(ain_parent_id, ain_id) any time a row is inserted into the database. Here's an example of the method for hierarchical content table package LOGICAL_WORKPLACE:

```
FUNCTION create_id_context(
ain_parent_id                    in       LOGICAL_WORKPLACES.parent_id%TYPE,
ain_id                           in       LOGICAL_WORKPLACES.id%TYPE)
return                                    varchar2 is

v_id_context                              LOGICAL_WORKPLACES.id_context%TYPE;

begin
  v_id_context := get_parent_id_context(ain_parent_id);

  if v_id_context is not NULL then
    return substr(v_id_context||'.'||to_char(ain_id), 1, 2000);
  else
    return to_char(ain_id);
  end if;
end create_id_context;
```

Let's work through an example using the primary key ID values for the organizations represented in Figure 10-5. Table 10-3 lists the primary key values for some of the organizations shown in that figure.

Table 10-3. *Selected LOGICAL WORKPLACE Entries*

Code	Name	logical_workplace_id	id_context
VDMI	Very Dirty Manufacturing, Inc.	1	1
MFG	Manufacturing	5	1.5
CHEM	Chemicals	8	1.5.8
BIO	Biologicals	9	1.5.9
METL	Metals	10	1.5.10
RUSE	Reusables	11	1.5.11
DISP	Disposables	12	1.5.12

The Chemicals department (ID = 8) is part of the Manufacturing business unit (ID = 5). So when FUNCTION create_id_context() is called, its parent's ID value, 5, is passed as ain_parent_id, and its ID value, 8, is passed as ain_logical_workplace_id.

First, the function retrieves the parent's ID context, 1.5. Then the method appends a period and the ID value, 8, to the parent's ID context, to get 1.5.8. This is the value returned by the function.

Once that value is stored in the database, if I want a list of everyone under Manufacturing, all I need to do is add the following SQL to a query:

```
where id_context like aiv_id_context||'%'.
```

get_code_context()

Method get_code_context() returns the hierarchical list of code values as a context string for the specified ID. For example, executing FUNCTION get_code_context(ain_id) will return the string VDMI.MFG.CHEM for the Chemicals department listed in Table 10-3. Here's an example of the method from hierarchical content table package LOGICAL_WORKPLACE:

```
FUNCTION get_code_context(
ain_id                      in      LOGICAL_WORKPLACES.id%TYPE)
return                              varchar2 is

cursor c_code_context(
ain_id      in     LOGICAL_WORKPLACES.id%TYPE) is
select upper(code) code
from   LOGICAL_WORKPLACES
connect by prior parent_id = id
start with       id       = ain_id
order by level desc;

v_code_context                      varchar2(2000);

begin
  for r_code_context in c_code_context(ain_id) loop
    v_code_context := substr(v_code_context||'.'||r_code_context.code, 1, 2000);
  end loop;
  return v_code_context;
end get_code_context;
```

In this case, I do use the CONNECT BY SQL clause in the method's cursor, c_code_context, to get the list of code values for the context string.

get_id_context()

Method get_id_context() returns the ID context for the specified ID. For example, calling FUNCTION get_id_context(ain_id) for Manufacturing (ID = 5) as in Table 10-3 will return the value 1.5. Here's an example of the method from hierarchical content table package LOGCAL_WORKPLACE:

```
FUNCTION get_id_context(
ain_id                      in      LOGICAL_WORKPLACES.id%TYPE)
return                              varchar2 is

v_id_context                        LOGICAL_WORKPLACES.id_context%TYPE;
```

```
begin
  if ain_id is not NULL then
    select id_context
    into    v_id_context
    from    LOGICAL_WORKPLACES
    where   id = ain_id;
  end if;

  return v_id_context;
end get_id_context;
```

This method is used by method create_id_context() to get the ID context for a new entry's parent entry.

get_name_context()

Similar to its sibling get_code_context(), get_name_context() returns the hierarchical list of name values as a context string for the specified ID. For example, executing FUNCTION get_name_context(ain_id) will return the string Very Dirty Manufacturing, Inc..Manufacturing.Chemicals for the Chemicals department listed in Table 10-3. Here's an example of the method from hierarchical content table package LOGICAL_WORKPLACE:

```
FUNCTION get_name_context(
ain_id                          in       LOGICAL_WORKPLACES.id%TYPE)
return                                   varchar2 is

cursor c_name_context(
ain_id                          in       LOGICAL_WORKPLACES.id%TYPE) is
select initcap(name) name
from    LOGICAL_WORKPLACES
connect by prior parent_id = id
start with      id       = ain_id
order by level desc;

v_name_context                           varchar2(2000);

begin
  for r_name_context in c_name_context(ain_id) loop
    v_name_context := substr(v_name_context||'.'||r_name_context.name, 1, 2000);
  end loop;
  return v_name_context;
end get_name_context;
```

As with get_code_context(), I use the CONNECT BY SQL clause in the method's cursor, c_name_context, to get the list of name values for the context string.

That's almost the entire list of table package or object TYPE methods. A few more are also used by most executables, so I will discuss them next.

The Black Box

The notion of a "black box" is something that you use but have no idea how it works. A lot of people drive cars, yet they don't actually know how they work. Even more people use electronic devices, yet they don't know how they work either. To these users, these are black boxes.

These black boxes have an interface. In the case of a car, the interface consists of an ignition switch, steering wheel, gas pedal, brake pedal, and so on. But beyond the use of the interface, users know little about how gasoline put in the tank turns into mechanical energy that takes them from place to place. And why should they?

In this section, I'm going to introduce you to a handful of methods that are used in almost every table package, object TYPE, or role package. Let's start with those that are common to all table packages and object TYPEs.

Table Methods

A couple methods are applicable to almost all, if not all, table packages and object TYPEs. They are get_id and inactivate(). The method get_id is shown without parentheses because it takes no arguments. From my point of view, these "black box" methods should exist in every table package and object TYPE. Let's start with get_id.

get_id

Method get_id allocates and returns a new primary key value from an underlying Oracle sequence. FUNCTION get_id() acts as an abstraction layer between the underlying Oracle sequence and PL/SQL. This abstraction layer allows you to later change the means by which you allocate a primary key value without having to recode any PL/SQL program units that call the method.

The following is an example of the get_id method from code table package WORKER_TYPE:

```
FUNCTION get_id
return                              WORKER_TYPES.id%TYPE is

n_id                                WORKER_TYPES.id%TYPE;

begin
  select WORKER_TYPES_ID.nextval
  into   n_id
  from   SYS.DUAL;

  return n_id;
end get_id;
```

inactivate()

Rarely have I encountered an application where I actually delete data from a table. Instead, applications work with the idea of inactivating or invalidating an entry. Method inactivate() handles inactivation.

If you have a code table, you can't delete a code value that's in use (one that has any relationships). Yet you may want to stop users from using an "outdated" code value. To do so, you write your code value's SELECT statement to utilize the code's inactive date, and then you set a code's inactive date so users can no longer select it from a list of values.

Along the same line of thinking, if you have a content table, and a particular entry has relationships, but you no longer want users to select the content table entry, you can set its inactive date and prevent it from appearing in the presentation layer. Just as with the code, the content entry has historical significance but is no longer to be used.

With an intersection table, the concept is slightly different. With an intersection, the assignment of a relationship between two tables exists for the period of time defined from its active date through its inactive date. So when you inactivate an intersection entry, you're simply defining the end of a historical relationship.

Regardless of the type of table for which an entry is inactivated, inactivate() does the same thing: it sets the inactive date. The following is an example of an inactivate() method from content table package LOGICAL_WORKPLACE:

```
PROCEDURE inactivate(
ain_id                          in      LOGICAL_WORKPLACES.id%TYPE,
aid_inactive_date               in      LOGICAL_WORKPLACES.inactive_date%TYPE) is

begin
  update LOGICAL_WORKPLACES
  set    inactive_date = aid_inactive_date
  where  id            = ain_id;
end inactivate;
```

That's straightforward enough. Now let's look at methods used by all packages and TYPEs.

Universal Methods

I expect some methods to exist in every package or TYPE. You've already been introduced to methods help and test. I have one new one here named initialize. Let's start with help.

help

Method help should display help text for the package or TYPE for which it is executed. PROCEDURE help was covered extensively in Chapter 9. You should code this method to display help text in whatever manner you find suitable. What I showed you in Chapter 9 was just an example. But, whatever you do, you must be consistent; otherwise, programmers won't consider the help as reliable documentation, and then you'll have defeated the purpose of coding the method altogether.

The following is an example of the method from code table package WORKER_TYPE:

```
PROCEDURE help is

begin
  TEXT_HELP.process('WORKER_TYPE');
end help;
```

In this example, PROCEDURE process in package TEXT_HELP will format and display the contents of the associated specification.

initialize

I know I have not talked about method initialize before, but I feel it's an important part of testing and should exist in any package that uses its initialization section. Just in case you don't know what I mean by "initialization section," let me elaborate.

A package body is a PL/SQL block. Because it is a PL/SQL block, it has a declaration section, which is where you code any instance variables, functions, procedures, and so on, and it has an executable section. Really, it does. If, after all the functions and procedures you coded, you add the keyword BEGIN, any code from the keyword BEGIN to keyword END at the end of the package body is executed once, and only once, any time the package is instantiated. By "instantiated," I mean loaded into memory and initialized. There it is, that word: *initialized*.

So for any package where I use the "initialization section," I add a public PROCEDURE initialize to the package. Why? So I can test the code in the initialization section.

One of the mysterious errors developers, support personnel, and end users encounter is NO_DATA_FOUND the first time they try to use a particular package, and then the error magically goes away. This is almost always caused by a SQL SELECT statement executed in the initialization section of a package that can't find a matching row in the database. It happens once, and only once, because the package is initialized once, and only once.

A problem like this can be quite elusive. You can go crazy troubleshooting the problem and then testing that your solution works. How do you fix it? Create a PROCEDURE initialize where you put your initialization code, and then execute that procedure in the initialization section of your package. Then, you can execute PROCEDURE initialize as many times as you like during testing, without having to log out and in, in order to get the database to initialize the package.

Here's an example of the method:

```
PROCEDURE initialize is

begin
  n_contractor := get_id(v_contractor);
  n_employee   := get_id(v_employee);
  n_unknown    := get_id(v_unknown);
end initialize;
```

Then add a call to initialize in the initialization section of your package, like so:

```
...
-- Initialization section
begin
  initialize;

end WORKER_TYPE;
```

Once this code is in place, any time you access the package the first time, the package will execute the code in method initialize. And any time you need to test the code from the initialization section of a package, all you need do is execute method initialize. Take a look at source file top_100_names.pkb for a complete example.

test

The test procedure should be coded so it performs all necessary tests on its package or TYPE's methods. I covered this method extensively in Chapter 8. Here's a partial example of the method from code table package WORKER_TYPE:

```
PROCEDURE test is

n_id                                    WORKER_TYPES.id%TYPE;
v_code                                  WORKER_TYPES.code%TYPE;
v_description                           WORKER_TYPES.description%TYPE;

begin
  -- Send feedback that the test ran
  pl('WORKER_TYPE.test()');

  -- Clear the last set of test results
  &_USER..TEST.clear('WORKER_TYPE');

  -- First, we need some test values

  -- Let's make sure they don't already exist: DELETE
  &_USER..TEST.set_test('WORKER_TYPE', 'DELETE', 0,
    'Delete test entries');
  begin
    delete WORKER_TYPES
    where  code in (
      &_USER..TEST.v_TEST_30,
      &_USER..TEST.v_TEST_30_1,
      &_USER..TEST.v_TEST_30_2);
    &_USER..TEST.ok();
  exception
    when OTHERS then
      &_USER..TEST.error(SQLERRM);
  end;

  -- Now let's add three test codes: INSERT
  &_USER..TEST.set_test('WORKER_TYPE', 'INSERT', 1,
    'Insert 3 test entries');
  begin
    insert into WORKER_TYPES (
          id,
          code,
          description,
          active_date,
          inactive_date )
    values (
          get_id(),
          &_USER..TEST.v_TEST_30,
          &_USER..TEST.v_TEST_80,
          &_USER..TEST.d_TEST_19000101,
          &_USER..TEST.d_TEST_99991231 );
```

```
    insert into WORKER_TYPES (
           id,
           code,
           description,
           active_date,
           inactive_date )
    values (
           get_id(),
           &_USER..TEST.v_TEST_30_1,
           &_USER..TEST.v_TEST_80,
           &_USER..TEST.d_TEST_19000101,
           &_USER..TEST.d_TEST_99991231 );

    insert into WORKER_TYPES (
           id,
           code,
           description,
           active_date,
           inactive_date )
    values (
           get_id(),
           &_USER..TEST.v_TEST_30_2,
           &_USER..TEST.v_TEST_80,
           &_USER..TEST.d_TEST_19000101,
           &_USER..TEST.d_TEST_99991231 );

  &_USER..TEST.ok();
exception
  when OTHERS then
    &_USER..TEST.error(SQLERRM);
end;

-- Now that we have test entries,
-- let's test the package methods
&_USER..TEST.set_test('WORKER_TYPE', 'get_id()', 2,
  'Get the ID for the specified code');
begin
  n_id := get_id(&_USER..TEST.v_TEST_30);

  if n_id > 0 then
    &_USER..TEST.ok();
  else
    &_USER..TEST.error();
  end if;
exception
  when OTHERS then
    &_USER..TEST.error(SQLERRM);
end;
```

```
&_USER..TEST.set_test('WORKER_TYPE', 'get_code_descr()', 3,
  'Get the code and description for the specified ID');
begin
  get_code_descr(
    n_id,
    v_code,
    v_description);
  if v_code         = &_USER..TEST.v_TEST_30 and
     v_description = &_USER..TEST.v_TEST_80 then
    &_USER..TEST.ok();
  else
    &_USER..TEST.error();
  end if;
exception
  when OTHERS then
    &_USER..TEST.error(SQLERRM);
end;

&_USER..TEST.set_test('WORKER_TYPE', 'get_code_id_descr()', 4,
  'Get the code, ID, and description for the specified code');
begin
  v_code := &_USER..TEST.v_TEST_30;
  get_code_id_descr(
    v_code,
    n_id,
    v_description);
  if v_code          = &_USER..TEST.v_TEST_30 and
     n_id            > 0                        and
     v_description   = &_USER..TEST.v_TEST_80 then
    &_USER..TEST.ok();
  else
    &_USER..TEST.error();
  end if;
exception
  when OTHERS then
    &_USER..TEST.error(SQLERRM);
end;

&_USER..TEST.set_test('WORKER_TYPE', 'get_code_id_descr()', 5,
  'Get the code, ID, and description for the specified date');
begin
  v_code := 'TEST';
  -- This test should raise a TOO_MANY_ROWS exception
  -- because at least three duplicate values will
  -- on the date specified
  get_code_id_descr(
    v_code,
    n_id,
    v_description,
    &_USER..TEST.d_TEST_99991231);
```

```
   if v_code            = &_USER..TEST.v_TEST_30 and
      n_id > 0                      and
      v_description     = &_USER..TEST.v_TEST_80 then
     &_USER..TEST.ok();
   else
     &_USER..TEST.error();
   end if;
exception
   when TOO_MANY_ROWS then
     &_USER..TEST.ok();
   when OTHERS then
     &_USER..TEST.error(SQLERRM);
end;

&_USER..TEST.set_test('WORKER_TYPE', 'help()', 6,
   'Display help');
begin
   help();
   &_USER..TEST.ok();
exception
   when OTHERS then
     &_USER..TEST.error(SQLERRM);
end;

-- Let's make sure they don't already exist: DELETE
&_USER..TEST.set_test('WORKER_TYPE', 'DELETE', 7,
   'Delete test entries');
begin
   delete WORKER_TYPES
   where  code in (
     &_USER..TEST.v_TEST_30,
     &_USER..TEST.v_TEST_30_1,
     &_USER..TEST.v_TEST_30_2);
   &_USER..TEST.ok();
exception
   when OTHERS then
     &_USER..TEST.error(SQLERRM);
end;

&_USER..TEST.set_test('WORKER_TYPE', NULL, NULL, NULL);
&_USER..TEST.success();
end test;
```

If you include and code method `test` in every package, then you can totally automate the testing of your PL/SQL executables, as I outlined at the end of Chapter 9.

Divide and Conquer

The traditional concept of "divide and conquer" is a tactic to destroy teamwork. Your actions cause dissention among team members, so they no longer work together toward a mutual goal, but instead each works on his own goals. Hence, they are no longer a team.

So where you had a team of discrete members working together at various tasks to achieve a common goal, you end up with a group of individuals competing with each other to achieve many goals. The latter is what we normally end up with in an application.

- The database tries to optimize its work around the overall use of reads and writes to the file system while maintaining a transaction context.

- SQL tries to optimize the overall access to data in the database.

- PL/SQL tries to optimize the overall performance of its executables.

- The communication network tries to optimize the overall consumption of bandwidth.

- The application server tries to optimize the overall performance of its hosted executables.

- The presentation layer tries to optimize the overall end-user experience.

What do these layers of technology all have in common? They are all optimized for a fictitious set of events: "the average." They work as a group of individuals competing with each other to achieve their own goals. So how can you turn them into a team whose members work together for a common goal? You divide and conquer. But this time, divide and conquer means you divide up a larger goal into tasks, and then have the best team member perform each task. I know, it's 180 degrees from the traditional definition of divide and conquer, but it works.

For example, if there is data-intensive work to be accomplished, it should be done in the database. Retrieving data from the database through a network to an application server, or worse, a presentation layer, in order to accomplish data migration or data processing is ludicrous. In addition, you should use SQL and PL/SQL to manipulate data. When you combine the use of these two languages, you have the easiest to code, yet most powerful combination for data processing that has ever existed.

In addition, if there is behavior related to data, like so-called business rules, it should reside in the database. Otherwise, each additional layer may have its own version of "the rules," and you'll end up with business rule anarchy. As I tried to convince you earlier, behavior is just as important to store as the data to which it "belongs."

Overall, I'm suggesting that you use PL/SQL and SQL to create actors—program units to fulfill particular roles—in order to accomplish the following kinds of tasks:

- Data migration

- Data processing

- Reporting

Accordingly, this section will cover each of these roles and the polymorphic commands they typically employ.

Data Migration

As I stated earlier, my concept of data migration (DM) is a one-time task where you move external data into a highly structured schema in a database. The notion of it being a "one-time" task is important here. If you needed to move external data into a database on a regular basis, I would call it *data processing* instead.

Here's the high-level idea: load the external data that is to be moved into an application's data structure into staging tables with whatever method is quickest, and then use a PL/SQL data processing program unit to move the data into the application's data structure.

As illustrated in Figure 10-6, you can use an Oracle database link if you're moving data from one database to another, or you can use C/C++ with the Oracle Call Interface (OCI) API, Java and JDBC, XML, or better yet SQL*Loader, if you're loading the data from a file system into the database. Use whatever method is the most efficient.

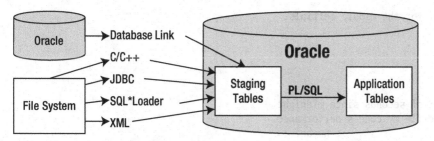

Figure 10-6. *An illustration of data migration*

After the data is loaded into the database, you can then write a PL/SQL package to move the data from the staging tables into a target application's schema. Such a package would have at least one public method: process. When executed, process would do the following:

1. Use the package's initialization section to load code value IDs that can then be used in a cross-reference IF statement to map external code values to ones in the target schema.

2. Initialize the set_row() counters—the public package variables n_inserted and n_updated—to zero for each target table.

3. Use a cursor and cursor FOR LOOP to read through the rows of the staging table.

4. Use the set_row() method on the target table(s) to insert the external data.

5. Display the n_insert and n_update counts upon completion in order to confirm that the data migration completed successfully.

After you've coded PROCEDURE process, all you would need to do is execute the method in order to move the data from a staging table to a (or set of) corresponding application table(s).

process

Method process is used to start an on-demand or polling process. The following is an example of the method from data migration package TOP_100_NAME:

```
PROCEDURE process is

-- This is the cursor for the last names.
cursor c_last is
select last_name
from   TOP_100_LAST_NAMES
order by 1;

-- This is the cursor for the first names.
cursor c_first is
select first_name,
       gender_code
from   TOP_100_FIRST_NAMES
order by 1;
```

```
-- This is the cursor for the middle initials.
cursor c_middle is
select letter
from    A_THRU_Z
order by 1;

-- This is the number of seconds since midnight
-- I'll use it to profile my code's performance.
n_start                            number :=
  to_number(to_char(SYSDATE, 'SSSSS'));

-- I'll use this to keep track of how many rows were selected
n_selected                         number := 0;

-- Here, I declare a record anchored to the table so
-- I can set the column values and then insert using
-- the record.
r_worker                            WORKERS%ROWTYPE;

begin
  -- Reset the insert/update counters for set_row()
  WORKER.n_inserted := 0;
  WORKER.n_updated  := 0;

  -- Loop through the last names
  for r_last in c_last loop

    -- While looping through the last names,
    -- loop through the first names
    for r_first in c_first loop

      -- While looping through the last and first names
      -- loop through the 26 letters in the English
      -- Alphabet in order to get middle initials
      for r_middle in c_middle loop
        n_selected                 := n_selected + 1;
        -- Initialize the record

        -- Set the PK to NULL so set_row() determines
        -- whether or not the entry already exists
        -- by it's unique keys
        r_worker.id                := NULL;

        -- Flip flop from contractor to employee and back again
        if r_worker.worker_type_id = WORKER_TYPE.contractor then
          r_worker.worker_type_id := WORKER_TYPE.employee;
        else
          r_worker.worker_type_id := WORKER_TYPE.contractor;
        end if;
```

```
        -- Set the External ID, UK1, to NULL so set_row() determines
        -- whether or not the entry already exists
        -- by it's unique keys
        r_worker.external_id      := NULL;

        -- The first, middle, and last names come from the cursors
        r_worker.first_name       := r_first.first_name;
        r_worker.middle_name      := r_middle.letter||'.';
        r_worker.last_name        := r_last.last_name;

        -- get the name using the table's package
        r_worker.name             := WORKER.get_formatted_name(
          r_worker.first_name, r_worker.middle_name, r_worker.last_name);

        -- get the date from determinate function create_birth_date()
        r_worker.birth_date       := create_birth_date(r_worker.name);

        -- select the corresponding ID value
        if r_first.gender_code = 'F' then
          r_worker.gender_type_id := GENDER_TYPE.female;
        else
          r_worker.gender_type_id := GENDER_TYPE.male;
        end if;

        -- Insert the row into the database
        begin
          WORKER.set_row(r_worker);
        exception
          when OTHERS then
            raise_application_error(-20001, SQLERRM||
              ' on call WORKER.set_row()'||
              ' in TOP_100_NAME.process()');
        end;
      end loop; -- c_middle

      commit;  -- commit every 26 rows

    end loop; -- c_first

  end loop; -- c_last

  -- Display the results
  pl(to_char(n_selected)||' rows selected');
  pl(to_char(WORKER.n_inserted)||' rows inserted');
  pl(to_char(WORKER.n_updated)||' rows updated');
  pl('in '||to_char(to_number(to_char(SYSDATE, 'SSSSS')) - n_start)||
    ' seconds.');
end process;
```

When migrating data, you should be able to take advantage of methods get_row() and set_row() on the target content or intersection tables. Now let's take a look at an on-demand, data processing PL/SQL program unit.

On-Demand Data Processing

If you have a task that needs to be done now, or on an hourly, daily, weekly, or monthly basis, you'll use some kind of external scheduler like cron in UNIX or Linux, or a Scheduled Tasks in Windows, or perhaps the internal Oracle job queue to execute the process. I call this kind of processing on-demand data processing (ODDP).

Just like its data migration sibling, on-demand data processing is executed through PROCEDURE process. What's different here is the fact that this is not a one-time event. You expect to use this process over and over again. Accordingly, I usually create a table to log when the process runs, along with any performance statistics like how long it took to run, how many rows it inserted, how many rows it updated, and so on.

Since I want to keep track of when a process executes, I now have three common method names used for an on-demand data processing program unit: process, start_logging(), and stop_logging(). Let's look at process first.

process

As before, process is used to start an on-demand or polling process. This time, process incorporates the use of a log so it can record that the process took place, along with some performance statistics. The following is an example of the method from package REPORT_STAGING_TABLE:

```
PROCEDURE process is

-- Get a list of all the tables that start with REPORT_ in the USER's schema
cursor c_table is
select table_name
from   SYS.USER_TABLES
where  table_name like 'REPORT\_%' escape '\'
order by 1;

n_selected                         number := 0;
n_deleted                          number := 0;

begin
  -- Start logging
  ON_DEMAND_PROCESS_LOG.start_logging(
    'REPORT_STAGING_TABLE', 'process');

  -- For each report "staging" table, delete any data over 2 days old
  for r_table in c_table loop
    n_selected := n_selected + 1;

    execute immediate 'delete '||
      r_table.table_name||
      ' where insert_date < SYSDATE - 2';

    n_deleted := n_deleted + nvl(sql%rowcount, 0);
  end loop;

  -- Stop logging
  ON_DEMAND_PROCESS_LOG.stop_logging(
    n_selected, NULL, NULL, n_deleted, NULL);
```

```
exception
  when OTHERS then
    -- Stop logging, but report an error
    ON_DEMAND_PROCESS_LOG.stop_logging(
      n_selected, NULL, NULL, n_deleted, SQLERRM);
    raise;
end process;
```

If you examine this example, you'll see that the process starts out by calling method start_logging() at the beginning, and then calls method stop_logging() at the end. The underlying log package, ON_DEMAND_PROCESS_LOG, keeps track of the start and stop time, and then records the statistics to table ON_DEMAND_PROCESS_LOGS when method stop_logging() is called.

The process itself deletes any staged reporting data that is over two days old. As with its data migration sibling, if processing data, you should be able to take advantage of methods get_row() and set_row() on any target content or intersection tables.

Now let's take a look at what supporting method start_logging() does.

start_logging()

Method start_logging() stores the time it was called, in memory, allocates and stores a new primary key value, and then inserts a "starting" row in a log table. In this case, it inserts a row into table ON_DEMAND_PROCESS_LOGS as defined in the following partial listing from script on_demand_process_logs.tab:

```
create table ON_DEMAND_PROCESS_LOGS (
id                        number                   not null,
object_name               varchar2(30)             not null,
method_name               varchar2(30)             not null,
rows_selected             number,
rows_inserted             number,
rows_updated              number,
rows_deleted              number,
result                    varchar2(256),
elapsed_time              number,
insert_user               varchar2(30)  default USER    not null,
insert_date               date          default SYSDATE not null,
update_user               varchar2(30)  default USER    not null,
update_date               date          default SYSDATE not null)
```

...

This log table holds information about how long it took to execute the process, row processing statistics, and the time when the process was started and stopped. The following is an example of the method start_logging() from package ON_DEMAND_PROCESS_LOG:

```
PROCEDURE start_logging(
aiv_object_name           in      ON_DEMAND_PROCESS_LOGS.object_name%TYPE,
aiv_method_name           in      ON_DEMAND_PROCESS_LOGS.method_name%TYPE) is

pragma AUTONOMOUS_TRANSACTION;
```

```
begin
  n_start := to_number(to_char(SYSDATE, 'SSSSS'));
  n_id    := get_id();

  insert into ON_DEMAND_PROCESS_LOGS (
        id,
        object_name,
        method_name )
  values (
        n_id,
        upper(aiv_object_name),
        upper(aiv_method_name) );
  commit;
end start_logging;
```

Variable n_start in method start_logging() is an instance (package body) variable used to capture the time when the method was called. Similarly, variable n_ id is used to capture the new log entry's primary key so the same entry can be updated in method stop_logging(). In addition, this method employs the use of pragma autonomous_transaction so a process that starts but fails will still leave a starting entry in the log.

Now let's look at stop_logging().

stop_logging()

Method stop_logging() takes the row processing information and a result description passed to it, and uses that information along with the stored start time and primary key to update the starting log entry. As part of updating the log entry, the method calculates the elapsed time in seconds between the start and stop of logging. The following is an example of the method from package ON_DEMAND_PROCESS_LOG:

```
PROCEDURE stop_logging(
ain_rows_selected              in      ON_DEMAND_PROCESS_LOGS.rows_selected%TYPE,
ain_rows_inserted              in      ON_DEMAND_PROCESS_LOGS.rows_inserted%TYPE,
ain_rows_updated               in      ON_DEMAND_PROCESS_LOGS.rows_updated%TYPE,
ain_rows_deleted               in      ON_DEMAND_PROCESS_LOGS.rows_deleted%TYPE,
aiv_result                     in      ON_DEMAND_PROCESS_LOGS.result%TYPE) is

pragma AUTONOMOUS_TRANSACTION;

n_elapsed_time                         number;

begin
  n_elapsed_time := to_number(to_char(SYSDATE, 'SSSSS')) - n_start;

  update ON_DEMAND_PROCESS_LOGS
  set    rows_selected          = ain_rows_selected,
         rows_inserted          = ain_rows_inserted,
         rows_updated           = ain_rows_updated,
         rows_deleted           = ain_rows_deleted,
         result                 = aiv_result,
         elapsed_time           = n_elapsed_time,
```

```
           update_user          = USER,
           update_date          = SYSDATE
  where  id = n_id;
  commit;

  n_id := NULL;

  -- Display the results
  if ain_rows_selected is not null then
    pl(to_char(ain_rows_selected)||' rows selected.');
  end if;
  if ain_rows_inserted is not null then
    pl(to_char(ain_rows_inserted)||' rows inserted.');
  end if;
  if ain_rows_updated is not null then
    pl(to_char(ain_rows_updated)||' rows updated.');
  end if;
  if ain_rows_deleted is not null then
    pl(to_char(ain_rows_deleted)||' rows deleted.');
  end if;
  if aiv_result is not null then
    pl(aiv_result);
  end if;
  pl('Elapsed time: '||to_char(n_elapsed_time)||' seconds.');
end stop_logging;
```

In addition to recording the log statistics, stop_logging() also echoes those statistics to the screen if serveroutput is set to on in SQL*Plus. Like its sibling start_logging(), this method employs the use of pragma autonomous_transaction, so a process that fails can still leave a completed log entry.

Having log information about when on-demand processes execute is an important part of managing their use. Access to statistics about each on-demand process is even more invaluable. Using these statistics, you can determine whether a process is fast and efficient, and make adjustments accordingly.

If you find you're running an on-demand process every few minutes, or if you're interested in offloading a long-running process from the presentation layer, then the process is probably better done as a polling process. Let's look at that next.

Polling Data Processing

Unlike an on-demand process, a polling data process (PDP) just keeps running. It follows three high-level steps.

1. Check a queue for commands.

2. Process the "next" command.

3. Sleep for a predetermined period of time, then go back to step 1.

I'll give you three common examples here of using "divide and conquer" to offload a portion of data processing to the database rather than the presentation or application layer. Doing so makes the presentation or application layer appear to be fast and efficient. And, since the best place to perform data processing is in the database, the offloaded portion of the larger process is fast and efficient. First, let's look at an example with the application layer.

Let's say you have web or message services that, in turn, update your database whenever there is a transaction on an external system. Rather than tie up the services with the entire business process, you can have your services update a set of staging tables in your database, and then have a polling process on your database wake up every so often and finish processing the staged data.

A second example is one where you have a long-running process in the presentation layer. Let's say you have a security system where an administrator can assign access to worker data based on business organization, location, and so on. Rather than tie up the administrator's computer while the mass assignments take place, you can have the presentation layer submit the processing request to your polling process's queue. Then, when your polling process wakes up from its sleep period, it will process your long-running request in the background. What's the result? To the end user using the presentation layer, the application appears easy, fast, and efficient.

A third example is along the same line of thinking. This time, however, you set up your end user's reporting subsystem to submit long-running reports to your polling process's queue, and then have your polling process email the end user with a link (URL) to a completed report when it finishes executing the report in the background. Once again, the end user's experience is one where submitting the report is easy, fast, and efficient.

Using a polling process requires a different design than an on-demand process. Instead of logging each time a process executes (which you can still do), you need to create a queue for process and processing-related commands, and possibly a table to hold the current status of the polling process. I'll start out by showing you an example of the process method, and then follow up with discussions on each of the supporting methods.

process

Once again, process is used to start an on-demand or polling process. In this case, it's a polling data process. A polling process is one that does its thing, goes to sleep, and then wakes up to do its thing all over again and again. A polling process is dependent on a queue, at the very least, so you can tell the process to quit executing.

The queue can also be used to indicate what needs to be processed. For example, if you have a long-running process that must take place as part of inserting an entry into a particular table, you could have a trigger on that table insert a row into a polling process's queue, like a primary key ID value, and then have the polling process finish the long-running process asynchronously.

The following is an example of a polling process that you can find in package POLLING_PROCESS:

```
PROCEDURE process is

r_polling_process_queues                 POLLING_PROCESS_QUEUES%ROWTYPE;

begin
  DEBUG.set_text('POLLING_PROCESS', 'Starting');

  -- perform a manual loop until it recieves a command to quit
  loop
    DEBUG.set_text('POLLING_PROCESS', 'Getting next command');

    -- Get the next command from the queue
    r_polling_process_queues :=
      POLLING_PROCESS_QUEUE.get_next(r_polling_process_queues);
```

```
    -- If it's time to quit, pool the queue once more to delete
    -- the quit command, and then exit
    if r_polling_process_queues.command =
        POLLING_PROCESS_QUEUE.v_QUIT then

      POLLING_PROCESS_STATUS.set_status('Quiting');

      DEBUG.set_text('POLLING_PROCESS', 'Quiting');

      r_polling_process_queues :=
        POLLING_PROCESS_QUEUE.get_next(r_polling_process_queues);
      exit;
    elsif r_polling_process_queues.command = 'DISABLE' then
      DEBUG.disable('POLLING_PROCESS');
    elsif r_polling_process_queues.command = 'ENABLE'  then
      DEBUG.enable('POLLING_PROCESS');
    end if;

    -- *** Now do all your groovy data processing here! ***

    POLLING_PROCESS_STATUS.set_status('Processing');

    DEBUG.set_text('POLLING_PROCESS',
      'I''m doing some groovy data processing at '||
      to_char(SYSDATE, 'HH:MI:SS'));

    -- *** End of your groovy data processing section.   ***

    POLLING_PROCESS_STATUS.set_status('Sleeping');

    DEBUG.set_text('POLLING_PROCESS', 'Sleeping');

    -- Sleep for 10 seconds
    SYS.DBMS_LOCK.sleep(10);

    DEBUG.set_text('POLLING_PROCESS', 'Awake');
  end loop;
end process;
```

This example currently has many lines that employ the use of DEBUG.set_text() to record what's going on in the process as it runs. The debug logging, as it is called, can be turned on before running the process, or it can be turned on by executing method enable. Conversely, debug logging can be turned off by executing disable. This means you can enable and disable debug logging on this process from any other database session at any point in time while the process is running. That's helpful when it comes to troubleshooting a new polling process.

This example also employs method quit to tell the polling process to stop executing. In addition, it updates a status table POLLING_PROCESS_STATUSES with the current status of the process, so you can determine what it's working on at any point in time while it's executing.

In this example, it's sleeping for only 10 seconds in between processing. I've just coded it that way in order to make it easy to demonstrate. In practice, I normally have a polling process sleep 3 to 5 minutes (180 to 300 seconds).

Let's look at method get_next() next.

get_next()

Method get_next() deletes the last item processed from the queue as specified by the passed parameter, and then retrieves the next command from a queue. In this case, it deletes and selects an entry from table POLLING_PROCESS_QUEUES. The following is an example of a queue table definition from file polling_process_queues.tab:

```
create table POLLING_PROCESS_QUEUES (
id                              number                        not null,
command                         varchar2(256)                 not null,
insert_user                     varchar2(30)  default USER    not null,
insert_date                     date          default SYSDATE not null)
```

...

FUNCTION get_next(air_queue_entry) is the "heart and soul" of the polling process. Here's an example of the method from table package POLLING_PROCESS_QUEUE:

```
FUNCTION get_next(
air_polling_process_queues      in        POLLING_PROCESS_QUEUES%ROWTYPE)
return                                    POLLING_PROCESS_QUEUES%ROWTYPE is

pragma AUTONOMOUS_TRANSACTION;

r_polling_process_queues                  POLLING_PROCESS_QUEUES%ROWTYPE;

begin
  delete POLLING_PROCESS_QUEUES
  where  id = air_polling_process_queues.id;

  begin
    select q.*
    into   r_polling_process_queues
    from   POLLING_PROCESS_QUEUES q
    where  q.id = (
    select min(n.id)
    from   POLLING_PROCESS_QUEUES n);
  exception
    when NO_DATA_FOUND then
      r_polling_process_queues := NULL;
  end;

  commit;

  return r_polling_process_queues;
end get_next;
```

The way that this method is written, an entry is removed from the queue only after it has completed successfully.

Let's look at the one method that always uses the queue, quit, next.

quit

Method quit is used to tell a polling or long-running process to quit before its next round of processing. With a polling process, this method stores a quit command in the polling process's queue, so the next time it wakes and starts processing, it quits executing.

PROCEDURE quit inserts a new message into its queue table with a primary key value of –1 so the command jumps to the top of the queue. Here's an example of the method from table package POLLING_PROCESS_QUEUE:

```
PROCEDURE quit is

pragma AUTONOMOUS_TRANSACTION;

begin
  begin
    insert into POLLING_PROCESS_QUEUES (
            id,
            command,
            insert_user,
            insert_date )
    values (
            -1,
            v_QUIT,
            USER,
            SYSDATE );
    pl('Queued to quit.');
  exception
    when DUP_VAL_ON_INDEX then
      pl('Already queued to quit.');
  end;

  commit;
end quit;
```

A convenience method quit also exists in package POLLING_PROCESS, because it's easier to remember to execute POLLING_PROCESS.quit to stop the execution of POLLING_PROCESS.process than it is to remember the name of the queue's table package.

So you can now start and quit the process. Wouldn't it be nice to be able to see what the process is doing whenever you need to? Well that's what method enable is for. Let's look at it next.

enable

Method enable is used to enable something—in this case, the logging of debug information at any desired point in time. PROCEDURE enable inserts a new command into the queue with a primary key value of -2, so enabling debug logging has an even higher priority than quitting. Here's an example of the method from package POLLING_PROCESS_QUEUE:

```
PROCEDURE enable is

pragma AUTONOMOUS_TRANSACTION;

begin
  begin
    insert into POLLING_PROCESS_QUEUES (
            id,
            command,
            insert_user,
            insert_date )
    values (
            -2,
            v_ENABLE,
            USER,
            SYSDATE );
    pl('Queued to enable logging.');
  exception
    when DUP_VAL_ON_INDEX then
      pl('Already queued enable logging.');
  end;

  commit;
end enable;
```

After executing PROCEDURE enable, and after the polling process's next access to the queue, PROCEDURE process enables debug logging. As with its sibling method quit, a convenience method enable also exists in package POLLING_PROCESS.

And disable?

disable

Method disable is used to disable something—in this case, the logging of debug information at any desired point in time. PROCEDURE disable inserts a new command into the queue with a primary key value of -3, so disabling debug logging has an even higher priority than enabling debug logging and quitting. Here's an example of the method from package POLLING_PROCESS_QUEUE:

```
PROCEDURE disable is

pragma AUTONOMOUS_TRANSACTION;

begin
  begin
```

```
    insert into POLLING_PROCESS_QUEUES (
            id,
            command,
            insert_user,
            insert_date )
    values (
            -3,
            v_DISABLE,
            USER,
            SYSDATE );
    pl('Queued to disable logging.');
  exception
    when DUP_VAL_ON_INDEX then
      pl('Already queued to disable logging.');
  end;

  commit;
end disable;
```

After executing PROCEDURE disable, and after the polling process's next access to the queue, PROCEDURE process disables debug logging. As with its sibling methods quit and enable, a convenience method disable also exists in package POLLING_PROCESS.

Now let's look at the methods used to record and read the current status of a polling process.

set_status()

Method set_status() is used to record a process's current status in a status table. In this case, set_status() is updating a row in table POLLING_PROCESS_STATUSES, as defined from following partial listing of file polling_process_statuses.tab:

```
create table POLLING_PROCESS_STATUSES (
status                          varchar2(256)                      not null,
update_user                     varchar2(30)   default USER        not null,
update_date                     date           default SYSDATE     not null)

...
```

This table is supposed to have one, and only one, row at any point in time. PROCEDURE set_status(aiv_status) updates or inserts an entry in this table as needed. The following is an example of this method from table package POLLING_PROCESS_STATUS:

```
PROCEDURE set_status(
aiv_status                      in       POLLING_PROCESS_STATUSES.status%TYPE) is

pragma AUTONOMOUS_TRANSACTION;

begin
  update POLLING_PROCESS_STATUSES
  set    status      = aiv_status,
         update_user = USER,
         update_date = SYSDATE;
```

405

```
  if nvl(sql%rowcount, 0) = 0 then
    insert into POLLING_PROCESS_STATUSES (
            status,
            update_user,
            update_date )
    values (
            aiv_status,
            USER,
            SYSDATE );
  end if;

  commit;
exception
  when OTHERS then
    raise_application_error(-20002, SQLERRM||
      ' on update or insert POLLING_PROCESS_STATUSES'||
      ' in POLLING_PROCESS_STATUS.set_status()');
end set_status;
```

So how do you get the status? Come on now . . .

get_status

Method get_status returns the current status for the associated process from its status table. FUNCTION get_status retrieves the one, and only, row from the table, and then returns the value of column status. Here's an example of the method from table package POLLING_PROCESS_STATUS:

```
FUNCTION get_status
return                             POLLING_PROCESS_STATUSES.status%TYPE is

v_status                           POLLING_PROCESS_STATUSES.status%TYPE;

begin
  select status
  into    v_status
  from    POLLING_PROCESS_STATUSES;

  return v_status;
exception
  when NO_DATA_FOUND then
    return 'UNKNOWN';
  when OTHERS then
    raise_application_error(-20001, SQLERRM||
      ' on select POLLING_PROCESS_STATUSES'||
      ' in POLLING_PROCESS_STATUS.get_status()');
end get_status;
```

And finally, the last polling process method: status.

status

Since we are in such a "commanding (or demanding) mood" with this section, status is a convenience method that exists in the polling process's package that executes method get_status from the table package for the status table. Once again, it exists in the polling process package because it's simply more intuitive to execute commands for a given process from its own package.

Here's an example from polling process package POLLING_PROCESS:

```
PROCEDURE status is

begin
  pl(POLLING_PROCESS_STATUS.get_status);
end status;
```

With the queue and status tables and their associated table packages in place, you can now tell the polling process to do the following:

- Quit
- Enable debug logging
- Disable debug logging
- Process a given command
- Display its current status

A common use for on-demand or polling processing is to build interfaces between systems. Let's discuss some common method names used for just that next.

Interfacing

Interfacing, systems integration, or whatever you want to call it, is just data processing. It is commonly a multistep data process (MSDP) that follows a fairly standard set of tasks.

1. Log that you are going to attempt to download data from a source to your target system.

2. Download data from the source to your target system.

3. Log that you downloaded the data successfully.

4. Verify that you have cross-reference values for all mapped fields.

5. Upload data from its staging tables to its target tables.

6. Log that you uploaded the data successfully.

As you can see, interfacing consists of two high-level steps: downloading and uploading (for lack of better terms). Figure 10-7 shows a visual representation of this division of tasks. These steps can be accomplished synchronously or asynchronously. Regardless, I like to separate the major steps by recording their success or failure in a status table. This allows me to rerun the process, as needed, until both steps are completed.

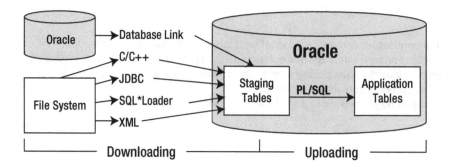

Figure 10-7. *Interfacing with external systems, two steps: downloading and uploading*

Whether or not I use a program external to the database to move data from a source to destination staging tables, the "download" program can record when it starts its processing and when it completes. Then when the upload process starts, it can check to see if the download process has been completed. If the download has been completed, the upload process can log when it starts and when it completes.

Dividing a long-running process into multiple smaller processes like this not only allows you to do asynchronous processing, but also provides you with a framework to build robust processes that can be rerun over and over again until they finish there processing.

For example, if you build an interface with multistep processing that should move data into your database once a week, it can be scheduled to run every day of the week with cron or Scheduled Tasks, and it will just quit if the weekly work has already been completed.

Here, I'll discuss commonly used method names for a multistep interface on-demand process. Let's start with process.

process

Again, process is used to start an on-demand or polling process. In this case, it's a multistep data process. A multistep process is one that checks which portion of a process needs to be done and (re)starts the process at the required step. A multistep process is dependent on a status table that is used to record when a step is completed successfully.

The following is an example of a multistep process that you can find in package WEEKLY_INTERFACE:

```
PROCEDURE process is

begin
  if not WEEKLY_INTERFACE_STATUS.is_downloaded() then
    download();
    if not WEEKLY_INTERFACE_STATUS.is_downloaded() then
      pl('WARNING: download() did not complete successfully.');
    end if;
  end if;

  if WEEKLY_INTERFACE_STATUS.is_downloaded() then
    if not WEEKLY_INTERFACE_STATUS.is_uploaded() then
      upload();
```

```
    if not WEEKLY_INTERFACE_STATUS.is_uploaded() then
      pl('WARNING: upload() did not complete successfully.');
    end if;
  end if;
end if;

pl('process() completed successfully.');
end process;
```

As you can see from this example, PROCEDURE process is concerned only with the status of the multistep process and calls other procedures to accomplish its required steps.

Let's take a look at the supporting methods. We'll start with is_downloaded.

is_downloaded

Method is_downloaded returns a Boolean value that indicates whether the first step, downloading, has been accomplished. FUNCTION is_downloaded returns TRUE if the download process has been completed; otherwise, it returns FALSE.

The following is an example of the method from supporting table package WEEKLY_INTERFACE_STATUS:

```
FUNCTION is_downloaded
return                              boolean is

pragma AUTONOMOUS_TRANSACTION;

d_download_date
  WEEKLY_INTERFACE_STATUSES.download_date%TYPE;

begin
  begin
    select download_date
    into   d_download_date
    from   WEEKLY_INTERFACE_STATUSES
    where  id =
      WEEKLY_INTERFACE_STATUS.get_week();
  exception
    when NO_DATA_FOUND then
      d_download_date := NULL;
  end;

  if d_download_date is not NULL then
    return TRUE;
  else
    return FALSE;
  end if;
end is_downloaded;
```

PROCEDURE WEEKLY_INTERFACE.process calls this method directly from package WEEKLY_INTERFACE_STATUS. In addition, I've added a convenience method, is_downloaded, which returns the number 1 for TRUE and 0 for FALSE to package WEEKLY_INTERFACE, because external programs that might want to know the status of the download process, such as a Java JDBC program, cannot call a stored procedure that returns a Boolean value. Here's an example of the is_downloaded convenience method from package WEEKLY_INTERFACE:

```
FUNCTION is_downloaded
return                                      number is

begin
  -- A function that returns a 1 or 0 from TRUE and FALSE
  -- from WEEKLY_INTERFACE_STATUS.is_downloaded()
  return to_boolean_number(WEEKLY_INTERFACE_STATUS.is_downloaded());
end is_downloaded;
```

Next, let's take a look at the download method.

download

Method download is used to start a download process—that is, a process to move data between systems—from a data source to your target staging tables. PROCEDURE download can be utilized in your multistep process if the data can be moved from its source to the destination staging tables from inside the database. You can do this in a variety of ways, using the following:

- A database link between systems

- An embedded JDBC program to access an external database

- Package SYS.UTL_MAIL to access an email server

- Package SYS.UTL_HTTP to access a web server

- Package SYS.UTL_FILE to access the database server's file system

If you need to perform this step externally with another program, you can simply code a put_line() message that reminds the user that this step is accomplished externally. By handling the external process in this fashion, you don't need to modify the code in method process.

The following is an example of the method from package WEEKLY_INTERFACE:

```
PROCEDURE download is

begin
  pl('Executing download()');
  -- You can code this procedure to move data between systems
  -- using an Oracle database link, loaded JDBC driver and class,
  -- etc. Or, you can change this message to remind the user
  -- that this is an asynchronous process handled by an external
  -- program.

  set_downloaded();
end download;
```

If you code this method, then you'll call set_downloaded upon a successful download. If, on the other hand, you code the download process externally, that program will need to call WEEKLY_INTERFACE. set_downloaded in order to let process know that the first step of the multistep process has been completed asynchronously.

While we're on the topic, let's look at set_downloaded next.

410

set_downloaded

Method set_downloaded is used to set the status of the download process to complete. Supporting table package's PROCEDURE WEEKLY_INTERFACE_STATUS.set_downloaded is called from inside download, if the download method is actually coded to perform the download process.

The following is an example of the supporting status table WEEKLY_INTERFACE_STATUSES from script weekly_interface_statuses.tab:

```
create table WEEKLY_INTERFACE_STATUSES (
id                        number                          not null,
download_date             date,
upload_date               date,
insert_user               varchar2(30)  default USER      not null,
insert_date               date          default SYSDATE   not null,
update_user               varchar2(30)  default USER      not null,
update_date               date          default SYSDATE   not null)
```

...

And, here's an example of the method set_downloaded supporting table package WEEKLY_INTERFACE_STATUS:

```
PROCEDURE set_downloaded is

pragma AUTONOMOUS_TRANSACTION;

begin
  update WEEKLY_INTERFACE_STATUSES
  set    download_date              = SYSDATE,
         update_user                = USER,
         update_date                = SYSDATE
  where  id =
    WEEKLY_INTERFACE_STATUS.get_week();

  if nvl(sql%rowcount, 0) = 0 then
    insert into WEEKLY_INTERFACE_STATUSES (
           id,
           download_date )
    values (
           WEEKLY_INTERFACE_STATUS.get_week(),
           SYSDATE );
  end if;

  commit;
end set_downloaded;
```

I've also created a convenience method set_downloaded in package WEEKLY_INTERFACE, which can be called by an external download program in order to set the download process to complete, as follows:

```
PROCEDURE set_downloaded is

begin
  WEEKLY_INTERFACE_STATUS.set_downloaded();
end set_downloaded;
```

Enough with the download business. Now let's talk about uploading, starting with method is_uploaded.

is_uploaded

Method is_uploaded returns a Boolean value that indicates whether the second step, uploading, has been accomplished. FUNCTION is_uploaded returns TRUE if the upload process has been completed; otherwise, it returns FALSE.

The following is an example of the method from supporting table package WEEKLY_INTERFACE_STATUS:

```
FUNCTION is_uploaded
return                                boolean is

pragma AUTONOMOUS_TRANSACTION;

d_upload_date
  WEEKLY_INTERFACE_STATUSES.upload_date%TYPE;

begin
  begin
    select upload_date
    into   d_upload_date
    from   WEEKLY_INTERFACE_STATUSES
    where  id =
      WEEKLY_INTERFACE_STATUS.get_week();
  exception
    when NO_DATA_FOUND then
      d_upload_date := NULL;
  end;

  if d_upload_date is not NULL then
    return TRUE;
  else
    return FALSE;
  end if;
end is_uploaded;
```

PROCEDURE WEEKLY_INTERFACE.process calls this method directly from package WEEKLY_INTERFACE_STATUS. Unlike its sibling, is_downloaded, there's no need for a convenience method, because the whole point of the multistep process package is to upload the data from staging to application tables. So no external process will ever be used, and hence no convenience method is required.

Now let's look at upload.

upload

Method upload is used to start an upload process—that is, a process to move data from staging tables to an application's tables. This is where you code all your groovy data processing.

Here's an example of the method from package WEEKLY_INTERFACE:

```
PROCEDURE upload is

-- Add cursor(s) used to loop through the staging data here.

begin
  pl('Executing upload()');
  if is_verified() then

    -- Add your data migration code here.

    WEEKLY_INTERFACE_STATUS.set_uploaded();
  end if;
end upload;
```

And last, but not least, is set_uploaded.

set_uploaded

Method set_uploaded is used to set the status of the upload process to complete. Supporting table package's PROCEDURE WEEKLY_INTERFACE_STATUS.set_uploaded is called from inside upload, if the upload method completes successfully.

The following is an example of the method from supporting table package WEEKLY_INTERFACE_STATUS:

```
PROCEDURE set_uploaded is

pragma AUTONOMOUS_TRANSACTION;

begin
  update WEEKLY_INTERFACE_STATUSES
  set    upload_date               = SYSDATE,
         update_user               = USER,
         update_date               = SYSDATE
  where  id =
    WEEKLY_INTERFACE_STATUS.get_week();

  if nvl(sql%rowcount, 0) = 0 then
    insert into WEEKLY_INTERFACE_STATUSES (
           id,
           upload_date )
    values (
           WEEKLY_INTERFACE_STATUS.get_week(),
           SYSDATE );
  end if;

  commit;
end set_uploaded;
```

413

Using the `WEEKLY_INTERFACE` package as a framework for your database destination interfaces, you can provide a consistent treatment to all interfaces and at the same time have the freedom to perform each high-level step in a manner that is suitable for solving the associated business requirements.

Next, let's look at the polymorphic use of method names in support of the reporting presentation layer.

Reporting

It has become quite fashionable in our industry to develop or implement the data-entry portion of an application and then throw a reporting utility—like Cognos Impromptu, Business Objects, Crystal Reports, BIRT, and so on—at the application's relational database or data warehouse for reporting needs. Since I'm not selling any of these "solutions," I can share my honest opinion. Throwing a reporting utility at an application for its reporting needs is a poor idea. Suddenly, we've decided to give our customers half of a solution. What's with that? I know that it's all about the money. But I've never seen much large-scale reporting success with end users with this strategy. Here's why:

- Most end users know very little about how the information they work with is actually organized and related.

- Most end users know very little about how information is input into their application and how it is consequently stored in the application's database.

- Most end users have no time to spend trying to engineer a set of complex reports to help them run the business.

That's not to say that there aren't exceptions. But for the most part, reporting requirements and deliverables should be a required part of any application's development or implementation (depending on whether you build or buy).

For those exceptional end users who are information and system architects, when they do use reporting utilities, they usually get poor performance from the database. It's not necessarily the database's fault; it's a matter of physics.

A well-designed relational or object-relational database will have tables that are all in their third normal form. Accordingly, any `SELECT` statements written against a well-designed database will have many tables in the `FROM` clause of a given `SELECT` statement. The more tables, the more data must be physically read from physical devices, the more physical devices have to work, the longer it takes. It's not a database problem; it's a physics problem.

Now if you recall from previous chapters, I've spent some time showing you the consequences of physics and a database. You can use the following tactics to "divide and conquer" in order to improve the speed and efficiency of retrieving data for reporting:

- Use pseudo-constants and PL/SQL IF statements to replace code tables in a `FROM` clause of a `SELECT` statement. This reduces the use of physical devices.

- Retrieve data from the smallest table that will produce the smallest set of results, and then do programmatic nested loops with cursors to retrieve the "rest" of the data. This reduces the use of physical devices.

- Create thin (narrow) row extracts of data, and then join them together in a `SELECT` statement. This reduces the use of memory and physical devices. For example, if the source table has an average row size of 297 bytes, you may extract data from it into a temporary table that has an average row size of 13 bytes. The temporary table is what I call a *narrow* row table.

- Post-sort results. Sort the rows for a report after the report data has already been placed in a staging table(s). This reduces the use of memory and CPU cycles.

However, you can use these tactics only if you write stored procedures to produce the result sets for your reports, placing the results in staging tables, which are then later queried by the presentation layer. What I'm advocating here is heresy to some, and bliss for others. I know many of you may want to send me an email explaining why this is such a bad idea. Do it. I would love to argue with you about it. Here's what I do know:

- In applications with well over one million rows in each content table, I'm able to produce short reports in less than 3 seconds, most in less than 1 second. That's compared to over 3 minutes trying to accomplish the same task with a large, complicated SQL SELECT statement.

- In the same large enterprise applications, I've been able to produce large reports in less than 3 minutes. That's compared to 20 minutes to 28 hours for some of the largest reports. Yes, even reports that took 28 hours to produce using a very large and complicated SQL SELECT statement took less than 3 minutes when these "divide and conquer" principles were applied. And no, there were no accidental Cartesian products in the SELECT statement.

- When this architecture is adopted, the business intelligence on how to produce the report permanently resides in the database where it is easiest and most efficient to process data. This means that any presentation layer can be used to produce the result set for a given report by executing it in the database, and then simply formatting and displaying the data in whatever fashion is desired. Presentation layers come and go. Does the business knowledge that produces your reports have to go with it? No.

Figure 10-8 demonstrates the reporting architecture I'm advocating. In this architecture, producing a report consists of these three high-level steps.

1. The presentation layer calls a function get_report() in the database, passing it any required parameters for producing a report.

2. get_report() produces the result set for the report, placing the results in a staging table specific to the report. Then get_report() returns an ID for the results.

3. The presentation layer executes a SELECT statement against the report's staging table, where the report ID is the one returned from get_report(), and orders the results by the report's sequence.

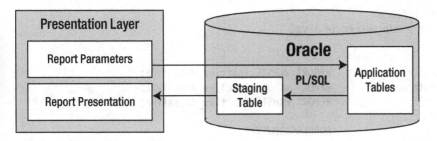

Figure 10-8. *A modular PL/SQL- and SQL-driven reporting architecture*

I call reports produced in this manner "staged data reports." In practice, I've used this architecture to impressively improve the performance and complexity of reports, while also reducing the consumption of server resources. That's a win-win situation. I've called the same report stored procedure from Oracle Reports, PowerBuilder, and a J2EE, Python Django or Ruby on Rails application on the Web. Here, the same result set is used by six different presentation layers. This means you can consistently produce the results for a report, and present the results in whatever way you see fit.

Accordingly, in this section, I'm going to cover the polymorphic method names I use in this reporting architecture. Let's get started with get_report().

get_report()

Method get_report() produces a report result set by retrieving data from application tables, placing the results in a report-specific set of staging tables, and then returning an ID to the result set. FUNCTION get_report(...) takes runtime parameters passed to it from the presentation layer and uses those to efficiently retrieve and stage the data for a report. Most often, you'll use get_report() to simply improve the performance of a report. However, some reports cannot be created with just SQL statements, and that's where the use of get_report() becomes critically important.

Here's an example of the method from a report stored procedure that produces a work history report for a given worker_id. This method is from package REPORT_WKHST:

```
FUNCTION get_report(
ain_worker_id                   in      REPORT_WKHSTS.worker_id%TYPE)
return                                  REPORT_WKHSTS.report_wkhst_id%TYPE is

cursor c_date(
ain_worker_id                   in      REPORT_WKHSTS.worker_id%TYPE) is
select v1.active_date
from ( select active_date
       from   LOGICAL_ASSIGNMENTS
       where  worker_id = ain_worker_id
       UNION
       select active_date
       from   PHYSICAL_ASSIGNMENTS
       where  worker_id = ain_worker_id
       UNION
       select active_date
       from   WORK_ASSIGNMENTS
       where  worker_id = ain_worker_id ) v1
order by 1;

d_logical_inactive_date                 REPORT_WKHSTS.inactive_date%TYPE;
d_physical_inactive_date                REPORT_WKHSTS.inactive_date%TYPE;
d_work_inactive_date                    REPORT_WKHSTS.inactive_date%TYPE;

r_worker                                WORKERS%ROWTYPE;

r_report_wkhsts                         REPORT_WKHSTS%ROWTYPE;
```

```
begin
  r_report_wkhsts.report_wkhst_id  := get_id();
  r_report_wkhsts.report_wkhst_seq := 0;

  r_worker.id                      := ain_worker_id;
  r_worker                         := WORKER.get_row(r_worker);

  r_report_wkhsts.worker_id   := r_worker.id;
  r_report_wkhsts.worker_name :=
    WORKER.get_formatted_name(
      r_worker.first_name,
      r_worker.middle_name,
      r_worker.last_name);

  for r_date in c_date(ain_worker_id) loop
    r_report_wkhsts.active_date := r_date.active_date;

    get_logical_workplace_name(
      r_report_wkhsts.worker_id,
      r_report_wkhsts.active_date,
      r_report_wkhsts.logical_workplace_name,
      d_logical_inactive_date);

    get_physical_workplace_name(
      r_report_wkhsts.worker_id,
      r_report_wkhsts.active_date,
      r_report_wkhsts.physical_workplace_name,
      d_physical_inactive_date);

    get_work_name(
      r_report_wkhsts.worker_id,
      r_report_wkhsts.active_date,
      r_report_wkhsts.work_name,
      d_work_inactive_date);

    r_report_wkhsts.inactive_date :=
      least(
        d_logical_inactive_date,
        d_physical_inactive_date,
        d_work_inactive_date);

    set_report(r_report_wkhsts);
  end loop;

  commit;

  return r_report_wkhsts.report_wkhst_id;
end get_report;
```

If you examine the listing, you'll notice that I call three private methods: get_logical_workplace_
name(), get_physical_workplace_name(), and get_work_name(), which are used to get the data in a
programmatic nested loop fashion. I suppose if I spent enough time, I could write a SQL SELECT statement to
get these results, but in this case, it's much easier and faster to use PL/SQL.

The following script, report_wkhst.get_report.sql, is a test unit I use to run the report from SQL*Plus
during development and troubleshooting:

```
rem report_wkhst.get_report.sql
rem by Donald J. Bales on 2014-10-20
rem Test Unit for REPORT_WKHSTS_TS.get_report()

column worker_name                format a21 trunc;
column logical_workplace_name     format a11 trunc;
column physical_workplace_name    format a11 trunc;
column work_name                  format a11 trunc;
column active_date                format a8;
column inactive_date              format a8;

execute pl('report_wkhst_id='||to_char(REPORT_WKHST.get_report(11649889)));

select worker_name,
       logical_workplace_name,
       physical_workplace_name,
       work_name,
       to_char(active_date,   'YYYYMMDD') active_date,
       to_char(inactive_date, 'YYYYMMDD') inactive_date
from   REPORT_WKHSTS
where  report_wkhst_id = &report_wkhst_id
order by report_wkhsts_seq;
;
```

When executed with worker_id 11649889, the script produces the following output:

```
WORKER_NAME            LOGICAL_WOR PHYSICAL_WO WORK_NAME   ACTIVE_D INACTIVE
---------------------- ----------- ----------- ----------- -------- --------
PATTERSON, MICHELLE D  BIOLOGICALS GRAVITRON 1 ENGINEER1   19740520 19850507
PATTERSON, MICHELLE D  BIOLOGICALS GRAVITRON 1 ENGINEER2   19850508 19960425
PATTERSON, MICHELLE D  BIOLOGICALS GRAVITRON 1 ENGINEER3   19960426
```

In practice, every report has a different package name that starts with REPORT_, whose associated
table is the plural form of the package's name. All reports use the same method name, get_report(), with
the presentation layer passing the method any required parameter values. Since a report package has an
associated table, it's only fitting for it to have an associated method name for inserting values into that table,
and that name is set_report().

set_report()

Since you're an astute reader, you're probably thinking, "Why doesn't he just use the method name set_row()?" It's because set_report() does something different than set_row(), so I consistently use the name set_report() in order to emphasize that difference.

Before I get into an explanation of the difference, let's look at an example of the definition of an associated report staging table. This is the report staging table definition for the work history report. You can find this listing in script report_wkhsts.tab:

```
create table REPORT_WKHSTS (
report_wkhst_id                 number                          not null,
report_wkhst_seq                number                          not null,
worker_id                       number                          not null,
worker_name                     varchar2(100)                   not null,
active_date                     date,
logical_workplace_name          varchar2(80),
physical_workplace_name         varchar2(80),
work_name                       varchar2(80),
inactive_date                   date,
insert_user                     varchar2(30)  default USER      not null,
insert_date                     date          default SYSDATE   not null)
nologging
```

And here is an example of method set_report() that inserts the data into the report staging table:

```
PROCEDURE set_report(
aior_report_wkhsts              in out REPORT_WKHSTS%ROWTYPE) is

begin
  aior_report_wkhsts.report_wkhst_seq := aior_report_wkhsts.report_wkhst_seq + 1;

  if aior_report_wkhsts.inactive_date = DATE_.d_max then
    aior_report_wkhsts.inactive_date  := NULL;
  end if;

  aior_report_wkhsts.insert_user      := USER;
  aior_report_wkhsts.insert_date      := SYSDATE;

  insert into REPORT_WKHSTS values aior_report_wkhsts;
exception
  when OTHERS then
    raise_application_error(-20004, SQLERRM||
      ' on insert REPORT_WKHSTS'||
      ' in REPORT_WKHST.set_report()');
end;
```

In contrast to method set_row(), which selects and then inserts or updates, PROCEDURE set_report(air_row) strictly inserts. In addition, set_report() increments the value of the report's sequence number. The sequence number is the second half of a two-column primary key for the staging table. With this design, get_report() can return a single value, an ID, that will allow the presentation layer to select all the subject rows for a report, and then sort against the sequence value.

This means that the order of the information on the report is driven by a given report's engine in the database, not the presentation layer. This is also what allows you to, as I mentioned earlier, post-sort.

You can code a report stored procedure so that, after it places all of its data in its staging table, you sort the data in the table by opening a cursor against the staging table with an ORDER BY clause, and then update the sequence numbers in the same staging table so the results will have a new sort order.

Now you have a means to get the presentation layer to use a modular and efficient approach to creating reports, but what if you want to email a report from the database? That's the purpose of method report().

report()

Not all reports need human interaction to produce them. Sometimes, an application has a list of reports that should be produced on an hourly, daily, weekly, or monthly basis. Why should you require users to run them? A better design is to provide end users with a set of batch-processed report distribution screens, where they can configure who gets what report, and then have the application produce the reports for them.

If the database produces the reports, it can send the report via email as fixed-length text, HTML, PDF, and so on, or as a link. The following is an example of an HTML emailed report from report procedure REPORT_WKHST:

```
PROCEDURE report(
ain_worker_id                    in      REPORT_WKHSTS.worker_id%TYPE,
aiv_to                           in      varchar2) is

cursor c_report_wkhsts(
ain_report_wkhst_id              in      REPORT_WKHSTS.report_wkhst_id%TYPE) is
select initcap(worker_name) worker_name,
       active_date,
       initcap(logical_workplace_name) logical_workplace_name,
       initcap(physical_workplace_name) physical_workplace_name,
       initcap(work_name) work_name,
       inactive_date
from   REPORT_WKHSTS
where  report_wkhst_id = ain_report_wkhst_id
order by report_wkhst_seq;

n_line                                number;
t_lines                               EMAIL.LINES;
n_report_wkhst_id                     REPORT_WKHSTS.report_wkhst_id%TYPE;
v_worker_name                         REPORT_WKHSTS.worker_name%TYPE;

begin
  n_report_wkhst_id := get_report(ain_worker_id);

  t_lines(incr(n_line)) := '</pre><table>';
  for r_report_wkhsts in c_report_wkhsts(n_report_wkhst_id) loop
    if c_report_wkhsts%rowcount = 1 then
      v_worker_name           := r_report_wkhsts.worker_name;
      t_lines(incr(n_line)) := '<tr><td align="center" colspan="5">'||
        '<big>Work History Report</big></td></tr>';
      t_lines(incr(n_line)) := '<tr><td align="center" colspan="5">'||
        'for '||v_worker_name||'</td></tr>';
      t_lines(incr(n_line)) := '<tr><td align="center" colspan="5">'||
        '</td></tr>';
```

```
        t_lines(incr(n_line)) := '<tr>'||
          '<th align="left">Logical</th>'||
          '<th align="left">Physical</th>'||
          '<th align="left"></th>'||
          '<th align="left">Active</th>'||
          '<th align="left">Inactive</th>'||
          '</tr>';
        t_lines(incr(n_line)) := '<tr>'||
          '<th align="left">Workplace</th>'||
          '<th align="left">Workplace</th>'||
          '<th align="left">Work</th>'||
          '<th align="left">Date</th>'||
          '<th align="left">Date</th>'||
          '</tr>';
      end if;
      t_lines(incr(n_line)) := '<tr>'||
        '<td align="left">'||
          r_report_wkhsts.logical_workplace_name||'</td>'||
        '<td align="left">'||
          r_report_wkhsts.physical_workplace_name||'</td>'||
        '<td align="left">'||
          r_report_wkhsts.work_name||'</td>'||
        '<td align="left">'||
          to_char(r_report_wkhsts.active_date, 'MM/DD/YYYY')||'</td>'||
        '<td align="left">'||
          to_char(r_report_wkhsts.inactive_date, 'MM/DD/YYYY')||'</td>'||
        '</tr>';
    end loop;
    t_lines(incr(n_line)) := '</table><pre>';

    EMAIL.send(
      EMAIL.get_username,
      aiv_to,
      'Work History Report for '||v_worker_name,
      t_lines);
end report;
```

In this case, PROCEDURE report(ain_worker_id, aiv_to) calls get_report() to produce the result set, and then queries the staging table to produce an HTML report. report() then calls supporting package EMAIL.send() to send the report.

The following is an example of a test unit for report(). This is from script report_wkhst.report.sql:

```
rem report_wkhst.report.sql
rem by Donald J. Bales on 2014-10-20
rem Test Unit for REPORT_WKHSTS_TS.report()

execute REPORT_WKHST.report(11649889, 'don@donaldbales.com');
```

After I execute this test unit, I get an email report, as shown in Figure 10-9. In practice, I even use this functionality to send an email report to the support personnel any time a user encounters an error. That way, support personnel can start troubleshooting a given problem before the customer even calls. How's that for customer service?

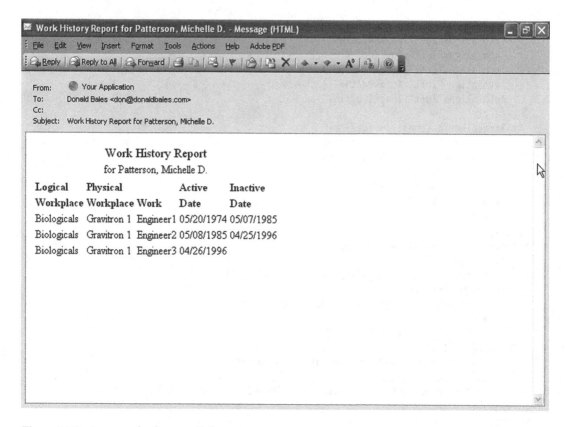

Figure 10-9. *An example of an emailed report*

Well, that's it for polymorphism. I hope you can appreciate the power and simplicity that the use of polymorphic command names provides when used in the development of software. I also hope you take the time to sit down and think about what method names you should use before you start coding your next program.

Summary

In this chapter, I introduced the concept of organizing the nature of behavior behind a common set of method names. In addition, I demonstrated how I've used each method name in the past. With all the content you've seen in this book, you should be well on your way to solving business and science problems with the use of SQL and PL/SQL in a relational of object-relational setting.

Some have given me the feedback that perhaps the object-relational stuff should be treated as an advanced topic. Phooey! There's nothing advanced about object-relational. It's actually the correct and natural way of thinking. We should have been doing it this way for at least the past 20 years. So I hope you'll find yourself in a position to use it.

Just how astute are you? Did you notice that I even used polymorphism with table column names? Normally, I even use id for the primary key column name, and then the singular of the table name concatenated to _id for the corresponding foreign key column name. I used the same names in this book in order to make the relationships obvious. By treating column names polymorphically, you can implicitly note what the column is for in every table, just as you do with method names in executable code.

Wow! That was fast, wasn't it? Did I make you work hard? Did you learn anything? I sure hope so. As I stated in the introduction, this was a tutorial—a place to get started. The only way you can learn how to program is to discover the possibilities of a programming language and start mimicking someone else's work by writing programs.

I've been extremely successful in my career when working with Oracle and PL/SQL, so if you mimic my coding behavior, I'm guessing that you will be successful, too. But you've just started. Here's what I suggest you do next:

- Browse the *Oracle Database SQL Reference*, so you can get an idea of what can be accomplished using SQL. You don't have to remember it all; you just need to remember where to look for the information when you realize you can put a possibility to work!

- Read Oracle's *PL/SQL User's Guide and Reference*, or Steven Feuerstein's *Oracle PL/SQL Programming* (O'Reilly, 2014). These are both good references. Once again, you don't need to remember everything you read, just the possibilities. You can always refer to the reference later. You have better use for your memory, like remembering your lover's birthday or your anniversary!

- Browse Oracle's *PL/SQL Packages and Types Reference*. Why should you build something that's already been built by experts? Just catalog the possibilities in your gray matter.

- Check out Oracle's *Application Developer's Guides*.

- Share your ideas by writing an article, a white paper, or at least an email about your experience. After you do, go back and write an INSERT statement in order to add yourself to the list of database geniuses from Chapter 1.

As I said before, good skill. Luck is for losers.

■ ■ ■

How to Download, Install, and Use Oracle

Since knowing Oracle SQL is a prerequisite for learning PL/SQL, I could simply assume that you already have resource-level access to Oracle (you can create objects like tables, views, and so on), already have access to SQL*Plus, and already know SQL. But that might not be the case.

Just in case you don't have access to Oracle, I'm going to give you some advice on the following subjects:

- How to download Oracle Database software

- How to install Oracle Database software

- How to use Oracle SQL*Plus

This should get you started in the right direction. Keep in mind that I have no idea what the Apress and Oracle web sites or the Oracle software will look like by the time you read this. Nothing may have changed, but I kind of doubt that. It's more likely that everything will have changed. So my directions will probably no longer be correct, but I think some direction is better than none.

How to Download Oracle Database Software

At the time of this writing, you can download a trial copy of Oracle Database software from Oracle's web site. You can use this trial software for learning purposes only. If you decide to do something commercial with it, like write software that you can then sell, then you'll need to pay for a license. Keep that in mind. Play for free, but earn a fee and you must pay. You should read the license agreement so you know exactly what you can do.

The URL you use to download trial software at Oracle changes all the time. Try www.oracle.com/technetwork/index.html. When you get to that web page, as in the example in Figure A-1, look for a menu item that says Downloads.

425

Figure A-1. *An example of an Oracle Technology Network web page*

When you find the Downloads link, click it. When you do, a web page like the one in Figure A-2 may appear. I say "may appear" because who knows how this web site will be organized in the future.

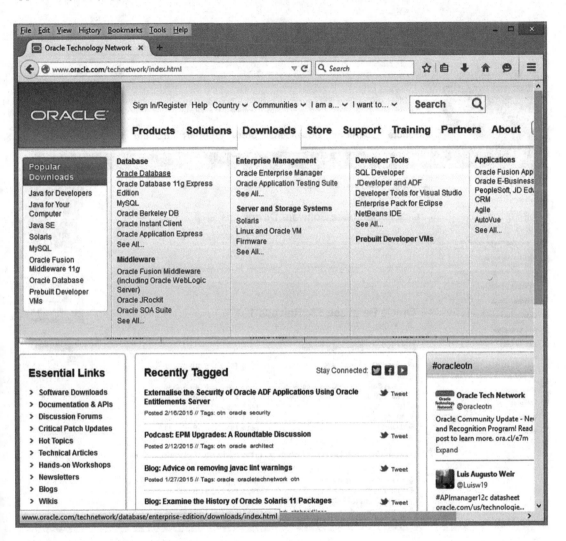

Figure A-2. An example of an Oracle Downloads menu

On the Oracle Software Downloads menu, click the *Oracle Database* option. When you do, a web page like the one in Figure A-3 may appear.

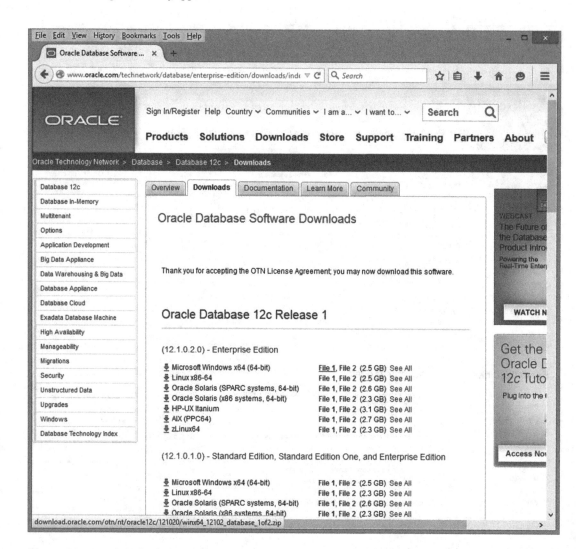

Figure A-3. *An example of an Oracle Database Software Downloads web page*

On the Oracle Database Software Downloads page, first click the *Accept License Agreement* radio button. Next, find the latest version of the database software (currently Oracle Database 12c) and click the link for File 1. A file download dialog like the one in Figure A-4 may appear.

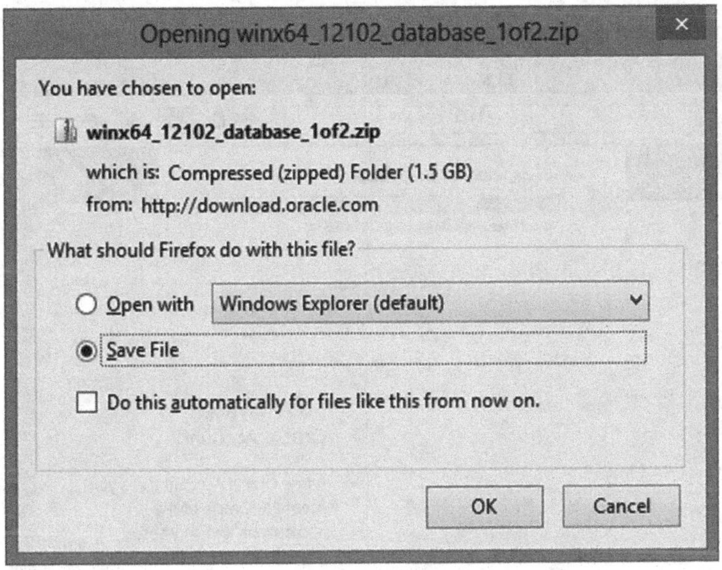

Figure A-4. *An example of a Firefox File Download dialog*

Write down the name of the archive so you know it when you go to install the software. Click the OK button in the File Download dialog box. When you do, the Oracle Single Sign On web page will appear, as in Figure A-5.

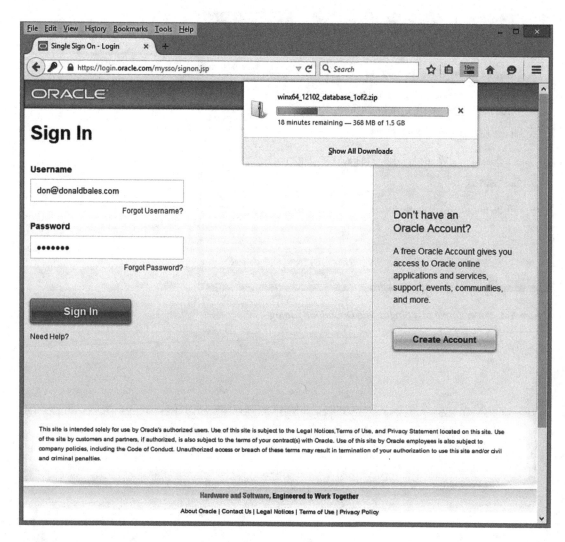

Figure A-5. *An example of Oracle's Single Sign On web page*

At this point, if you already have an account, sign in, and then Firefox will save the file in your Downloads directory. If you don't have an Oracle Technet account, you'll need to create one. Just click the Create Account button, and then return to this page to sign in and continue the download.

Once the download is complete, return to the Oracle Database Downloads web page and repeat the process for File2, as shown in Figure A-6.

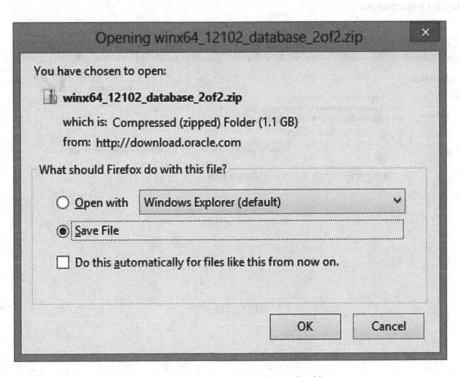

Figure A-6. *An example of a Firefox file download dialog for file 2*

Once again, write down the name of the archive so you know it when you go to install the software. Click the OK button in the File Download dialog box.

After both files have been downloaded, you can move on to the next step, which is to install the Oracle Database software. But first, I suggest you go back to the Downloads link web page and download the installation instructions. Read them before you start the installation.

How to Install Oracle Database Software

I'm going to show you an overview of installing the Oracle database software on a Windows machine. On a computer running the Windows OS, here are the steps.

1. Unzip the archives in the Downloads directory.

2. Navigate to the directory where you unzipped the files with Windows Explorer, and then run setup.exe in the database directory.

3. Follow the instructions on the installation screens, answering any prompts as required.

The following screen shots are from an installation I made on one of my desktop PCs called windows8-pc. It's important that you name your machine (in the OS) before you install Oracle because this is the name that will be used to specify the machine's network address throughout the installation process.

When you execute setup.exe, the Oracle Universal Installer will start and display the Configure Security Updates screen, as shown in Figure A-7. Specify your email address and uncheck "I wish to receive security updates via My Oracle Support."

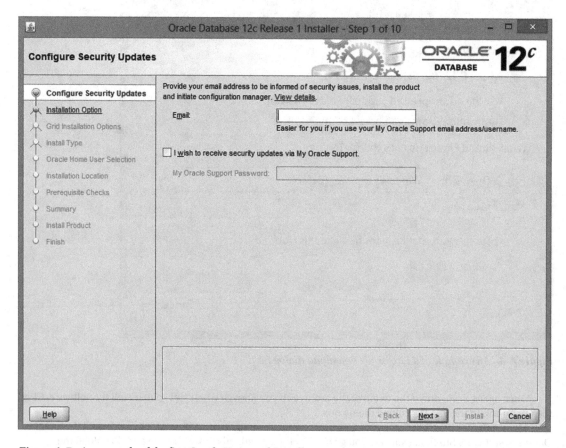

Figure A-7. *An example of the first Oracle Universal Installer screen*

Click Next and the Installation Option screen will appear, as shown in Figure A-8. Here, I suggest you specify "Create and conFigure 1 database."

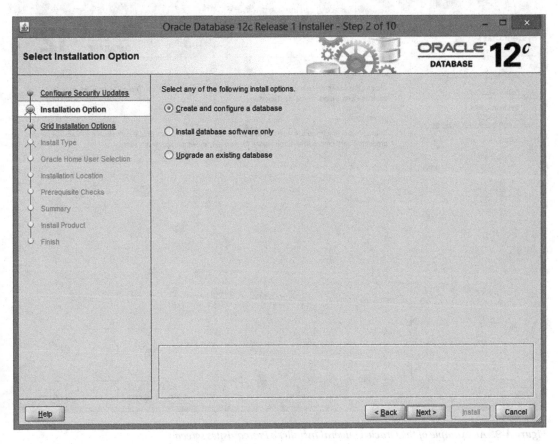

Figure A-8. *An example of the second Oracle Universal Installer screen*

Click Next and the System Class screen may appear, as shown in Figure A-9. Select Desktop class.

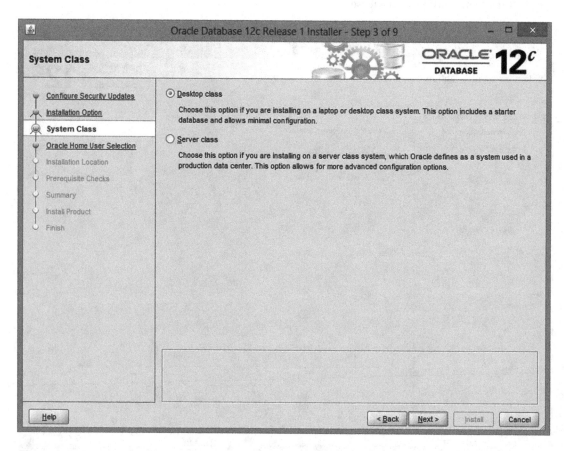

Figure A-9. *An example of the Oracle Univeral Installer's Prerequisites screen*

Click Next and the Oracle Home User Selection screen may appear, as in Figure A-10. Select Use Windows Built-in Account.

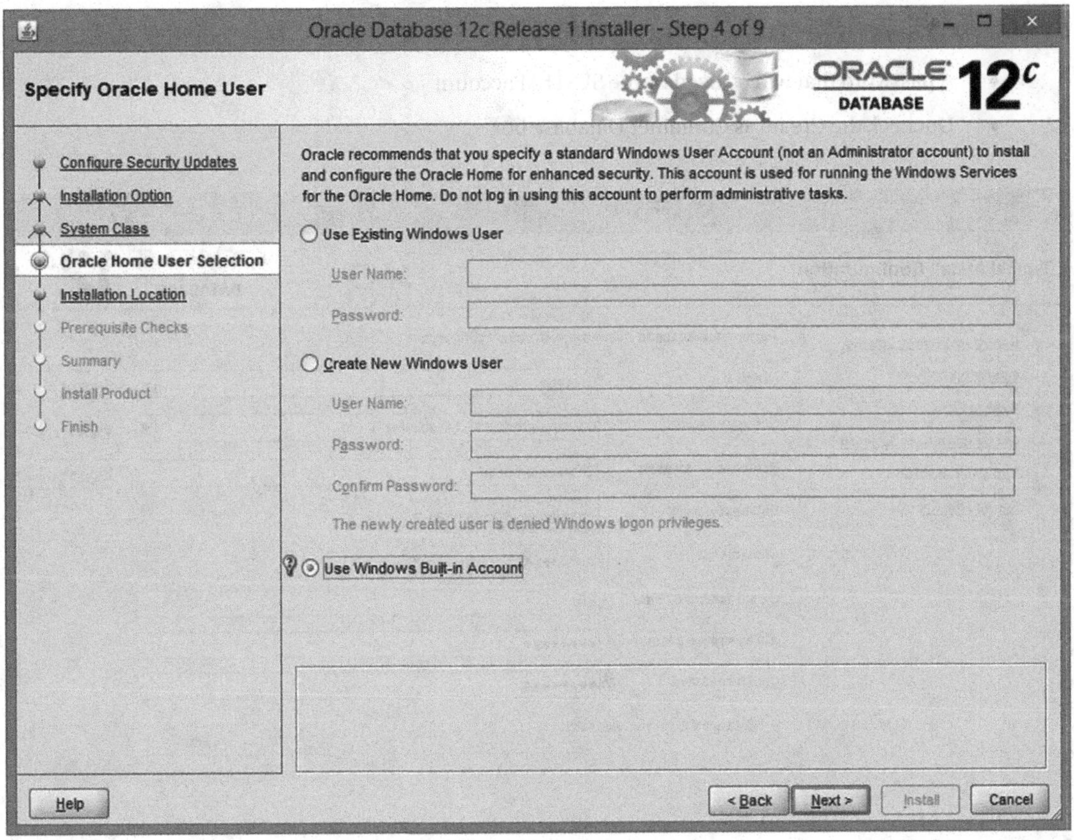

Figure A-10. An example of the Oracle Universal Installer's Oracle Home User Selection screen

Click Next and the Typical Installation Configuration screen may appear, as in Figure A-11. Here I suggest you specify the following:

- An Oracle base of C:\oracle

- A Character set of Unicode (AL32UTF8)

- A password that will be used by the SYSTEM account

- Uncheck the Create as Container Database box

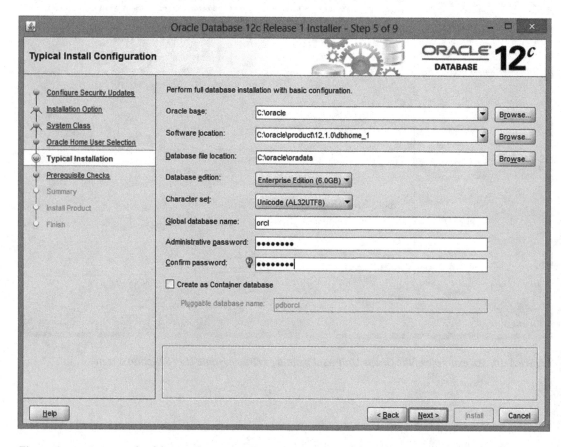

Figure A-11. *An example of the Oracle Universal Installer's Typical Installation Configuration screen*

Click Next and the Summary screen may appear, as in Figure A-12.

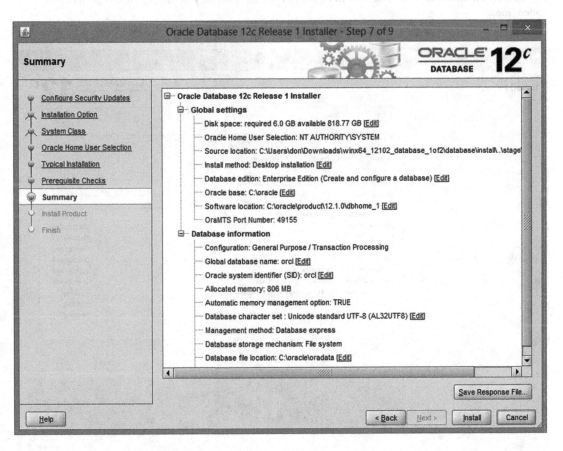

Figure A-12. An example of the Oracle Universal Installer's Summary screen

Assuming that the summary is correct, you should click the Install button. Clicking the Install button may display the Install screen, as shown in Figure A-13. This is where you can get up and get a cup of coffee (joe).

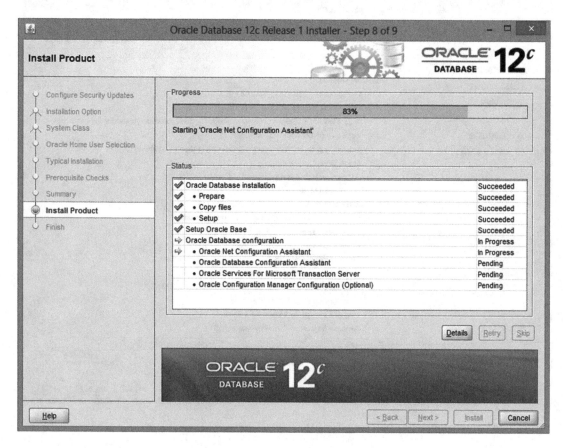

Figure A-13. *An example of the Oracle Universal Installer's Install Product screen*

After some annoying period of time, the Database Configuration Assistant screen may display, as shown in Figure A-14.

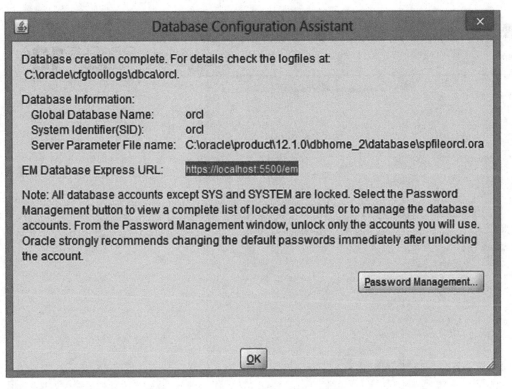

Figure A-14. *An example of the Oracle Universal Installer's Configuration Assitant screen*

Write down the URLs on this screen. You will need them!

You're on the home stretch now! After you click the OK button to dismiss the summary screen, the Finish screen may appear, as shown in Figure A-15.

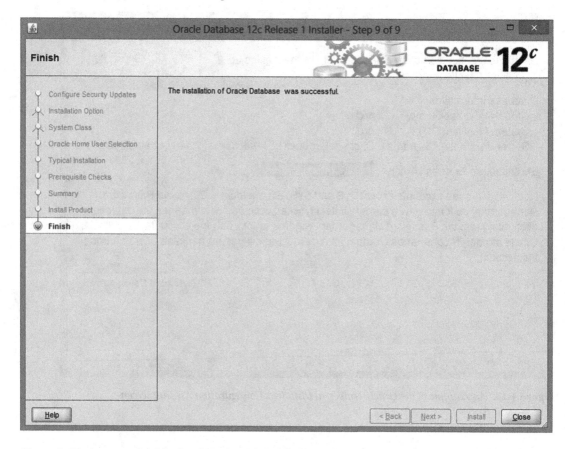

Figure A-15. *An example of the Oracle Universal Installer's Finish screen*

Click Exit to complete the installation. At this point, Oracle should be installed, and up and running on your computer. Congratulations!

To manage Oracle from this point forward, access the Enterprice Manager from your browser using the URL displayed on Figure A-14 of your installation, which is typically https://localhost:5500/em.

Now you need to open SQL*Plus to create a resource-enabled account.

How to Use SQL*Plus

You are going to be using SQL*Plus as your primary user interface to the Oracle database. With it, you will do the following:

- Create two usernames to use when doing the assignments in this book: rps and ops.

- Execute Data Definition Language (DDL) in order to create tables, indexes, views, types, and stored procedures.

- Execute Data Manipulation Language (DML) in order to insert into, update, delete from, and select data from tables in the database.

To get started, create a directory named \bps on your file system. You'll download this book's source code and solutions to that directory.

How to Download This Book's Source Code

To download the source code for this book, go to the Apress web site at www.apress.com, which may look something like Figure A-16. Click the Source Code menu item, and then search for and download the source code for this book.

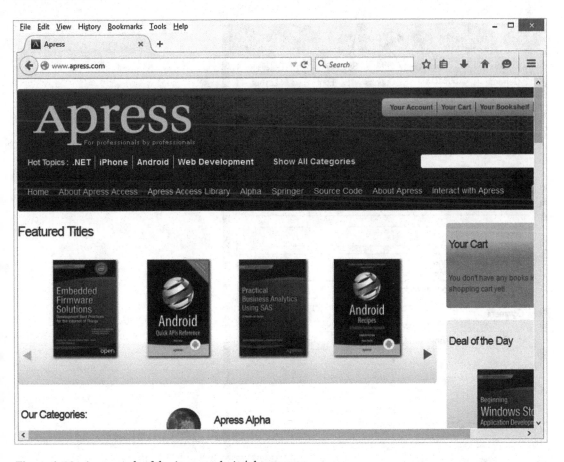

Figure A-16. An example of the Apress web site's home page

Next, decompress the archive (unzip it) into a \bops directory.

Now that you have the book's source code in place, you can create a shortcut to SQL*Plus in directory \bops\Appendix.

1. Navigate to directory Appendix using Windows Explorer.

2. Right-click any empty part of the directory's listing window.

3. Select New ~TRA Shortcut.

4. Specify the location of the SQL*Plus executable, sqlplus.exe, and then click the Next button. The SQL*Plus executable should be in the "Oracle Home" BIN directory, such as c:\oracle\product\12.1.0\dbhome_1\BIN\sqlplus.exe.

441

5.   Specify the name for the shortcut. I name the shortcut after the database, so I suggest `orcl`. Click the Finish button.

6.   Right-click your new shortcut and select Properties.

7.   Delete the entry for the Start-in directory, then type in one space character, as in Figure A-17, and then click the OK button. This will make SQL*Plus use the directory where the shortcut exists as the default source directory when running a script, and that will make your life a lot easier.

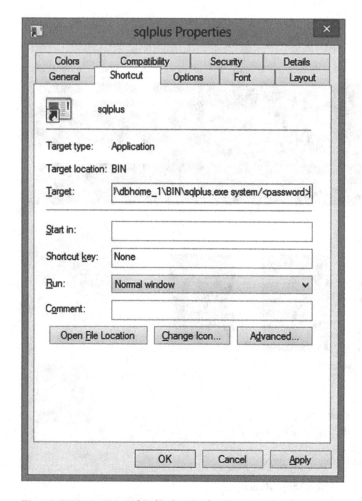

Figure A-17. *An example of a shortcut's Properties dialog box for SQL*Plus*

At this point, you should have a SQL*Plus shortcut icon in directory `\bops\Appendix`. Double-click the icon to start SQL*Plus. When you do, SQL*Plus will display a Login dialog box, where you specify the following:

•   The username SYSTEM

•   The password you decided to use

•   Host string `orcl`, or whatever you decided to name the database

After you specify the login information, SQL*Plus should log you in to the database as user SYSTEM. If you see a screen like the one shown in Figure A-18, you have successfully logged in to your Oracle database.

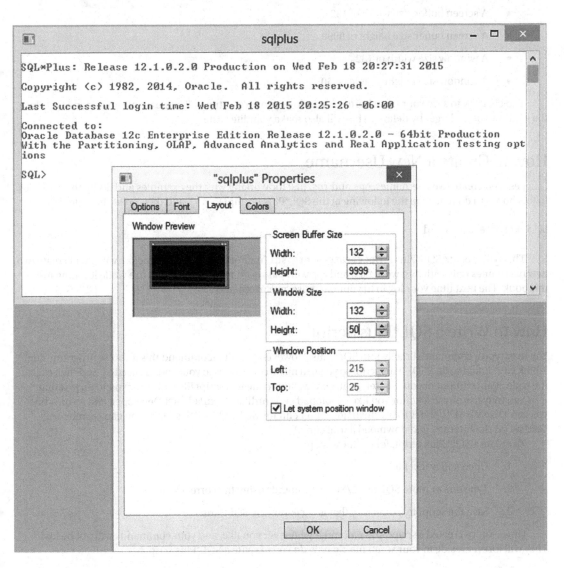

Figure A-18. *An example of a SQL*Plus screen and the window's Properties screen*

The reason you create the shortcut in the same directory that contains the example source code files is to give yourself easy access to those files. When you invoke SQL*Plus using the shortcut that you've just created, the source code directory becomes the default directory that SQL*Plus will search when you invoke a SQL script.

If you click the icon in the upper left hand corner, the window's Properties screen will appear, as in Figure A-18. Here I suggest you specify the following:

- A screen buffer size width of 132

- A screen buffer size height of 9999

- A window size width of 132

- A window size height of at least 50

The click OK to save your new shortcut's windows property settings. The next time you open SQL*Plus the window will be larger by default. This will also make your life easier.

How to Create a New Username

I suggest you create two usernames, ops and rps, just for working with the examples and doing the exercises in this book. To do that, type the following at the SQL*Plus prompt (SQL>), and then press the Enter key:

```
SQL> @create_users.sql
```

This will execute SQL*Plus script create_users.sql in directory \bops\Appendix, which will create two new usernames (ops with password ops, and rps with password rps) that you can use while learning from this book. The next time your log in to your database, use username rps.

How to Write a SQL*Plus Script

You may type a command directly into SQL*Plus. However, I don't recommend this if you're programming. I think you should write a SQL*Plus script so you can make corrections to your code as needed, and then execute the code again without needing to retype it. Having your code in a script file will allow you to do just that.

You may use any text editor you like—Notepad++, WordPad, TextPad, SQLDeveloper, and so on—but you can't use Word. (I prefer to use TextPad when I edit my SQL or PL/SQL scripts. You can search for TextPad on the Internet, and download a trial copy.)

To create a SQL*Plus script, follow these steps.

1. Open a new text file.

2. Type one or more SQL or PL/SQL commands using the correct syntax.

3. Save the script to a directory that is accessible by SQL*Plus.

Once you've created a script, you can run it whenever you like, and your commands will not be lost. They will forever reside in your script file. So how do you execute a SQL*Plus script?

How to Execute a SQL*Plus Script

I had you execute a SQL*Plus script earlier in order to create usernames ops and rps for this book. To execute a SQL*Plus script, you type an at sign character (@) followed by the name of the script to execute. SQL*Plus expects this script to exist in the SQL*Plus startup directory.

If the script isn't in the startup directory, you must specify the entire path and filename. If the path or filename has space characters in it, you need to enclose the path and filename in double quote characters ("). Here's an example:

```
SQL> @"c:\Program Files\Not a convenient location\my script.sql"
```

So I suggest you be lazy and create a shortcut with a blank (space) "start in" directory in every directory where you have scripts. This way, you can start a SQL*Plus session with the default directory set to where your script files exist.

How to Describe Your Tables and Stored Procedures

While you're in SQL*Plus, you can use the describe command to display the definition of a table or stored procedure. For example, you can type the following to get a definition for view SYS.USER_OBJECTS:

```
SQL> desc SYS.USER_OBJECTS
```

SQL*Plus will respond with the following:

```
Name                                      Null?     Type
----------------------------------------- --------- -------------
OBJECT_NAME                                         VARCHAR2(128)
SUBOBJECT_NAME                                      VARCHAR2(128)
OBJECT_ID                                           NUMBER
DATA_OBJECT_ID                                      NUMBER
OBJECT_TYPE                                         VARCHAR2(23)
CREATED                                             DATE
LAST_DDL_TIME                                       DATE
TIMESTAMP                                           VARCHAR2(19)
STATUS                                              VARCHAR2(7)
TEMPORARY                                           VARCHAR2(1)
GENERATED                                           VARCHAR2(1)
SECONDARY                                           VARCHAR2(1)
NAMESPACE                                           NUMBER
EDITION_NAME                                        VARCHAR2(128)
SHARING                                             VARCHAR2(13)
EDITIONABLE                                         VARCHAR2(1)
ORACLE_MAINTAINED                                   VARCHAR2(1)
```

However, SQL*Plus has this annoying feature: it aligns the right portion of a table description to the right side of the line width, and that usually prevents you from seeing the Type, so I use a script, desc.sql, to describe a table or stored procedure instead. For example, to describe utility package SYS.DBMS_OUTPUT, I type the following at the SQL*Plus prompt (SQL>):

```
SQL> @desc SYS.DBMS_OUTPUT
```

SQL*Plus will respond with the following:

```
SYS.DBMS_OUTPUT
SQL> @desc SYS.DBMS_OUTPUT
SYS.DBMS_OUTPUT
PROCEDURE DISABLE
PROCEDURE ENABLE
Argument Name                       Type                     In/Out Default?
--------------------------------    ---------------------    ------ --------
 BUFFER_SIZE                        NUMBER(38)               IN     DEFAULT
PROCEDURE GET_LINE
Argument Name                       Type                     In/Out Default?
--------------------------------    ---------------------    ------ --------
 LINE                               VARCHAR2                 OUT
 STATUS                             NUMBER(38)               OUT
PROCEDURE GET_LINES
Argument Name                       Type                     In/Out Default?
--------------------------------    ---------------------    ------ --------
 LINES                              TABLE OF VARCHAR2(32767) OUT
 NUMLINES                           NUMBER(38)               IN/OUT
PROCEDURE GET_LINES
Argument Name                       Type                     In/Out Default?
--------------------------------    ---------------------    ------ --------
 LINES                              DBMSOUTPUT_LINESARRAY    OUT
 NUMLINES                           NUMBER(38)               IN/OUT
PROCEDURE NEW_LINE
PROCEDURE PUT
Argument Name                       Type                     In/Out Default?
--------------------------------    ---------------------    ------ --------
 A                                  VARCHAR2                 IN
PROCEDURE PUT_LINE
Argument Name                       Type                     In/Out Default?
--------------------------------    ---------------------    ------ --------
 A                                  VARCHAR2                 IN
```

This description looks different from the first one, not because I used @desc.sql, but because the described object is a stored procedure, not a view. All that @desc.sql does for you is set the SQL*Plus linesize property to 80, use the describe command, and then return the linesize to its prior length.

At this point, you should know how to do the following:

- Download Oracle

- Install Oracle

- Create usernames ops and rps

- Write a SQL*Plus script

- Execute a SQL*Plus script

- Describe a table or stored procedure

So now it's time for you to get started with Chapter 1. I wish you good skill on your journey. Feel free to contact me if you have any questions about the book.

Index

■ U

■ V, W, X, Y, Z

Printed in the United States
By Bookmasters